NÎMES AT WAR

Robert Zaretsky

NÎMES AT WAR

Religion, Politics, and Public Opinion in the Gard, 1938–1944

The Pennsylvania State University Press
University Park, Pennsylvania

Library of Congress Cataloging-in-Publication Data

Zaretsky, Robert, 1955–
    Nîmes at war : religion, politics, and public opinion in the Gard, 1938–1944 /
Robert Zaretsky.

        p.   cm.
    Includes bibliographical references and index.
    ISBN 0-271-01326-5. — ISBN 0-271-01327-3 (pbk.)
    1. Gard (France)—History.   2. France—History—1914–1940.
3. France—History—German occupation, 1940–1945.   4. Conservatism
—France—Gard.   5. Communism and Christianity—France—Gard.
6. Antisemitism—France—Gard.   7. Church and social problems
—France—Gard.   I. Title.
DC611.G217Z37   1995
944'.830815—dc20.   93-41182
                                                                             CIP

Published by The Pennsylvania State University Press,
University Park, PA 16802-1003

CONTENTS

ABBREVIATIONS

ANAR	Association nationale des anciens de la Résistance
CDL	Comité departemental de libération
CIMADE	Comité d'Inter-Mouvement auprès des évacués
CGT	Confédération générale du travail
FFI	Forces françaises de l'Intérieur
FTP	Francs-tireurs et Partisans français
GERAL	Groupement des évacués et réfugiés d'Alsace et Lorraine
GMR	Gardes mobiles de réserve
JFOM	Jeunesse de France et d'outre-mer
LVF	Légion des volontaires français contre le bolchévisme
MUR	Mouvements unis de la Résistance
PCF	Parti communist français
PPF	Parti populaire français
PSF	Parti social français
SFIO	Section française de l'internationale ouvrière
SNCF	Société nationale des chemins de fer
SOL	Service d'ordre légionnaire
STO	Service du travail obligatoire
UFC	Union fédérale des combattants
UNC	Union nationale des combattants

If we consider what the work of attention is like, how continuously it goes on, and how imperceptibly it builds up structures of value round about us, we shall not be surprised that at crucial moments of choice most of the business of choosing is already over.

—Iris Murdoch, *The Sovereignty of Good*

Data?
What about the data
we lost when we didn't press "Save"
and a surge from the thunder brought down the system.
Could we regroup
and reconstruct the narrative as it was . . .

—Tony Sanders, *The Warning Track*

PREFACE

In the winter of 1987–88, while living in Nîmes and gathering the material for this monograph, I twisted my ankle. At first I ignored it, but my foot soon rivaled a healthy eggplant in size and color, and my limp caught the notice of Madame Debant, the assistant director of the archives. She urged me to visit the city's Maison de santé protestante. With a good deal of diffidence, I agreed and when the archives closed for lunch, I hobbled the few blocks to the clinic. Upon entering the quiet emergency room, I noticed the plaque on the office door: "Docteur Viala." The name was fairly common in the Midi, but I nevertheless found it curious: in a few accounts, I had heard and read of the efforts made by a certain Doctor Frank Viala to save the lives of members of the local Jewish community from the police of the Vichy regime.

After signing in and answering a few questions in my faltering French, I was shown into the examination room, where my foot was X-rayed. I was then directed to an examining table and asked to wait. After ten minutes or so, a young, dark-haired man in a white smock, in the company of a nurse, strode in and directed me to lie down on the table. As he turned my ankle this way and that in a firm and businesslike fashion, I asked him if his father happened to be a doctor as well. He gave me a funny look and said yes, he had been a doctor. He then returned to the business at hand, telling me that though I had a sprain and not a fracture (the X-rays were negative), I would most certainly need a cast. When I protested, he said sternly, "Perhaps this is not how things are done in America, but this is France." As he continued the examination and the nurse prepared the cast, I asked, more to distract myself from my predicament than out of any professional calling, if his father happened to have been involved in efforts to save French Jews during the Second World War. I then went on to recount, in a garbled fashion, the few stories I had read in the archives. By then, Viala *fils* had dropped my foot and was staring at me. When I finished the little I had to tell, he asked how I had come by this knowledge. I explained and after a moment's silence he replied (more or less), "My father never talked about his war experiences. I've learned more from his associates and friends than I ever did from him. And to think that a foreigner has to appear in my hospital in order to add to my knowledge."

Historical knowledge, personal or professional, is a terribly problematic thing. This is especially the case with the history of Vichy France. During the last forty years, Nîmes and the Gard have changed a great deal. The Esplanade Maréchal Pétain is now the Esplanade Charles de Gaulle. The Avenue Jean Chiappe has reverted to its original and sweeter name of Rue des Biches. The Café de la Bourse, which served as the watering hole for members of the Action française, now caters to the city's high school students and tourists. The former headquarters of the Milice on Rue Emile Jamais has long been an insurance office, and the benches near the war memorial, the site of battles between protesters and police, now attract only the city's homeless and young backpackers hunched over their maps. And Germans again sit next to Frenchmen on the stone benches of *les arènes,* the Roman arena, during the summer bullfights, but this time as invading tourists and not as touring invaders.

These and countless other cosmetic changes may be symptomatic of more profound transformations in the character of the Gard. Accordingly, the events and experiences of the Vichy years may soon be irretrievably submerged. Whether this is the case will only be known to future historians. It is, however, still possible to doubt the depth and endurance of these changes. As this study tries to underscore, peoples and mentalities change more slowly than we are wont to believe. The history of the Gard under Vichy reminds us that men are fashioned by their past, and that we are less free of history than we sometimes believe. The responses of the Gardois to the situation in which they found themselves between the summers of 1940 and 1944 may well contain certain lessons for us today, particularly the imperative needs for humility and sympathy. I received one such lesson in the emergency room of the Maison de santé protestante of Nîmes, and it is my hope that the following study carries at least a distant echo of the understanding and recognition I felt that day.

A number of organizations, institutions, and individuals have helped in the research and writing of this work. My thanks to the French government for their generous Chateaubriand Fellowship, which allowed me to spend the year 1987–88 at the archives in Nîmes. The Woodrow Wilson Institute awarded me a Charlotte Newcombe Fellowship in 1988–89, which permitted me to remain in France and write the bulk of the manuscript. I am especially grateful for the kindness shown by the office's director, Judith Pinch. A summer travel and research grant from the University of Houston in 1990 gave me the chance to attend the 1990 colloquium on Vichy held at the IHTP (Institut d'histoire du temps présent) in Paris, as well as do additional research in Nîmes.

The men and women of the Archives départementales du Gard provided more

than an ideal atmosphere for my work; they provided a home. My gratitude to
M. Robert Debant, the director of the archives, and his assistant director, Mme
Debant, for their elegant professionalism. My special thanks to four of the
archivists—Lise Carretero, Jacqueline Lebert, Michel Vielzeuf, and Alain Paul—
for their advice and friendship: I lost count long ago of all the kindnesses they
continue to show me.

During the last four years, the Honors College at the University of Houston
has furnished wonderful colleagues and bright students, all of whom have made
the work of revision remarkably painless. My particular thanks to Dr. Ted Estess,
dean of the college, for his unstinting support and friendship. I also wish to thank
my colleague Sarah Fishman who has always, despite her own busy research and
teaching schedule, found the time to read my own work, share her insights, and
encourage me along.

Patrick Hutton, my master's thesis adviser at the University of Vermont,
introduced me to modern French history, and his scholarship and encouragement have served as sources of inspiration ever since. Lenard Berlanstein of
the University of Virginia first suggested the topic for this book, and has
since maintained a friendly and critical eye on its evolution. John Sweets of
the University of Kansas has provided important counsel and shown a spirit of
generous criticism for which I am very thankful. Patrice Higonnet of Harvard
University made a number of useful suggestions, both on the manuscript and
during a memorable lunch a few years ago in Nîmes. Most important, I wish to
thank Hans Schmitt of the University of Virginia, who was instrumental in
shaping earlier drafts of this manuscript. His devotion to the writing and teaching of history, his breadth of knowledge, and his abiding concern for the work
and lives of his graduate students will always serve as my guides. I hope this book
meets his high expectations. Family and friends have provided crucial support
during the past several years. Bets, Michael, Susan, and El have furnished love,
encouragement, and, at critical moments, roofs over my head. Cécile and John
Danehy, Tony and Linda Sanders, Paula Moya, Tanya Lunstroth and Irene
Guenther have been good friends, excellent readers, and providers of poetry,
word processors, and encouragement. My editor at Penn State, Peter Potter, has
been both a friend and a gracious critic. His interest, encouragement, and sharp
eye have been vital. This book is dedicated to my mother, Roslyn Zaretsky, who
has been the best and most dedicated of readers; my father, Max Zaretsky, and to
the memory of two friends: Millie Neiland and Frédèrique Bouvier. Lastly, were
it not for Silvia Kersusan, this book surely would never have existed. I will
always be grateful to her.

I would also like to thank Armand Cosson and Aime Vielzeuf for their kind
permission to use the photographs on the front cover. I wish to thank Ray
Barr for his help in compiling the index.

DEPARTMENT
OF THE GARD

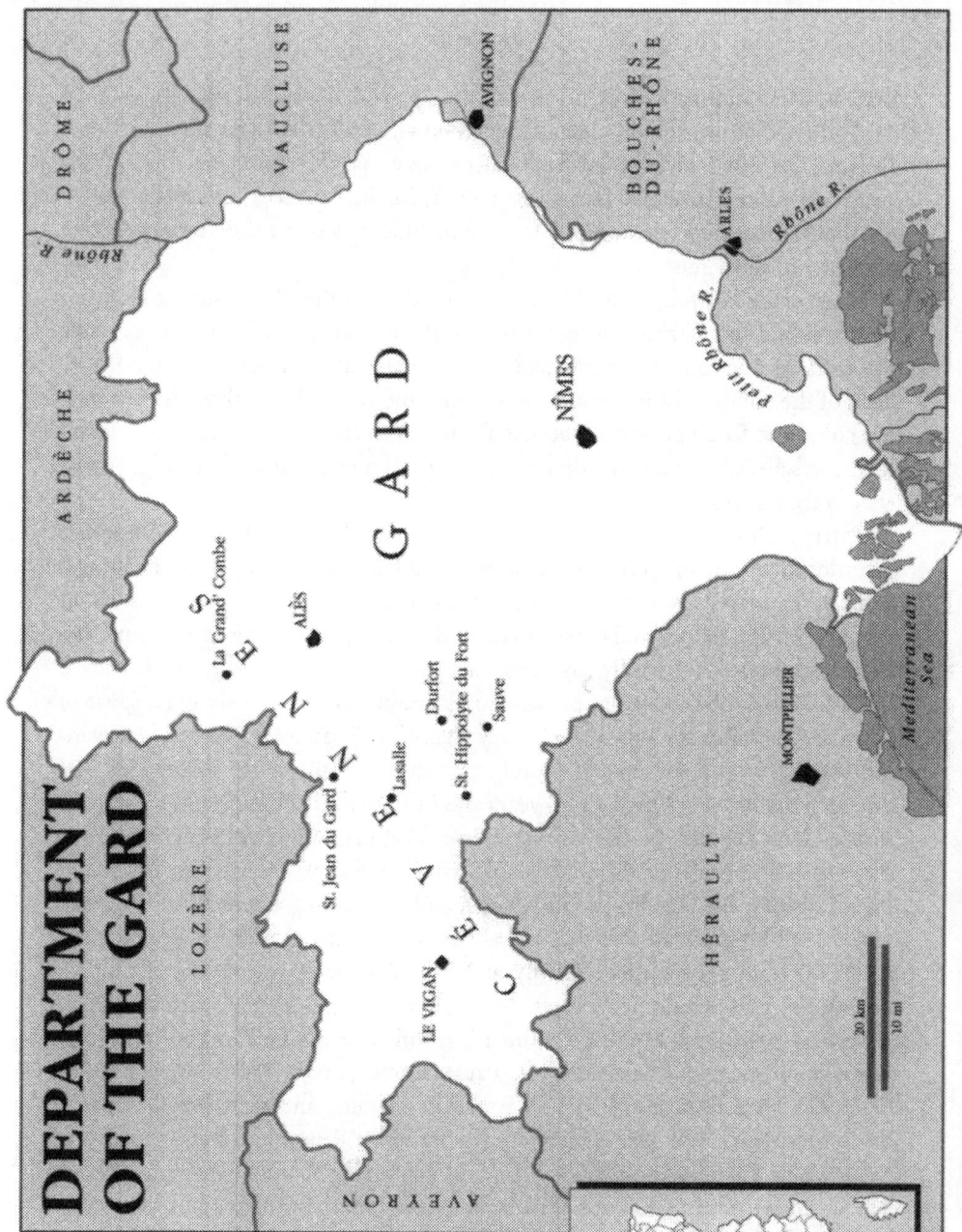

DRÔME

VAUCLUSE

AVIGNON

BOUCHES-
DU-RHÔNE

Rhône R.

ARLES

Rhône R

Petit Rhône R.

NÎMES

ARDÈCHE

Rhône R

Mediterranean
Sea

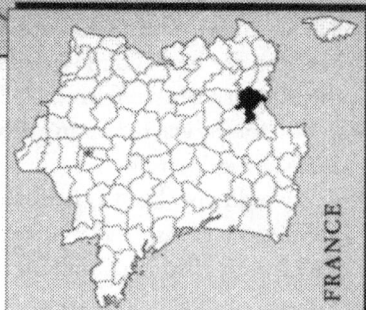

LOZÈRE

la Grand' Combe
Alès

C É V E N N E S

Durfort
Sauve
St. Hippolyte du Fort

Lasalle

MONTPELLIER

St. Jean du Gard

G A R D

LE VIGAN

HÉRAULT

AVEYRON

20 km
10 mi

FRANCE

INTRODUCTION

Vichy will not go away. As I write, France is in the throes of the Paul Touvier affair. Touvier was an officer of the Milice, a French paramilitary organization created by the regime of Vichy, which collaborated with the Gestapo in the savage repression of the Resistance and the deportation of Jews. Sentenced to death in absentia in 1946 for war crimes, Touvier was hidden by a network of monasteries and Catholic "safe houses" for the next forty years. Though he temporarily resurfaced in 1971, when President Georges Pompidou granted him a pardon, he was then charged with crimes against humanity and disappeared a second time. In 1989 he was found in a Savoyard monastery and arrested. Three years later, in April 1992, his case was dismissed by an appeals court in Paris.

The decision stunned France not only for the acquittal granted to Touvier, but for its finding concerning the past. Vichy, affirmed the court, was neither a regime that sought to impose "ideological hegemony" upon the nation—a juridical sine qua non of France's revised statute of crimes against humanity—nor was it an officially anti-Semitic regime. The case, following on the heels of the Klaus Barbie trial, and falling in the midst of cases being considered against several former Vichy officials including Maurice Papon and René Bousquet, forced France once again to confront the ghosts of her past. Not only did the great majority of political leaders condemn the verdict, but it also prompted a petition signed by several dozen French historians, who voiced outrage over the meretricious reasoning and shoddy history of the three judges sitting on the *cour d'appel*. Touvier may have been acquitted, but thanks to the attending controversy, Vichy has found itself once again in the docks.[1]

---

1. An SS officer stationed in France, Klaus Barbie was known as "the butcher of Lyons." His most notorious crimes were the deportation and death of forty-four Jewish children hidden at a home in the town of Izieu and the torture and death of the Resistance leader Jean Moulin. He was extradited from Bolivia to France in 1983 and stood trial for crimes against humanity in 1987. He was found guilty and sentenced to life imprisonment. For a sobering critique of the trial and its "lessons," see Alain Finkielkraut's *La Mémoire vaine* (Paris, 1989), trans. Roxanne Lapidus and Sima Godfrey as *Remembering in Vain* (New York, 1992). The English version carries a fine introduction by Alice

The Touvier affair is just the most recent expression of what the historian Henry Rousso has called the Vichy syndrome.[2] For this reason alone, research on the period is important: it may not prevent future efforts to whitewash Vichy, but the record itself, maintained and refined by historians, will always stand as proof and reproof against such attempts. This is not, however, the sole justification for our attention and study. Vichy is one of the last manifestations of the *guerres franco-françaises,* or the Franco-French Wars. The phrase, popularized by the political scientist Stanley Hoffmann, points to the series of civil conflicts between the French right and left since the Revolution. The examination of this period will thus cast light on aspects of France that long predate the brilliant, disastrous summer of 1940.

And, of course, the four long years of Vichy are themselves worthy of study and reflection. It was a time when men, women, and children were faced with choices—sometimes stark, more often confused, almost always bleak—freighted with ethical and political consequences. The consideration of such issues may remind American readers that their status is privileged and precarious, and that we are accountable to the past no less than to the future. Vichy laid bare the human predicament. The questions posed by this period are perennial, and we can no more escape them than we can dodge our shadows. This is why Vichy will not go away.

Over the last twenty years, the subject of Vichy France has been well served by a number of historians who have treated it in broad and synthetic terms, or have focused instead on specific lives or ideas. The result has been the construction of a model or paradigm, the lines of which were largely drawn by Robert Paxton in

---

Kaplan. The Bousquet trial has been adjourned, apparently for good, with the murder of the accused by a disturbed publicity hound in June 1993. For a profile of the former prefect of police in Paris, see Jean-Pierre Husson, "L'itinéraire d'un haut fonctionnaire: René Bousquet," in *Vichy et les Français,* ed. Jean-Pierre Azéma and François Bédarida (Paris, 1992), 287–301. See also the summaries in *Le Monde* (10 June 1993), 12–15; and "Bousquet: Les pièces du procès . . . qui n'aura pas lieu," in *Le Nouvel Observateur* (10–16 June 1993), 28–33. Finally, the Touvier affair has taken yet another twist since the writing of this introduction. The *cour d'appel* of Versailles has recently ordered the return of the case to a *cour d'assises,* where it will probably not be adjudicated before 1994. But given the fairly minor status of Touvier, it is arguable that, with the death of Bousquet, "il n'y aura donc pas de procès de Vichy." See Eric Conan's "Mort d'un collabo," *L'Express* (17 June 1993), 11–17. For a history of the affair, see Laurent Greilshamer, *Un certain Monsieur Paul: L'Affaire Touvier* (Paris, 1989) and the findings of the committee of historians, commissioned by Cardinal Decourtray of Lyons and led by René Remond, in the church's role in this affair, in *Touvier et l'église* (Paris, 1992).

2. Henry Rousso, *Le Syndrome de Vichy, 1944–198. . .* (Paris, 1987), translated as *The Vichy Syndrome: History and Memory in France since 1944,* trans. Arthur Goldhammer (Cambridge, 1991). For an examination of the recent flowering of organizations, journals, and individuals engaged in refurbishing the image of Vichy, see *L'Express* (17 July 1992), 21–27.

his work *Vichy France: Old Guard and New Order.* The Paxton paradigm supplanted a welter of competing myths. There was, most famously, the Gaullist portrayal of France as a nation of resisters, a myth that wafted like incense from the general's war memoirs. Coexisting uneasily with this version was the Pétainist myth, which received its greatest defense in the massive *Histoire de Vichy* of Robert Aron, who argued that there were two Vichys: that of Pierre Laval, collaborating shamelessly with the Nazis, and that of Marshal Pétain, seeking to place a shield between France and Germany until the sword of de Gaulle liberated the nation. By the end of the 1960s, another somewhat more diffuse and subversive legend appeared. Fed by the rebelliousness and skepticism of the generation of '68, it portrayed Vichy France as a nation of collaborationists and cowards and opportunists—a perspective glimpsed, for example, in Marcel Ophul's documentary film *The Sorrow and the Pity.*

Though no less captive to certain moral concerns than were the earlier makers of myth, Paxton wrote a marvelously nuanced, complex, and critical history of the regime. Through the study of German and American documentary sources, along with a careful gleaning of the available French sources, Paxton described the many and often competing ideological, economic, and social groups that, indigenous and independent of Nazi influence and pressure, had no less "a certain idea of France" than did General de Gaulle. The independent initiatives of the regime, the search for a role in a German-dominated Europe, the ideological drives to both modernize and recover a traditional France, the several institutional, individual, and ideological continuities between Vichy and the Third and Fourth Republics: these are the major axes of the Paxton model. It has withstood the test of time and, for the last twenty years, most historians have worked within its interpretive boundaries. The fact that the model has been criticized for certain details reveals, paradoxically, its fundamental health. New siding, a new window or two, perhaps even a new addition, but no one has considered asking the architect to raze the house and build from scratch a new one.

One of the merits of local studies is that they offer the material for such a revision. The Gard and its capital Nîmes are particularly rich in this regard. Bordered on the south by the Mediterranean and the north by the rugged Cévennes mountains, the central plains of the Gard are carpeted with vineyards. Apart from the parenthesis of the phylloxera epidemic of the late nineteenth century, the Gard's principal export has long been wine, as plentiful as it had been, until very recently, nondescript. Though other crops were cultivated— especially rye, chestnuts, and potatoes in the Cévennes, and various vegetables along the Rhône—the grape remained the crop of choice in the Gard and the magnet for local investment. As a result, the department imported most of its food staples, and as late as 1939 was buying half of its flour from outside its borders. The local monoculture would have, in the wake of war and defeat, catastrophic consequences for the Gardois.

Nevertheless, the Gard was home to other industries. The local economy had been buoyed by a growing textile industry in the first half of the eighteenth century, and though it began a slow and inexorable decline in the earlier years of the Second Empire, there remained, especially in the region of Le Vigan, a few firms specializing in hosiery, and Nîmes still sheltered a few ateliers producing gloves, shawls, and ready-made clothing. Yet it was mining that represented, after viticulture, the second major industry in the department. Judged in terms of sheer expanse, the mining *bassin* of Alès and La Grand Combe, located in the north-central section of the department, was the third largest in the country, and generated the growth of a number of metallurgical industries. Drawing workers from as far as Poland and Algeria, the basin had a relatively high population density. Alès was, in fact, the second largest city in the department, its population of 42,000 slightly less than half that of Nîmes.[3]

The religious traits of the Gard, no less than its economic characteristics, entailed serious consequences for the officials of Vichy. The region had long been an arena of religious conflict as massive and elemental as the *garrigues* and *causses* that mark the land. From the sixteenth century onward, the region was repeatedly thrown into turmoil by warring Protestants and Catholics. As a number of monographs have shown, these struggles continued to play an important and bloody role in the Gard from the Revolution through the Second Republic.[4] By the end of the nineteenth century, Catholics and Protestants were no longer shedding one another's blood, yet the many layers of mutual distrust and fear remained. Indeed, as late as 1870 Nîmes was described by one local notable as an "old volcano" of religious controversy.[5]

By the 1930s, with a population roughly three-quarters Catholic and one-quarter Protestant, the volcano was quiet, but not entirely dormant. One of this study's conclusions is that, with the advent of Vichy, a regime that was, if not overtly clerical, at least deeply deferential to the Catholic Church, there occurred in the Gard a significant revival of confessional tension and conflict. Four

3. According to the 1936 census, the Gard had 395,300 inhabitants, ranking it 53rd in the nation. Nîmes had a population of 93,700, followed by the two mining centers to the north, Alès (41,800) and La Grand-Combe (12,400). The historic Protestant stronghold Le Vigan, though along with Alès a subprefecture of the department, had a population of just 3,700.

4. See Gwynne Lewis, *The Second Vendée: The Continuity of Counterrevolution in the Department of the Gard, 1789–1815* (Oxford, 1978); and Brian Fitzpatrick, *Catholic Royalism in the Department of the Gard, 1814–1852* (Cambridge, 1983).

5. Quoted in *L'Histoire de Nîmes* (Aix-en-Provence, 1982), 294.

hundred years of mutual fear and antagonism, often flaring into political and literal bloodlettings, were not, even in 1940, entirely forgotten. The study of the ways in which these religious souvenirs were recognized and retrieved by the Gardois will, I hope, inflect our understanding of not only the specific nature of the Vichy years, but also this period's place in the *longue durée,* or "long haul" of French history.

Religion was not the sole particularity of the Gard. Ideologically, the department was also something of a curiosity, if not an anomaly. On the one hand, the Gard continued to send monarchist deputies to the National Assembly until the elections of 1936, thus setting it apart from its neighbors, all of whom had fully converted from royalism to radicalism as early as 1849. This tendency found expression in the relative flourishing, at least until the papal ban of 1926, of the departmental section of Action française. This was a movement which was born in the turmoil of the Dreyfus Affair and, led by Charles Maurras, sought a France cleansed of Jews, Freemasons, Protestants and other "alien" elements held responsible for the tragedy of the Revolution and fall of the monarchy. Along with Maurras's movement was the Association Sully, an ideological oddity that flowered for a time in the soil of the Midi. A group of Protestants more royalist than the Pretender himself, the Sullyists' sole objection to the Maurrasian vision of France was their own exclusion from it. They rivaled and often outdid their Catholic colleagues in reactionary dogma and anti-Semitic rhetoric.

On the other hand, radicalism and socialism both commanded widespread followings in the Gard. The Radicals had reigned in Nîmes from the turn of the century until the mid-1920s, when the Socialists (Section française de l'internationale ouvrière, or SFIO), led by Hubert Rouger, captured the mayor's office. In the wake of the right-wing riots in Paris on 6 February 1934, the left joined forces in the Gard as elsewhere in France. This movement was symbolized by the 14 July 1935 celebrations, when the rank-and-file of the Socialists, Communists (Parti communist français, or PCF), and Radical-Socialists massed behind more than a hundred red and tricolored flags and marched down the Avenue Jean Jaurès and spilt onto the Esplanade, where they joined in taking an oath to the Republic. The following year, electoral accords between the Communists and Socialists allowed the latter to win (with a number of dissident Radicals) thirty-six general council seats. In the subsequent legislative elections of 1936, the left carried the department: the Socialists won 32 percent of the vote, while the Communists, based firmly in the mining basin of Alès, claimed 27 percent. Nevertheless, the Radical Party maintained a certain presence in the department, thanks to the tacit support of royalists (as was the case in Uzès) or anticlerical Protestants (as in Le Vigan).

Thus, on a political no less than a religious plane, the Gard represented a challenge for the authorities of Vichy. For the historian, it presents no less a challenge, for it may force him to revise, if only in certain details, the blueprint of the house built by Paxton. The builder's specifications, I will argue, need to be revised in areas other than the durability of tension between French Catholics and Protestants. The evolution of public opinion, particularly in regard to the popularity of the regime and the person of Philippe Pétain, must also be reconsidered. My study confirms the thrust of some other recent monographs, which argue that popular disaffection was more widespread and precocious than suggested by Paxton. Indeed, the evidence from the Gard indicates that the revised chronologies are themselves too conservative.[6]

Finally, there are the profoundly difficult questions of resistance and collaboration. Though I offer clear examples from the two extremes, the overwhelming bulk of evidence does not permit me the generalizations and austere judgments made by some other historians. Most often, the cases are too complex and shot through with ambiguity to allow such straightforward declarations.[7] It will be for the reader to decide if the acknowledgment of this confused and confounding state of affairs represents a step forward or back. In the end, to provoke such questions, and suggest certain readjustments to the blueprint, is the modest ambition of this work.

6. A summary of these works can be found in Jean-Maire Flonneau, "L'Evolution de l'opinion publique de 1940 à 1944," in *Vichy et les Français,* 506–22.

7. In this regard, I have been influenced by the work of John Sweets, who has done valuable work in deepening our appreciation of the complexity of the times and the ways in which resistance should be understood. See especially his *Choices in Vichy France* (New York, 1986), and "Hold That Pendulum! Redefining Fascism, Collaborationism and Resistance in France," in *French Historical Studies* (Fall 1988), 731–58.

1

CRISES ABROAD AND AT HOME

Despite the waves of different epidemics and the plague which struck her during the Middle Ages; and despite the wars of religion, perhaps more terrible than the epidemics, which consumed so many men and so much energy, Nîmes valiantly survived these trials.
—Max Raphel, *académicien* of Nîmes, 1939

The last days of September 1938 found the residents of the Gard bent over their radios. It was neither Charles Trenet nor Edith Piaf, but rather Adolf Hitler to whom they were listening so intently. Delivering a speech during the Munich crisis, the Nazi leader held his distant audience transfixed. A moving scene, an odd scene: as a reporter from *Le Républicain du Gard* observed, "ignorant of German, [the Gardois] understood absolutely nothing" of the speech.[1] Yet the tone of his voice, the modulations of his harangue, the very quality of the static were freighted with meaning. Through a radio transmission darkly, parsing the sound of Hitler's language, the Gardois hoped to glimpse the future.

They can be forgiven if they were less than optimistic. By the time of the Munich Conference, on 29 September 1938, France had been led by Nazi

1. *Le Républicain du Gard* (30 September 1938).

Germany through an escalating series of crises. The illusions spawned by Versailles had received their first battering with the German reoccupation and remilitarization of the Rhineland on 7 March 1936. Hitler's gamble—he described the twenty-four hours following his move as the most nerve-wracking of his life—paid off handsomely. For military as well as political reasons—the Radical government of Albert Sarraut was facing an election and the military high command discouraged a forceful response—France declined to parry the German move, thus granting Germany control of the strategically critical Ruhr area and front-row seating for her army on the French border.[2]

French attention to the Rhineland soon shifted to events south of the Pyrenees. In July 1936, there occurred the military revolt against the government of the Spanish Second Republic, sparking the Spanish Civil War. A complex and tragic struggle that lasted three years, the war quickly assumed international significance, pitting the forces of democracy and socialism against those of fascism. Though a war fought among Spaniards, it was soon joined by men and material from beyond the country's borders. Franco's forces received crucial support from Nazi Germany and Fascist Italy, while the Republican forces were aided (and hobbled) by the Soviet Union, as well as committed idealists from the liberal Western democracies.

At very nearly the same moment that the Spanish Civil War exploded into history, an event of nearly equal seismic strength occurred in France. In June 1936, the Popular Front government, led by the Socialist Léon Blum, took office. The electoral victory of the left—the Popular Front had the participation of the Radicals and Socialists, as well as the tacit parliamentary support of the PCF (Parti communist français)—was accompanied by an unprecedented wave of strikes that swept across the country and paralyzed the national economy. A largely spontaneous and festive movement, the workers' occupation of the factories caught the trade unions and the PCF no less by surprise than it did the ranks of industrialists and bankers. Startled and anxious, the latter quickly agreed to a series of labor concessions, negotiated by Blum and codified in the Matignon Accords. Nevertheless, the Blum ministry was, by the following year, obliged to call a "pause" to its agenda of social and economic reform. In July 1937, the government fell, and though followed by an abbreviated return to power in early 1938, the experiment of the Popular Front soon came to an end with the formation of the Radical government of Edouard Daladier.[3]

---

2. For a provocative reevaluation of the event, see Stephen A. Schuker, "France and the Remilitarization of the Rhineland, 1936," *French Historical Studies* (Spring 1986), 299–338.

3. For a recent analysis of this period, see David A. L. Levy, "The French Popular Front, 1936–37," in *The Popular Front in Europe*, ed. Helen Graham and Paul Preston (New York, 1987), 58–83.

Yet the memory of the Popular Front—the delirium of the first days, the factory sit-downs, the dizzying succession of laws passed, the banners and proclamations—endured. So, too, did the fears and hopes inspired by the event. With the advent of the Munich crisis, the mutual fear and incomprehension between left and right, already charged by the events of 1936, grew even deeper. Already stunned by the *Anschluss* of Austria with Germany in February 1938, France was then confronted with German claims on the Sudeten region of Czechoslovakia. From early spring through early fall, Europe teetered on the edge of war. Tied since 1924 by explicit treaty obligations to Czechoslovakia, France would have no choice but to respond in case of German aggression. Hence, the British government, allied to France yet loath to consider the prospect of war with Germany over, in Prime Minister Neville Chamberlain's phrase, "a quarrel in a faraway country between people of whom we know nothing," scrambled for a diplomatic settlement. On 29 September 1938, on the eve of the expiration of Hitler's ultimatum that the Sudetenland be transferred to Germany or he would invade Czechoslovakia, there took place a meeting at Munich between Daladier, Chamberlain, Hitler, and the Italian Fascist leader Benito Mussolini. It was the result of this conference that the Nîmois, along with the rest of France, were following so carefully.[4]

In sum, burdened by the specter of World War I, harried by the provocative behavior of the Third Reich and dependent upon the diplomatic support of a reluctant Great Britain, the French Third Republic never settled upon a cogent and resolute foreign policy. The paralysis was, moreover, sharpened by the lack of domestic consensus as to who the true enemies of France were. For the political right, the mortal threat was posed by the Soviet Union and, by extension, the French Communist Party. As for the left, the menace was fascism and *its* domestic expression, the extremist "leagues" that to varying degrees challenged the very legitimacy of the Republic. The threat of war in 1938 thus revealed and honed psychological and ideological fault lines in France. In the starkest manner, the crisis framed two intertwined dilemmas that had confronted the nation since the early years of the decade. In international terms, did bolshevism or national socialism present the more immediate danger to France? Similarly, in domestic terms, which political extreme posed the greater danger to the life of the nation? A consensus was never reached on either question, and the ensuing disputes over the nature of the real and present danger helped pave the way for defeat and occupation in 1940.

4. See Jean-Baptiste Duroselle, *La Décadence, 1932–1939* (Paris, 1979) and for a cogent overview, Maurice Larkin, *France Since the Popular Front* (Oxford, 1988).

The department of the Gard, with certain nuances, shared the political confusion that plagued the rest of France. In the pages of the royalist paper *L'Eclair,* the right, a boisterous minority, clamored over the threat of international communism guided by a conspiracy of Jews, Freemasons, and assorted *métèques* (a right-wing coinage that denoted all those elements of foreign or mixed birth whose alleged aims were inimical to French racial and cultural purity). The local Socialists were, as elsewhere in France, divided between pacifists and realists over the appropriate response to Nazi Germany. Only the Communists consistently denounced the peril represented by Nazism—a position, however, suddenly abandoned in the wake of the Non-Aggression Treaty signed by Nazi Germany and the Soviet Union in 1939. The men of the center showed the same agonizing indecision as did their representatives in Paris. The pages of *Le Républicain du Gard,* the local organ of the Radical Party, reflected the emotional kaleidoscope of dread and hope, bluster and rationalization that affected good republicans throughout the nation during the fateful days of September 1938. When Georges Pujolas, the paper's editor, greeted the announcement of the accords with the exultant questions "Was there one who made demands? Was there one who gave ground?" the public already knew and accepted his answer: "It does not matter! Only the result matters for us, and henceforth the details are unimportant."[5]

It does appear that the men and women of the Gard were, like Pujolas, indifferent to the details. The police reports on public morale dating from the last week of the month are punctuated repeatedly with words like "resignation," "gravity," and "fatalism." According to one local official, "although the politics of the German chancellor spark legitimate indignation, [the Gardois] nevertheless remain partisans of peace at any price."[6] Prefect Martin could find no phrase more positive for the Gardois than that they were ready to "respond without hesitation to the appeal of France's leaders."[7] He went on to emphasize, however, the widespread enthusiasm for France's abandonment of Czechoslovakia. They greeted the accords with a mixture of joy and, in the sad phrase of the Socialist leader Léon Blum, "cowardly relief."[8]

The leaders of the local Protestant and Catholic communities were no more exempt from this confusion than the rest of the population.[9] Like many of their

5. *Le Républicain du Gard* (1–2 October 1938).
6. IM 625, commissaire central to préfet (24 September 1938).
7. IM 625, préfet to Interior (3 October 1938).
8. Given the unremarkable nature of the reactions of the local political parties to these events, they are not discussed in this study. For those who wish to have a detailed evolution of local responses to Munich, see Robert Zaretsky, *Nîmes and the Gard under Vichy, 1940–1944* (Ph.D. diss., University of Virginia, 1989), esp. chap. 1.
9. A comparison between the two religious communities, based on the press, is an extraordinar-

parishioners, they often were caught at the crossroads between deeply held illusions and hard geopolitical realities; they too, in Stanley Hoffmann's phrase, suffered from a form of cognitive dissonance.[10] Yet their opinions bear examination: the positions they eventually adopted under Vichy, in regard to the issues of collaboration and resistance, were not random. Rather, they were the result of a process, often confused and halting, of political, ideological, and theological reflection inflected by the dramatic events of the mid- and late 1930s. Interestingly, the journals often shared, at the outset, the same concerns and fears. There was on the part of local Catholics and Protestants, throughout the decade, a common preoccupation with the moral state of France, the decline of religious observance, the anxiety in face of the social question, the stubborn slide of the birthrate, and the flight from the countryside to the cities. These mutually held concerns were to bridge the rupture of defeat in 1940 and carry over into the first months of Vichy's existence.

Yet the common ground that existed at the level of social diagnosis gave way when prognoses and cures were offered. This divergence was emblematic of mutual distrust and irritation, despite, or perhaps because of, the occasional calls for ecumenism. A commonplace of French historiography is that, by the opening decades of the twentieth century, Catholic-Protestant relations had lost their ancient edge. Robert Paxton, for example, states that by the 1930s the "religious issue that divided Catholic and Protestant in 1900 had long since given way to an antisocialist issue that united them."[11] In Nîmes, this claim finds support in the creation of the Industrialist and Merchant's Union, an organization of businessmen founded in 1910. Their credo was "Neither politics nor religion: nothing other than the defense of commercial and industrial interests." Formed by both Protestant and Catholic entrepreneurs, the union was far less concerned with religious issues than by the economic threat posed by the nearby cities of Montpellier and Avignon or, come 1936, by the advent of the 40-hour workweek.[12]

Nevertheless, at the very moment that the Industrialist and Merchant's Union was girding for battle with the proletariat, there were signs of simmering religious tension. Evidence for this is found, for example, in the pages of *La*

---

ily thorny affair. It is impossible to gauge how deeply the sentiments of the respective groups were reflected in their journals. There were no opinion polls and only after 1940 are police reports on public morale broken down into confessional categories. As a result, there are no parallel sources against which to measure the representativeness of the positions taken by the religious press. The historian is left with the obvious, yet unavoidable conclusion that the newspapers were both a mirror and molder of public opinion.

10. See Stanley Hoffmann, "Le Désastre de 1940," in *Etudes sur la France de 1939 à nos jours* (Paris, 1985), 24.

11. Robert Paxton, *Vichy France: Old Order and New Guard, 1940–1944* (New York, 1972), 171.

12. *L'Histoire de Nîmes*, 347.

Semaine Religieuse. An official and national weekly of the Catholic Church, *La Semaine Religieuse* was managed by the local bishop and church administration of each city and carried official communications (pastoral letters, directions to the clergy, etc.) and sermons from the bishop, as well as homilies and diverse reports on conferences and publications. Moreover, *La Semaine Religieuse* was the journal from which the parish bulletins took the majority of their articles and the general direction of their thoughts. Under the guidance of the bishop of Nîmes, Jean Girbeau, the journal assumed a distinct, if not unique, position on the political and moral questions of the day.

An article by C. Cantaloube in *La Semaine Religieuse* referred to this muffled conflict. The journalist noted the difficulties that history placed in the way of Christian unity, given the legitimate reluctance felt by "French Protestants, and first and foremost those of the Cévennes, whose last and most bitter memories date from the Camisards." Despite his silence over the even more recent and no less bitter memories of the White Terror, Cantaloube showed a relatively keen sympathy for the refusal of many Protestants to forget the past. "How many years, or maybe centuries, will be necessary to efface the heritage of an undeniably unhappy past?" One deplores, he declared, "with all one's soul the fatal misunderstandings which formerly separated men of good will. The mere glimpse of a signature of 1685 in a register of abjuration, studded with spurts of ink from a savagely-handled goose quill, is distressing. There is no need for learned discourses to understand the error of those who, believing that they served God and king, exerted pressure on the conscience of their fellowmen." But neither Protestants nor Catholics, according to Cantaloube, could afford to continue to dwell on the past: the threat of "paganism," from both within and without France, demanded the unified effort of all those "who believe that Christ's coming into the world is not a vain word. . . . Whether one likes it or not, Christianity has, since the Reformation, been in a state of mortal sin."[13]

Despite this appeal to men of goodwill, mutual distrust and incomprehension were simply too deeply rooted to disappear altogether. Bishop Girbeau himself gave proof of this inability to overcome the past. In 1936, *La Semaine Religieuse* printed a sermon from the bishop condemning the practice of local Catholics to organize trips to Lourdes independently of the church's direction or control. Such a trend not only contradicted the spirit of pilgrimage, Girbeau declared, but was also contrary to the spirit of the diocese. Unity was essential to the life of the church and all of her dioceses, "principally that of Nîmes, where the majority of parishes are mixed and the Catholics mingle with Protestants. The latter have

13. *La Semaine Religieuse* (14 March 1937), 105–7.

their own rules and laws. The Catholics recognize authority and submit to it. To break away from this unity and organize separate movements on the margins of those of the diocese reveals a lack of Catholic spirit *and allows oneself to be penetrated by the spirit of Protestantism.*"[14]

In the eyes of Girbeau, if there was to be unification, it would be on the terms of the Catholic Church. This was an improbable event for several reasons, not least being the very lack of doctrinal agreement among the Protestants. French Protestantism, as one Nîmois pastor proudly affirmed, comprised a "corps of pastors whose diversity of opinions on strictly religious questions sometimes leads to the most radical divergences, from an extreme liberalism to the most narrow and rigid of orthodoxies"—the very spirit, in short, against which Girbeau inveighed.[15] Moreover, the Protestants of the Gard were far from prepared to lower their guard against Catholicism. In an essay in *Le Foyer Protestant*, L. A. Gervais responded to Jules Lemaître's assertion that, had it not been for the Reformation, Europe would have been blessed with just one Christianity. Such a belief, Gervais held, reveals the obstacles in the way of "attempts at contact between them [the Catholics] and us. In having expressed himself in the way he did, Jules Lemaître was the echo of the Catholics of his time—and let us have no illusions on this point—of Catholics of our time."[16]

Obviously, there remained an abiding, mutual mistrust between the two communities—and this despite the dawning mutual recognition that the enemy was no longer one's neighbor but rather the totalitarian and "pagan" powers to the East. Yet a distinction needs to be drawn between the different social classes within the two cults. This is especially the case with Protestantism. If the antisocialist issue rallied Protestants, they were largely those who belonged to the *haute société protestante* of Nîmes; that is, the bankers, merchants and professionals who continued to play a dominant role in the city's commercial life. André Siegfried has underlined this general evolution, remarking that the "traditional positions issuing from the eighteenth century tended to shift, with the Protestant bourgeoisie evolving in a different direction from that of the popular class of Protestants."[17] Even if the *haute bourgeoisie* remained liberal, they nevertheless "increasingly slid into a position of 'resistance,' in the sense that they had become opposed to 'movement.'"[18] In sum, the differences between the two confessional communities had been bridged by a mutual fear of the "social question." But a

---

14. *La Semaine Religieuse* (31 May 1936), 231–32. My emphasis.
15. *Le Foyer Protestant* (December 1937), 254.
16. *Le Foyer Protestant* (February 1938).
17. Marc Boegner and André Siegfried, eds., *Le Protestantisme Français* (Paris, 1945), 43.
18. *Le Protestantisme Français*, 48.

bridge is precisely that, a bridge; it spans a gulf that cannot be filled and, at times of natural or political disaster, is liable to collapse. The divisions between the two groups had not disappeared entirely, and the bridge moreover touched only the more cosmopolitan segment of the Protestant community.

With little variation or difference in emphasis, the Catholic press depicted a France under siege by the forces of laity, socialism, and communism—movements that, in the eyes of the journalists, were often interchangeable. For example, the parish bulletin of Sauve, a town in the Protestant Cévennes that harbored a significant Catholic minority, published an article in 1938 titled "The Eternal Exile." It underlined the "mysterious paradox" of Christ's having mobilized the most disparate hatreds against himself: "The Soviets banish him in the name of the proletariat; the Nazis hound him in the name of a racism; the esthetes scorn him in the name of culture; secularists refuse him the right to self-expression in the name of free thought; and in the name of free thought, the advocates of the new morality advise us to do without him."[19] The bulletin repeatedly took pokes at the Popular Front; one issue carried a photograph of a woman holding an (apparently) smaller than normal loaf of bread with the caption "The beneficial effects of the Popular Front: everything is shrinking, including the bread!"[20] Yet the advent of the Popular Front was but one symptom of an underlying illness: the dechristianization of France. The weakness of France issued from moral as well as economic and political sources; indeed, in the eyes of the Catholics of Sauve, these various ills could not be separated. The bulletin thus warned that France could maintain her strength only if she rebuilt "her military, economic and moral forces, which have been weakened by her declining birth-rate and financial mismanagement. . . . We observe above all that the public and secular school, by the total absence of all religious or simple moral instruction, is suppressing, along with faith, the spirit of sacrifice and devotion to the nation. This is deforming the very notion of good and evil, and destroying those virtues which make for good citizens."[21]

The bulletin's conclusion was that if France was to be strong and prosperous, she "must again become Christian and learn again to pray to God, who so loved the Franks." The Catholics in this isolated corner of the Cévennes were not alone in this belief: it was a message also hammered home by *La Semaine Religieuse* of the diocese of Nîmes. Bishop Girbeau repeatedly called his flock's attention to the danger of communism. As early as the spring of 1936, in the days before the victory of the Popular Front, Girbeau was ringing the tocsin. In his Easter

19. *Bulletin paroissial de Sauve* (March 1938).
20. *Bulletin paroissial de Sauve* (April 1938).
21. *Bulletin paroissial de Sauve* (October 1938).

communion appeal of that year, he demanded that his parishioners awaken to the gravity of the times: the hour was "grave for religious belief, and especially Catholic belief. Look at Mexico, Spain, Russia, Germany. Will it be France's turn tomorrow to see her churches and convents torched and her priests massacred? Are you for or against God? Are you for or against Christ? You cannot remain neutral. Declare your faith. Like a wounded soldier entering a hospital, the events are posing the question: 'Do you have a religion, and which one is it?' "[22] In general, the bishop and journal refrained from directly criticizing the Popular Front or giving explicit voting instructions. Still, there was no need for great exegetical skills in order to know the bishop's opinion on the elections. In the paper's account of a departmental tour in the summer of 1938, an anonymous writer accompanying Girbeau praised the voters of Sauvignargues who "harmonized their civic duty with their religious faith. The believer and the citizen joined in front of the voting urns and, in one voice, cast the same vote." How unlike so many other Catholics in the same diocese who "burn in front of the urns that which they had adored at the altar. Then they weep like willows on the [banks of the] torrent of impiety and anarchy which is carrying everything, religion and society, towards the abyss."[23]

The preoccupation of the French Catholic Church with the Soviet Union and communism has been well documented by historians. The Gard proved no exception: *La Semaine Religieuse* abounded, in the late thirties, with references to the threat posed by Moscow and its minions in the West. In a New Year's address to his parishioners in 1937, Girbeau devoted significant attention to this theme. He noted that the Communists promised "to wipe out suffering and to turn the earth into a paradise. In the meantime, they fill the world with hatred, tears and blood." He then recounted a visit the year before to Pius XI. The pope declared to the gathered bishops that "not a day goes by that bad news does not arrive from Germany. And then there is Russia, Spain, the flood of Christian blood with which communism is bathing the earth and her peoples."[24]

22. *La Semaine Religieuse* (5 April 1936), 144.
23. *La Semaine Religieuse* (30 August 1938), 312–13. The tour was actually undertaken two months before in June. The pieces were unsigned, but it is obvious that even if they were not written by Girbeau, they required his imprimatur. J.-M. Mayeur and Claude Langlois note, in this regard, that by the end of the nineteenth century, the French dioceses witness a transformation from a "limited monarchy" to one which was "universal and absolute ... the bishop governed alone, surrounded by a council of vicar generals whom he has chosen." See "Les Eglises comme sociétés religieuses," in J.-M. Mayeur, ed., *L'Histoire Religieuse de la France: Problèmes et Méthodes* (Paris, 1975), 16. See also Janine Boisson, "Les réactions des chrétiens d'après *Les Semaines Religieuses* de zone libre," in Xavier de Montclos et al., eds., *Eglises et chrétiens dans la deuxième guerre mondiale* (Lyon, 1982), which emphasizes the "decisive importance" of the individual prelate in the positions assumed by the journal.
24. *La Semaine Religieuse* (2 January 1938), 2.

La Semaine Religieuse appeared noticeably more worried by the horrors of communism than of national socialism. In this context, the paper's reaction to *Kristallnacht* — the Nazi-led street riots of the night of 10 November against Jews, their businesses and synagogues — was telling. Following a silence of two weeks, the journal published an article by its editor, Canon C.-R. Bastide, which was titled "Hitler." For two full pages, Bastide described in detail how Hitler was the realization of Nietzsche's prediction that a man would one day appear embodying an "atheistic religion." He portrayed the German leader as a "medium who is always in a trance," and is a "nervous and hypersensitive individual." Bastide concluded his article with the serene observation that "even here on Earth, our God will have the last word with Hitler."[25] Pious, irrelevant, and complacent, the article did not refer once to either *Kristallnacht* or the lot of Germany's Jews. This omission was the rule for the paper: the official organ of the diocese remained stubbornly mute over the fate of the Jews. Even such obvious occasions to confront the issue, such as the publication of Pius XI's 1937 encyclical *Mit brennender Sorge,* elicited no response from either Bishop Girbeau or the staff of *La Semaine Religieuse.* The little that did appear only serves to confirm the observation of one historian that Catholic confessional journals, when expressing indignation over anti-Semitism, preferred "rhetorical tinsel to the analysis of the causes [and] stigmatized German barbarism rather than [trying to] comprehend the anti-Semitic logic of national socialism."[26]

We will have occasion to see that this silence would deepen with the advent of Vichy and the torment of French Jewry. For the moment it will suffice to note that the Catholic Church's silence that surrounded the fate of German Jews was tied in part to the relative indifference inspired by Nazi Germany when compared to that of the related dangers of atheism and communism. *La Semaine Religieuse* was obsessed by the events in Spain and incessantly conjured up gory images from France's own past to drive home the imminence of the threat from the other side of the Pyrenees. In commenting upon the victory of the Popular Front, the paper lamented the nation's slide to the left: "Moscow is winning. Poor France! What will tomorrow bring? Passing before our eyes are the sinister visions from Spain of heads paraded on the end of poles and of burned churches."[27] The journal asked its readers to pray for Spain because "she is the lightning rod against communism. For having attracted its great violence, she may have preserved us."[28]

---

25. *La Semaine Religieuse* (27 November 1938), 473–75.

26. C. Ponson, "L'Information sur le nazisme dans la presse catholique française entre 1933 et 1938," in *Eglises et chrétiens dans la deuxième guerre mondiale,* 27–28.

27. *La Semaine Religieuse* (10 May 1938), 200–201.

28. *La Semaine Religieuse* (13 September 1938), 335.

The paper pointed to communism as the principal danger threatening France. Rejecting the "outstretched hand" of the PCF as a trap, *La Semaine Religieuse* cited Pius's assertion that communism is our "greatest and most widespread enemy . . . as it threatens everything [and] undermines the dignity of the individual, the sanctity of the family, the order and safety of society, and above all else, religion, since it flatly denies the existence of God."[29] As a consequence, though the paper came to uneasy terms with the Popular Front governments, it remained alive to the perceived threats inherent in the doctrines of socialism as well as communism.[30] Indeed, according to Bishop Girbeau, the social and moral order was already tottering dangerously. In a sermon delivered to the *Ligueuses du Gard* (a Catholic youth movement for girls), Girbeau intoned: "At this moment all is in danger in France: the family, riven by divorce, weakened by indiscipline, exhausted by selfishness and the thirst for sensual pleasures; the trades and professions, sabotaged by ineradicable conflicts of interests and the decline of confidence between employer and employee; the earth, which is in agony through the lack of willing arms and battered by the lack of foresight of certain social legislation and the irresistible attraction that the cities exercise upon the countryside; and society, whose very pillars — justice, authority, private property — are shuddering under the repeated blows delivered by the doctrines of destruction and revolutionary passions."[31]

The simplistic analysis of the social problem, the idealization of the countryside and scorn for the city, the preoccupation with the family, the overriding fear of internal enemies — in short, the overwhelming sense of living under a political, spiritual, and social siege by occult forces — marked the discourse of Bishop Girbeau during the period of Munich. The emphasis on the urban threat is especially striking. Girbeau often spoke eloquently, as did so many conservative contemporaries, on the role to be played by the countryside and the peasant in France's salvation. In an appeal to young farmers, the bishop declared that "since the best reserves of the French race come from the countryside, it is upon you, young farmers, even more so than the young workers, that an imperiled France founds her hopes for the future."[32] As for the urban workers, *La Semaine Religieuse* could not hide, despite the church's efforts at addressing the labor issue, stubbornly

29. *La Semaine Religieuse* (5 July 1938), 269.

30. For example, in commenting upon the "pause" imposed in the implementation of its economic program by Léon Blum's government, the paper warned that despite the decline of tension between the state and church, "we must not return to the deceptive peace of a sleeping Church. We have learned our lesson too well, we who have lived those sad days during which the Church was woken by secularism, separation and war." *La Semaine Religieuse* (7 March 1938), 97.

31. *La Semaine Religieuse* (25 April 1937), 165.

32. *La Semaine Religieuse* (11 April 1937), 143–44.

rooted fears and revulsion. In an article titled "Visions of May," C. Veyras offered
a revealing portrayal of the celebration. "The ideal offered to the worker is that
of idleness, with all that this entails by way of wild activities and unleashed
instincts . . . the gatherings, speeches, marches, swarming of crowds . . . the
Internationale bellowed over the course of the day by men, women, children with
clenched fists and twisted faces . . . and the reason for this orgy, the source of this
crush of people, is the brutal, wild and driven passion of hatred. A vision of
horror! A vision of hell!"[33]

There is a striking similarity between the themes dwelt upon by Bishop
Girbeau and those that would subsequently be taken up by Marshal Pétain and
the ideologues of Vichy; one like the other brandished the values of "travail,
famille, patrie." This is unsurprising, since the future seemed less than rosy for the
church and the nation. There was the stubborn decline of the birthrate, a sharp
drop in the number of young Gardois entering the priesthood and a general
decrease in church attendance. As Girbeau lamented during one of his tours of
the department, the Catholic town of Montpezat was now reduced to a "desert,"
and at Aramon the ringing of the church bell "dies out in emptiness . . . and the
voice of the curé laments the futility of his zeal."[34] But Aramon, unlike many
towns, at least had a priest to witness its decline: the Gard was critically short of
men of the cloth. Girbeau often returned to this menacing trend. Referring to a
report on departmental recruitment to the church, which warned that an insufficient number of Gardois were taking sacred orders, Girbeau declared: "I do not
know of any document more painful to read, nor of any truth sadder to confess:
the parishes of this diocese . . . have failed in their duty."[35]

Yet the interpretation of the causes of this condition was fundamentally
reactionary and hazily expressed. At one moment, the bishop accused politics—
this "cursed sower of ill-feeling, this eternal divider"—as the culprit; at the next
moment, he pointed his finger at the nation's leaders. "Those who today hold
the rudder have lost control, and overwhelmed by the torrent of the Revolution,
the ship of state is in imminent danger of breaking against the rocks."[36] In
1936 Girbeau warned that even if the frontiers of France still stood, the frontiers
of her soul had already been invaded and the "sickness was already profound.
All of her living forces threaten to dissolve under the corrosive doctrines
of ruin and destruction." And in a peroration that would be "fulfilled" a few
years later, the bishop declared that "if a revival [*redressement*] does not soon

33. *La Semaine Religieuse* (9 May 1937), 194.
34. *La Semaine Religieuse* (21 June 1936), 235–36.
35. *La Semaine Religieuse* (16 August 1936), 301.
36. *La Semaine Religieuse* (2 May 1937), 180.

occur in the moral health of France, the worst events are to be feared for the near future."[37]

Neither Girbeau nor the staff of *La Semaine Religieuse* ever presented a political solution to the crisis afflicting France; their suggestions were limited to the realm of prayer and faith—and to the occasional, veiled allusion on how one's faith ought to be expressed when marking the ballot. For those local Catholics, however, incapable of reading between the lines, there was the monthly *L'Eveil du Gard.* The paper was launched in early 1937 and had official ties to the Church; the editor, Abbé Steven, was appointed by Girbeau and *La Semaine Religieuse* encouraged its readers to support "an undertaking whose importance cannot be underestimated."[38] The paper soon made clear its political allegiances. Paul Thoulouze, a member of the "pleiad of talented and experienced collaborators" hailed by *La Semaine Religieuse,* and who would soon reveal himself to be a virulent anti-Semite, struck a comparison between Portugal and France in his column on political affairs. Intrigued by the multitude of similarities between the two countries, Thoulouze noted that Portugal's recovery was "due to a good dictator, M. Salazar," and quoted the latter's endorsements of religion and tradition. Wondering why France should not experience a similar recovery, Thoulouze replied that "lacking such a statesman (we will not have ourselves accused of fascism!), all we need do is feel, think, and act like Christians."[39] Despite concentrating the rest of his article on a discussion of Catholic youth movements, it was obvious that Thoulouze's reference to Salazar was not capricious and that he would have welcomed a solution similar to Portugal's.

The Protestant journals of the Gard revealed a greater variety of responses to the political and social situation at the time of Munich than their Catholic counterparts. Clearly, this diversity of opinion was partly due to the diversity of Protestant churches. French Protestantism was divided between the National Union of Reformed Churches and the Union of Reformed Evangelical Churches. (In addition, there were two smaller sects, the Union of Free Evangelical Churches and the Methodist Evangelical Church.) The two major tendencies had been at theological loggerheads since the second half of the nineteenth century, the reform Protestants advocating a liberal exegesis of Holy Scripture, while the evangelicals embraced a literalist interpretation. The prominent pastor A.-N. Bertrand examined the schism in the liberal Protestant journal *Le Soc,* a regional monthly of Social Christian orientation edited by, among others, two Nîmois

37. *La Semaine Religieuse* (15 August 1936), 331.
38. *La Semaine Religieuse* (15 November 1936), 423.
39. *L'Eveil du Gard* (January 1938).

pastors, Maurice Albaric and Elie Lauriol. According to Bertrand, the evangelicals believed that Christianity was "essentially a doctrine to profess, and that neither faith nor life could take the place of fidelity to this doctrine," while the liberals considered Christianity to be "fundamentally a way of life to be spread: one is Christian not because of what one thinks, but because of what one lives, or rather what one is."[40] Unity between the two churches was achieved in 1938 with the creation of the Reformed Church of France; this merger, however, did not do away with the stubborn differences between the two tendencies. It was less a complete fusion than a "reunion of members separated by the heat of quarrels. . . . Different currents still existed, but they no longer posed obstacles to ecclesiastical unity."[41]

Beyond the institutional and theological divisions reflected in their respective political stances, there was also the very spirit of Protestantism, which rebelled against political and spiritual conformism. It has become a commonplace of religious history to cite the Protestant's emphasis upon the individual—in his reading and interpretation of the Bible, his personal relationship with his God and, at least in France, his long and troubled relationship with the state—to create what the historian Janine Garrisson has called the "éternel contestataire," an individual relentlessly suspicious of the establishment. Such a propensity leads to a society of believers prone, at best, to tolerate differences of opinion, and at worst, to provoke either individual exile or group schism. Yet it is important to keep in mind Garrisson's insistence on the paradoxical influence of Protestantism: even when its adherents "swerve off the track, even when they are engaged in extreme movements, it is in the spirit of Protestantism that they proceed, believing that they simply constitute one more sect. For there remains in the soul and the heart of the escapee something of the morality and principles of the religion."[42]

This paradox received its most extreme expression from Sully, an association of Protestant royalists. Gauging the actual significance of the group is difficult. Though the number of active members in the Gard was estimated at some one hundred and fifty, the group's paper announced that it had a distribution of 2,700 (which presumably included the Hérault and the Bouches du Rhône, the two other departments where it was based). One police official even considered it to have been "perhaps the most important" extreme-right organization in the city, a significant attribution given the former role and importance of Action française.[43]

40. *Le Soc* (May 1938).

41. André Dumas, "Courants théologiques dans le protestantisme français entre 1930 et 1939," in Pierre Bolle and Jean Godel, *Spiritualité, théologie et résistance* (Grenoble, 1987), 73.

42. Janine Garrisson, *L'Homme Protestant* (Brussels, 1986), 221.

43. CA 777, commissaire principal, report on Royalist propaganda, 9 March 1943. The reference is to the prewar role of the organization.

And though the editors often recounted tales of financial woe, which would lead the historian to suspect that *Sully* was a marginal journal, they nevertheless published a paper of sixteen pages on a monthly basis, as well as special issues approximately once a year, which were double the usual length and devoted to special themes. As a result, though the association was on the political fringe, its significance cannot be entirely dismissed. Moreover, it provides a fascinating instance of the way in which the peculiarities of the Gard nurtured such exotic forms of political extremism.

In the paper's early issues, the editors sought to square the circle of a Protestantism that swore allegiance to the French monarchy. They asked the reader to recall that "the king of France is neither the Very Catholic King nor the Apostolic and Roman Sovereign, but the Very Christian King."[44] The editors explained that they sought not an obsolete and outworn monarchy, but "a modern royalty adapted to our present needs which alone can meet the context of rediscovered liberties." As for the widespread belief that Protestantism was, intellectually and historically, opposed to such ideas, *Sully* countered that there was absolutely no historical or dogmatic tie between Protestantism and the spirit of democracy: "To the contrary, the formation, Calvinist traditions and organization of our Church are clearly opposed to the principles and erring ways of democracy."[45]

Given their allegiance to the monarchy and repudiation of democracy, the Sullyists were perplexed by the guarded attitude shown toward them by the ideologues of Action française. The period of outright rejection and scorn on the part of Maurras and his followers for *Sully,* if not for French Protestantism, seems to have ended by the mid-thirties. The paper noted solemnly that Action française no longer pinned the label of *métèque* on the Protestants, and was now aware that there "existed but one order of Christians . . . those whose mission is to serve against the sectarians and the godless, the Jews and the Freemasons."[46] Yet even more perplexing in their eyes was that despite the shared values and common enemies of the two organizations, and Action française's "occasional homage to our patriotic attitudes," most fellow Protestants "still refused to forgive" Maurras and his followers.[47] *Sully* was thus puzzled by the response of a liberal Protestant journal that having listed the history of massacres and crusades that the monarchy had carried out against the Huguenots, asserted that it was one thing to forgive, but quite another to join the camp of the monarchists. The paper declared: "Does one have the right to erase all of that from History

44. *Bulletin l'Association Sully* (June 1934), 3.
45. *Sully* (15 December 1933), 1–2.
46. *Sully* (April 1938), 2.
47. *Sully* (15 December 1933), 2.

and forget? When we hear Protestants defend the Monarchy, we are stupefied."[48] *Sully*'s effort at political proselytization promised to be an uphill struggle.

As the above passages suggest, among the shared values of the two royalist organizations was a doctrinal anti-Semitism. The violence of *Sully*'s anti-Semitism, in fact, may have been an effort to repress the fact that the Protestants, no less than the Jews, were at one time considered to be *métèques*. Was this a case of denouncing a fellow alien in order to gain acceptance? Whatever the answer, it remains that the anti-Semitic proposals of the men of *Sully* often eclipsed those of Action française. For example, the entire issue of April 1937 was devoted to the "Jewish question." Noël Vesper, the pen name of the Provençal pastor Noël Nougat, who would subsequently become a fervent collaborationist, contributed a "Meditation" in which he contrasted the "Jew of the Revelation"—acceptable insofar as he served as a foil to the truth of Christianity—and the "Jew of this world." According to Vesper, the latter, due to his "universalist vocation, which the particularism of race transforms into a necessarily hidden imperialism," is responsible for the "terrible ideological idols that are shattering Western Christian civilization."[49] Such obscure exegeses (and mixed metaphors), when coupled with declarations that the Jew, having denied revelation, "must pay for an exceptional and enormous crime," constitute more than a tacit acceptance of the legal harassment of Jews. When someone declares that the Jews, necessarily guilty, "must pay" for the greatest of crimes, it requires no great leap of juridical imagination to assign the greatest of punishments—or, at least, satisfaction when they are leveled and carried out by another party, as would occur after 1942 in France.

Yet Vesper was not alone in the enormity of his proposals. Contorted theological ramblings aside, *Sully* engaged in the gutter anti-Semitism found in other extreme-right journals like *Gringoire* and *Je Suis Partout*. Michel Montaud, in an article titled "The Causes of Our Decadence," portrayed a France in the last stages of a ghastly illness and subjected to "all variety of scandals, odious dealings, profound anarchy, disastrous laws, a debased civil service, the total reign of the Jew, Freemason, and *métèque*, treasonous activity carrying into the Catholic and Protestant churches, and flagrant and unpunished immorality flaunting itself in the bright light of day." Such a state of affairs, according to Montaud, was only to be expected when teaching is in the hands of "revolutionaries using Jewish methods," the press was "judaicized," the radio was "governed by an invisible Jewry," the cinema had become "the empire of international Jewry," and sports were limited to a handful of *métèques* who performed for the profit of "the son of

48. *Sully* (July 1938), 10. *Sully* quoted the paper, but did not identify it.
49. *Sully* (April 1937), 2.

Jacob." The only realm of culture which, in Montaud's diagnosis, seems to have escaped the epidemic was the theater.[50]

Sully's coarse anti-Semitism was typical of a significant element of French reactionary thought. It revealed an obsession with the perceived incapacities of France—a condition indissolubly linked to the Jew. From her decline in foreign affairs and her domestic political chaos to her declining birthrate, the common denominator to France's decadence was clear: "All could be attributed to the Jews, so notoriously not French yet so vividly evident in so many spheres of French activity."[51] The literature on the nature and uses of anti-Semitism, in France and elsewhere, is immense; here, we shall simply observe that certain Protestants of the Midi, no less than many neighboring Catholics, were not immune to a conspiratorial vision of the world that, in times of crises, yielded great "explanatory" powers. As Raoul Girardet underlines, the myth of the conspiracy, be it Jewish, Freemason, or even Jesuit, is all the more convincing and seductive as it pretends "to a complete and exemplary clarity: all the facts, regardless of the order in which they are taken up, are reduced by an apparently inflexible logic to a single and unique source, simultaneously elementary and all-powerful."[52] Nevertheless, there is a certain surprise in discovering that a minority within French Protestantism, a religion bound to Judaism by a history of religious discrimination, its status as a threatened minority, and its emphasis upon the Old Testament, could be such exemplary anti-Semites. *Sully*, to paraphrase Samuel Johnson, was like a dog walking on its hind legs: one is not so much astonished that it walks so well, but that it walks at all.

As with most of their colleagues on the right and extreme right, the staff of *Sully* considered that Moscow posed a greater threat to France than Berlin. This position is clearly revealed in a review by Roger Darolle, a local journalist, of *Français, Voici la guerre!* by Henri de Kerillis, one of the rare French nationalists who denounced the Munich accords. Darolle agreed with de Kerillis's irrefutable observation that there existed a German danger as well as a Communist one; however, he could not accept that this entailed a "temporary convergence of interests" between the Soviet Union and France. Indeed, whatever the circumstances, Darolle lectured, "there are people with whom one cannot and must not

50. *Sully* (March 1938), 8–9.
51. Michael R. Marrus and Robert O. Paxton, *Vichy France and the Jews* (New York, 1981), 41.
52. Raoul Girardet, *Mythes et mythologies politiques* (Paris, 1986), 55. *Sully* did not spare Freemasonry, either. For example, in its December 1934 issue it lamented that though Germany was burdened with Hitler, France was stricken by Freemasonry: "Identical despotism, similar crimes, the former's committed in broad daylight, the latter's planned in the shadows."

deal. . . . 'Better to perish,' Marie Antoinette declared a hundred and fifty years ago, 'than be saved by La Fayette and the Constitutionals.' All the more reason for France, which cannot perish, to refuse Soviet assistance." He then went on to question whether the German threat was as great as de Kerillis pretended, suggesting that it was understandable that France did not have "Hitler's respect . . . since the man who is supposed to represent us is a Jew."[53] Darolle's conclusion that the danger was from within and that, above all else, "it was essential to get rid of the Jews and *métèques* who are poisoning France," is anticlimactic: it is the predictable response of an individual who saw himself as a faithful retainer of Marie Antoinette. His use of her memorable phrase is, in fact, fundamentally identical to that of the notorious and widespread "Better Hitler than Blum."[54]

Given its political perspective and choice of enemies, *Sully* was an unhesitating champion of Munich. Montaud depicted Czechoslovakia as both an indefensible geographical aberration ("this monster wrought from bits and tatters") and as a political menace ("it is a democratic, Marxist and fanatically Freemason state").[55] His colleague Hubert Rohte noted that though it was ostensibly a question of preventing the dismemberment of Czechoslovakia, "Blum gave the game away when he asked what would become of the 100,000 Jews who are in the Sudeten."[56] In short, Munich was a potential trap that would lead to a war waged on behalf of all those elements inimical to the health and security of France. These elements were composed of Jews, Freemasons, and *métèques;* groups that were advocates of ideologies—democracy and parliamentarianism—that, to echo Karl Kraus's gibe about psychoanalysis, were the diseases for which they pretended to be the cure. As Montaud phrased it in the summer of 1939: "Through the course of her long history, France has known just one implacable enemy, which she has always nourished at her breast: the liberal and democratic spirit."[57]

In a well-known, and admittedly loose definition, André Siegfried described the Protestant of the Midi as one who "votes to the left."[58] In this instance, *Sully*

53. *Sully* (April 1938), 11.

54. The Catholic thinker Emmanuel Mounier remarked after Munich that the "behavior of this element of the French bourgeoisie will never be understood if one did not hear it murmuring at the time 'Better Hitler than Blum'"; quoted in Jean-Pierre Azéma, *De Munich à la Libération,* 22.

55. *Sully* (October 1938), 5.

56. *Sully* (October 1938), 7.

57. *Sully* (June 1939). This was the last issue of *Sully* until December 1942. Neither the departmental archives of the Gard, the Bibliothèque nationale, nor the library of the Société historique du protestantisme français carry any issues between these two dates. Pierre Bolle assumes *Sully* had stopped publication during this period.

58. Boegner and Siegfried, *Le Protestantisme français,* 29. For a more recent refinement of this observation, see Aline Coutrot and F.-G. Dreyfus, *Les Forces religieuses dans la société française* (Paris, 1965).

represented the exception that proved the rule. The other principal Protestant journals of the Gard largely conform to Siegfried's observation: they were all vessels of the "liberal and democratic spirit" denounced by their religious brethren on the far right. Yet it is a remark that needs to be nuanced, as the Protestant press of the Gard was not immune to the concerns and confusion of the late 1930s.

"From the muddy wells of the press, the Truth cannot emerge in its naked purity; it is stained, painted over, disguised under the rags of comedy . . . or, rather, tragedy!" wrote J. Jouanen, in *Le Foyer Protestant,* one of the two principal Protestant journals of Nîmes. He went on to observe that it seemed as if France had been flung back to the Middle Ages: "The social and political dogmatisms, which we today call ideologies, confront one another with even more violence than did the theological variety. . . . And the blood runs, and an atmosphere of civil war, more or less heavy depending on the region, weighs on the people."[59] In the face of this grim portrayal of events, Jouanen advocated that the Protestant churches follow the Vatican's lead in addressing the social question. "While remaining outside and above the political parties, our churches can and must, like the Pope and the Roman Church, offer advice, seek to inspire and nurture in their fold authentic Christians . . . thanks to whom the world will be saved from corruption."[60]

Jouanen's disclaimer of political involvement underscores the dilemma that confronted the Protestant community (as well as Catholics) during this period: they had an acute sense that the social and political institutions were no longer holding, yet were held back from directly participating in their salvation. As a result, time and again in articles, reviews, and messages, the writers made explicit that they were not entering the political arena. Yet the very frequency of such assertions suggests the contrary: there is a thin line, occasionally transgressed, between social and political action. As the editor of *Le Foyer Protestant,* G. Fayot, pointed out, when one begins an appeal by declaring the intention to abstain from all political action, this is "a rhetorical precaution which leads us to believe that politics will be *talked* about. And when one talks about politics . . . is not one already *acting* politically?"[61]

Le Foyer Protestant often talked politics. The journal did not belong to the Social Christian movement—a powerful element within French Protestantism during the interwar period that sought to fuse the religious conversion of the individual with the social transformation of the nation. It did share, however,

---

59. *Le Foyer Protestant* (1–16 June 1937), 125–26. Through 1937, the journal, which was founded in 1886, appeared twice a month; from 1938, it converted to a monthly format.

60. *Le Foyer Protestant* (1–16 June 1937), 128–29.

61. *Le Foyer Protestant* (1–16 March 1936), 67. Emphasis in original.

many of the same concerns: as the paper announced in its New Year issue of 1938, it intended to continue in the line of a Protestantism "concerned before all else with evangelical faithfulness, but also broad-minded, liberal, open and fearless," both with regard to the advances of science and "fraternal reconciliation between Protestants and Catholics in an atmosphere of sincerity, confidence and mutual tolerance."[62]

Liberal concerns are evident, for example, in the paper's position on the Popular Front's legislating the 40-hour week. In a long piece, Fayot recognized the wisdom in waiting for the other European nations to adopt similar laws, so as not to place France at an economic disadvantage. Yet, in contrast to *La Semaine Religieuse*'s fears of the moral effect of increased leisure time on the workers, Fayot responded that it was no more just to condemn such free time than it was to criticize literature or science because they were liable to abuse. Besides, he added, "it suffices to go to the train station on Saturday or a Sunday morning to see the joyful families leaving to relax together at the sea or the countryside."[63] Fayot concluded that the fourth commandment ought to be revised so as to read, "You shall work . . . and you shall do all that is required. You shall repose on the days which shall be given to you and you shall sanctify them." The article is a model of common sense with a dash of the higher criticism, marking an attempt to come to terms with a new and promising social and political order.

Indeed, the Nîmois journal had occasion to take the Council of the Protestant Federation to task for intentionally ambiguous positions taken on political issues. In a critical dissection of one of the council's appeals, in which it advanced the need for Christian love and understanding as part of the solution to the social ills that confronted France, Fayot was skeptical and impatient. He asked if the "always indispensable and insufficient brotherly love" encouraged by the council "contains the solution . . . to the disastrous state of society? The victims of this state of affairs are rather exasperated by such protestations of love." He also criticized the council for having lumped together civil violence and class conflict in the same condemnation. Whereas violence was obviously condemned by the Bible, Fayot argued that class confrontation was a natural consequence of modern society and will "show itself wherever conflicting interests of different social groups collide with one another."[64] Pious sentiments were simply not enough, according to Fayot; clearly expressed principles serving as a basis for effective policies were also necessary.

Just as the *Foyer* largely shared the political views of the Socialists, so too

62. *Le Foyer Protestant* (January 1938), 4–5.
63. *Le Foyer Protestant* (November 1937), 226.
64. *Le Foyer Protestant* (1–16 March 1937), 61.

did it share their political and emotional confusion at the moment of Munich. The paper praised the accords, but did so with a distinct uneasiness. Fayot described the agreement as both a "human triumph" and a "Christian triumph," for it was the "only SOLUTION which could have avoided armed conflict."[65] Yet his joy was far from unalloyed: Fayot hailed the "heroic resignation" of Czechoslovakia, the party that "has paid the highest ransom for peace." Though a relatively small price to pay when compared to that of war, "it nevertheless remains a painful mutilation, pregnant with difficulties and dangers."[66] Fayot concluded that the threat of war persisted and that "it would be a disastrous illusion to think that the method inaugurated at Munich . . . will always suffice to guarantee peace!"[67]

The response of French Protestants to the rise of anti-Semitism in Germany and elsewhere in Europe has been the subject of much study.[68] The consensus of these inquiries is that the Protestant community in France was more disturbed by anti-Semitic persecution in Germany and its manifestations in France, and more outspoken in its condemnation, than were the Catholics. The several reasons that have been advanced for this difference in reactions will be discussed and judged from the perspective of the Gard in Chapter 4. Here it will only be noted that *Le Foyer Protestant*, despite its Social Christian orientation, was, in this regard, something of an anomaly. The violence of *Kristallnacht* had wrenched a sharp protest from French Protestantism; the Council of the Protestant Federation condemned the massacre and appealed to Frenchmen to aid the refugees fleeing Germany. It was, moreover, an event that has been cited as the spark to a renewed critique of anti-Semitism in the pages of the *Revue du christianisme social* and other journals of the same persuasion.[69] Yet the Nîmois monthly passed over it in complete silence—a silence all the more striking since the journal did not hesitate to comment on other positions taken by the council. Nor was *Le Foyer Protestant* mute on other victims of Nazi persecution. For example, it closely followed the persecution of the dissident pastor Martin Niemoller, as well as the

65. *Le Foyer Protestant* (November 1938), 227–28.
66. *Le Foyer Protestant* (November 1938), 229.
67. *Le Foyer Protestant* (November 1938), 231.
68. The pioneering work in this field has been done by Pierre Bolle; see, "Les protestants et leur églises durant la seconde guerre mondiale," in *Revue d'histoire moderne et contemporaine* (April–June 1979), 286–97; and "L'Influence du barthisme dans le protestantisme français," in de Montclos et al., *Eglises et chrétiens dans la deuxième guerre mondiale*, 59–66. See also the contribution of André Dumas, "Courants théologiques dans le protestantisme français entre 1930 et 1939," in Bolle and Godel, eds., *Spiritualité, théologie et résistance*, 72–78.
69. Patrick Cabanel, "Veillée d'armes face à l'antisémitisme: Le Mouvement du christianisme social (1933–1940)," in Philippe Joutard et al., *Cévennes: Terre de Refuge, 1940–1944* (Montpellier, 1987), 216.

28 NÎMES AT WAR

fate of the German Confessional Church.[70] But the only reference to the lot of German Jewry is found in L. A. Gervais's article on the conflict between Mussolini and Pius XI, in which the author approvingly quoted the pope's declaration that for Christians, "man has value not only because he is tall and blond, strong and handsome, but because of the nobleness of his soul," and concluded with a verse from the New Testament affirming that "there is neither Jew, nor Greek, slave nor free man, man nor woman. We form but one person in Christ."[71] Inexplicably, this passage betrays the same brand of ambiguous and insufficient Christian love that Fayot himself had earlier condemned in one of the council's letters.

However, the other major Protestant journal of the Gard, Le Soc—which would change its name to Semailles in April 1939—quickly assumed a clear and unflinching position on anti-Semitism. Prior to the summer of 1939, the journal, despite its allegiance to the Social Christian movement, paid scant attention to the burgeoning of anti-Semitism and racism. Its great preoccupation, particularly during 1938, seemed to be the difficult path to Protestant unity. Exasperated by the hesitation and distrust of certain Cévenol communities, Louis Atger exclaimed "Have we not the same religious habits, the same customs, the same austere temples, the same worship? Have not four centuries of Protestant life sculpted our mentality? Is there a Protestant family that is more unified than that of the Midi?"[72] The cascade of articles on unity also distracted from a strong reaction to Munich: it is not until November 1938 that a short article appeared on the subject. Written by A. Gall, it is unexceptional in its contents and form; pessimistic and solemn, the writer asked if, during the respite given by God to the world, the latter would be able to "turn around, repentant, toward God?"[73] His answer, however, was already implicit in the autumnal quality of his tone.

In the summer of 1939, Semailles published an essay by Auguste Lemaître titled "Israel's Persecution: A Short History." A two-part article, its point of departure was the "indescribable suffering inflicted upon the Jews of the German Reich" and the assertion that "the impact of our indignation has everything to gain from a better knowledge of Israel's tragic destiny over the past nineteen centuries of history." Lemaître then launched into a critical review of Christianity's relations with Judaism, and praised the "resistance" of the latter—a "miracle of history that is founded more on the unity of their religion than that of their race."[74] The contributions to Western civilization of Bergson, Einstein, and

70. See the issues of Le Foyer Protestant of April and August–September 1938.
71. Le Foyer Protestant (August–September 1938), 178.
72. Le Soc (May 1938), 4.
73. Le Soc (November 1938), 1.
74. Semailles (June 1939), 3. The issue of July 1939 is missing from the departmental archive collection.

Freud were praised by Lemaître, who concluded with an appeal of great conviction and power. Issuing a "unreserved condemnation" of the policies of Nazi Germany, Lemaître declared that the anti-Semitism of the Nazi regime is "a crime against God and against humanity that affects us all and forces us to assume a double attitude. First, an attitude of faith, which prophesies heavenly punishment, and finds a degree of reassurance in the certitude that there is a form of iniquity that ineluctably calls upon its authors a curse not merely from the judgment of the historian, but also from that of History itself. . . . And second, the attitude of our heart, which must open itself to all our generous impulses, even if they lead to hardship and sacrifice."[75]

Lemaître's essay is notable for several reasons. First, it displays a defense of Judaism free from hesitation, ambiguity, condescension, or self-interest—an observation that, in the context of the late thirties, is less trivial than it ought to be. Second, the piece has an oracular character: both in Lemaître's reference to "crimes against humanity" and in his warning of the eventuality of the need for sacrifice, there is a moral and historical lucidity that borders on prophecy. There is, lastly, the impact that such an article had upon its audience. The Cévenol historian Patrick Cabanel has noted that whereas prominent journals like the *Revue du christianisme social* and *L'Avant-Garde* had relatively limited readerships, *Semailles* was widely distributed and read in both the Cévennes and the cities of Nîmes and Alès.[76] The reflections of Lemaître and others assumed a dramatic relevance after the advent of Vichy—hence, the importance of the didactic role they played in the late thirties. Exercises in ethical imagination that would have such important consequences under Vichy, they renewed the historical and moral attention long nurtured by Protestant culture. The pastor Jacques Martin has underlined that interest in the Jews was not born spontaneously in 1940, but was instead preceded by a "long preparation and reflection in opposition to those Protestant theologies that considered the Jews and Judaism to be a mere prelude to Christianity."[77] Although the actual degree of influence cannot be ascertained, it seems clear that articles such as Lemaître's played a critical role in preparing the Gardois Protestants for the approaching trials of war and defeat.[78]

75. Quoted in P. Cabanel, "Veillée d'armes face à l'antisémitisme," 223.

76. P. Cabanel, "Veillée d'armes face à l'antisémitisme," 223. Cabanel writes that a "majority" of Protestant households in the two departments subscribed to *Semailles,* but neglects to offer any statistical evidence (215).

77. Personal testimony in Joutard et al., *Cévennes: Terre de refuge,* 239–40.

78. Still, any conclusion must remain tentative. For example, the pastor of Mandagout, Georges Gillier, asserts that it was only in 1942 and Marc Boegner's activity that he and his Cévenol parishioners became aware of the lot of the Jews. Prior to that, "the Jews were for us something of a myth . . . something rather vague" (Joutard et al., *Cévennes: Terre de refuge,* 240).

Nevertheless, it is important to emphasize that even *Semailles*'s attitude toward Judaism was not entirely unambiguous. Thus G. Debu's comment upon an article written by Albert Einstein, in which the latter confessed his error in having once disdained the church, the sole institution now protesting anti-Semitism in Nazi Germany. Debu wondered if "this great Jew" could go even further and "discover Him who is head of the Church and after having admired Him, bow before Israel's messiah?"[79] And in an article in *Le Foyer Protestant,* the missionary F. Faure was particularly alive to the soul-winning bonanza represented by the Nazi persecution. Not only was he more sympathetic to the lot of those Jews who had converted to Christianity, but nevertheless "are treated like Jews" by the Germans; but he also considered that this "tragic trial can be a favorable circumstance to witness an awakening of a great number of Jews." He concluded: "Christians! It is the moment to show our Christianity."[80]

In the twilight years before the outbreak of war, there was yet room for a variety of motives, some less honorable than others, for Christian charity toward the Jews. The philo-Semitism shown by Lemaître was perhaps exemplary, in the waning years of the decade, even among the Protestants of the Gard. Yet, come the defeat of France and the advent of Vichy, the Protestant community experienced the shock of state anti-Semitism; the initial seismism and aftershocks of official policy swept through society with vibrations and casualties no one could ignore. As we shall see, the blend of accounting and missionary zeal found in the reasoning of a Faure or Debu by and large soon gave way. Instead, disinterested generosity and a deep assurance in the moral rightness of one's actions became the hallmarks of Protestant behavior. Before we examine this period, though, we must first consider the phony war and the battle for France. For it is only when these events have been properly situated that we can begin to understand the reasons for the initial popular acceptance of the regime, if not all the policies, of Vichy.

79. *Semailles* (November 1939), 2.
80. *Le Foyer Protestant* (June 1939), 132.

2
WAR AND DEFEAT

Truth, justice and right, coming as they do from God, cannot vary in time and space.
Two plus two equals four on both sides of the border.

—Pastor Paul Brunel, 1939

The evils which [this war] will drag in its wake—in the tears and sobbing of mothers, the abandonment of orphans and the despair of widows, the rivers of blood which will bathe the fields of battle, and in the cries of the dying and wounded—His justice will be the ransom of our blasphemy and scorn of his eternal laws.

—Bishop Jean Girbeau, 1939

In the winter of 1940, the police of Nîmes arrested Auguste Vigne. Emboldened by one too many *pastis*, Private Vigne, on furlough from his regiment, had been holding forth on the questions of war and peace. From the makeshift lectern of a bar counter, the soldier complained that "six million of us have to have our faces smashed in for the gun merchants. That bastard Raynaud [the transcript's misspelling of the prime minister's name] is raking in our money but is careful to protect his own. Our colonel, with his eyes on a promotion, treats us like animals. We're in the mountain artillery, yet are doing the work of the open country artillery. We're fighting for the capitalists who have stayed behind. . . . Why break our necks and fight blokes who've never done anything to us: the *boches* [Germans] are as decent as the rest of the universe's inhabitants."[1]

1. CA 300, commissionnaire divisionnaire to préfet, 7 February 1940.

How did Vigne's monologue play with his audience? We are not told, unfortunately. Similarly, we cannot know the reviews he would have received had he done a tour of the department. In a word, it is difficult to say how representative Auguste Vigne's philipic was of public opinion. The destination and detailed nature of the police report, however, underlines the gravity of Vigne's remarks and the administration's sensitivity to such sentiments. It is as if the prefecture was aware that the Gardois were increasingly unenthusiastic about a war declared but not yet engaged, undertaken for reasons that had been much debated but never made clear. Vigne's ramblings were perhaps extreme when they were uttered, but six months later, in the shambles of defeat, they would represent the mainstream of public opinion in the Gard.

During the Munich crisis, not only was there a fatal blindness in France to the actual issues at stake; there also existed a tendency that may be described as pre-Pétainist—the belief that France was unprepared both materially and spiritually for a battle with Nazi Germany. In his radio address of 20 June 1940, Philippe Pétain, the octogenarian hero of Verdun who had assumed leadership of the Vichy regime, presented in his lapidary fashion his well-known trinity of causes of France's defeat: "Not enough children, not enough weapons, not enough allies." In the same appeal, he underlined that "Since the victory [of 1918] the spirit of pleasure prevailed over that of sacrifice. We demanded more than we offered; we sought to avoid sacrifices; and today we confront a calamity." Less an analysis than a judgment, Pétain's words echoed a general impression of moral malaise already evident in 1938. Clearly, the moralism of the Pétainist discourse did not rise, new and unexpected, from the intellectual rubble of the summer of 1940. Important elements were common currency two years earlier in the departmental press and in public opinion. It would require only the impact of war and defeat to provide the ground for the erection of this worldview.

The first rumblings of war were felt on 23 August, when to a shocked world, Nazi Germany and the Soviet Union, two nations held to be at ideological and geopolitical loggerheads, announced the signing of the Non-Aggression Pact. Poland was especially startled by the pact, for it now found itself wedged between the two hostile, totalitarian states. Poland's greater vulnerability, in turn, had fatal ramifications for European diplomacy. Following the debacle at Munich, the British government, under intense public pressure, had been compelled to offer diplomatic guarantees to Poland against foreign aggression. This declaration of collective security had initially found a guarded reception in France, whose foreign policy was in the hands of the pro-appeasement Georges Bonnet. Equally important, there was a fairly widespread sentiment that Poland held less strategic importance for France than did Czechoslovakia, which, after all, had already been sold down the river by the Allied powers.

The guarantees were nevertheless affirmed, and on 1 September 1939 the French found that they would indeed be asked, in the infamous phrase of the French fascist Marcel Déat, "to die for Danzig." On that day, German Panzer divisions plowed across their eastern frontier, overrunning the Polish defenses, while the Luftwaffe quickly dominated the skies. Two days later, on 3 September, both Great Britain and France declared war on Germany. Yet the declaration, though it surprised Hitler, who had hoped that the Allies would limit their response to the usual diplomatic protests, had no effect on the course of the invasion. The staggering impact of the German blitzkrieg was mirrored in the east by the advances of the Soviet army, and on 27 September, with Warsaw reduced to rubble by air strikes, Poland sued for peace.

French military thought since World War I had given primacy to defensive strategy, based on the axiomatic belief that firepower was more effective than movement. This strategic worldview, embodied in the construction of the famed Maginot Line, along with the obstacle of the German chain of fortifications known as the Siegfried Line, explains in part the absence of a serious French riposte in September. But as all historians agree, a second factor also weighed heavily: the memory of World War I, where much of the bloodletting occurred on French soil. The French military command, no less than its political class, was determined not to relive the bleak years of 1914–18, and thus held to a firm defensive posture. As a result, there followed the so-called *drôle de guerre*, or phony war.[2]

Just as with the partial mobilization during the Munich crisis, the French government's declaration of war against Germany on 3 September 1939 was welcomed by "firmness" and "resolution" in the Gard. The previous day's announcement of mobilization had left the Nîmois "unsurprised." As the report of the central commissioner explained, the population, which had been swinging "between the extremes of pessimism and optimism," had expected that "a solution, probably the worst for those countries seeking peace, was going to intervene." Hence, the Nîmois prepared for the future "in an atmosphere of calm which did not lack

---

2. Barry Posen provides a detailed comparative analysis in *The Sources of Military Doctrine: France, Britain, and Germany Between the World Wars* (Ithaca, 1984).

a certain serene *grandeur.*" Clearly partial to this last word, the official went on to portray a people who gave the "very clear impression that whatever the *grandeur* of the sacrifice demanded, they will accomplish it with a firmness that nothing will be able to weaken."[3]

In fact, the apparent resolve of the Nîmois was such that, two weeks after the declaration of war, one police official was rather astonished: "Surprisingly, rather than discussing the war, the public simply goes about its affairs."[4] This apparent lack of interest may have been the result of the population's "firm determination." But it is no less possible that the impression of calm resolution was the product of sheer lassitude or deep disengagement from the issues at hand. The inability to recognize the reasons for the war and the refusal to accept the sacrifices such a war would exact were widespread phenomena. The public had been mercilessly tossed and turned over the preceding year by the vagaries of the French government's policies and the "Scottish shower" (*une douche écossaise,* a rare literary term, referring to an alternately hot and cold shower) applied by Hitler. There was, moreover, the population's desperate belief, cultivated by the French government, that no matter the cost, peace would prevail in their lifetimes. The result of such willful blindness on the part of both governors and governed was not a grim determination to fight the good fight. Rather, once the illusion was exploded, there followed a state of profound resignation and incomprehension — sentiments conveyed by, but rarely acknowledged or analyzed in the police reports.

The press clearly reflected this state of joyless acceptance. Georges Pujolas, the editor of *Le Républicain du Gard,* thought that even if these "feverish hours [were] saturated with electricity," there was "absolutely no enthusiasm on the faces" of the Nîmois.[5] A couple of days later, his paper dwelt on the difference between the spirit of the soldiers mobilized in 1914 and those now reporting to their regiments. Rather than the "great enthusiasm" of that earlier generation, there now existed an "energetic resolution" on the faces of the departing men. However, the reporter concluded with the wish that "in the next few days all the mobilized members of the great French family will turn back on the path to their homes."[6] A laudatory desire, but one that not only contradicted the insistence on the "energetic resolution" of one and all, but also bespoke a continued and alarming unwillingness to confront reality. This attitude was aptly summarized by a front-page editorial of *Le Républicain du Gard* in early September: "However it

3. CA 565, commissaire central to préfet, 2 September 1939.
4. CA 565, commissaire divisionnaire to préfet, 14 September 1939.
5. *Le Républicain du Gard* (28 August 1939).
6. *Le Républicain du Gard* (30 August 1939).

may be, we must be done with a situation that has gone on too long."[7] Less a fervent rallying to the flag than a resigned shrug of the shoulders, it was to such blandishments that the Gard slouched toward war.

The leader of the local diocese, Jean Girbeau, echoed the ambivalence of his parishioners. In a sermon delivered in early September, the bishop lamented the futility of the efforts for compromise and the disappointment of hopes for peace. In a gesture of national reconciliation he remarked that "it would be fruitless and untimely to look, in our own recent past, for those who are responsible for the bloody tragedy in which we are now engaged. This is the moment not for recrimination, but for *union, confidence, and prayer.*"[8] The following week, Girbeau wondered what would be the results of the coming war. He warned his listeners that, unlike the years after the First World War, this time the "needs of the home front" must be attended to, namely, "the Christian education of our children." He concluded by emphasizing the "necessity, after the war, to remake a Christian France."[9] Girbeau did speak occasionally in terms of the days following France's "victory" rather than "war," and it would be unjust to accuse him of defeatism. Nevertheless, there is an inescapable impression in his sermons that refashioning France in the image of the church was more important than the nature of the opportunity which would permit it.

This sentiment is evident in the bishop's New Year sermon. After having condemned the secularization of the household and the dechristianization of the family, Girbeau warned that "there are no laws where there are no sanctions. That the divine laws have been broken on every step of the social ladder invites divine punishment." He asserted that God had allowed this war so that through "the evils which it will drag in its wake—in the tears and sobbing of mothers, the abandonment of orphans and the despair of widows, the rivers of blood which will bathe the fields of battle, and in the cries of the dying and wounded—His justice will be the ransom of our blasphemy and scorn of his eternal laws."[10] Clearly, if the value of this "ransom" was proportionate to the pain it entailed, a defeat would prove even more salutary than a victory. This consequence of Girbeau's soteriology would become explicit only after the fall of France—the very event that confirmed Girbeau's baleful visions.

7. *Le Républicain du Gard* (2–3 September 1939). It is far from certain, in Henri Guillemin's phrase, that in 1940 it was merely "the fear of arrest and the fright of the War Council which made [the soldiers] obey"; see his *Nationalistes et nationaux, 1870–1940* (Paris, 1974), 327. Nevertheless, the Gard does, at the very least, accord with Henri Michel's depiction of the "resigned, impassive faces" of the soldiers called to the colors; see his *Drôle de guerre* (Paris, 1966), 23.
8. *La Semaine Religieuse* (10 September 1939), 348. Girbeau's emphasis.
9. *La Semaine Religieuse* (17 September 1939), 357–58.
10. *La Semaine Religieuse* (31 December 1939).

The Catholic hierarchy of the Gard was not alone in its analysis of the underlying reasons for the outbreak of war; to a certain degree, the Protestant churches embraced the same interpretation. In a sermon delivered in Nîmes, Pastor Elie Lauriol claimed that the "shortcomings of this world have permitted the unleashing of evil forces."[11] And like their Catholic peers, the Protestants also declared this was the time for union and not mutual recrimination. The Catholic weekly Le Viganais had announced that, despite local history, where "we have often been divided by the bitter struggles between parties," France's future now demanded unity.[12] Similarly, the Protestant journals referred to the region's divisive past in order to underline the present need for Christian unity. Henri Devaux described a France that, only yesterday, had been "composed of individuals living their own lives shorn of close ties to their neighbors. Today, these same men are united in the same thought, the same conviction and same supreme will—to save the Homeland and Civilization."[13]

Girl au gave an intriguing proof that winter of his devotion to the quest for unity. On 1 November, a Gardois priest had given a sermon at the war memorial for Action française. That the event caused a stir in the department was clear when La Semaine Religieuse published an unsigned article that took the unnamed priest to task. The editorial criticized the priest both for his political associations and for his dubious theology (he apparently revived the church's theology of the Crusades, which promised eternal recompensation for those Christians who fell in a just cause—a clear reference to the camelots du roi of Action française). The article rejected the priest's contention that the 1926 papal ban of Maurras's group was a "misunderstanding from which everyone has suffered." This statement was intolerable on two counts. First, it implied that the pope was mistaken in an ex cathedra statement. Second, it was proof of ecclesiastical insubordination: the discourse was delivered without prior episcopal approval. As the article explained, if "M. l'Abbé had dutifully gone to the diocesan authorities concerning his plans, he would have been advised to put away his speech and remain quiet." The article concluded that it was the priest's affair if he wished to remember "the living and the dead of Action française," but that his public role as priest and educator required that these political ties be expressed "more thoughtfully and discreetly."[14]

The priest's reaction is unknown, but he may well have been surprised, for Bishop Girbeau himself had once been sympathetic to Maurras's movement—a

---

11. Bulletin de l'église reformée de Nîmes (November 1939).

12. Le Viganais (9 September 1939).

13. Foi et éducation (December 1939), 229. A Protestant journal edited in the Cévenol town of Anduze, it was, as its rubric affirmed, devoted to "Christian inspiration and documentation for education."

14. La Semaine Religieuse (10 December 1939).

sympathy that survived the papal ban. In the summer of 1928, three years after Girbeau's arrival in the Gard as bishop and two years after the papal condemnation of Action française, an editorial appeared in Le Républicain du Gard under the headline "Monseigneur Girbaub [sic] reported to be leaving Nîmes." The piece referred to the "unfortunate" administrative and personnel changes made by the newly arrived bishop, which broke with the liberalism of his predecessor, Msgr. Beguinot. Although Girbeau had acquiesced in the Vatican's condemnation of Action française, he nevertheless committed the imprudence of supporting a member in the local elections. The paper asserted that the bishop's position, compromised between the royalists and liberals, had become untenable: "No longer able to master events . . . his transfer is being seriously considered."[15]

The transfer never took place, and the apparent absence of subsequent controversies lend support to the observation that Girbeau "gave great proof of loyalism vis-à-vis Rome."[16] But this points to an important difference between the Catholic and Protestant hierarchies in France concerning the ultimate source of submission and obedience. Whereas Girbeau made clear that the church was the one and only source of authority for Christians, the Protestants during this period reemphasized the primacy of the individual's faith and the direct and independent relationship between God and one's conscience. The editor of Le Foyer Protestant, Pastor Paul Brunel, summed up this attitude in the winter of 1939. For the Christian spirit, he wrote, "the truth remains the truth, justice remains justice whatever the circumstances and land. . . . Truth, justice and right, coming as they do from God, cannot vary in time and space. Two plus two equals four on both sides of the border."[17]

This passage, which would be transformed in less than a year's time from a solemnity bordering on cliché to an existential and imperious truth, marks one reason for the different comportments of the two churches under Vichy. As we have already observed, the Catholic Church largely contented itself to belittle Hitler. The parish bulletin of Sauve, for example, described Hitler in February 1940 as "the liar par excellence, the most frightening monster that Satan has placed on earth. . . . He is crime made man."[18] As a source of emotional release, this tantrum — representative of the Catholic press in the Gard — perhaps served a purpose, but it fell tragically short as either an analysis or guide to future action. The Protestant press, on the other hand, generally abstained from such attacks

15. Le Républicain du Gard (9–10 June 1928).
16. Private communication of Father Aptel, of the Archives de l'évêché de Nîmes, to the author (September 1988).
17. Le Foyer Protestant (November 1939), 218–19.
18. Bulletin paroissial de Sauve (February 1940), 4.

and instead reminded their readers of their Christian duties and responsibilities. In so doing, the journals reinforced the moral foundations on which the local Protestants, both collectively and individually, would base their actions between 1940 and 1944. Thus E. Guillierme, in the October issue of *Foi et Education*, wrote that just as "Caesar demanded payment from the Lord Jesus, so does the *patrie* now demand your devotion and the possible sacrifice of your earthly life. But Christ encourages you: 'Do not fear those who kill the body but cannot kill the soul.'"[19] How could one justify such a sacrifice? The *Foyer Protestant* provided the answer in a quote from Montesquieu: "An injustice committed against one man is a danger to all."[20]

Montesquieu's axiom has relevance for the actions of the Republic no less than Vichy. On 26 September 1939, the French Communist Party was dissolved by the government, an act followed two weeks later (8 October) by the arrest of the PCF deputies. These events, which mark the institutionalization of an obsession with the enemy within, have been emphasized by the historian Pierre Laborie. In his study of the Lot during the Second World War, Laborie argues that this officially encouraged obsession, mirrored in the local media and public opinion, with the PCF (and by extension, the Soviet Union) was an important element in France's collapse. He concludes that the chase after the Communists, considered to be an even greater evil than Nazi Germany, distracted the French from the declared enemy—the enemy with whom they were in a state of war—and clouded the aims pursued through this conflict.[21]

Laborie's observations shed important light on the evolution of public opinion in the Gard, as well. In terms of sheer numbers, the department was heavily represented by the PCF. According to a prefectoral report, only the departments of the Seine, the Seine et Oise, and the Nord had more Communist officials (all deprived of office by the time the report was written). There were in the Gard 6 Communist *conseillers généraux*, 8 *conseillers d'arrondissement*, and some 400 *conseillers municipaux*.[22] The actual rank and file of the PCF numbered some 25,000, concentrated in the mining and industrial towns of Alès and La Grand-Combe. Outside of the Alesian mining basin, it appears that the party's presence was less imposing; there were cells in some 20 *arrondissements* in Nîmes and Le Vigan,

19. *Foi et éducation* (October 1939), 177.
20. *Foi et éducation* (February 1940).
21. Pierre Laborie, *Résistants, vichyssois et autres* (Paris, 1980). See especially part 2, chap. 2.
22. CA 355, 13 March 1940. By 19 March 1940, the national "tableau de chasse"—the phrase was that of Sarraut, the minister of the interior—counted 2,778 Communist officials deprived of their posts, along with 3,400 arrests and 8,000 legal sanctions directed at party members.

three-quarters of which counted "a very weak number of members" and virtually disappeared after the general mobilization.[23]

The police reports of late September and October all maintain that the measures taken against the Communists were unanimously welcomed by the population. In Nîmes, the party's dissolution "was the subject of every conversation and the government is congratulated for the measure it has taken."[24] The arrest of Communist officials created, at least in Nîmes, "absolutely no public reaction."[25] In fact, the list of arrested deputies, "which grows every day, attracts the nearly unanimous approval of the middle and working classes. There was no reaction among the members of the party in Nîmes to the arrest of two representatives from the Gard."[26]

The local press was relatively silent on the subject. *Le Républicain du Gard* neither praised nor criticized the government's actions; it limited itself to a dry accounting of the news and maintained a list of those elected officials who fell under the law of 8 October 1939 (the arrest of PCF deputies) and that of 20 January 1940 (their deposition from office). On the other hand, *Le Languedoc Socialiste* reported an address given by the Socialist deputy F. O. Frossard, in which he asserted that "if communism is a licit opinion like any other, Stalinism is an act of high treason [*applause*] and the Communist Party, be it legal or illegal, since the approval it has given to the Russo-German Pact, has become a foreign army camped on our territory [*applause*]."[27] *Le Journal du Midi* jettisoned the qualifications of Frossard and joyfully threw itself into the hunt for "cocus." The paper congratulated the government for the expulsion from parliament of the "mobilized Moscowteers" and announced the need of undying vigilance against these "internal enemies."[28]

It is difficult to know in any detail the reaction of the local Communists following the signing of the Non-Aggression Pact between the Soviet Union and Germany, the subsequent invasion of Poland, and the declaration of war. It appears, though, that they experienced the same confusion and shock that their comrades felt elsewhere in France. The central commissioner reported on 20 October that the party militants "are abstaining from all public expression and give the impression of being embarrassed by their past political activity."[29] The various unions, moreover, were "repudiating the old directives of the ex-

23. CA 383, préfet to Interior, 20 October 1939.
24. CA 565, commissaire divisionnaire to préfet, 28 September 1939.
25. CA 565, commissaire central to préfet, 7 October 1939.
26. CA 565, commissaire central to préfet, 8 October 1939.
27. *Le Languedoc Socialiste* (21 January 1940).
28. *Le Journal du Midi* (23 January 1940).
29. CA 565, commissaire central to préfet, 20 October, 1939.

Communist Party and support the CGT in the position it has taken against the Soviets."[30] Remarkably enough, the repressive measures taken by the government in the mining region aroused no overt opposition. The subprefect of Alès reported that the PCF's dissolution and police searches have "been followed by no reaction whatsoever."[31] The passivity and acceptance by the working class seem to support the observation made by the prefect in December that "the mass of workers, disoriented since the treason of the Communist Party, seems to distrust everything and everyone."[32]

However, the absence of any demonstration or protest was not necessarily tantamount to a lack of concern, much less a surrendering of political beliefs on the part of the Communist rank and file. It is very difficult to measure the actual number and strength of those Gardois who continued to remain faithful to the party—or, at least, to what they thought the party continued to represent. Still, the number of party faithful seems to have been substantial. The police reported that although there were no incidents at the national railway (*Société nationale des chemins de fer*, or SNCF) workshops in Nîmes-Courbessac, there was nevertheless the "impression that almost all the workers who belonged to the Communist Party conserve the same ideology, and it is only through fear of public criticism or of being drummed into the army that they do not express themselves."[33] The lack of support for the former Communist deputy and mayor of Alès, Fernand Valat, is also telling. Having renounced his ties to the PCF during the one-month grace period offered to the party's deputies, Valat joined Marcel Guitton's Worker and Peasant Party. Despite, or because of this shift, Valat lost the support of at least some voters. In the winter of 1940, the central commissioner of Alès reported that the renegade Communist "does not have the confidence of Alès's workers on the extreme left."[34] The police official offered neither exact figures nor a definition of the "extreme left," but this episode does suggest that there was an important number of miners and industrial workers unwilling to surrender their political allegiance to the PCF.

Did the dissolved PCF, beyond sporadic and inconsistent attempts at propaganda, pose the threat to national security claimed by the local administration? It is beyond the scope of this work to add to the growing literature on the complex of attitudes the outlawed party assumed on the question of France's defense.[35]

30. CA 565, commissaire central to préfet, 20 October 1939.
31. CA 565, commissaire central to préfet, 24 October 1939.
32. CA 565, préfet to Interior, 8 January 1940.
33. CA 565, commissaire central to préfet, 11 October, 1939.
34. CA 300, commissaire central of Alès to sous-préfet, (n.d.).
35. For the most recent studies on the positions taken by the PCF during the period between the

Yet it can be observed that though a good deal of time and concern was spent keeping close tabs on the Communist threat, it seems that the local administration, at least after the initial crackdown, was chasing ghosts. For example, an investigation of a certain Gaston Pascal was undertaken by the police following the receipt of an anonymous denunciation. He was accused of being a militant Communist who, by spreading subversive information, sought to provoke the desertion of troops stationed in the barracks at Jonquières–Saint Vincent. Yet the inspector assigned to his case concluded that these charges were groundless, and suggested that they were woven "by an individual living on bad terms with Pascal's wife."[36] Similarly, in the winter of that same year, a rumor began to spread that the outbreak of minor acts of insubordination among a garrison of troops from the 27 Regiment de Tirailleurs Algériens had, as its source, leftist agitation. An inspector was dispatched to Pont Saint-Esprit, the town where the troops were stationed, and reported that he observed nothing out of the ordinary. However, he did remark that the Algerian soldiers "did not have the sympathy of the locals and that some women were frightened." Moreover, the acts of insubordination, far from being attributable to the PCF, instead resulted from a "lack of body linen, the turnover of officers, and primitive living conditions."[37]

These examples reveal that certain social and intellectual reflexes normally associated with the regime of Vichy, such as anonymous letters of denunciation and a rooted xenophobism, were already apparent during the last days of the Third Republic. This is also manifest in the prefect's report on the strength of the PCF in the Gard, which tallied "25,000 Communists and 35,000 foreigners of all nationalities and tendencies."[38] The fact that the prefect lumped Communists and foreigners in a single phrase reveals a certain attitude firmly rooted in France during the late thirties: the common danger represented by the Other, be it through the premeditated allegiance to a "foreign" ideology or simply through the accident of birth. The police reports during this period reveal a deep concern with the presence of foreigners in the Gard—a concern the Gardois seemed to share. In the eyes of many inhabitants, foreigners, be they Spaniards, Italians, Germans, or East Europeans, represented a potential political and economic danger.

Yet, upon the declaration of war, there were several instances where foreign

---

declaration of war and Germany's invasion of the Soviet Union, see Jean-Pierre Azéma et al., eds., *Le Parti communiste français des années sombres, 1938–1941* (Paris, 1986).

36. CA 565, commissaire divisionnaire to préfet, 28 September 1939.
37. CA 565, inspecteur to commissaire central, 29 November 1939.
38. CA 355, préfet to Interior, 13 March 1940.

nationals sought to show their solidarity with France. For example, on 3 September the Beaucaire section of the Union Populaire Italienne distributed flyers announcing that "in the grave circumstances which France is undergoing, [we] invite all Italians to attend the mass demonstration of Franco-Italian friendship."[39] Or, again, there was the case of a certain M. Beekman, a baker in Alès, who published a flyer at his own expense. Apparently of German origin, the baker declared: "Friends, fellow workers, and patrons of foreign origin: a foreigner, a small baker-proprietor of Alès and friend of France urgently appeals to all foreigners to enroll as volunteers in the French Army for the sake of our rights, peace, and liberty. As France has nourished us, it is our duty to defend her."[40]

Despite such displays of patriotism, there remained a good deal of distrust and friction between the Gardois and foreigners. Three days after the declaration of war, a fruit store in Nîmes was sacked by city residents. It was alleged that the store's owner, a woman of Spanish nationality named Mme Sastre, "loudly displayed her total indifference to France's rallying to Poland's defense." The good woman's opinion led to a volley of words "devoid of amiability" and the eventual pillaging of the store.[41] The incident, reported on the front page of *Le Républicain du Gard,* appeared to be the fulfillment of a warning that the paper had uttered just a few days before, stating that foreigners, "who are so numerous in Nîmes, must show themselves very prudent in their opinions and avoid displaying in public their material well-being while the French are called upon to fulfill their duty."[42]

Indeed, the local presence of Spaniards had been a source of controversy since the outbreak of the Spanish Civil War. We have already seen, in the apocalyptic sermons of Bishop Girbeau, reflections of the divisions created by this conflict. Unsurprisingly, the staff of *Sully* found themselves in full agreement with the Catholic hierarchy. As one of their journalists, Eugène Gaeckle, warned: "Moscow has sought from the beginning of the civil war in Spain to provoke an incident that would unleash a world war. It is doing this in cahoots with our Popular Front, which wants to turn us into soldiers for a communist revolution in its death throes."[43] On the other side of the political chasm, *Le Combat Social* and *Le Républicain du Gard* maintained an unwavering sympathy for the Spanish Republican forces, but neither paper advocated the active participation of France in the conflict. By the autumn of 1938, moreover, the attention of the Gardois

39. CA 565, commissaire de police de Beaucaire to préfet, 3 September 1939.
40. CA 565, sous-préfet of Alès to préfet, 3 September 1939.
41. *Le Républicain du Gard* (5 September 1939).
42. *Le Républicain du Gard* (31 August 1939).
43. *Sully* (April 1938), 8.

Radicals and Socialists had become almost wholly absorbed by the events in Munich and Prague. Local support for the Spanish Republic had become, more than ever, "platonic."[44]

Everyday relations between the Gardois and Spaniards, however, were often less than platonic. The Catholic weekly of Le Vigan, *Le Viganais*, gave vent to its fears concerning the arrival of a quarter-million of Spanish refugees on French soil. "By their physical contamination and their revolutionary aims," the paper exclaimed, these foreigners constitute a "permanent moral, financial, and social danger."[45] The paper tied the presence of the refugees and the alleged role they played in the strikes of 1938 to the existence of a Communist conspiracy. The sudden bellicosity of those who yesterday were still pacifists, averred the paper, meant that these elements hoped that a war would present a "favorable occasion for the foreign garrison [i.e., the Spanish refugees] established in France to impose a Bolshevist regime at the very moment that the French armies were massed on the border."[46] As a result, it was imperative to staunch "this invasion, which has cost us so dearly, tarnished our image in the eyes of the world and burdened our citizens with an unmerited mortgage."[47]

During the first weeks of September, relations between the local population and Spanish refugees became increasingly strained. In general, the sources of this tension were both economic and nationalist. There was a muted discontent on the part of those Gardois and their families who, called to active service, saw able-bodied Spaniards stay behind. Friction was also reported in the mines of Alès. The presence of young Spanish militiamen in the workforce led the French miners to protest that the Spanish workers prevented the return of mobilized comrades. It was a striking display of national and corporate unity placed before

44. This was the phrase of the central commissioner describing the various demonstrations in favor of Republican Spain. 1M 625 (16 July 1938).

45. *Le Viganais* (11 February 1939).

46. *Le Viganais* (18 February 1939).

47. *Le Viganais* (25 February 1939). The influx of Spanish refugees presented *Sully* with the opportunity to pontificate on the general question of foreigners. In an article by Mercier Calvairac La Tourrette, the axiom was immediately posed that "it is neither good nor normal that a human being should forever abandon the land where he was born: between the two there exist bonds that cannot be broken heedlessly." The inevitable corollary was the mutual inability of a host country and foreigner to understand one another. No less inevitably, the journalist then took the opportunity to tie this general observation to the "Jewish question." With a remarkable tolerance for a contributor to *Sully*, Calvairac La Tourrette exempted from this veritable law of nature those Jews who had lived in France "for several generations and were an integral part of our nation." Instead, he concentrated on those Jews fleeing Nazi persecution, and after considering and dismissing the various proposed solutions, concluded that "the Jewish problem is one of those enigmas that prove to be indecipherable; the mind and the heart remain overcome in front of a unique situation which seems to be without a satisfactory solution for all concerned" (December 1938, 11–12).

that of class solidarity, for as the subprefect emphasized, this dissatisfaction existed "even among those Frenchmen who share the same political ideas as the militiamen."[48]

These confrontations were not limited to the mines of Alès: in the immediate wake of the mobilization the Cévenols living in the mountainous region of Le Vigan were also "very worked up" against those Spanish men young enough to carry arms.[49] Indeed, Spanish and Italian women, no less than their husbands and sons, were the target of local anger and distrust. For example, certain farmers, themselves of Spanish or Italian extraction, would hire only their own for fieldwork. This practice led to an incident near St. Gilles, where an Italian farm manager had been taking on only fellow countrywomen for the grape harvest. Cornered by a delegation of local women whose husbands had been mobilized, he was ultimately forced to fire the Italian laborers.[50] Although such confrontations were minor and sporadic, they nevertheless displayed an undeniable irritation that the locals felt for the foreigners. According to one police report, the department's inhabitants had the "keenest desire" to see the Spanish refugees "turned back to their country of origin."[51] There would be happy exceptions to this tendency in the days to come. Nevertheless, thanks in part to this influx of refugees in the final days of the Third Republic, Vichy's xenophobism was to find an initially receptive audience in the Gard.

The question of refugees was not the only one to weigh upon the public during the first months of the war; there were also the everyday irritations that accompany national mobilizations. The street lighting of Nîmes, for example, was curtailed, a pointless defense measure considering the city's geographical position. Unhappily, it dovetailed with the approach of autumn and the shortening of the days. The blackout converted the city streets into obstacle courses and the local papers abounded with complaints of heedless drivers, twisted ankles, and missed turns. In *La Vie Nimoise,* a local journal devoted largely to human-interest stories, a reporter suggested that dog owners leave their pets home after nightfall, because the leashes served as a "very convenient means to trip pedestrians—a source of accidents which have become countless."[52] Even if one avoided such traps on the sidewalks, it was far from certain that he was groping along in the right direction since, with the fall of night, the street signs were impossible to read. Night life in Nîmes suffered; cafés and cinemas, usually

48. CA 565, sous-préfet of Alès to préfet, 18 January 1940.
49. CA 565, commissaire divisionnaire to préfet, 26 September 1939.
50. CA 565, commissaire divisionnaire to préfet, 16 November 1939.
51. CA 565, commissaire divisionnaire, to préfet, 5 October 1939.
52. *La Vie nîmoise* (11 September 1939).

crowded with locals and tourists, now emptied by sundown and an unusual calm would fall over the town.[53]

There also existed a certain nervousness that provided fertile ground for tall stories and rumors. The passage of hospital trains through the station at Nîmes, barely a week after the declaration of hostilities, was immediately transformed in the public imagination into a convoy of cars filled with wounded soldiers.[54] Or there was an incident involving a soldier named Riboulet, entrusted with the maintenance of public order in one of Nîmes's *arrondissements*. Having already succeeded in fraying the nerves of the quarter's inhabitants by blowing his whistle incessantly and ordering the dousing of lights, Riboulet went overboard when he informed a certain Mme Fabregoul of disastrous French military reverses, adding that the city hall had just received the bodies of forty soldiers from a single regiment. The story was sheer fantasy, but Riboulet's stunned listener fainted on the spot: her husband was a member of the cited regiment. Riboulet was called upon by a gendarme, who concluded that the soldier clearly "did not have full use of his mental faculties" and advised that he undergo a medical examination.[55]

There was a more serious and crippling aspect to public credulity: just as the Gardois were vulnerable to such rumors, so too were they the victims of an official propaganda that often was as fantastic as the ravings of Riboulet. The shortcomings of state-directed propaganda in France are well-known. First, it was only in the summer of 1939 that a Commissariat Général à l'Information, charged with the coordination of all the information services, was finally established. Second, there was the choice of Jean Giraudoux to head the agency. A playwright, novelist, and essayist of great ability, Giraudoux was by the same token poorly equipped to bolt together the blunt, repetitive, and emotionally charged phrases that could rally a nation.[56]

The deficiencies in both state propaganda and the local censorship became quickly apparent in the Gard. During the fall of 1939, the papers were replete with egregious articles on the invincibility of the army and the inevitability of victory. The headlines in *Le Journal du Midi* were typical. "We shall be victorious," guaranteed one, while a second explained why: "We shall win because we are the

53. CA 565, commissaire central to préfet, 23 September 1939.
54. CA 565, commissaire divisionnaire to préfet, 10 September 1939.
55. CA 565, commissaire de police, ler arrondissement to commissaire central, 16 September 1939.
56. As Pierre Lepape has written, "propaganda requires that one write crudely; Giraudoux tried, but never succeeded. He was by nature too elegant" (review of Giraudoux's collection of wartime writings, *Messages du Continental,* in *Le Monde* [23 October 1988]).

strongest." This phrase, considered felicitous by the office of propaganda, enjoyed
wide currency—and wider scorn.[57] Somewhat less vacuous were the stories and
headlines in *Le Petit Marseillais,* a regional paper distributed in Nîmes. Yet here,
too, was a certain speciousness to the majority of reports. The paper transformed
bleak events into optimistic ones by judicious quotations and turns of phrase.
Thus, as German Stukas were reducing Warsaw into a flaming pile of rubble, the
paper headlined: "City's civil defense commander says: 'The enemy's bombs do
not scare us.' "[58] Past French military errors were also recalled, if only to predict
that the *Germans* would now repeat them. Hence, it was asserted that "just as
Napoleon encountered 'General Winter' in Russia, the Germans will now have to
struggle against 'General Swamp.' "[59] The stories in *Le Républicain du Gard*
during this period were equally optimistic, stressing the irrelevant actions of the
French troops massed along the Maginot Line, in which minor skirmishes were
transformed into tactical successes.

The vapid optimism of the news stories was at least partly the result of the
official censorship. Over the course of the winter the confrontations between
those who reported and those who clipped became increasingly heated. The
columnist of *Le Républicain du Gard,* Le Rachalan, affirmed that while censorship
was imperative in time of war, it was a profession unhappily practiced by
censors—and "censors are men, which is to say that they are prone to exaggeration,
unthinking zeal and error."[60] The columnist's upbeat conclusion—"We nevertheless have one right: the right to smile over all this"—was not shared by his
editor. In early March, following a series of articles that were liberally sprinkled
with blank spaces left by the scissors of the censor, Pujolas finally revolted.
Following the censoring of a piece on wintry weather conditions, Pujolas, at
wit's end, confessed his inability to understand why the Nazis needed "to read *Le
Républicain du Gard* in order to know that it was cold in Nîmes . . . and that the
whiting-out of Le Rachalan's article [on the weather] prevented them from
learning that it snowed in Provence!"[61]

The impact of propaganda and state censorship on public opinion in the Gard
is difficult to assess. French propaganda, first of all, did not measure up to its
competition east of the Rhine. Numerous police reports attest to the impact that

---

57. The writer Jean Dutourd, then a young soldier of twenty years, wrote that the phrase
ought to have been "We shall win because we are the bravest." Apart from its being "more noble, it
would also have been more just since war is not a question of arithmetic"; *Les taxis de la Marne* (Paris,
1956), 14.

58. *Le Petit Marseillais* (9 September 1939).

59. *Le Petit Marseillais* (11 September 1939).

60. *Le Républicain du Gard* (24 February 1940).

61. *Le Républicain du Gard* (9 March 1940).

German propaganda had upon part of the population. The central commissioner of Nîmes remarked that "a certain number of listeners" were impressed by French editions of German radio propaganda, and suggested that ways be found to jam the programs—an act that "would certainly be welcomed by a large number of our fellow citizens."[62] Returning the following day to this problem, the official observed that the German programs continued to have a "demoralizing effect on certain Nîmois, particularly the popular class, which is more sensitive to this kind of propaganda."[63] At the turn of the new year, the prefect worried that the "depression" that had overtaken the population in December would persist through January. He wondered if the "perfidious and constantly repeated allegations of the German radio have not finally had a certain effect," and underlined the need to "carefully watch over the morale of the population" and to impose "as soon as possible truly effective radio jamming."[64]

Though the government did eventually succeed in jamming the German broadcasts, this technical success was no substitute for a positive and cogent policy of propaganda. The reports on public morale during the winter and spring of 1940 reveal an unsettling absence of political acumen and emotional malaise on the part of not just the population, but those who were responsible for informing and leading it. In his study, Laborie underscores the government's efforts to maintain the population in a reassuring and comfortable ignorance of the gravity of events.[65] It was a mentality that had as its concrete corollary the Maginot Line: just as the French were lulled by the advertised invincibility of this defensive wall, so too were they comforted by the no less invincible barrier of ignorance and disbelief. Thus, in late November it was observed that despite recent technological advances made by the German Navy, the Gardois "preserved their entire confidence in the technicians of the French and English admiralties to annihilate all future German naval attacks."[66]

Le Languedoc Socialiste dealt harshly with such blind optimism. The paper lambasted the French government's chipper assessments which claimed that "absolutely all that we possess is flawless, and that absolutely everything which the Germans use is either worthless or defective." The paper argued that the French deserve better: "The nation agrees that she be told only what can be told in time of war, but not that she be fed a lot of hogwash."[67] In the long run, the

---

62. CA 565, commissaire central to préfet, 20 October 1939.

63. CA 565, commissaire central to préfet, 21 October 1939.

64. CA 565, préfet to Interior, 8 January 1940. The prefect did not specify the nature of these "allegations."

65. Pierre Laborie, *Résistants, vichyssois et autres.* See especially part 2, chaps. 1 and 2.

66. CA 565, commissaire central to préfet, 25 November 1939.

67. *Le Languedoc Socialiste* (21 January 1940).

amateurishness of official propaganda and the simpleminded optimism of most news stories— betraying a certain scorn or condescension on the part of the molders of opinion for their audience—rendered the population either skeptical or cynical. As Jean Giraudoux himself once wrote, "Nations, like men, die from imperceptible acts of rudeness." The Gardois, like the rest of France's population, were the victims of state-directed disrespect.

The population was affected not only by the technical incompetence and political confusion of the media, but was also undermined by the internal tensions created by the mobilization and prolonged inactivity following it. The "drôle de guerre," as Georges Bernanos wrote, "n'est pas drôle, elle est funèbre" (an untranslatable pun based on the double meaning of "drôle," which can mean either funny or peculiar). The suspicion and conflicts that appeared between the Gardois and foreigners were replicated *en famille* as well. As early as the first week of October signs of tension were signaled by *L'Eclair*'s publication of a letter denouncing those young men who, thanks to connections, escaped active service. "The real scandal concerns these hopeless incorrigibles who have been transformed from gardeners and laborers into lawyers, police commissioners and municipal paper-shufflers. Why are these individuals more indispensable to the rear lines than a farmer whose work at least has the merit of feeding our boys in the front lines?"[68] Though a police official described the letter as "venomous" and thought it ought to have been censored (not altogether surprising, given that his bureau was one of the targets), it seems that the anger expressed was fairly widespread and cut across class lines. The letter revealed that one need not be a bourgeois or professional in order to have the right connections in provincial France: networking was the patrimony of all classes. Thus a long letter sent to the subprefecture of Alès by a group of local mothers whose children had been mobilized: the women were upset over the attending irregularities of the call-up. There is anger, the subprefect of Alès warned, "especially in our industrial region, from the existence of special dispensations. The problem is very delicate, and if the hostilities go on, I believe that a serious revision of this practice . . . will be necessary."[69]

If there was a line of demarcation between those who did and did not benefit from exemptions, it was the one that separated the town from the countryside. During the final days of the Republic certain social and professional conflicts began to heat up; a notable instance in the Gard was that between those who worked the land and those who worked in the mines and the factories. Since the exemptions were often accorded for reasons of national defense, those workers in

68. CA 565, commissaire divisionnaire to préfet, 6 October 1939. *L'Eclair* letter quoted in report by the official.
69. CA 565, sous-préfet of Alès to préfet, 25 November 1939.

the Alesian region involved in defense-related industries benefitted the most from this policy. The rural population, however, refused to accept this ordering of priorities. According to the subprefect, the farmers who "just as in 1914 are most affected by the mobilization, are clearly jealous of the industrial population, whose special dispensations are a source of envy. The small landowner cannot easily accept the often disastrous consequences of the requisitions."[70] Moreover, the requisitions involved not only manpower, but horsepower as well. In early September a "certain nervousness" was observed in the countryside and was attributed to the sudden shortage of horses to assist in the imminent harvest.[71] The response of a farmer who, having just left his two workhorses at the requisition center in Nîmes, collapsed into tears on the sidewalk, is representative. "I understand . . . it's necessary . . . but, still, it's hard. I've only them to help me in the fields. . . . Who will pull my 'pastiero' [Provençal for plough]." He then walked up to his horses, tapped them on the nose, told them to "serès bravas" [be brave], and returned home alone.[72]

These everyday inequalities and hardships were imposed by a government that appeared increasingly indecisive in leading an increasingly dubious cause. The doubts and confusion sown from the time of Munich were to blossom in March 1940 with the fall of the Daladier government and its replacement by one led by Paul Reynaud. Le Rachalan compared the impact of the news on the Nîmois to that of a stone thrown in the city park's frog pond, and urged his readers to show some confidence: "A ministry led by Chautemps, Daladier or Reynaud: what does it matter since 'France goes on.' "[73] The calm and insouciance shown by the columnist was not, however, shared by the public. It judged the moment to be less than opportune for another turn of the ministerial revolving door. The central commissioner confirmed that the city was surprised by the news of Daladier's fall, and that although the new government under Reynaud was "favorably received," there existed nonetheless a "certain atmosphere of disquiet." He reported that "due to the gravity of the hour, all circles of society find it regrettable that these political antics have not ended."[74]

It is difficult to describe with any certainty the mood of the population after the Germans began their offensive on 10 May 1940: the monthly reports on public morale for April and May have been either lost or destroyed. It is probable,

70. CA 565, sous-préfet of Alès to préfet, 29 January 1940.
71. CA 565, commissaire divisionnaire to préfet, 11 September 1939.
72. Le Républicain du Gard (29 August 1939).
73. Le Républicain du Gard (21 March 1940).
74. CA 565, commissaire central to préfet, 23 March 1940. Along with those of April and May, the monthly police reports on public morale for October, November, and December of 1940 are missing, thus rendering difficult a sustained study of the population's attitude during this critical period.

however, that the Gardois were largely unaware of the magnitude of the threat until the end of May and the first days of June. This state of ignorance was partly due to the optimistic glosses the local press continued to apply to the reports from the front line, as well as to the sheer speed with which the events succeeded one another. Thus, *Le Républicain du Gard,* which by the final week of May had been reduced to a single page, continued to apply optimistic twists to the bad news from the north. On 29 May—the day following the start of the Allied retreat from Dunkirk—the paper reported that "our troops are resisting courageously in the north against the determined efforts of the enemy." The valor shown by the French and English armies at Dunkirk was undeniable, but the headline clearly sinned by omission, thus underlining the old maxim that, in time of war, truth is always the first casualty. As late as 1 June, the journal still strove to pluck out and emphasize the rare pieces of good news in what was becoming a military defeat of epic proportions, reporting that "the Allies have reoccupied the area of Abbeville and have crossed the Somme at one point."

For the Gardois, far removed from the thundering of the Panzer divisions and whine of low-flying Stukas, the news of the capitulation of Leopold III of Belgium on 28 May was the first irrefutable sign that the Allied cause was mortally threatened. The fury of the local papers directed at this "act of treason" and "stab in the back" was shared by the public. Yet, despite the shock of Belgium's surrender and the growing number of air alerts, it appeared that the Gardois remained calm and confident that the Allied armies would carry the day.[75] This calm soon gave way to growing bewilderment, if not anxiety, in the face of unrelenting air alerts and the changing character of the news stories. From the determined optimism of the last days of May, the headlines in *Le Républicain du Gard* became increasingly neutral and noncommittal. On 3 June it was reported that "No new event occurred over the course of last night," and four days later it blandly announced that "the battle was taken up this morning in the same circumstances as yesterday."

Le Républicain du Gard succeeded, if only for a time, to remain "above the battle," and rarely stooped to partisan brawling and frantic demands for popular justice. It sharply contrasted with *Le Journal du Midi,* which in its issue of 1 June displayed the banner headline "For the country's salvation." Announcing the news that Reynaud had placed General Weygand in overall military command and had named Pétain as minister of state and vice-president of the council, the paper also showed a sudden flair for Jacobinism. Obsessed with the existence of

75. CA 565, commissaire central to préfet, 1 June 1940.

treason, the paper declared that normal sanctions and punishment no longer sufficed: "We are not afraid to say it: the country is waiting for executions, on the condition, of course, that they be just and deliberate. The new tumbrels and merciless repression that are called for should be public so that everyone can profit from the examples." For its part, *L'Eveil du Gard* had no doubts for whom the tumbrels ought to be reserved. In its May issue, the Catholic journal managed to divert its attention long enough from the front lines to criticize the Socialist paper *Le Populaire* for its "odious campaign" against the church. It asserted that these attacks dovetailed with the insidious work of civil strife that Hitler's agents—"and we know they are there"—were trying to foment. Clearly, the calls for union could not withstand the shock of the German advance, and that there existed, well before the birth of Vichy, an ingrained and reactionary impulse to identify the enemy within as the cause for the defeat.

Neither the studiously optimistic news stories nor the repeated calls for confidence could hide from the Gardois the most convincing symptom of France's mortal condition: the influx of refugees from the north. It was not the first time that the Gard had played host to a press of humanity fleeing battle. During the First World War, nearly 11,000 refugees, the great majority from Alsace and Lorraine, flowed into Nîmes alone, and were sheltered either in the former Assumptionist school or parceled out among the neighboring communes.[76] Many Nîmois undoubtedly remembered this previous wave of refugees. Nonetheless, the experience of 1914–18 did little to prepare them for the unending tide of humanity that flooded the city and the department in the summer of 1940. By 20 June, the prefect Martin reported the influx of 120,000 refugees.[77] This was, moreover, an estimate that accounted for neither the personnel of the French bureaucracy and armament factories, nor the Belgian civilians and military recruits who had fallen back to the Gard. The number of the latter was thought to top 30,000, thus bringing the total refugee population, at its most conservative estimate, to some 150,000.[78] As the indigenous population of the Gard was barely 400,000, this sudden, massive influx of men, women, and children placed extraordinary strains on the infrastructure of the department, the ingenuity of its administrators, and the everyday lives of its inhabitants.

The "exodus" of 1940, a social and demographic upheaval of epic proportions, has been the source of a good deal of literature. Jérôme Tharaud described it as a

76. *Histoire de Nîmes,* 330.
77. CA 684, telegram of préfet to government in Bordeaux, 20 June 1940.
78. Figure of number of Belgian refugees based on report of préfet to Interior. CA 689 (17 July 1940).

"phenomenon unknown since the barbarian invasions of the fourth century."[79] Yet the other side to the exodus is often neglected: the experience of the communities of central and southern France, still largely rural and fairly insular, lying in the path of the tidal wave.[80] The Gard was not spared the shock, yet reacted in a remarkably effective manner. Nevertheless, the crisis helped cultivate those conditions favorable to the installation of Vichy and, at least initially, aspects of the regime's ideology.

The first wave of refugees to wash over the Gard were retreating Belgian civilians and military recruits. As early as the third week of May their presence began to weigh heavily on the departmental and municipal services, and on 18 May, Hubert-Rouger issued an urgent appeal to the residents of Nîmes. In a moving statement, the mayor, referring to "the tragic hours which we are now passing through," urged the Nîmois to open their homes as well as their hearts to their fellow men "chased to these privileged regions of France by the stampede of barbarians." He asked that landlords make known to the city officials the number and size of vacant properties in their possession and that those Nîmois willing to take in children or entire families also immediately notify the authorities.[81]

Though they posed serious logistical problems, the Belgians were warmly welcomed by the Gardois. Rapidly lodged and amply fed by the locals, the Belgians were unanimously pleased by their reception.[82] Perhaps such treatment was to be expected; after all, the Belgians were allies. A significant demonstration of this sentiment was given on 31 May in the Cévenol commune of Anduze, when a group of 700 young Belgians participated in a spontaneous ceremony at the town's *monument aux morts* (war memorial). Having placed flowers at the base of the pedestal, the men marched to city hall, where in twenty detachments, they offered the mayor "a motion of sympathy for France and the people of Anduze, who have done so much to welcome warmly [the Belgians] and nurse their bruised morale." The twenty motions, some of which were written in Flemish, thanked the French for their hospitality and swore attachment to their common cause. The sincerity of the ceremony and speeches was such that the crowd was visibly moved and several young people cried.[83] Similar demonstrations took

79. Quoted in H. R. Kedward, "Patriots and Patriotism in Vichy France," *Transactions of the Royal Historical Society* 32 (1982), 181. See also Jean Vidalenc, *L'Exode de mai–juin 1940* (Paris, 1957) and Nicole Ollier, *L'Exode sur les routes de l'an 40* (Paris, 1970).

80. It must be recalled that forty percent of the Gardois were, on the eve of the war, still involved in agriculture. See Roger Bourderon, *Libération du Languedoc Méditerranéen* (Paris, 1971), 21.

81. CA 459 (poster).

82. CA 689, commission de contrôle postal summary of letters sent by Belgian refugees, 2 June 1940.

83. CA 689, commission de contrôle postal, 1 June 1940.

place over the course of the next few days in the nearby villages of Cassagnoles and Massillargues-Atuech.

This demonstration took place less than a week after the monarch of these young Belgians had capitulated—an event that shocked the Belgians in the Gard no less than their hosts. The intercepted letters from the recruits provide overwhelming proof of their consternation and anger. One recruit wrote that he had not written "since our treasonous king made us ashamed of our nationality. When the village priest told us the news yesterday, we were overcome with dismay." Another wrote in a disbelieving tone that "we have received an unbelievable piece of news: King Leopold is said to have betrayed the Allies. We're losing our minds. . . . The shame for our soldiers, for us all."[84] Yet, given the surprise and shock of the news, the gravity of its ramifications, and the extraordinary violence with which the local press reacted to it, relations between the Belgians and Gardois predictably grew strained. One recruit reported that even after his officers, veterans of 1914, had torn off their decorations, there was a "rumbling anger in the city and fights have already taken place this morning."[85] On the same day as Leopold's surrender, a resident of Sommières described some two hundred Belgian soldiers in disparaging tones: they are "basking in the sun in Soussines, while the children from this same village are somewhere in Belgium, defending their soil against the Germanic hordes."[86] As one Belgian soldier concluded, "even though the folks around here are very kind and received us like brothers, we are no longer welcomed in the same manner . . . [the locals] are saying that the king should not have abandoned his soldiers and country."[87]

The press and local authorities strove to distinguish between the king and his subjects, violently condemning the cowardice of the former while praising the courage and fidelity of the latter. The departmental authorities deliberately sought to maintain the morale of the Gardois by maintaining a positive image of Belgium. An example of this is provided by a prefectoral press release titled "Heroic Belgium." It was a short piece on the Belgian combatants in the north, and though already quite upbeat, an anonymous official in the prefecture attempted to apply yet another coat of mad optimism to it. Over a passage that read "Sergeant G. and his two comrades," the official scrawled in purple ink "these three energetic men." And following a passage on the enlistment of 450 young Belgian recruits in a Gardois village, the copyreader added "In various departmental communes . . . similar demonstrations unfolded in the same atmosphere of

84. CA 689, commission de contrôle postal, 2 June 1940.
85. CA 689, commission de contrôle postal, 2 June 1940.
86. CA 689, commission de contrôle postal, 2 June 1940.
87. CA 689, commission de contrôle postal, 2 June 1940.

fervent patriotism."[88] The violently underlined phrases "Vive la France" and "Vive la Belgique," followed by long series of exclamation points, hint at the desperation, rather than confidence, of this particular official. And one can only speculate on the reader's effort to reconcile the contents of the release with the reality of tens of thousands of young Belgian recruits, idle and not visibly thirsting for action, that surrounded him.

Moreover, Leopold's act provided the compost for a flowering obsession with treason and subversion. The transition from assertions of invincibility to intimations of total collapse occurred too rapidly to be easily negotiated. Philippe Laborie's observation for the Lot holds equally true for the Gard: public opinion "had great need for exceptional explanations for a situation it could not master," and thus pounced upon Leopold's act as the key to the burgeoning mystery.[89] The notions of conspiracy and treason as explanatory concepts had long been part of the ideologies of both left and right. These notions had been common political currency since the early 1930s and received, with the dissolution and hounding of the PCF in 1939, a recognition tantamount to an official imprimatur. At the very moment Leopold was preparing his capitulation, the *Journal du Midi* was warning its readers about the continuing existence of Communist agitation. It affirmed that the party's propaganda was omnipresent, reaching the farmers, merchants, and soldiers, and demanded that the country be given "the conviction that an energetic and thorough repression is being undertaken which will protect it from the stab in the back which [the nation's] enemies from within and without are preparing."[90] That the stab came from the Belgian king rather than Communist militants was irrelevant; the stab itself was the central act in the ritual of treason.

The Belgian recruits were soon followed by an ever-deepening river of French refugees, cascading down from the northern departments, Alsace and Lorraine. After 10 June and the entry of Italy in the war, this human torrent was bloated by another tributary of refugees coursing in from the southeast. The rising watermark demanded extraordinary measures on the part of the departmental administration. On 15 June, the prefect dispatched a circular to the mayors of the Gard, informing them that they had his entire support and confidence "to settle all the difficulties" that the arrival of the refugees would entail. They were given the power to requisition and impose the lodging of refugees on the residents, as well as take over all public buildings and public and private schools. The prefect

88. CA 626, *arrêté à la presse*, 1 June 1940.
89. Laborie, *Résistants, vichyssois et autres*, 143.
90. The story first appears 2 May, and is reprinted in every issue until 15 June.

concluded that "one sole rule [*sic*] will inspire your conduct: humanitarian duty and social solidarity."[91]

Despite the near anarchic conditions in France and the meager material and human resources available to the prefecture, the local authorities ably acquited themselves. By the end of the second week of June, a report had been submitted to the prefect by M. Thibault, director of the municipal reception center, in which he surveyed the various options open to Nîmes for sheltering the incoming refugees. If, in addition to the sites specifically designated as temporary residence centers, one were to add the public and private schools and cinemas, Thibault estimated that there would be place enough for 8,500 people to lie down at night and for another 6,500 who would have to remain seated. Adding that there remained the hotels to be requisitioned, Thibault concluded that Nîmes could meet the needs of lodging if one kept in mind that the city was not a permanent stationing center, but "only a temporary residence from which, after a pause, the refugees will have to be directed either to the departmental communes or other departments to which they have been assigned."[92]

Yet there inevitably were conflicting directives and orders from the authorities in Nîmes and outlying villages, to which were added the sheer material limitations of the communal resources. Thus when the mayor of Le Vigan, the seat of the mountainous and austere subprefecture, was confronted by the new wave of refugees provoked by the Italian intervention, he sent an urgent note to the prefect. He warned that there is a "humanitarian duty to shelter families with young children who thought that they had been assigned to Le Vigan or the region as their center of retreat; consequently, the number of available sites for the evacuees is diminishing. I wanted to point this out to you so that the disappointments I foresee will surprise no one."[93]

As for the Belgians, there were increasing signs of irritation and anxiety on the part of their hosts. As early as 6 June, the subprefect of Alès warned that the presence of young Belgian recruits was creating serious friction in the villages whose men (from the ages of 18 to 48) were in uniform. He predicted that the Belgians' continued presence would deepen an "atmosphere of criticism, indeed anger, as the women do not understand why their husbands or sons should be fighting while these young men, most of whom are idle, hang about the roads and in their camps."[94] These warnings found a clear echo in the Cévenol valleys:

91. CA 684, préfet to mayors, 15 June 1940.
92. CA 459, Thibault to préfet, 14 June 1940.
93. CA 459, sous-préfet of Le Vigan to préfet, 12 June 1940.
94. CA 689, sous-préfet of Alès to préfet, 6 June 1940.

more than a month after the subprefect's warning, the police commissioner of Anduze and St. Jean du Gard reported that the tension was, in fact, worsening. He observed that the complaints lodged against the Belgians had become universal; having little to occupy them, some "distinguish themselves by their rowdy behavior in town and others by the petty crimes they commit in the countryside (stealing of fruit, potatoes, etc.), more often for the sake of destruction than for profit." With admirable understatement, the police official concluded that the Belgians had lost the goodwill with which they had been originally welcomed.[95] The welcome was wearing all the thinner with the prospect of the grape harvest and the growing fear on the part of the locals that the Belgians would damage or destroy the crops. André Pallier, a resident of St. Jean du Gard, warned that "our rural population has until now been able to conserve its sang-froid. But I am afraid that . . . if the refugees are still in our villages when the grapes begin to ripen, extremely serious incidents will occur."[96]

The prefect strove to respond to these multiple warnings by alerting a government in the midst of flight. His telegrams followed the caravan of French officialdom migrating from Bordeaux to Clermont-Ferrand and finally to Vichy. Repeated requests in late June for the removal of the Belgian recruits went unheeded; the authorities, clearly, were simply incapable of responding to any such demand. On 17 July, the prefect renewed his warning, affirming that the Belgian officers themselves admitted their inability to control their men, and that the "attitude of certain Belgians has given rise to numerous incidents that risk to worsen and spark a sharp response from the farmers."[97] Interestingly, the prefect singled out the Flemish as the major source of trouble, as did several other reports that arrived from all parts of the department. It is difficult to ascertain the validity of these observations, but it is probable that the inability of many Flemish to speak French, or by speaking in a "barbaric accent," played against them. A good distance had been traveled from the days that the motions of sympathy written in Flemish were found "quaint" by the residents of Anduze.

In fact, there was a certain fear on the part of the departmental officials that the Belgians, and in particular the Flemings, presented a security risk for unoccupied France. In a report of early July, the subprefect of Alès reported the attempt of nearly two hundred Belgians to leave their camp at St. Jean-du-Gard and return to their homes. After having forced them back to their camp, the subprefect wrote that while most of the restive Belgians sincerely desired to return to their country, "it is not impossible that there are certain elements among them, notably among the Flemish, who are looking for any possible occasion to sow disorder

95. CA 689, commissaire de police of Anduze to préfet, 10 July 1940.
96. CA 689, letter to préfet, 5 July 1940.
97. CA 689, préfet to Interior, 17 July 1940.

within free France." He concluded that such a tendency would serve the purposes of the German authorities, "who would not fail to take advantage of these demonstrations, perhaps in order to impose punitive expeditions and increase the burden of the armistice."[98]

It is obvious that the restlessness, if not subversiveness, of the Belgians was real. As early as June, there are reports of their growing discontent; certain recruits began to worry about missing the upcoming harvest, others simply missed their homes and families. The morale of the *chasseurs belges* stationed in Goudargues was singled out as particularly bad; many were miners and complained that they wanted to return to their children: "French fathers of four children haven't been mobilized and we don't see why we should be."[99] Leopold's surrender clearly incensed and shamed the great majority of Belgians in the department; yet once the initial shock began to recede and the German Army approached, a significant number of Walloons as well as Flemish questioned the utility of remaining under uniform in the Gard. It is only toward the end of July, however, that the Belgians, both civilians and soldiers, began to return home—an *exode* undoubtedly as welcomed by the departing guests as well as the worried hosts.[100]

Yet the homesickness of the Belgians never rivaled that of the refugees from Alsace and Lorraine, who were now strangers in their own country. Unlike the other refugees who had fallen back upon the Gard, the Alsatians and Lorrainers were there to stay: their region was eventually annexed and placed under the administrative control of Nazi gauleiters. M. Damnert, the president of the Groupement des évacués et réfugiés d'Alsace et Lorraine (GERAL), underlined this point in early October. The German designs on the two provinces now manifest, the Alsatian patriot referred to the annexation of these two provinces in 1870–71. At least then, he affirmed, "there were protests raised in Bordeaux by several representatives from Alsace-Lorraine. However, in 1940 not a single deputy from our two provinces had the courage to protest the pure and simple annexation of Alsace and Lorraine by the Third Reich."[101]

---

98. CA 689, sous-préfet of Alès to préfet, 3 July 1940.

99. CA 689, commissaire divisionnaire to préfet, 3 June 1940.

100. "Exode" is the word used by the commander of the gendarmerie in his report of 20 July 1940 (CA 689). The documents I have read concerning the Belgian presence in the Gard clash sharply with the participants' memories of this period collected by the pastor W. Marichal in "Des Belges en Cévennes," in *Causses et Cévennes*, no. 4 (1976), 264–67. Although the pastor acknowledges that "a certain local xenophobism weighed on our friends [the Belgians]," the accounts he introduces all emphasize the warm welcome and continuing ties of friendship between the Cévenols and visiting Belgians.

101. CA 686, commissaire divisionnaire to préfet, 13 October 1940. Although the departments of the Moselle, Upper Rhine, and Lower Rhine were never annexed de jure by Germany, they were

The stated aims of the refugee association were mutual aid (both moral and material), the safeguarding of individual and collective interests of the members, the preservation and promotion of French ideas, and the remembrance of Alsace and the department of the Moselle. It would only be over the course of the next several months that the contradictions inherent in this kaleidoscope of goals would appear. The "French ideas" of the Alsatian and Lorraine refugees eventually diverged from those of Vichy, and their stubborn embrace of the souvenir of the "lost provinces" would undermine the very legitimacy of the regime by underscoring the latter's diplomatic and political impotency. The continued worship of the provinces had no place in the "new Europe" advocated by the representatives of Vichy, and the continued existence of such an association challenged the raison d'être of the new French state. It is for this reason, among others, that the local authorities kept extremely close tabs on the activities of the association and would eventually suspect the group of "anti-national" (i.e., Gaullist) sentiments.

The arrival of the Alsatian and Lorraine refugees served as a tragic reminder of an earlier, overwhelming defeat seventy years before. In fact, the sudden appearance of the refugees clashed with the continued optimism of the closely monitored press. The refugees were the petrels preceding a storm of unprecedented intensity. It was not until the second week of June that the news accounts in *Le Républicain du Gard* became unmistakably pessimistic and bleak. On 8 June the paper announced that "enemy tank divisions, observed last night in the upper valley of La Bresle, have speeded up their advance." During the next week, the paper offered fewer details and more moral exhortation. For example, on 9 June it urged the Gardois to have confidence: "The leaders we need are now where they are needed." A poor choice of headlines: twenty-four hours later, few knew where the "leaders" were, as they had quit Paris for Bordeaux. In a week's time they would be suing for peace.

In a powerful condemnation of the leadership of the Third Republic from Munich to Vichy, Pierre Laborie affirms that there can be found, at least within the Lot, no evidence that officials demanded sacrifices and encouraged realism among the inhabitants. There was no identification of the war with a grand cause and no expression of realistic hope to which the public could cling. Within a very short period, the French were swung by their government from one extreme to the other, reeling from a succession of false assumptions: there was "the false guarantee of security, the false hope for peace after Munich, the false notion of

---

placed under the control of Nazi gauleiters in August 1940, and administered as if part of the Reich, thus amounting to an annexation de facto.

military security . . . [and] the considerably falsified depiction of the reality of the war."[102] Laborie goes on to underline the continuities between these last days of the Republic and Vichy: "The old marshal and his cortege of anachronisms and reactionaries seem to be the logical continuation . . . of the abdications that had preceded them. The disconcerting episode of the 'phony war' reinforced the settling in of collective attitudes that anticipate the acceptance of the French State."[103]

Laborie's observations apply to events in the Gard during this same period. After the Maginot Line of cement and steel was easily circumvented by the German blitzkrieg, and the "Maginot Line" of illusions proved equally frail before the onslaught of reality, the Gardois were all too prepared for the comforting visions and simple truths of the Pétainist discourse. The creation of Vichy and its initial legitimacy were rooted in the local reaction to the manifest failures and shortcomings of the men and institutions of the Republic.[104] Stanley Hoffmann has written that Vichy was "a great revenge of minorities"—of those conservative political and social forces, in other words, increasingly perturbed over the previous sixteen years by the leftward drift of the Republic.[105] In an unhappy twist to Adolphe Thier's ultimatum in somewhat similar circumstances seventy years before, these forces declared in the summer of 1940 that the new regime would be conservative—and that the republic of 1875 would no longer be at all. Yet it must be reemphasized that the reaction of most Gardois, like the overwhelming majority of their fellow countrymen, was not the end result of a process of political reasoning. Theirs was instead a visceral reaction to two years of perceived incompetence and impotence of the Third Republic's leaders, culminating in the abdication of power and perceived abandonment of the institutions and ideals of the Republic. This is the soil in which Vichy attempted to take root.

102. Laborie, *Résistants, vichyssois et autres,* 155.
103. Laborie, *Résistants, vichyssois et autres,* 334.
104. That the French military were not implicated in what Georges Bernanos called "The Big Bust" had less to do with their innocence—indeed, they must carry a large responsibility for France's defeat—than with the demand for an armistice rather than a capitulation, which consequently left the moral and legal burden of defeat on the shoulders of the government.
105. Stanley Hoffmann, *Decline or Renewal? France Since the 1930s* (New York, 1974), 5.

3

THE ADVENT OF VICHY

They told me to chose between being an oppressor or a victim. / I embraced unhappiness and left them to commit the crime.
— Condorcet, quoted by Charles Corbière, 1940

We banished God from France and the Germans have taken his place
— Bishop Jean Girbeau, 1940

On 17 June, Philippe Pétain, head of the French government formed that same day in Bordeaux, announced in a radio broadcast that he was seeking an armistice with Germany. *Le Républicain du Gard* reprinted the marshal's address under the headline "France is in mourning." Yet, the great majority of the Gardois were already wearing their Sunday best. Scorched by the onslaught of events and battered by the torrent of refugees carrying countless stories of the horrors of the exodus and the absence of authority, the inhabitants of the Gard were ripe for Pétain's message. Two days before, the central commissioner had reported, in a passage studded with prudent qualifications, that if further resistance became futile, "the population, and especially those families with members at the front, would support those steps necessary to obtain the best deal for the cessation of hostilities."[1] The great diarist of the Occupation, Jean Guéhenno, was certainly a minority when he wrote: "It's over. An old man who no longer even has the voice of a man, but speaks like an old woman, told us at twelve-thirty this afternoon that he is seeking peace."[2] The experience of the exodus, and the shock of defeat and the anger at those institutions and men held responsible for these events, had prepared the Gardois for the marshal's address, regardless of its octave.

Although the local authorities had acquitted themselves ably of their administrative tasks, and notables like Hubert-Rouger retained the support and sympathy of the population, the influx of fleeing civilians, soldiers, and politicians nevertheless helped prepare the department for the accession of Pétain. Given the political and administrative vacuum left by the Republic, to believe that someone was prepared and willing to take the affairs of the nation in hand was not necessarily a call for dictatorship or the return of the Bourbons. It may instead have been the reflex of a frayed and desperate patriotism, the response of a population that was profoundly unprepared for the drama and tragedy of 1940.[3] As Pétain himself was to ask that same autumn, "Is it understood that I found myself, and continue to find myself, confronted by a vacuum [le néant]? A vacuum is above all else the absence of authority—and authority, when I came to power, did not exist anywhere."[4] It is in the light of this observation that we will consider the course of events in the Gard during the summer of 1940.

In the years immediately leading up to the war, Pétain's potential as a national leader and symbol had already stirred a certain amount of sympathy and active support among the right in the Gard. In 1936 the nationalist Gustave Hervé had published his pamphlet "C'est Pétain qu'il nous faut," in which he made the case for placing the hero of Verdun in power. As Hervé wrote, Pétain's very name "speaks to the mind and heart; it is a popular and prestigious name, an illustrious name that does away with the need for long introductions and discourses."[5]

1. CA 565, commissaire central to préfet, 15 June 1940.
2. Jean Guéhenno, *Journal des années noires* (Paris, 1947), 14.
3. H. R. Kedward makes this point when he writes that the embrace of Pétain was a response to the "images of personal authority and leadership, and to invest them with all the sanctity of patriotism, still more the desperate patriotism of crisis"; see his "Patriots and Patriotism in Vichy France," 183.
4. Quoted in Miller, *Les pousse-au-jouir du maréchal Pétain,* 31. On the fall of France, see Alistair Horne, *To Lose a Battle: France, 1940* (London, 1969), Henri Michel, *La Défaite de la France* (Paris, 1980), Jean-Baptiste Duroselle, *L'Abîme 1939–1945* (Paris, 1982), and Marc Bloch, *Strange Defeat* (New York, 1968).
5. On Hervé's campaign, and the nature of Pétainism before 1940, see Richard Griffiths, *Marshal Pétain* (London, 1970). Henri Guillemin has pointed out that the title of Hervé's tract referred to a popular Boulangist refrain of 1888: "C'est Boulanger, Boulanger, Boulanger / C'est Boulanger qu'il nous faut"; *Nationalistes et nationaux* (Paris, 1974), 370.

In a review of Hervé's work, *Sully* allowed that Hervé's proposal "certainly would not be the worst in this period of crisis." But the reviewer, Roger Darolle, warned that even were France driven to disaster, *Sully* would accept Pétain only as a provisional chief of the government, insisting that the only satisfactory and permanent solution to France's problems was the return of the monarchy.[6]

Three years later, *Le Viganais* hailed Pétain's nomination as ambassador to Franco's Spain. The paper quoted an address given by the marshal, in which he affirmed that the major cause of France's decline was "the abandonment of the nation's spiritual life . . . by which I mean the respect for authority and discipline, the taste for work well done, the worship of art, and the sentiment of duty." The Catholic journal cheered France's great fortune to have a man of Pétain's moral fiber who "remains in the breach up to the very end of his life, not for his own ends, [but] to *serve* once again."[7] *Le Viganais* thus anticipated one of the arguments for the legitimacy of the Vichy regime, for which the verb *servir* would become a principal theme.

Quite apart from these specific, early and scattered homages, the person of Pétain in the Gard, as throughout France, had long attracted universal respect, thanks to his reputation as a republican in politics and a humanitarian in war. Hence, when Pétain gave the "gift" of his person to the country in the critical days of June 1940, the gesture was gratefully accepted. Pétain was depicted as a modern-day Cincinnatus, shouldering the burden of government at the very moment when he should have instead been enjoying a well-earned rest. In the eyes of the Gardois, the old marshal, despite his long career of national service, reluctantly accepted the responsibility thrust upon him by the feeble men of the Republic. He thus followed a succession of saviors or providential men: from Napoleon Bonaparte and General Boulanger, to Raymond Poincaré and Gaston Doumergue (a native of the Gard) who all donned the mantle of leadership at those very moments when France found herself short of leaders and long on danger.[8]

As Raoul Girardet has noted, the ostensible virtues of these "providential men" correspond, in the public's imagination, to the Latin notion of *gravitas*:

6. *Sully*, April 1936, 11–12.

7. *Le Viganais* (11 March 1939). Paper's emphasis.

8. See the recent biography by Marc Ferro, *Pétain* (Paris, 1987). Ferro's work is the basis for the controversial film "Pétain" now in production. See also the work by the American biographer Herbert Lottman, *Pétain: Hero or Traitor, the Untold Story* (New York, 1985). For a concise review of the works consecrated to Pétain's career, see Bernard Laguerre, "Les Biographies de Pétain," in *Vichy et les Français,* ed. Azéma and Bédarida, 45–56.

"firmness under fire, experience, prudence, sang-froid, moderation."[9] These very qualities would be emphasized ad nauseam by the propagandists of Vichy; yet, based upon the sparse evidence available, they seem to have been anticipated spontaneously by the inhabitants of the Gard. In its issue of 19 June, *Le Républicain du Gard* affirmed that the Gardois had placed their confidence in the "towering figure of Marshal Pétain [which] dominates the terrible struggle that will determine the fate of our country." Yet such exhortations on the part of the press were unnecessary. The central commissioner reported that Pétain's decision to accept the terms of the armistice, "which the glorious soldier himself had the courage to announce, has caused a great stir [*une immense sensation*]."[10] Following the announcement of the actual cessation of hostilities, the divisional commissioner observed that the public acknowledged "the futility of continuing the struggle, particularly after the explanations of . . . Marshal Pétain." The desire of some to see France continue the struggle from overseas "seems to have found little enthusiasm," and from the moment the public learned that the armistice had been signed, it "felt a sentiment of relief provoked by the fear of seeing the continuation of an invasion that risked becoming total."[11]

First and foremost, then, for the Gardois, Pétain symbolized the savior. But not only did he save France from complete devastation and occupation: his advent also marked the end of one era and the birth of a new and more promising one. Thus the central commissioner of Nîmes reported that after "the hard truths told to the French by the authoritative voice of Marshal Pétain, everyone seems to have understood that the era of discussions and sterile debates, like the regime of comfort and insouciance, must be abolished."[12] Pétain's personality was beyond discussion: "It is held that there is no one better than he to gather all those of good will, to tell the French those truths that need to be said and open the way to France's new destinies."[13]

Both the religious and lay press took up almost immediately many of the themes that would become staples of the ideology and propaganda of the Vichy regime. Thus, the repeated religious and political mea culpas; the condemnation of politics and mores under the Third Republic; the call for political and spiritual renewal; the praise of traditional values, rising from soil, family, and labor; and a rekindled interest in regionalism are the major themes intoned by the press during this period. Yet it would be misleading to portray all papers as responding

---

9. Girardet, *Mythes et mythes politiques,* 74.
10. CA 565, commissaire central to préfet, 22 June 1940.
11. CA 565, commissaire divisionnaire to préfet, 27 June 1940.
12. CA 565, commissaire central to préfet, 29 June 1940.
13. CA 565, commissaire central to préfet, 13 July 1940.

with equal alacrity and enthusiasm to the turn of events. In the period between the ebb of defeat and flow of state censorship, there appear telling differences in the tenor and direction of the articles in the various journals. In fact, important nuances were to remain even after freedom of expression had disappeared.[14]

Le Journal du Midi, which had been trumpeting the old refrain of *le patrie en danger* up until the very end, abruptly changed register on 20 June. It reprinted an article on "The heroism of the French soldiers," taken from the *Hamburger Tageblatt.* Apart from this piece—which paid homage to "the valor of [Germany's] defeated adversary," but whose origin spoke more eloquently than its text on the course of events—there was but a handful of other articles, innocuous padding on subjects ranging from the oldest veterinary school in the world to a millionaire-for-a-day club in the United States. This change from Jacobinism to distraction lasted but one issue. On 26 June, the paper carried a piece on the causes and responsibilities of the defeat, which echoed the Pétainist analysis: too few children, too little work, too much joy. In a foretaste of the puritanism of the National Revolution, the paper attacked those Nîmois who were calling for the reopening of the outdoor cafés. To what end, the article asked: "To once again see women seated at tables, smoking nonchalantly their cigarettes and mocking passers-by?" The paper denounced any such return to the decadent manners of the past and demanded that "we each examine our conscience and realize that we must better ourselves and abandon all of our past illusions."[15]

During the days immediately following Pétain's assumption of power, *Le Républicain du Gard* struck a prudent position. On 23 June, in an article titled "The Struggle Continues," it sought to emphasize the "correctness" of the behavior of the occupying German troops, and at the same time, underline the tenacity of the French Army. Upon the signing of the armistice on 22 June, the paper remained cautious. Echoing Pétain, it asserted the need for a "redressement moral" and exhorted its readers to "remake France, despite the hard conditions which will be imposed, through an effort that will not know any respite."[16]

In the wake of the armistice, the paper nevertheless betrayed an indecisiveness as profound as that exhibited during the Munich crisis. From 25 June, the day the armistice took effect, to the end of the month, Pujolas's paper limited itself to

14. Censorship, which applied the stick of suspension, grew increasingly heavy-handed, and by 1942 papers generally had their entire content dictated by Vichy's secrétariat général de l'information. On the nature of censorship under Vichy, see Michele Cointet-Labrousse, *Vichy et le fascisme,* 73–82. See also "Propagande et modelage des esprits," by Claude Lévy and Dominique Veillon, in *Vichy et les Français,* ed. Azéma and Bédarida, 184–202.

15. *Le Journal du Midi* (26 June 1940).

16. *Le Républicain du Gard* (23 June 1940).

carrying the messages of the government without comment. This neutral stance was also assumed in the paper's reports on the continuing struggle of Great Britain, as well as in the printing of both Churchill's address to France, in which the British leader expressed his consternation concerning France's surrender, and Pétain's tart response: neither side received the paper's approbation nor its condemnation.

Should such reticence be interpreted as resistance to the new government? The answer is far from certain. On 29 June the journal carried a large article devoted to Salazar's regime in Portugal. No particular event in Portugal justified such an article; rather, it found its justification in France's current situation. An antirepublican allegory of childish transparency, the piece recounted the history of republican Portugal which, prey to no less than sixteen revolutions and forty changes of government during its life, "knew great misery and anarchy." The parallel thus drawn between Portugal in 1926 and France in 1940, the article went on to strike a second one between Salazar and Pétain. The former, described as a modest and unknown individual, at first resisted when asked by the members of the Portuguese government to assume the reins of government. Yet, though "sickened by politics . . . he was conscious that his patriotic duty must take precedence [and] he gave in to the pleas." The piece concluded, "This man, extraordinary in his simplicity, this ascetic of iron in a velvet glove was able to impose his will upon his fellow citizens to the extent that, just like sheep led by their shepherd, they obey him without hesitation." Despite the farrago of mixed metaphors and potted history, the point of the article was clear: Pétain, no less than Salazar in Portugal, was the individual sent by providence to France at her moment of great need.

Yet the apparent reorientation of the paper in favor of an authoritarian form of government was halting: the republican scruples of the staff were not quickly overridden. The day after Pétain had been invested with the power to modify the constitution, *Le Républicain du Gard* gave only its guarded approval. The paper allowed how the constitution of 1875 foresaw the possibility of modifications, and concluded with the wish that such changes would make France a "new country of peace, of Work, of Family and of Liberty!" The final trait underlined by the paper is significant. A leftover from the trinity of revolutionary values, liberty would not figure on the list of the commandments of Vichy's National Revolution. Yet the anonymous journalist clung to it, though it was only a matter of days before the paper, under the eyes of the censor, jettisoned the word, if not the hope behind it.

The paper returned to this theme the following day, announcing that Pétain had been given the power to promulgate a new constitution. In an editorial titled "Confidence"—a headline marking the very absence of the quality it denoted—

the journal betrayed its disquiet with the heralded changes. It worried that the only attributes of the new constitution were the guarantees and rights of work, family, and homeland. Whistling in the dark, the editorial expressed its "confidence in the government to present a viable project that nevertheless respects the core of democratic liberties." Yet the editorialist then affirmed that "any regime that will guarantee an honest administration, equality in the division of financial burdens, the integrity of those who govern and the impartiality of the law will be welcomed with satisfaction." Thus erasing with his right hand what he had just written with his left, the anonymous writer concluded that "we still do not know the face of the new France. We are ready to greet it if it imposes upon us new disciplines, shared by all, beneficial to all."[17] The writer still clung to the words of 1789, but had already begun to reinterpret their sense. It had now become the equality of hardships, a fraternity in collective responsibility, and the liberty to deny liberty's utility.

The absence of commentary and the appearance of neutrality or objectivity in the press can be interpreted in more than one sense. For example, the British attack on the French fleet anchored at Mers-el-Kebir on 3 July did not push *Le Républicain du Gard* into a flurry of hysterical anglophobia. In a noncommittal fashion, it reported on the sea battle, and on 6 July carried the headline "Response of M.-J. Prouvost to M. Churchill after the attack on Mers-el-Kebir," under which was the text of the French propaganda chief's declaration. The paper, though as shocked by the attack as were most Frenchmen, distanced itself from any attempt to turn the drama into fuel for the fire of anti-English sentiment.[18] The relative calm of the paper contrasted sharply with the hysteria of *Le Journal du Midi,* which published a diatribe on France's "defunct friendship" with the British and approvingly quoted Maurras's comment that at the moment "the real nation [*le pays réel*] has just found its true expression, London continues its abominable campaign against the reborn French State."[19]

Indeed, in the early days of July, *Le Républicain du Gard,* in subtle ways, seemed distrustful of the new order. The columnist of "Votre opinion ce soir?" observed, in a piece on the weather, that "it is better to speak of the rain, the wind and the heat rather than to speak maliciously . . . of one's neighbor"—a fairly clear reference to the growing phenomenon of anonymous denunciation.[20] And as late as 15 July, the paper succeeded in slipping anti-German pokes past the

17. *Le Républicain du Gard* (11 July 1940).
18. On this aspect of the attack, see J.-P. Azéma, "Le Drame de Mers-el-Kebir," in *Etudes sur la France de 1939 à nos jours* (Paris, 1985), 38–53.
19. *Le Journal du Midi* (9 November 1940).
20. *Le Républicain du Gard* (2 July 1940).

censor. Along with an article announcing the nomination of the tennis champion Jean Borotra as secretary general of physical education and sports, there appeared a photograph of the French star in action. The caption read: "A shot of Borotra (the bouncing Basque) during a Dawis [sic] Cup match won against the German Henkel."[21]

There were few such subtleties in Le Journal du Midi. The paper gave itself completely to the National Revolution, as well as to the hunt for scapegoats. In an article titled "France Again Becomes French," the paper hailed the first racist laws passed by Vichy, and affirmed that though "it will be necessary to go further along this path, the way is already traced."[22] The same article also mugged Georges Mandel, the former minister of the interior, disciple of Georges Clemenceau, and not uncoincidentally, Jewish. He was branded as "the agent of England . . . charged with conspiring against the security of the State." Just two months before, the journal had praised Mandel as the legatee of Clemenceau's reputation as the "premier flic de France [France's top cop]" responsible for the "vast cleaning-up of spies and communists."[23] It is pointless to multiply the "before" and "after" articles of Le Journal du Midi; this one example suffices to show its rapid and total adhesion to the ideology of the new regime.

In an article published the week before, titled "The Return to the Soil," Le Journal du Midi took up a theme dear to French nationalists. Anchored in the notion of la terre et les morts (the land and the dead), coined at the turn of the century by the French nationalist writer Maurice Barrès, this motif would become a touchstone of the Vichy ideology.[24] As Pétain was to declare in one of his early addresses, "The soil does not lie. It remains your haven. It is the patrie itself." The departmental journal that most wholeheartedly embraced this notion was Le Vigneron du sud-est. The official organ of the General Confederation of

21. Up until November 1942 and the German occupation of southern France, the press in the unoccupied zone generally enjoyed greater flexibility in its attitude toward Germany than the press in occupied France. See Claude Bellanger et al., Histoire de la presse française (Parıs, 1972), 4; chap. 1.

22. Le Journal du Midi (17 August 1940). The paper is referring to the law of 22 July, which created a commission to review all naturalizations granted after 1927.

23. Le Journal du Midi (14 June 1940). Le Républicain du Gard showed a certain ambiguity on the arrest of Mandel. Le Rachalan wrote that those who had thought that nothing new could appear under the sun were mistaken: "Who would have thought that one of the passengers of the Massilia [the ship on which those notables of the Republic who refused to follow Pétain had attempted to land in French North Africa] would become a passenger on a . . . tumbrel" (27 July 1940).

24. Le Journal du Midi (10 August 1940). For the background to this element of the ideology of Vichy, see Paxton, Vichy France, 200–209. See also Miller, Les Pousse-au-jouir du maréchal Pétain, 132–37. The latter points out that, in the Pétainist discourse, the soil is more than just the soil; it is the guarantee of France's perennity and the moral foundation of the French state.

Southeastern Winegrowers, the journal, both administered and published in Nîmes, was understandably the most enthusiastic proselyte for such an appeal. France's defeat provided the occasion for a lesson in morality and politics not only from the church, but also from the winegrowers. If the peasantry were to be the motor of France's rebirth, as the journalist Roger Rouviere asserted in the paper, "it is essential that they no longer be refused that which they've never been accorded: the right to have their voice heard and to participate in the management of public affairs."[25]

Rouviere's affirmation undoubtedly found a sympathetic and wide audience in the Gard. In 1940, agriculture was the department's dominant economic activity, employing approximately 40 percent of the Gardois. The principal crop was the grape: though it was less widespread in the Gard than in the neighboring departments, winegrowing nevertheless accounted for some 60 percent of the cultivated land.[26] Thus, in commenting upon a motion presented by Paul Barthe, a deputy from the Hérault, to suppress the sale of contreband alcohol (a competitor of wine) Le Rachalan saw cause for congratulation: "We know, as does every good Nîmois, that 'All's well in Nîmes when wine sells well.' "[27]

The local monoculture would cause massive food-supply difficulties once the era of rationing and scarcity began under Vichy. Yet in the summer of 1940, the preponderance of viticulture in the Gard provided a tailored audience for a regime that praised the values of the land and enthused over the virtues of the peasant. As the *Vigneron*'s monthly columnist, Louis Fourmaud, made clear, governments may come and go, but the earth and traditional values abide. After a storm, "the peasant has always rebuilt his house, replanted his trees and reworked the land in order to plant his seeds. France's soul is not dead and she will do like the peasant." In fact, the earth became, for Fourmaud, the source of the country's salvation; he declared that though France "gave way under the weight of [German] numbers and material, yet sooner or later, just as the soil saves the peasant . . . so too will it save France."[28]

The paths to salvation being blazed left and right during those summer months were religious no less than secular. Catholics and Protestants were equally busy

25. *Le Vigneron du sud-est* (May–June 1940).
26. Bourderon, *Libération du Languedoc Méditerranéen*, 21. In contrast, in the neighboring Hérault, it accounted for 66 percent of the farmland. See Roger Austin, "Propaganda and Public Opinion in Vichy: The Department of the Hérault, 1940–44," *European Studies Review* 13 (October 1983), 457.
27. *Le Républicain du Gard* (24–25 March 1940).
28. *Le Vigneron du sud-est* (May–June 1940). It is interesting to note that Fourmaud here anticipated Pétain himself, who in his address of 23 June used the same metaphor of the passing storm and the persistence of the peasant, who does not lose hope and "plows with the same faith the same furrow for next season's harvest."

with their spiritual maps and compasses. Both communities confronted the same riddles: why was France defeated and why did God permit it? The speed and thoroughness of France's collapse convinced a majority of her clergy that the defeat was nothing less than divine punishment for the dechristianization and decadence of the French—a historical commonplace that applies no less to the two confessions of the Gard than to the rest of France.[29] Yet it is a generalization that, in this particular case, requires minor but important qualifications.

Following Pétain's call for an armistice, Bishop Girbeau strove to maintain a certain optimism. Acknowledging the immensity of France's reverses, he nevertheless refused to despair; as he reminded his flock, to surrender all hope would be neither Christian nor French. He then inveighed against declining French morality, demanding that the Vaillantes, members of the Church's movement for young girls, dress more modestly: "If the present fashion pushes [the girls] to take a few more liberties, will anything remain of their dresses?" The moment was not right, he concluded, to irritate God's justice by taking such pagan license.[30]

It was not coincidental that Girbeau worried over the length of dress hems at the very moment that France had been brought to her knees. In the eyes of the bishop, the ties were obvious between the corrupted state of politics and society in republican France and her crushing military defeat. Though a number of lay leaders made the same connection, the ecclesiastical hierarchy in particular exhibited what one historian has called the "temptation of reductive reasoning"; namely, the tendency to reduce or transform political questions into religious, social, or moral ones. When discussing the causes of defeat, the clergy declared itself to be interested solely in the moral and religious sources, which "led to striking . . . and worrisome shortcuts."[31]

Girbeau took this exegetical shortcut in his first full statement on the causes of France's defeat. In a letter addressed to his flock, Girbeau repeated the themes of moral decay and religious indifference that had laced his sermons since the period of the Popular Front. Changed circumstances, however, now lent a prophetic character to these earlier warnings, and the bishop sought to profit fully from the turn of events. Posing the question whether God could come to terms with a France ignorant of the principles of morality, the duties of the family, and the proper education of its youth, Girbeau replied with a firm "No." The bishop said that God "has put an end to his silence and forbearance. Who can deny that his

29. See, for example, Yves-Marie Hilaire, "L'été 40: L'effondrement et le saveur," in *Eglises et chrétiens dans la deuxième guerre mondiale,* ed. Montclos et al. (Lyon, 1982), 79–90.

30. *La Semaine religieuse* (23 June 1940), 207.

31. Claude Langlois, "Le Régime de Vichy et le clergé d'après les 'Semaines religieuses' des dioceses de la zone libre," *Revue française de science politique* 22 (August 1972), 766.

response has been the collapse of our front on the Meuse, the heroic but bloody retreat from Flanders, the complete routing of an army famed for its legendary bravery and valor, and most humiliating of all, the occupation by an insolent conquerer of the most beautiful provinces of our country. We banished God from France and the Germans have taken his place."[32]

A riveting conclusion, both in the brutal simplicity of its expression and the seeming irrefutability of its logic: after all, had not the Church long warned of the dire risks France ran by denying her religious vocation? Girbeau then placed a special burden on the shoulders of his parishioners. Deaf to the warnings of the church, the Christian voter had failed "in the accomplishment of his civic duty [and so] brought to power those who demolished the Christian conscience of France." Yet the bishop saw potential good resulting from the catastrophe: the defeat would be a "godsend if it opens the eyes of the French and puts them back on the path to the House of our Father."[33] This politico-theological gloss, which transformed the state of defeat into one of grace, resembled the notorious observation of Cardinal Gerlier, archbishop of Lyon, that "if we had remained victorious, we would probably have remained the prisoners of our errors. Through being secularized, France was in mortal danger."[34]

This critique of the men and institutions of the Third Republic echoed through the various departmental parish journals. The July issue of the parish bulletin of Le Vigan published a representative article. In a flight of patriotic bravado, the anonymous author first insisted that the French Army would succeed in defeating "the filthy and bloody Beast who is polluting and tearing apart French soil."[35] But he then suddenly changed register, and worried about the spiritual struggle confronting France. It was "useless to entertain any illusions: the *redressement* of France will be long and will require the aid of all good souls." To condemn those responsible for France's plight was inadequate; instead, "evil must be attacked at its source: irreligion. . . . Will France return to her God, her traditions and her vocation?"[36]

Examples of this line of analysis, summarized by the curé of Lasalle—"France's soul was killed by dechristianizing her"—could be multiplied many times over.[37] The intellectual approach of the local clergy merged with their antebellum preoccupations and fears. As Jean-Marie Mayeur has noted, just as the National

32. *La Semaine religieuse* (21 July 1940), 291.
33. *La Semaine religieuse* (21 July 1940), 291–92.
34. Quoted in Paxton, *Vichy France*, 147.
35. *Bulletin paroissial du Vigan* (July 1940), 6.
36. *Bulletin paroissial du Vigan* (July 1940), 11–12.
37. *L'Echo Paroissial de Lasalle* (September 1940).

Revolution was not born in July 1940, neither was the attitude of the Catholic hierarchy new or unexpected. To the contrary, the "necessity of a *redressement* was already present in the spirit [of the clergy] before the world war, and in this regard June 1940 is less a rupture than a tragic confirmation." On this somber vision the church founded a critique of society and politics that would dovetail with the ideology of Vichy.[38]

The local Protestant press, no less concerned during the 1930s by the decline of religious observance than their Catholic colleagues, posed the same questions and partially shared the same answers for the defeat, though foregoing the same vehemence in framing them. Pastor Paul Brunel, a leader of the Nîmois Protestant community, echoed Pétain's diagnosis of France's ills: "Lulled by our memories and dreams of victory, we thought only to sample as many pleasures as possible—and the deluge struck."[39] The tenor of Brunel's statement found a sharper edge in the evangelist journals. In *Christ et France,* E. Ponsoye asserted that the principal cause of defeat was France's declining birthrate. Would Germany have risked war, either in 1914 or 1939, against a France of equal population? Ponsoye attributed the problem to decadence. "Shall God be faulted that France in 1914 and 1939 had an inferior number of soldiers? Is not the fault attributable to the men and women of France?" He concluded that France's choice was either to grow or disappear: "Now that it is a question of France's existence and the future of our Churches, let us finish with our egotistical and cowardly behavior."[40]

Yet in neither the liberal nor evangelical Protestant press did any explicit political references appear to the possible causes of defeat. This contrasts not only with *La Semaine religieuse,* but also with past practice among some of the Protestant journals as well—certain papers, like *Le Foyer Protestant,* despite avowals to the contrary, had not hesitated to throw their support behind the Popular Front government in 1936. Hence, the context of this silence is telling. It speaks to French Protestantism's historical concern over the notions of individual liberty, political democracy, anticlericalism, and a secular state and lay education. Though no less overwhelmed than other Frenchmen by the rapidity of events, most Protestants were not prepared to condemn the ideas that many conservatives held responsible for their country's collapse.

The journalist Charles Corbière expressed this early resistance of many Gardois Protestants to shirt-rending and acquiescence in an article on the eighteenth-century thinker Condorcet. Published in *Foi et éducation,* the article listed several

---

38. J.-M. Mayeur, "Les évêques dans l'avant guerre," in *Eglises et chrétiens,* ed. Montclos et al., 16.
39. *Le Foyer protestant* (July–August 1940), 104.
40. *Christ et France: Journal des eglises reformées évangeliques* (August 1940), 57–58.

reasons for writing about the *philosophe:* apart from his Protestant background, Condorcet was known for his "open-mindedness, generosity, devotion to freely chosen principles and his absolute sincerity."[41] Each of these traits was, of course, threatened with extinction in the autumn of 1940. In discussing Condorcet's philosophy of history, Corbière noted that his subject never treated material and moral progress as inevitable. Instead, mankind's progress depended upon individual initiative, which placed a heavy burden on man's shoulders. Yet, Corbière wondered, is that not "our most glorious title—to feel ourselves to be the collaborators of God and the artisans of the future?" After drawing the parallels between Condorcet's principles and Christian tradition, Corbière concluded his essay with a quotation from Jeremiah: "Practice justice and equity; deliver the oppressed from the hands of the oppressor; do not mistreat the foreigner, orphan, and widow; do not use violence."[42]

Corbière's message demands as little exegesis for the historian as it must have required for his readership. Writing when Vichy began to translate its political and social ideas into law, the journalist provided a sharp reminder that one could not escape the choices imposed by the times and that obedience to secular authority must satisfy the dictates of one's conscience. To underscore this last point, Corbière quoted from a poem that Condorcet had written to his wife: "They told me to chose between being an oppressor or a victim. / I embraced unhappiness and left them to commit the crime."[43] The reasons behind such an article, be they reflective or reflexive, reveal a mentality fundamentally different from that of most Gardois Catholics. Corbière's essay breathed the spirit of critical thought, identification with the oppressed, and the autonomy of the man's conscience. Thus, even at this earliest and most hopeful stage of Vichy, the Cévenol Protestant's "instinctual resistance to power" was evident.[44]

Yet it is important to avoid reading backward the history of this period, and attribute ideas and motives to the actors that they did not yet possess. In the summer of 1940, it is very difficult to speak of "resistance," not just as an organized movement, but also as a state of mind. The brute reality of national defeat had numbed the great majority of the French. Moreover, it was far from clear *what* needed to be resisted. The creation of the government of Vichy, voted into existence by a Parliament that, through this act, voted itself out of existence, was apparently undertaken in due legal form. Hence, at least until the govern-

---

41. *Foi et éducation* (September–October 1940), 37.
42. *Foi et éducation* (September–October 1940), 43.
43. *Foi et éducation* (September–October 1940), 38.
44. The phrase is André Siegfried's. See *Le Protestantisme Français,* ed. Boegner and Siegfried, 40–42.

ment began defining itself through its legislation, both the left and right, Protestants and Catholics, could, with few qualms, rally to its standard.[45]

This was especially the case when the standard-bearer was Marshal Pétain. During the first months of Vichy's existence, the Protestants of the Gard appear to have been no less Pétainist than their Catholic neighbors. Both communities initially cheered the ascension of Pétain, and there is little evidence that the Gard was divided over the wisdom of his assumption of power. Concerning his Cévenol parish of Saint-Privat-de-Vallonge, Pastor Marc Donadille recalled that even "all the old Communists in my parish, including the vice president of the presbyterial council, were one hundred percent for Pétain! They had fought in the war of 1914–18; they had been with Pétain at Verdun."[46]

The attitude of Marc Boegner is no less telling. Though not a native Gardois, Boegner passed the years 1940–42 in Nîmes in his double capacity as president of the Protestant Federation of France and the National Council of the Reformed Church of France—positions that imposed a certain "representativeness" on the part of their holder. The biographer of Boegner, Roger Mehl, has written that the death of the Third Republic did not sadden the Protestant leader: "He was too conscious of [the republic's] sorry state and its responsibility in our defeat to shed any tears over it."[47] Moreover, Boegner thought that the early addresses of Pétain responded to the many errors and shortcomings of the Third Republic. Yet Boegner's attitude toward the newly installed regime was ambivalent; the "instinctual resistance to power" showed itself in the pastor's discomfort with the potential abuses open to such a government. As Boegner wrote in his journal when the first articles of the new constitution were announced: "They accentuate the nature of personal power that had already been glimpsed. It's literally the negation of the democratic regime. It would matter little if spiritual, civil, and individual liberties are safeguarded. But will they be? And will not racism be introduced step-by-step?"[48] Mehl justly remarks that Boegner's initial error was his belief that such liberties could exist outside a democratic form of government— an error that was shared for a short time by many of his co-religionists in the Gard.

---

45. Pierre Laborie's reminder is salutary in this context: given the indescribable political, emotional, and material confusion of the time, to "speak of public opinion . . . makes little sense"; *L'Opinion française sous Vichy* (Paris, 1990), 223.

46. "Table ronde," in Joutard, *Cévennes: Terre de refuge,* 236. Although the village of Saint-Privat-de-Vallonge is just across the border between the Gard and the Lozère, its Cévenol and Protestant character qualifies it for this study.

47. Roger Mehl, *Le Pasteur Marc Boegner* (Paris, 1987), 135. See also Boegner's autobiography, *The Long Road to Unity* (London, 1970) and his recently published journal from the war years, *Carnets du pasteur Boegner, 1940–1945,* ed. Philippe Boegner (Paris, 1992).

48. Quoted by Mehl, *Le Pasteur Marc Boegner,* 135.

A France of forty million Pétainists: the phrase, batted about as an insult more often than as a description, retains all of its force a half century later. The attitude of Boegner and the Cévenol Protestants underscores the comprehensiveness of the *ralliement* of Frenchmen to Pétain in 1940: the hero of Verdun attracted the near unanimous support of the Gardois. Yet let us recall that, if there were in fact forty million Pétainists during this period, they worshiped different images of their hero with different degrees of fervor. The person of Pétain was polyvalent; he represented different things to different men—a fact perhaps better understood by the French of that period than by many subsequent observers.

As a result, the apparent unanimity claimed by Pétain is deceiving; given his protean nature as a symbol, the possibility of arriving at hermeneutic loggerheads or confrontation was great. Many Gardois may well have sought "new destinies," but it is doubtful that they were all scanning the same horizon. It does appear that a small number of Gardois were early adherents of the National Revolution and hoped that Pétain would prepare the country for her proper role in the new European order. Thus the surprise of some when the first government was named; less a gathering of new and promising individuals, it was more a collection of deeply conservative retreads. There was, according to one report, "a marked astonishment [over] the presence of veteran politicians, [since] one had expected to find only new men, technicians with new and bold ideas who are likely to find the solutions to the great problems we now confront."[49] This disappointment was clearly expressed in a letter that a certain Roger Chabaud of Pont St. Esprit sent to Marcel Déat, the socialist-turned-fascist ideologue and columnist. After having first announced his attitude on the issue of collaboration with Germany— "You said that certain rapes finish in marriage. There are some that even leave deliciously troubling memories"—Chabaud went on to denounce the traditionalist and conservative nature of the government. "Either France will be remade with new men and new ideas, or it will be necessary to stop reasoning in terms of France—as France, for me, is not this strange mosaic of moustachioed generals, greedy bankers, selfish industrialists, bribed journalists, and duped masses."[50]

The two confronting tendencies of the Vichy administrations underlined in this sampling of observations—a polarity referred to by one participant as that of "anciens Romains et nouveaux cyclistes"—would extend through the life of the regime and be reflected in departmental politics.[51] Yet the truly revolutionary element remained a minority; for most Gardois in 1940, Pétain instead promised forgetfulness. As a police report from early July observed, the public's confidence

49. CA 565, commissaire central to préfet, 13 July 1940.
50. G 355, commission de contrôle postal, letter of 28 August 1940.
51. Quoted in Azéma, *De Munich à la libération*, 86.

in the government was "the product of a profound desire for peace and tranquility."[52]

In the hearts of the great majority of Gardois, this desire for peace coexisted with a marked sympathy for Great Britain and her continuing battle with Germany. The authorities occasionally identified this anglophilism with the Protestant community—a nearly reflexive association, more than partially justified, that becomes ever more explicit with the growth of the Resistance. In general, the Gard displayed the same resistance to the official sponsorship of a permanent anglophobism that Pierre Laborie observes in the Lot.[53] Barely two months after the British attack on the French naval ships at Mers el-Kébir, it was reported that there was a widespread pessimism concerning the country's future and that the public hoped for a British victory.[54] In one intercepted letter, a Nîmois wrote that the English, having witnessed the cowardly behavior of the French army during the battle of France, were right to abandon the continent. The correspondent concluded, in a clear allusion to Mers el-Kébir, that it would be better to "recognize our own faults rather than pick an argument with the English."[55]

The peace and tranquility sought by the Gardois were also menaced by the material situation, which began to unravel during this period; and by the political climate, which, if only for the prescient, forecast the trends of the newly installed regime. As for the first, there was a clear link between the gradual eclipse of security and confidence, the collapse of the network of food transportation and provision and the concomitant growth of a black market and mounting prices of those items still available legally or illegally. Scarcity and inflation were to become two of the fundamental preoccupations of both the general public and the local administration, and it would be largely through the prism of food availability and distribution that the governed would judge the legitimacy of the governors.

Due to its dependence upon viticulture, which led to its categorization as a "deficit department," the Gard secured most of its food products from elsewhere in France. It was far more vulnerable, as a result, than most other departments to the material penury and sheer lack of means and organization ushered in with Vichy. In fact, the originality of the Gard was not only that it had urban areas easily prey to shortage (especially the Alesian mining basin), but that the countryside was only marginally more secure. Dependent upon viticulture, the rural cantons, no less than the urban centers, were constrained to ship in "most of their

---

52. CA 565, commissaire central to préfet, 7 July 1940.
53. See Laborie, *Résistants, vichyssois, et autres,* 171–74.
54. G 355, commission de contrôle postal to préfet 8 September 1940.
55. G 355, commission de contrôle postal, August, 1940. Letter written 28 August 1940.

meat, dairy products, flour and, on occasion, even their vegetables."[56] Hence, though the Gardois peasantry would be indisputably better off than the town-dwellers during these four years, their lot was often markedly inferior to that of their peers in other departments.

By the last days of July, the issue of food was paramount in the lives of the Gardois. The price of the basic necessities, warned the central commissioner, had reached the "extreme limit" of most Gardois' "budgetary possibilities."[57] The situation, however, had not yet created much tension among the populace; the police commissioner of Uzès, a town famed for its medieval center, remarked that the restrictions had not caused undue agitation.[58] This relative calm was in part due to the widespread belief that once the refugees returned to their homes, the market stalls would again creak under mounds of fresh produce. Thus a police report noted that, upon the normalization of the situation—that is, resettlement of the refugees, demobilization of the army and reestablishment of the rail service—the population of Nîmes would once again be provided for: "It's simply a question of days and patience."[59]

The problem would, however, remain irremediable; awash in wine, the Gard would be barren of basic food stuffs during the Vichy years. As two wine specialists declared in *Le Républicain du Gard,* the concentration on viticulture had led to a situation where the inhabitants "are subjected to bread ration cards while the storehouses are flooded with wine."[60] The situation was worsened almost immediately by the commercial blockages imposed in July by most departments in order to preserve those staples already in their possession. By the end of the month, the Gard was no longer able to find essential supplies in those departments that normally exported their produce. In response, the prefect ordered a freeze on all Gardois exports. The move was revealed to be ineffective when, less than two weeks later, *Le Républicain du Gard* called for the lifting of departmental barriers concerning food distribution, confessing that for the Gard it was "a vital question which needs to be quickly resolved."[61]

The first concrete sign that the presumed abnormality of the situation was instead becoming the norm was the appearance of rationing cards. On 30 June, Le Rachalan warned that the coming month would be one of cards—"for bread,

56. Roger Bourderon, "Le Ravitaillement et les prix dans le département du Gard (été–automne 1940), *Revue d'histoire de la deuxième guerre mondiale* (July 1970), 39.

57. CA 565, commissaire central to préfet, 20 July 1940.

58. CA 565, rapport moral, 13 July 1940.

59. Quoted in Bourderon, "Le Ravitaillement," 42.

60. *Le Républicain du Gard* (22 July 1940). René and Raymond Gourgas wrote a regular viticulture column for the paper.

61. *Le Républicain du Gard* (29 July 1940).

for food, for this and that."[62] His prediction was followed by a prefectoral decree of 31 July imposing restrictions on sugar, coffee, rice, and soap. In the gap of five days between the announcement of the decree and its application, however, the stores in Nîmes were besieged by housewives who, according to one police report, made off with "stocks of whatever they could get their hands on and carry off."[63] More ominously, cards for meat were issued on 23 September, those for milk on 14 October, and for potatoes for 20 December—signs that the "temporary" shortages were settling in for the duration.

The Gardois confronted a situation for which there existed few, if any, precedents. This was certainly the case for the local administration. At the departmental and municipal levels, officials were overwhelmed by relentless waves of needs and demands. In addition to the emptying of the markets and anarchy of transportation and distribution, the administrators also had to wrestle with the feverish rise of prices. Although Vichy had invested the prefects with extraordinary powers to control prices and punish black marketeers, the proliferation of declarations and warnings, police surveillance, and exemplary arrests had a minimal impact.[64] The prices of most staples continued to balloon: from the summer of 1939 to the late fall of the following year the price of oils and fats doubled, more than doubled for eggs, and tripled for potatoes.[65] These and similar statistics, moreover, are misleading since the items themselves were not always available on the open market. Despite the existence of contingency plans, the shock of the food crisis took everyone by surprise.[66]

The situation was, of course, as novel for the man in the street as it was for the administrators. In fact, the men of Nîmes *were* on the street, hesitant and bemused, shopping alongside the women. According to Le Rachalan, never had so many men been seen who, with grocery baskets in hand, made the rounds of the food stands. As the columnist declared, "Sign of the times! Never before had the head of the family deigned to participate in the business of the 'biasse' [bread basket]."[67] Another sign of the times was the appearance of gardens in Nîmes. Praised by *Le Journal du Midi* as a place where "there reigns wisdom and tranquillity of mind,"

---

62. *Le Républicain du Gard* (30 June 1940). Then, in a play on the French word for card—*carte* meaning both "card" and "map"—Le Rachalan added that there were also the *cartes* which "M. Molotov is in the midst of . . . 'demarquer' with Bukovinia and Bessarabia."

63. Quoted in Bourderon, "Le Ravitaillement," 55.

64. For example, Marie-Thérèse Martin, the owner of a grocery store in Nîmes, was arrested and hauled into court at the end of June for "selling potatoes at a scandalous price. Moreover, her store has been closed for a month" (CA 626, 28 June 1940).

65. Bourderon, "Le ravitaillement," 45.

66. Bourderon, "Le ravitaillement," 47.

67. *Le Républicain du Gard* (8 August 1940).

the garden was no doubt also a place that provided respite from increasingly empty vegetable stands and monotonous meals.[68]

Tending one's garden for spiritual or material reasons was not limited to the city; there also dates from this period a rediscovery of the virtues of the *maset*. A small house located in the countryside, the *maset* served as a weekend retreat for the Nîmois. A phenomenon that appeared in the nineteenth century and enjoyed by the worker as well as the bourgeois, the *maset* was a place to reclaim one's ties to the soil.[69] Beyond these cultural and social aspects, however, was an important material consideration: the *maset*, by providing oil, some wine, dried fruits, firewood, and the like, allowed workers during the interwar period to supplement their meager food budget.[70] During this era of want and scarcity, the *maset* thus took on an even greater importance. As a result, it not only conformed to the ideological obsessions of the regime, dovetailing with the theme of a return to the land, the nobility, and "Frenchness" of rural life, but also helped meet the material demands of the times.

The *maset* was just one sign of Gardois particularism during the general revival of regionalism under Vichy. A movement supported by the regime's traditionalists, the issue of regionalism would not be taken up until mid-1941 by the National Council of Vichy. Moreover, as Paxton has written, truly effective reorganization of France's departmental character was imposed by Admiral Darlan through the creation of regional prefects in April 1941—a decision inspired by administrative efficiency rather than the nostalgia of folklorists.[71] Nevertheless, the Gard's place in the new map of France, based upon both the urgent needs of the present and the dreams of past historical associations, became a widespread topic of discussion.

The provincial status of the Gard had long been debated by the local literati. Some contended that the Gard belonged to Provence, others argued that its roots lay in Languedoc, and one and all brought up batteries of historical, economic, cultural, and linguistic arguments to support their respective positions. That the Gard straddled these two historic provinces led not only to a continuous tug-of-war for rightful ownership, but also to the formation of a third camp, one that affirmed the Gard's unique identity and refused its assimilation by either of the

68. *Le Journal du Midi* (7 December 1940).

69. Thus one member of the Académie de Nîmes wrote that to have a *maset* "for all Nîmois, rich or poor, bourgeois or worker, is a common dream and . . . the supreme recreation." Quoted in *L'Histoire de Nîmes*, 345.

70. *L'Histoire de Nîmes*, 293.

71. *Vichy France*, 199. See also Cointet-Labrousse, *Vichy et le fascisme*, 185–89; Pierre Barral, "Idéal et pratique du régionalisme dans le régime de Vichy," *Revue française de la science politique* (1974), 911–39; and Christian Faure, *Le Projet culturel de Vichy* (Lyon, 1989).

other provinces. This position had been defended during the late 1920s by the local academician Paul Giran. Noting that the political and economic changes following the First World War had rendered obsolete the administrative map of France, Giran asked if it would be in the Gard's interest to remain tied to either Marseilles (Provence) or Montpellier (Languedoc). The academician rejected both possibilities. He asserted that the Gard's horizon embraced just three other departments: the Ardèche, Vaucluse, and Lozère. Citing economic, historical, and topographical arguments, Giran concluded that "it is time to construct in this area a definitive region which, named *la région Bas-Rhône,* would fit admirably in the plans for a future territorial reorganization that . . . cannot fail to materialize soon."[72]

Giran could not have known just how soon, and under what conditions, that day would arrive. With the advent of Vichy, the question of regionalism found its way to the front page of the departmental press and became the topic of local debates and discussion. In part, no doubt, this flurry of attention was an effort to divert attention from the harshness of defeat and a partial military occupation that had disfigured the face of France. It cannot, moreover, be known with any certainty just how taken the Gardois were by the public debate. Common sense suggests that, in the disarray of defeat and the daily challenge of meeting basic needs, many inhabitants paid little attention to such matters. On the other hand, the fact that the Chamber of Commerce and various professional corporations took an active interest in the course of the debate underlines that important stakes were involved, and that the debate was not mere entertainment or the hobby-horse of a handful of folklorists and fantasists.[73]

The debate concerning the Gard's administrative future quickly gave way in late October to the news of Montoire. It was this event, along with domestic legislation passed during the same period, that first revealed the true political character and aims of Vichy. We have already noted that even after the British attack on Mers el-Kébir, the Gardois did not swing into the collaborationist camp. This refusal hardened after the meeting between Pétain and Hitler on 24 October 1940 at the small railway station of Montoire. As Paxton has rightly observed, the meeting was more notable for its public effect than for any concrete issue or agreement that resulted from it.[74] The photograph of the handshake between Hitler and Pétain, displayed prominently on the front pages of depart-

72. Paul Giran, "Le Régionalisme vu de la Tour-Magne," *Mémoires de l'Academie de Nîmes* 48 (1928–30), x.
73. See Zaretsky, "Nîmes and the Department of the Gard under Vichy, 1940–44," 175–78.
74. Paxton, *Vichy France,* 75.

mental newspapers, symbolized the aspirations of the new regime. A week later, determined to dismiss any possible ambiguities, Pétain made clear the reasons for the encounter: "It is with honor and in order to maintain French unity . . . that, in the context of constructive activity for the new European order, I enter today on the path of collaboration."[75]

Given the paucity of police reports for the months of October and November, any attempt to portray the public's reaction to Montoire is hazardous. It is possible, nevertheless, to sketch public reaction from the tenor of the coverage in *Le Républicain du Gard.* Both the articles and the headlines in the week following the meeting revealed a certain caution, if not actual mistrust. On 25 October, the paper simply announced the meeting between Hitler and Pétain, giving no information on the contents of the discussion. The following day the paper quoted Hitler's remark to Pétain: "I know that you did not want the war and I am sorry that we meet under these circumstances." It was a judiciously chosen quotation: the handshake and "apology" between warriors suggests an equality of status; and the observation that it was a battle not sought by Pétain alludes to the clarity of the marshal's vision. The headline of 27 October was, for a different reason, no less revealing: "Fully confident in Marshal Pétain and M. Pierre Laval, the French public follows with interest, but also with calm, the rapid evolution of political events." The article was a banal account of activities in Vichy since the meeting, but the very inclusion of the word "calm" and its juxtaposition with "interest" in the headline implied that serenity was probably the last emotion felt by the Gardois in the wake of these events.

A widespread lack of serenity and a queasy curiosity in Montoire led Pétain to make the famous message of 30 October, reprinted the following day in *Le Républicain du Gard:* "The first duty of every Frenchman is to have confidence. It was my own decision to meet the Führer, and I was subjected to neither *diktat* nor pressure." With a great deal more emphasis, the rest of the departmental press urged the Gardois to maintain its trust in Pétain. In an article titled "Confidence in the Chief," the *Journal du Midi* underlined that Pétain would not, could never dishonor France.[76] The argument failed to convince the readers; two weeks later the paper acknowledged that there were "troubling" questions raised by Vichy's desire to collaborate with Germany. Nevertheless, the article concluded that "all of France, clearly excited, and keen to serve, waits with sang-froid and confidence."[77]

75. Quoted in Azéma, *De Munich à la libération,* 110.
76. *Le Journal du Midi* (9 November 1940).
77. *Le Journal du Midi* (20 November 1940). It is important to note once again that the *Journal du Midi* appeared irregularly throughout this period; consequently, it is difficult to use it for a piece of sustained research.

L'Eveil du Gard outdid the *Journal du Midi* in its attempt to convince the Gardois of the wisdom of Vichy's foreign policy. In an explicit appeal to its Catholic readership, the paper printed an assortment of Pétain's moralistic chestnuts, declaring that they "vibrate with a Christian tone. . . . We can attain [these goals] by giving to the Great Soldier the active and loyal collaboration that he demands of all the French."[78] Paul Thoulouze added his voice to the chorus when he affirmed that Pétain was France's "man of providence." Every Frenchman's duty was to lend Pétain his absolute confidence: the marshal "is our CHIEF [and] Catholics are familiar with the phrase in the Holy Scripture: give to Caesar that which belongs to Caesar."[79]

The slant of these articles suggests that the actual amount of public confidence in Vichy's foreign policy was inversely proportionate to the huzzahs in the press. Le Rachalan hinted at this in an article written shortly after the meeting at Montoire. Titled "In the Bath," the journalist commented on a report concerning the per capita number of bathtubs in the United States, noting that France was a close runner-up to the record-holding Americans. However, he concluded, the Americans seemed unaware of the fact that "for some time now, everyone [in France] has been in the bath."[80] "To be in the bath," in French argot, means to be compromised. Le Rachalan spoke for the great majority of his fellow Gardois: they were one and all in the bath.

Yet some were deeper in the tub water than others. This was the case for the Freemasons and especially the Jews of the Gard. Both groups represented, in the gospel according to the founder of Action française, Charles Maurras, elements fundamentally opposed to the nature and well-being of the real France. The natural bent of Vichy was toward this conspiratorial view of the world—a tendency that, through the determination of the Maurrasian minister of justice, Raphaël Alibert, and the minister of the interior, Adrien Marquet, was translated quickly into policy. By the late summer and early fall of 1940 the new regime's will to transform France according to this ideological blueprint had become manifest.

The Freemasons were affected first. On 13 August, a law was passed forbidding the existence of secret societies. In compliance with that law, all departmental civil servants, during the last ten days of that month, had to sign a declaration stating that they had never and did not currently belong to a Masonic lodge.[81] At the same time, the lodges in Nîmes and the other towns were searched and

78. *L'Eveil du Gard* (November 1940). There is a gap of four months in the archival holdings, with no extant issues between June and November.
79. *L'Eveil du Gard* (November 1940).
80. *Le Républicain du Gard* (2 November 1940).
81. Unfortunately, it is impossible to ascertain the exact number of Freemasons in the Gard, not to

closed down by the police. On 17 September, for example, the Nîmois lodge of the *Echo du Grand Orient* was turned upside down, its contents and furnishings inventoried and sequestered. A sampling was subsequently gathered and carried off to Paris by Gueydan de Roussel, assistant to Bernard Fäy, the director of the Archives Nationales and Vichy's "expert" on the Masonic conspiracy.[82]

The public reacted ambiguously to the purge. A "deep sensation in all quarters" was reported to have followed the law's announcement.[83] Yet, whether the measure actually received the support of the public is left unsaid. The public may have been unenthusiastic over the news, or their apparent reticence was the work of the investigating police official, A. Legrand, who had himself been a Freemason. (In a letter of denunciation, sent directly to the minister of the interior on 25 August 1940, and signed "Victims of Freemasonry," a handful of important civil servants in Nîmes, including Legrand, were accused of Masonic activities. In the subsequent investigation ordered by the ministry, all of the officials named in the letter were found to have once been Freemasons, but all had also signed the declaration of 13 August, breaking ties with the organization. Moreover, not only did Prefect Martin defend Legrand, but so too did Martin's successor, Angelo Chiappe, who never doubted his subordinate's loyalty to Vichy.) In sum, even if the measures against Freemasonry did not spark widespread support, neither did they provoke condemnation. The public most probably accepted the law as one necessitated by the circumstances.

The Gardois held to the same crouch in the undertow of the initial wave of anti-Semitic measures. On 3 October 1940 the first *statut des juifs* was promulgated. The statute forbade French Jews to hold positions in the civil service, the officer corps, and services, such as the press, film, radio, and teaching, which shaped and influenced public opinion. Moreover, a quota was promised that would limit the number of Jews in the liberal professions. (Exceptions were made for those Jews who had served in the First World War, or who had served with distinction in 1939–40.) "Jewishness" was defined racially: anyone with more than two Jewish grandparents, or simply two grandparents and a Jewish spouse, fell under the statute.[84] A second law, announced the following day, invested the prefects with

---

mention those who refused to sign the declaration, since the departmental archives have conserved only the signed statements. Michel Vielzeuf of the departmental archives of the Gard has nevertheless pieced together partial lists of those who were investigated by the Vichy authorities. I am indebted to him for these lists and other information on Gardois Freemasonry during this period.

82. CA 565, commissaire divisionnaire to préfet, 12 October 1940.

83. CA 565, commissaire central to préfet, 17 August 1940.

84. As Marrus and Paxton, among others, have pointed out, the French statute carried a more severe racial definition than the German ordinance which had been issued a week before in the Occupied Zone. See *Vichy France and the Jews* (New York, 1981), 12.

the power to intern foreign Jews in concentration camps or place them under police surveillance in isolated villages. Also, a law was passed on 22 July, which created a commission to review, and empowered to annul, all naturalizations issued since 1927. The commission ultimately deprived some six thousand Jews of French citizenship (and, thus, the dubious protection of the French state).[85]

This salvo of anti-Semitic legislation found a significant number of victims in the Gard. A Jewish community had taken root in Nîmes at the end of the eighteenth century; originally formed by natives from nearby Comtat Venaissin (the former papal territory of Avignon and the outlying areas), the ethnic balance of the community shifted over the course of the next century as a growing number of Jews from the Balkans settled in the city. The population stabilized at approximately four hundred throughout the nineteenth century.[86] By the eve of the Second World War, the head-count had declined by one-quarter (approximately 0.33 percent of the overall population), and was roughly divided between native-born Jews and recent immigrants from the Balkans and eastern Europe.[87] Nevertheless, the community had an influence far beyond its numerical strength. Among the illustrious offspring of the city were Bernard Lazare (born Lazare Bernard), the nineteenth century Dreyfusard and Zionist; and Adolphe Crémieux, the Second Republic's minister of justice and author of the landmark 1870 law that granted French citizenship to Algerian Jews (which was repealed by the Vichy regime on 7 October 1940).[88] The community was well integrated in the life of the city, the earlier generations having carved places in commerce and the liberal professions, while recent arrivals tended to be petty merchants. Community leaders, as Vichy police reports observed, enjoyed the respect and esteem of their fellow townsmen.

The Jewish population of the Gard grew dramatically following France's defeat. By July 1941, the department sheltered nearly 1,700 Jews, roughly two-thirds of whom were French citizens.[89] It is probable that the great majority,

85. Marrus and Paxton, *Vichy France and the Jews,* 4.

86. *L'Histoire de Nîmes,* 296.

87. Lucien Simon, *Les Juifs à Nîmes et dans le Gard durant la deuxième guerre mondiale de 1939 à 1944* (Nîmes, 1987), 13–14. Simon notes that the community lacked a rabbi since 1931, a certain sign of diminishing numbers.

88. On the life of Lazare, see Michael Marrus, *The Politics of Assimilation: The French Jewish Community at the Time of the Dreyfus Affair* (New York, 1971) and Nelly Wilson, *Bernard Lazare: Antisemitism and the Problem of Jewish Identity in Late Nineteenth-Century France* (Cambridge, 1978). For Crémieux, see the biography of Daniel Amson, *Adolfe Crémieux: L'Oublié de la Gloire* (Paris, 1988).

89. CA 1473. Based upon census ordered on 2 June 1941 by Vichy. The *état numerique* contains a precise breakdown of the origin of the foreign Jews (738 in all), the immense majority of whom were Polish, German, Turkish, and "ex-Austrian." As for the French Jews (961 in all), the census, in a surprising lapse of bureaucratic precision, did not distinguish between native-born and naturalized citizens.

part of the numerous waves of refugees washing across the Gard, had arrived by the fall of 1940. Yet the only Nîmois who seemed to worry over the presence of the refugees were the city's native Jews. Partly as a reflex born from the desire to affirm their "Frenchness," and partly from a distaste for the exotic appearance of many of their coreligionists, the local Jews were loath to see the refugees remain in the city. The community's help was thus often limited to a small sum of money and a train ticket to another destination. It was a treatment that, according to a witness, prompted the curse of one refugee: "You will yourselves soon know what we are going through!"[90]

The absence of *rapports sur la morale publique* for October and November presents a major obstacle in the study of the Gardois's reaction to Vichy's anti-Semitic measures. Yet it does appear that by September 1940, the increasing difficulties with food distribution had already begun to exacerbate relations between the natives and refugees of all kinds. In the growing lines outside grocery stores, grumbling was now occasionally heard against the city's foreigners, all too distinguishable by their accents and customs, who competed for limited food supplies.[91] In the public imagination, possibly influenced by the anti-Semitic ravings of *L'Eclair, Action française,* and *Sully,* the image of the foreigner may have been confounded with that of the Jew—an amalgam increasingly held responsible for the food shortages. One official thus observed in early September that the Jews "seem to be increasingly [considered] undesirable."[92]

The great majority of Gardois, overwhelmed by their own everyday *travail* and problems, either paid the *statut* little mind or considered it an unfortunate but necessary measure. Moreover, its impact seems to have been limited, thus reducing any possible effect on the public's consciousness. It appears that only seven public servants in the Gard were dismissed as a result of the law: a legal counselor and a judge at the *cour d'appel,* four others attached to the Académie du Gard (as either teachers or administrators), and a police agent in Nîmes. The last, Gaston Fernand Creange, requested that his dismissal be delayed two months. He specified that his paternal grandfather was a Lorrainer and "un bon Français" and that his maternal grandfather had fought in the war of 1870. As for his own career, Gaston Creange had served as an infantryman in the First World War and received a decoration. The patriotic tradition was carried on by his son, who at that very moment was serving under the tricolor and had need of financial assistance from his father. The outcome of Creange's request is unknown, but the

---

90. The witness was Dr. Lucien Simon. See his *Les Juifs à Nîmes,* 14.
91. Simon, *Les Juifs à Nîmes,* 15.
92. CA 646, commission de contrôle postal, 9 September 1940.

odds were not in his favor since a first demand had already been turned down by his immediate superior, central commissioner Legrand.[93]

The character of Creange's appeal would be repeated a heartbreaking number of times over the next four years. As we shall see in Chapter 4, the reaction of the Jewish community in Nîmes to the anti-Semitism of Vichy would long remain a mixture of incomprehension, disbelief, rationalization, and wounded pride. There was a nearly ineradicable belief among the Nîmois Jews that, at best, a mistake had been committed somewhere in the bureaucracy or, at worst, that the Germans were applying pressure on an unwilling government. It would only be with the *rafles* (roundups) of Jews in Nîmes, and elsewhere in France in the summer of 1942, that the last illusions concerning Vichy's attitude would collapse.

In the fall of 1940, in sum, most Gardois were too concerned with their own worries to pay much mind to the cares of a relative handful of Jews. Yet, the officially sanctioned anti-Semitism of Vichy helped fuel the fire of denunciation in the department. This encouraged a minority of Gardois who, prompted by either ideological zeal or the desire to settle accounts, became no less preoccupied with the Jews than most others were with material cares. Letters began to arrive at the prefecture accusing individuals or groups of antinational activity; the accused were often Jewish or Protestant.

For example, in early November, the police investigated a building on the Boulevard Gambetta in Nîmes that had been fingered by an anonymous letter-writer as a center of antigovernment agitation. Not surprisingly, at the heart of the conspiracy was a Jewish family (the Bechoeffers), a single Jewish doctor (Levy), and a Jewish widow and her daughter (Mesdames Milhaud) who, along with a Protestant widow (Mme. Floutier) and three Catholic tenants (Mlle Demartin, Mlle Moreau, and the Proueze family), all resided in the building. The police official investigating the case reported that the Catholics all "lead normal lives" and did not frequent their Jewish or Protestant neighbors. On the other hand, Mme Floutier and Mme Milhaud were "very intimate" and maintained relations with the other Jewish neighbors, with whom they "get along perfectly." The investigator noted that the Protestant and Jewish residents were "all reputed to be partisans of the old Popular Front, admirers of Blum, and ardent anglophiles," but concluded that "no evidence could be found concerning the alleged conspiracy."[94]

A second letter of denunciation, this time sent directly to Pétain and subsequently referred to the authorities in Nîmes, singled out the local Conseil de l'Association

93. CA 339, commissaire central to préfet, 18 October 1940.
94. CA 300, commissaire de police to commissaire central, 5 November 1940.

des Israélites (CAI) as a "nest of agitation." The principal members of the council were André and Roger Simon, and Mssrs Horvilleur and Landauer. All four were important local businessmen and veterans of the First World War; in fact, André Simon was a *grand mutilé* [disabled veteran] and treasurer of the Association des mutilés et anciens combattants of Nîmes. They were, moreover, the heads of families who "are known honorably in our city and enjoy widespread respect." The investigator concluded that this charge was even less founded than the previous one (apparently leveled by the same individual), and dismissed it out of hand.[95]

The same letter also charged that several well-known Nîmois, including Pastor Elie Lauriol and the former mayor Hubert-Rouger, were members of this conspiracy. Along with the rest of the municipal council, Hubert-Rouger had been relieved of his functions by ministerial order on 14 November 1940 and replaced by E. Velay, the former director of a winegrowers' cooperative. The old Socialist nevertheless retained his popularity with the Nîmois: the division commissioner refused flatly to investigate the charges brought against him, citing that "apart from his well-known political ideas, he enjoys the esteem and respect of the great majority of the population of Nîmes."[96] As for Lauriol, the police official could not gather any precise information on a sermon in which the pastor allegedly criticized the government. It did appear, however, that Lauriol was known for his "rather advanced political sentiments," which he "sometimes let slip into his sermons." Moreover, the commissioner conceded the possibility that, even if Lauriol had not, as he was accused, attacked the government in one of his sermons, he did criticize its anti-Semitic policies. However, the commissioner concluded that even if Lauriol, Hubert-Rouger, and other public figures disapproved of the measures taken against the Jews, they nevertheless "do not hide their sentiments for the work of national rebuilding . . . and notably the goals of order and authority."[97]

These letters of denunciation underscore several important facts. First, they reveal the basic objectivity of the police investigators: the "state anti-Semitism" of Vichy did not noticeably skew their reports — an observation no less important for the actual individuals subjected to these investigations than it is for the historian. Second, they underline the ripening climate for the growth of popular anti-Semitism. The deepening crisis of food distribution had begun to rub a latent strain of xenophobia, if not outright racism, among the Gardois. Third,

95. CA 300, commissaire divisionnaire to commissaire central, 29 November 1940.
96. CA 300, commissaire divisionnaire to commissaire central, 29 November 1940.
97. CA 300, commissaire divisionnaire to commissaire central, 29 November 1940.

the example of the house on Boulevard Gambetta can serve as a metaphor for the evolution of relations between the three religious communities in Nîmes: Protestants and Jews found themselves sharing many of the same criticisms and fears concerning Vichy, while this is more rarely the case with the Catholics. The Protestants were markedly more sensitive to the plight of the Jews than their Catholic neighbors, and would be the first to react to the increasingly harsh anti-Semitic measures undertaken by Vichy.

Fourth and last, it is at this point that a clear picture of the true nature of the Vichy regime began to take shape. Montoire, the *statut des juifs,* the purge of the Freemasons, the critical food situation were all signs that the coming winter would be one of discontent for the Gard. By November, a watershed had been reached. In a famous phrase apropos of the 1848 revolution in Germany, A. J. P. Taylor remarked that the bourgeoisie, having arrived at a turning point, did not turn. With a small but important qualification, the same may be said of the Gardois in late 1940: they, too, had reached a turning point and did not turn—at least, not immediately. But the seeds of doubt had been planted, both as to the wisdom of Vichy's political program and as to her ability to protect the nation from the material sacrifices imposed by Germany. Yet the lingering confusion of the period and the effort to adjust to the new state of affairs helped disguise the existence of this turning point from all but the most lucid participants. There was, moreover, the looming figure of Pétain, which shrouded the realities of the period. Yet, at this very moment both the old marshal and his ministers began to squander the fund of goodwill and trust with which the Gardois had entrusted them. As Roderick Kedward has affirmed, Vichy started life with a "broad base of tolerance," a base eroded through the pursuit of its own sectarian aims.[98] This erosion dates from October 1940, and unmistakable fissures begin to appear in early 1941.

<hr />

98. H. R. Kedward, *Resistance in Vichy France: A Study of Ideas and Motivation in the Southern Zone, 1940–1942* (Oxford, 1978), 90.

4

PROTESTANTS, CATHOLICS, AND JEWS

It is incompatible with the dignity attached to the grade I still retain in the French Army reserves, to present myself to a bureaucrat in the next 48 hours in order to declare, after 45 years of service, that I am an Israelite.

—General André Boris, 1941

The public does not understand the necessity of arresting people who do not seem a priori dangerous.

—Departmental military commander, 1942

"Living with the enemy": thus read a headline in a late November issue of *Le Républicain du Gard.* There followed an advertisement for an herbal tea promising relief from constipation and its "procession of discomforts: heaviness, stuffiness, dizzy spells, nausea, headaches, belching and acidity."[1] It was a minor stroke of advertising genius: a message that confounded a sociopolitical with a physiological disorder, and guaranteed a cure. The advertisement is a reminder for the historian no less than it was for its intended audience: the Gardois were forced to live with the enemy. Not necessarily the Germans: their presence in the department was sparse and relatively low-keyed.[2] The immediate enemies were instead

1. *Le Républicain du Gard* (27 November 1940).
2. There was the permanent presence of German officers representing the German Armistice Commission, lodged at the prestigious Hotel Imperator. The commission attracted numerous Gardois searching favors and contacts, and posed a constant headache for the local administration, no less worried over the security of the officers as they were over the potential threat to Vichy's sovereignty.

material want, emotional distress, and political uncertainty. In the daily struggle against these conditions, one's fellow Gardois often became a threat or object of distrust, if not an outright enemy.

This chapter will concentrate on the evolution of relations between the different religious communities of the department—one of the most traditional sources of local conflict—and their attitudes toward Vichy. But we shall also see that it was a period that pitted town-dwellers against farmers, miners against industrial workers, *légionnaires* against the extreme right, *résistants* against the administration, and the administration against the Gardois. If these conflicts took forms falling short of outright civil and religious war, there was nevertheless a deepening chasm of distrust both between various social groups of the Gard and between the great majority of Gardois and the government. The winter of 1940–41 marked the beginning of a period of discontent and strife that would climax four years later.

In the fall of 1940, Marc Boegner, the chief representative of French Protestantism, met with Vichy's head of government, Pierre Laval. Though Boegner received Laval's assurance that the Protestants would have their "rightful place in the nation," not all Protestants were reassured by such guarantees. Boegner soon left for southern France in order to calm the anxiety provoked among the local Protestants by the clericalism of the new regime.[3] To little avail: a year after the first reports that sent Boegner to Nîmes, there was a new outbreak of fear, especially among Protestants in the region of Le Vigan. A resident of St. Hippolyte du Fort, an overwhelmingly Protestant town east of Le Vigan, wrote that the Protestant farmers were uneasy as they were "persuaded that the ruling party wants to expropriate them. On the order of the bishop, the priests have twice had to allay from the pulpit such fears."[4]

The fears over expropriation were baseless: the regime of Vichy never considered measures against Protestants similar to those aimed at Jews, Freemasons, and Communists. Laval had given his assurances to Boegner on this point, as would his successor Admiral Darlan. In addition, both men, as well as many other

---

3. Boegner refers to this in his memoirs, *The Long Road to Unity*, 155. See also Mehl, *Le Pasteur Marc Boegner*, 136. I have been unable to locate any police reports during the fall of 1940 confirming the existence of such popular fears.

4. CA 646, *synthèse* of commission de contrôle postal, 29 September–5 October 1941. This observation was confirmed in the monthly report of the commissaire principal, who affirmed that "certain Protestant milieus seem to fear a reinforcement of Catholicism in France" (CA 566, report to préfet, 29 October 1941).

members of the various Vichy administrations, were either nonpracticing Catholics or, as in Darlan's case, outright anticlericals.[5] Lastly, Protestants were themselves represented both in the government (for example, Maurice Couve de Murville, François Charles-Roux, Gaston Bruneton, and General Brécard) and on the National Council (for example, Marc Boegner). Robert Paxton has made clear that "among Maurras's *métèques*, Protestants [by 1940] no longer offered a target to conservatives."[6]

But why, then, these fears on the part of the Gardois Protestants? First, a certain Catholic traditionalism did characterize the initial phase of the Vichy regime. The most obvious representative of this tendency was Jacques Chevalier, a professor of philosophy at the University of Grenoble who served as minister of education from 14 December 1940 to 22 February 1941. Though of brief passage, Chevalier nonetheless left his mark on the public school system. Described by one historian as "a sort of Templar, a Leaguing monk," Chevalier succeeded in restoring a modicum of religious instruction in the state schools.[7] A law instructed that henceforth all public schools would offer a course in ethics based upon one's "duties toward God." Chevalier emphasized that it was not meant to introduce either dogma or confessional doctrine in the classroom, yet the measure was controversial, especially since it was soon followed by a law reinstating the option of catechism instruction in the state schools. Chevalier was soon thereafter removed from the ministry, replaced by Jérôme Carcopino, the rector of the Académie de Paris. Acting upon the commonsensical principle that a priest is most effective in the church and a teacher in the school, and that it was "ridiculous to have religion taught by atheist instructors," Carcopino watered down Chevalier's measures, simply leaving a certain amount of free time in the school curriculum for voluntary religious instruction off the premises.[8] Still, a breach had been made in the wall of secular education erected more than a half-century before by the Ferry reforms.

Many local Protestants, unnerved by Chevalier's attempt to overturn the secular character of public education, welcomed Carcopino's measures. The success of public and secular education in the Gard was largely due to the support given to it by Protestantism. Most of the department's public school teachers, in fact, were recruited at the turn of the century in the heavily Protestant Cévennes

5. G 354, commission de contrôle postal, October 1941. Letter from Jean Chaix, 15 October 1941. Chaix, a Protestant from the town of Vergèze, recounted a report given by Boegner in which the latter affirmed that both Pétain and Darlan "were categorically opposed to clericalism and deplore the excesses of some of its partisans."

6. Paxton, *Vichy France*, 171.

7. W. D. Halls, *The Youth of Vichy France* (Oxford, 1981), 67.

8. See Jacques Duquesne, *Les Catholiques français sous l'occupation* (Paris, 1966), 91–96.

and the Vaunage.[9] Thus, it is unsurprising that in 1941 a Protestant school
teacher hailed Carcopino's tolerance, claiming that it would help "calm certain
apprehensions born from the hasty interpretation of recent texts [presumably
Chevalier's measure]." By clearly marking and limiting the rights of both the
church and the school, Carcopino's edict "protects us from trespassing on one
another's territory, which would be as harmful for the one as for the other."[10]

A second reason for the apprehensions of local Protestants was their distance
from the seat of power in Vichy. The importance of a single region's history
cannot be overemphasized, for it is the past specific to that area that serves as a
prism for interpreting contemporary events. The divergence of responses to
Vichy's decrees, as Roger Austin has convincingly argued, was influenced by the
"particular contours of religious, political, and economic life within each
department."[11] If, in the succinct phrase of Michelet, history is first of all
geography, then the Gard's place on the map of religious mentalities cannot be
disregarded.

The local authorities were very sensitive to the religious particularities of the
Gard. A native Corsican and practicing Catholic, Angelo Chiappe, installed as
prefect on 25 September 1940, often returned to this theme in his reports. The
Gard, Chiappe reminded his superiors, had been the "fiery crucible of the wars of
religion since the seventeenth century [sic], and despite the appearance of mutual
concessions, anything that seems to favor one group is deeply resented by the
other."[12] Chiappe did not consider religious tensions a thing of the past, insisting
time and again on his efforts to have the two confessions work together for the
good of the National Revolution. It was at his request that Marc Boegner spoke
at the Grand Temple in Nîmes on the topic of French Protestantism and the
National Revolution. The talk, which created a good deal of controversy among
Protestants, was hailed by Chiappe, who claimed that he had thus succeeded "in
collaborating with Pastor Boegner to dull the opposing tendencies to the directives of the government."[13] Yet it seemed a Sisyphean task. Chiappe once
complained to a correspondent about his difficulties in Nîmes, "especially as the

9. Robert Gildea, *Education in Provincial France, 1800–1914: A Study of Three Departments*
(Oxford, 1983), 143. As M. Lafaye proudly declared in *Foi et éducation,* it is the Reformation that "has
the honor of proclaiming the necessity of universal instruction. France owes primary education to
Protestantism" (December 1942), 56.
10. J. L., in an article titled "Concerning Neutrality," in *Foi et éducation* (May 1941), 76.
11. Austin, "Propaganda and Public Opinion in Vichy France: The Department of the Hérault,
1940–1944," 457.
12. CA 566, préfet to interior, 1 October 1941.
13. CA 660, préfet to interior, 10 September 1941. Yet the prefect had no illusions as to the perma-
nence of such a change and noted that the Protestant circles were to be kept under "careful surveillance."

religious struggles are still strong in this area, and I have had a great deal to do concerning the Protestants."[14] He warned the ministry of interior that only "energetic action and especially an *intelligently handled propaganda* that takes into account the mentalities of the Catholics and Protestants, will prevent a slide towards anarchy."[15]

Chiappe's call for an intelligent campaign of propaganda was never answered by the regime. In fact, with the "Jeanne d'Arc affair" of 1942, Vichy actually succeeded in aggravating the unease of the Gardois Protestants. Yet before we turn to this event, the attitude of the local Catholic hierarchy must first be examined. Gardois Catholicism had maintained through the nineteenth century a remarkable missionary zeal and militancy. The memories of past religious struggles and the proximity of a vibrant Protestantism fueled the church's combativeness and nurtured the enduring myth that "the presence of a large Protestant minority in the region posed a permanent threat to the well-being and prosperity of the Catholic majority."[16] Provoked by the Ferry educational reforms and the Dreyfus Affair, anti-Protestantism remained a constant in local political and social conflicts and only began to disappear in the early years of the twentieth century.[17] Though the "Protestant peril" had become, by the late 1930s, a tattered and unconvincing scarecrow compared to communism, international Jewry, or even Freemasonry, its decline as a bugbear in the eyes of local Catholics was not replaced by the growth of mutual understanding or familiarity. There were the first hesitant steps on the road of ecumenism and the two communities were at peace, but it was largely the peace of separate tables. André Encrevé's general observation holds for the Gard: up until the Second World War, relations between the two churches "in the best of cases, took place at the level of polite ignorance, and at the level of polemic during times of tension."[18]

14. CA 561, "Note" attached to curriculum vitae sent by Chiappe to Vichy. No date, but probably written in late 1941.

15. CA 566, Chiappe to interior, 1 October 1941 (Chiappe's emphasis). Chiappe underlined in the same report that since his arrival, he had been in frequent contact with the representatives of the two churches. He then penciled in the margin that "Monseigneur Girbeau and Pastor Boegner are in constant touch with me."

16. Fitzpatrick, *Catholic Royalism in the Department of the Gard, 1814–1852,* 187.

17. See Jean Baubérot, "Les Principaux thèmes anti-protestants et la réplique protestante," (second half of two-part article), *Revue d'histoire et de philosophie religieuses,* no. 3 (1973), 178–221. See also Louis Secondy, "Question religieuse et enseignement au lycée de Nîmes entre 1850 et 1900," *Annales du Midi* (October–December 1982), 387–402; and Etienne Fouilloux, "Les Eglises contestées," in J.-M. Mayeur, ed., *L'Histoire religieuse de la France (19ème–20ème siècles): Problèmes et méthodes* (Paris, 1975).

18. André Encrevé, *Les Protestants en France de 1800 à nos jours* (Paris, 1985), 259.

Encrevé's chronology needs to be qualified in the case of the Gard: here relations remained distant and often tense at least through the first two years of Vichy. On the part of the Catholic Church, this strained tenor was cultivated. In a fall 1941 issue of *La Semaine Religieuse,* a message from the bishop condemned any form of collaboration between Catholics and Protestants except when authorized and directed by the hierarchy. Girbeau acknowledged that certain national and social tasks would be undertaken jointly with the Reformed Church, but that "the troops would carry out these campaigns separately, each in the context of their own confession." He concluded that Catholics, while professing a deep respect for individuals and their consciences, "will not and cannot compromise on the question of principles. The untouchable purity of our faith would inevitably suffer from regular and frequent contacts with those who do not share it."[19]

The importance of such sentiments lies not only in the language chosen by the bishop, but in the context of the times. The intransigence and distrust embodied in his declaration would have been unexceptional through the decade of the 1930s, but they assumed a different coloring against the background of Vichy France. Already shaken by the clerical impulses of the newly installed regime, the Protestants were all the more sensitive to the declarations of the local representatives of the Catholic Church. Hence, it is easy to imagine the reaction among the Gardois Protestants, for example, when Girbeau divided humanity into three categories—unbelievers, heretics, and Catholics—and asserted that if France wished to rediscover and recover its rightful place among other nations, it must "become again what it has ceased to be—a believing France, a Catholic France."[20]

Girbeau was not alone in making such provocative declarations. In his 1941 Easter sermon, the priest of Sumène praised his flock's resistance to Protestantism, which he described as a "pestilential poison" and bundle of "lies" invented five hundred years before by "the heretic of Geneva."[21] In August of that same year, the Protestant town of Lasalle was, for the first time in sixty-five years, the unlikely host to a Corpus Christi procession. Criticized by certain Lasallois as a deliberate provocation on the part of local Catholics, the parade was defended by the local priest, who asserted that the ceremony "sought to offend no one" and did not represent a danger to the liberty of belief. He emphasized his respect for the religious convictions of his "separated brothers," and concluded, somewhat

19. *La Semaine Religieuse* (28 September 1941), 425–26. In the same issue, Girbeau referred to a visit to the small Catholic minority of St. Jean-du-Gard, described as "submerged in a mass of Protestants." The Protestants were depicted as "separated brothers who divide and divide again in a multiplicity of sects . . . to the point that the father of a family is a pastor in one sect and his son a pastor in another" (426).

20. *La Semaine Religieuse* (5 October 1941), 432–33.

21. *Le Bulletin paroissial de Sumène* (May 1941), 5.

disingenuously, by expressing his astonishment that there "still exists such sectarianism in Lasalle in the midst of the twentieth century."[22]

Yet such religious sectarianism did exist, and it found striking expression in the rhetoric employed by the two communities when the subject was Pétain. The Christ-like imagery inspired by Pétain in both the secular and religious press has often been commented upon, and we have already seen the first examples of this reverential treatment in the previous chapter.[23] Yet the subtle differences that already existed between the Catholic and Protestant journals immediately following the defeat were to grow and become more insistent over the next two years. The contrast, however, often rested less in the words employed than in the spaces in-between; in certain cases, as we shall see, silences were as evocative as were several pages of exhortation.

The personality of Pétain and the program of the National Revolution were made to order for the Catholic Church. The traditionalism and religious deference of the marshal, when combined with the regime's determination to reintroduce God in the public schools and state subventions to parochial schools, understandably attracted the support of the Catholic hierarchy. This support, in fact, was not only found in the traditionalist wing of the church; the thoroughness of the defeat, which seemed to have swept away the prejudices of the past along with the insufficiencies of the Republic, helped rally Christian democrats to the new regime as well.[24] Although the church soon grew dissatisfied with the gains won from the regime, it remains true that for at least the first two years of Vichy's existence, a Catholic who referred to the teachings of his church "to enlighten his political conscience found the justification to place himself under the banner of Vichy rather than that of the Resistance."[25]

The Catholic hierarchy explicitly adhered to the goals of the National Revolution in the late summer of 1940, but only at the end of that year did it begin to participate actively in the cult of Pétain. In early November, Girbeau referred to Pétain not only as the father of the nation, but as its very source of life: the marshal's sole concern was "to give life to a dying France."[26] From the parable of Lazarus, Girbeau leapt a few weeks later to the theme of divine intervention: Pétain now embodied the "mysterious French miracle . . . whom we salute as the heaven-sent saviour of our suffering *patrie.*"[27] The better part of the bishop's

22. *L'Echo paroissial de Lasalle* (August 1941), 4–5.

23. See especially Miller's merciless dissection in *Les Pousse-au-jouir du maréchal Pétain*, 44–54.

24. Hence the initial support given to the regime by a thinker like Emmanuel Mounier, who established with the aid of Vichy the Ecole nationale des cadres at Uriage. This point is emphasized by Coutrot and Dreyfus, in *Les Forces religieuses dans la société française*, 89.

25. Coutrot and Dreyfus, *Les Forces religieuses*, 91.

26. *La Semaine religieuse* (10 November 1940).

27. *La Semaine religieuse* (12 January 1941).

sermons and letters addressed the need to support Pétain in his work of national restoration.[28] The local clergy were sensitive to their superior's sentiments. In an address in honor of Girbeau's birthday, they affirmed that the bishop's activities sought to respond to the expectations of Pétain. The vicar general, who presented the address, praised the fact that all of the bishop's letters, "regardless of the subject, reveal a stubborn concern to carry us along the path of the individual whom you have so clearly shown to be France's 'providential savior.' "[29]

Any rhetorical moderation shown by the bishop was completely discarded by the sectarian L'Eveil du Gard. The paper's Christmas message of 1940, penned by Paul Thoulouze, described Pétain as "watching over all of us with his fatherly solicitude." The marshal's ways, mysterious though they may appear, must not be questioned. Thus the December palace coup against Laval was handily explained: "We do not know the reasons; we do not have to know them. . . . We must have confidence in the marshal."[30] Just as the Catholic must accept unquestioningly the directives of the church, so too must Frenchmen bow before the decisions of Pétain. As a result, Thoulouze's position on whether France should practice economic or total collaboration with Germany was simple: "I follow the marshal just as a ship's passenger allows himself to be guided by the captain, because he has unlimited confidence in him. [Pétain] knows better than I do the implications of this question, which is why, whatever his opinion on collaboration should be, I share it."[31]

Neither Girbeaus's nor Thoulouze's enthusiasm for Pétain was exceptional for the period. In November 1940, Cardinal Gerlier declared solemnly that "Pétain, c'est la France; la France, c'est Pétain." Gerlier's declaration was echoed by the near totality of the Catholic hierarchy, and though the 1941 ecclesiastical assemblies carefully refrained from addressing the question of political legitimacy, they nevertheless did call on all Catholics to show a "sincere and complete loyalty to the established power" and declared their "veneration for the Chief of State and [their insistence] that all Frenchmen unify around him."[32] Yet, the rhetoric employed by the Catholic press—triumphalist, unquestioning, and inflexible— undoubtedly had a different resonance in the Gard than it had elsewhere in France.

28. Girbeau usually avoided the phrase "révolution nationale," preferring instead "restauration national." Clearly, the word "revolution," even when used to describe the agenda of Vichy, carried too many unhappy historical associations for the bishop.

29. La Semaine religieuse (29 June 1941), 318.

30. L'Eveil du Gard (January 1941), 2.

31. L'Eveil du Gard (October 1941), 2.

32. Quoted in Azéma, De Munich à la libération, 106. For a survey of the French episcopacy's initial attitude toward Pétain and the regime, see Duquesne, Les Catholiques français sous l'occupation, especially chaps. 2 and 3.

If Girbeau believed that Pétain was providence's gift to France, the local Protestants rightly wondered *whose* France the bishop had in mind. After all, the bishop asserted that Pétain was sent by the same hand that had sent Joan of Arc, and that in the heart of Catholics he "will find the most faithful echo, since it is we who, in the light of our faith, have reasons that the other French have not to embrace Marshal Pétain."[33] Such homilies seemed to stir the fears of the Gardois Protestants, necessitating the occasional intervention of the authorities. In the spring of 1941, the subprefect of Le Vigan spoke in the town of Avèze, a few miles south of the seat of the subprefecture. In his speech he insisted upon the need for national unity, asserting that "the ill-feelings and quarrels inspired by petty political or religious sectarianism" could no longer be tolerated.[34] The prefect had himself spoken on the same theme the month before in the Cévenol town of Valleraugue. Chiappe declared that the different churches had to rise above the "confessional differences that previously made for so much sorrow," and that it would be deplorable if "the old grudges and atavistic hatreds were to survive the present misfortunes of the country."[35]

On occasion, the police reports provide striking examples of the endurance of these "old grudges and atavistic hatreds." The small Cévenol village of Durfort—more than three-quarters of whose population of five hundred and forty was Protestant—was the object of official concern in 1942 because of religious divisions. The town council, described as politically leftist, consisted entirely of Protestants, and according to the police inspector dispatched to Durfort, "seems to administer the commune neither better nor worse than any other council." The Catholic residents thought otherwise, however, and accused the council of both anti-Catholic and antigovernment prejudice. The inspector found the accusations baseless, but conceded that the town's atmosphere was charged. The two confessions, he reported, lived "on very bad terms and total disunity reigns between [them]." He concluded that the population "shows a total lack of comprehension of current events and refuses to rise above local concerns."[36]

The town of Anduze spawned similar tensions. Constituting nearly three-quarters of the population and supporting one of the most active and important temples in the department, the Protestants of Anduze had long maintained a

33. *La Semaine religieuse* (5 January 1941).
34. *Le Viganais* (8 March 1941).
35. *Le Viganais* (1 February 1941).
36. CA 391, inspecteur de police to sous-préfet of Le Vigan, 20 July 1942. The pastor of Durfort, M. Cadier, was instrumental in the hiding of Jews and fabrication of false identity cards. Caught by the authorities and fined six hundred francs, Cadier was forced to leave the village, but the local police inspector complained that his attitude had "stigmatized [*sic*] the attitude of the population" (CA 391, inspecteur de police to sous-préfet of Le Vigan, 6 January 1944).

visible and powerful presence. After the advent of Vichy, however, the community was thrown on the defensive. During 1941 its members were accused by members of the Catholic minority of sympathizing with Great Britain, and, by extension, Gaullism. Following an investigation of the claims, Chiappe reported the presence of certain Catholics who were "certainly well-meaning, but overly excited [and who] delivered themselves to violent and baseless attacks against the Protestants."[37]

Other towns in the Cévennes proved troublesome. In the late summer of 1941, the subprefect of Le Vigan judged the state of public morale as generally good, but alluded to a certain hostility toward the government in several villages. The towns of Saint André-de-Valborgne, Quissac, Sauve, and Saint-Hippolyte-du-Fort were held to be especially restless. All four towns, situated on a northwest tangent cutting across the Cévennes, tended to express their hostility through support for Gaullism; the subprefect described this tendency as "much more accentuated in Protestant than Catholic circles."[38] Over the next three years this refrain would become increasingly intense in the police reports, and Saint-Hippolyte in particular would become feared for its resistance activity.

Diverse letters written during this period also bear witness to the friction between Catholics and Protestants. One correspondent questioned the wisdom of restoring the nuns of Saint-Vincent de Paul in Alès (from which they had been evicted in 1905), wondering whether it would be "diplomatic" to reinstall them so quickly. Besides, he continued, "by declaring its clerical sympathies so soon, wouldn't the work of the municipal council be compromised?" He concluded that revolutionary change in times of defeat ran certain risks: "What will happen to the nuns in the counterrevolution already rumbling and, in certain areas, promises to be bloody?"[39] Less than a year later, an intercepted letter from a Nîmois Protestant to the BBC dwelt on local religious tensions. The writer depicted as "fanatical Catholics" those individuals who most admired Pétain and supported collaboration, and suggested that most of them had their roots in the Cévennes. Moreover, it seemed that the Protestants in the youth camps begun by Vichy (*chantiers de la jeunesse*) were "very poorly considered" and that "group leaders are not easily promoted if they are Protestant."[40]

One of the greatest blows to the sensitivity of the Protestants was the Joan of Arc affair in 1942. Richard Cobb has remarked that regimes like Vichy are obliged to

37. CA 660, préfet to interior, 10 September 1941.
38. CA 566, sous-préfet of Le Vigan to préfet, rapport mensuel, 24 August to 24 September 1941.
39. G 354, commission de contrôle postal, October 1941. Letter sent from the Tarn, 1 October, 1941.
40. G 357, commission de contrôle postal, June 1942, Letter signed "a mother" and posted 16 June

"show an almost hysterical, querulous concern for the outward trappings and panoplies of nationalism."[41] The attention devoted by Vichy to Joan of Arc provides an obvious example of Cobb's observation; during the short life of the regime, the cult of the "Maid of Orleans" ranked second only to that of Pétain. The qualities incarnated by Joan included youth, sacrifice, and a faith that fused nationalism and Christianity. This last element became a point of contention for the Gardois Protestants, since Joan's faith had come to represent the faith of the Catholic Church.[42]

A harbinger of the affair appeared during the 1941 celebrations in Valleraugue. A governmental directive specified that the ceremony take place at Joan's statue rather than the local war monument. Unfortunately, in Valleraugue, as in so many other communes, Joan's statue stood inside the Catholic Church. The town's pastor, Laurent Olivès, noted the difference between "paying homage and veneration," and refused permission to the Protestant youth groups to enter the church. The parish priest eventually agreed to move the statue outside the church, and the celebration took place as scheduled. Yet, in his sermon, Olivès succeeded in subverting the aim of the ceremony by turning the heroine's symbolism on its head. Declaring that Joan had been put to death by the very same church now honoring her, he wondered if it would be the congregation's turn tomorrow. "Admired today, killed tomorrow; or hated today, killed tomorrow? While we wait for the answer: *Vive la France!*"[43]

This mark of Protestant sensitivity shown in Valleraugue led to a much more violent and widespread reaction during the celebrations of 1942. In the spring of that year, the propaganda services of Vichy printed a pamphlet, "Jeanne d'Arc: Sa mission et son exemple," which drew a variety of parallels between the condi-

---

1942. The writer thought that the connection between their Cévenol origin and their fanaticism was "bizarre," but it had in fact historical antecedents: their minority status in the Protestant Cévennes had often produced the most zealous of Catholics in the department.

41. Richard Cobb, *French and Germans, Germans and French* (Hanover, N.H., 1984), 169.

42. Conceived as a day of national concord, it became an occasion not only for the Protestants to show their mistrust of the regime, but also for the regime to show its scorn for its Jewish citizens. The Jewish general André Boris, who had settled in Nîmes in 1940, wrote a letter to the prefect to protest the exclusion of Jewish representatives from the ceremony at the préfecture in 1941. He went on to state that on the same day as the celebrations, there were a number of anti-Semitic tracts passed out in the city "too numerous to escape the attention of the authorities" and demanded an official acknowledgment of his letter so as to avoid the reproaches of a "poorly informed public" (CA 560, letter of General André Boris to préfet, 5 May 1941). See also Gerd Krumeich, "The Cult of Joan under the Vichy Régime," in *Collaboration in France: Politics and Culture during the Nazi Occupation, 1940–1944,* ed. Gerhard Hirschfeld and Patrick Marsh (New York, 1989), 92–102. Krumeich reviews the history of the cult, underscores the fundamental ambiguity of Joan's symbolism and concludes that Vichy's sole contribution to her image was to depict her as violently anti-English.

43. Laurent Olivès, "Valleraugue 1900–1940," *Causses et Cévennes,* no. 3 (1984), 209.

tions of fifteenth- and twentieth-century France and the respective destinies of Joan and Pétain. For the tract's anonymous author, a great deal had been at stake in Joan's struggle: the fate of not just France, he argued, but the entire West had hung in the balance. "If France had stayed in English hands, it would have become Protestant, and English would have replaced French. The language and spirit of Western civilization, embodied two hundred years later in the France of Louis XIV, would have been turned upside down."[44]

Reports from Le Vigan indicated that while the entire population had participated in the celebrations, "certain Protestant circles" had been shocked by the cited passage in pamphlet.[45] This shock created ripples in the Protestant press. *Semailles* duly noted the official clarification, which insisted that the author sought only to emphasize that the "cultural blossoming during the century of Louis XIV presupposes a French-speaking and Catholic France." Of course, the explanation only compounded the insult, yet the editorialist remained even-tempered. He pointed out the logical inconsistency of the argument, noting that had Racine become Protestant, he would have no more risked losing his poetic genius than Turenne jeopardized his military genius by converting to Catholicism. The writer warned against confounding the universality of Christianity with the specificity of national genius, and worried over the implicit assumption that Protestantism, as a foreign importation, was alien to the French spirit. Quoting the academician Emile Faguet's assertion that "there are no Frenchmen more French than French Protestants," the paper concluded with the reminders that "a country's greatness is measured by its spirit, and that Christ alone is savior."[46]

Le Messager, a journal published by the Gard's community of Protestant refugees from Alsace and Lorraine, addressed the affair in a more oblique fashion. The pastor Louis Dumas recounted the surprised reaction of his parishioners when, a few years earlier in Alsace, he had given a sermon devoted to Joan of Arc. Some church members responded that the anniversary was a Catholic one and expressed their anxiety that it might become a national holiday. He recalled that they had argued that such an eventuality would mark the resurgence of Catholicism and the reuniting of throne and altar.[47] As for the Reformed Church of Nîmes, its bulletin simply alluded to the "regrettable error" and limited itself to reprinting the passage from Faguet cited by *Semailles*.[48]

44. Pamphlet, CA 776. On the aims and organization of the regime's propaganda bureaucracy, see Claude Lévy and Dominique Veillon, "Propagande et modelage des esprits," in *Vichy et les Français*, ed. Azéma and Bédarida, 184–202.
45. CA 776, sous-préfet of Le Vigan to préfet, 23 May 1942.
46. *Semailles* (July 1942).
47. *Le Messager* (15 May 1942).
48. *Bulletin de l'Eglise réformée de Nîmes* (July–August–September 1942).

But did the local Protestant press perceive the offending remark as a mere error? Or, rather, was it considered an unintended revelation of the regime's true attitude toward their community? No clear answer exists since Protestant journals said little about either Vichy or Pétain. Rare explicit references were marked by a prudence and reserve that contrasted sharply with the patriotic broadsides in *La Semaine Religieuse* and *L'Eveil du Gard.* Yet, given the nature of the times — the cloak of state censorship and the unrelenting efforts to rally the French to the National Revolution — such a silence seems to imply political or spiritual resistance. The context of silence is, of course, all-important. At times, silence suggests acquiescence to, or even agreement with, the decisions and actions of a regime. Yet, in other situations, silence has a positive moral charge. At a moment when a veritable cult was forming around the person of Pétain, "the silence of the sea" — the title of the clandestine short novel, *Le silence de la mer,* written in 1941 by Vercors — represented a legitimate and eloquent form of protest.

The Gard's evangelical journals occasionally broke the mutism practiced by the mainstream Protestants. Unlike their "liberal" brethren, the evangelicals more readily threw their support behind Pétain, and though they never clothed him in the Christ-like imagery of the Catholic press, they were generous in their praise. Thus *Sois Fidèle,* the regional bulletin of the Evangelical Reformed Church, hailed the "chief who, at the very hour when all seemed to be collapsing, appeared to lead France along the rugged path of a lasting revival."[49] Yet even the evangelical enthusiasm for Pétain permitted the occasional hint of resistance. For example, *Christ et France,* the monthly journal of the Evangelical Reformed Church, published in late 1940 a sermon titled "Reform and Rebellion." In a long and carefully argued gloss on Peter's command — "Obey God rather than man" — M. Verseils simultaneously strove to defend Protestantism against the charge of "boycotting all human authority" and to maintain that God remained the ultimate authority. Despite his many qualifications, Verseils's point was clear: when the rule of man conflicts with the law of God, the Christian must choose the latter. As with Luther, so too with the evangelicals: their very conservatism could force them to disobey worldly authority.[50]

Protestants did not, of course, hold a monopoly on the ability to respond to higher laws. Despite the confessional divisions that existed in the Gard, there

49. *Sois Fidèle* (June–July 1941). It ought to be noted that even this journal showed a strain of traditional anti-Semitism. For example, in an editorial criticizing Christians for their materialism, they were likened to the "Jew who, in his characteristic way, loses his breath in chasing after and hoarding his riches" (August–September 1941).

50. *Christ et France* (1 November 1940).

were Catholics who became no less restless under the rule of Vichy than the Protestants. Moreover, neither community, even in the early stages of Vichy, presented a united front to the politics of the regime or the actions of their own representatives. The great historian of French Protestantism, Emile G. Léonard, has written that "in Protestantism as elsewhere there were traitors, cowards . . . and frightened property owners."[51] Yet the historian must avoid the moralism implicit in statements like Leonard's, and the *images d'Epinal* bred by such judgments. Obviously, neither of the two religious communities always conformed to its popular image, nor were the examples of dissension and conflict within each community always the product of cowardice or material greed. It is through the various reactions to Vichy's anti-Semitic legislation of 1941 and the *rafles* of foreign Jews in the Gard in the summer of 1942 that these two observations are best considered.

By March 1941, Vichy decided to address the "Jewish problem." The result was the Commissariat-General for Jewish Affairs, to which Xavier Vallat was appointed director. A veteran anti-Semite and devout Catholic, Vallat enacted several new measures in his first few months: the census in early June of all Jews living in unoccupied France (a census of those Jews living in the occupied zone had been ordered by the Germans the previous September), the announcement of a second and even more rigorous *statut des juifs* (it completed the purge of Jews from the civil service and imposed a Dranconian *numerus clausus* in the liberal professions), and at the end of July the "aryanization" of all Jewish property in the unoccupied zone.[52]

The census in the Gard stunned the local Jewish population: this was the first headcount based on religious criteria undertaken in France in over seventy years. Obliged to declare by 31 July that they "belonged to the Jewish race," many in the Jewish community were not content with a simple attestation. The declaration became a platform from which one's confusion, fear, shame, anger, or pride were expressed. Many respondents cited the several generations their family had lived on French soil and the wars in defense of France in which they and their ancestors had fought. Thus Freddy Benjamin Bedarrida wrote that he belonged to a Jewish family "established in the Comtat Venaissin *from before the fourteenth century,*" and Camille Horvilleur noted that he had begun the research "to prove

---

51. Quoted in Encrevé, *Les Protestants en France,* 238.
52. It is of some interest that the chef-adjoint of Chiappe's cabinet, Pierre-Jérôme Ullmann, was Jewish, but thanks to his decorated service during the campaign of 1939–40, remained in his post through the passage of both statutes. An embodiment of Hannah Arendt's Jew who tries to surpass his Jewishness, Ullmann signed on with Doriot's Légion des volontaires français contre le bolchevisme in August 1941 (CA 339, préfet to interior, 18 January 1941; and CA 785, préfet to interior, 23 August 1941).

that his family has been French for more than a century."[53] The Alsatian and Lorraine Jews who had taken refuge in the Gard were up against a double handicap: not only were they Jewish, but they had their roots in a region whose "Frenchness" was often debated. Hence, Simon Spiegel of Mulhouse underlined that his "ancestors lived in Alsace in 1784, and are listed in the census of Jews undertaken that year by King Louis XVI." This same proof was forwarded by Jean-Armand Hirsch, who added that his great-grandfather had served in Napoleon's army and fought in the Russian campaign of 1812.

Yet others declared that it was a case of mistaken identity: one was Jewish, but with extenuating circumstances. Robert Schreiber, a decorated pilot of the First World War, declared that he was a Catholic who had never practiced Judaism, but since two of his grandparents did so, he had no choice but to declare himself Jewish.[54] Mme Bertrand (née Cohen) asserted that her husband was an *aryen*, and that she had always been a practicing Protestant. An unusual case, in that he was not a convert to another religion, was presented by Louis Kalmanovitch. Though the child of Jewish parents, he had never practiced Judaism and had, since his childhood, "felt anti-Semitic sentiments and never belonged to a secret Jewish society." Inviting an inquiry to prove that he had avoided the company of other Jews during the five years he had lived in Nîmes, Kalmanovitch demanded a dispensation on his behalf. Although Kalmanovitch's protestations were of a different order than those of Bertrand or Schreiber, all three (along with innumerable others) shared the same basic inability to grasp that, since Jewishness was defined "racially" and not sociologically, they were one and all irremediably guilty in the eyes of Vichy.

Wounded patriotism was expressed by others. General André Boris, who had fallen back upon Nîmes during the exodus of 1940 and assumed a de facto role as representative of the local Jewish community, sent a letter of protest to the prefect, in which he declared that it was incompatible "with the dignity attached to the grade I still retain in the French Army reserves, to present myself to a bureaucrat in the next 48 hours in order to declare, after 45 years of service, that I am an Israelite."[55] But despite the hesitations and incomprehension felt by the

53. Emphasis in original. These and all subsequent declarations date from June 1941 and are filed in G 57.

54. There is some question as to the religion of Schreiber, the chatelain of Montfrin and a member of the eminent family into which Jean-Jacques Servan-Schreiber was born. He had asked M. Amat, the prison chaplain, to baptize him and his family in order to avoid deportation, but Girbeau refused to permit it. (Personal communication of Father Aptel to author, September 1988.)

55. As with his previous intervention after the 1941 anniversary of Joan of Arc, Boris demanded a letter written *personally* (a word he underlined) by Chiappe acknowledging receipt of his letter. In neither case have I seen proof that Chiappe did so.

targets of the census, it appears that the great majority of Jews in the Gard complied with the law.[56] Given their protestations that they were "Français et bien Français," such obedience is not surprising.

There is little evidence of public reaction in the Gard to the Jewish census. In late May, a police report remarked that the announcement of a definitive Jewish statute was welcomed "with satisfaction by all those French who are imbued with the spirit of order. It is held that there are too many foreigners and profiteering Jews whose personal interests come before those of the *patrie,* and who use and abuse France's hospitality, occupying posts that should be given first of all to the French."[57] The report's reference to those French "imbued with the sense of order" limits its usefulness, for we do not know who these individuals were or what percentage of the population they represented. There is, moreover, a paucity of letters referring to the anti-Semitic legislation. One letter sent from Nîmes expressed satisfaction that the "Yids are finally being swept out," even if "it was only with the help of the *boches* that we are getting rid of these *métèques.* "[58] On the other hand, there are occasional letters of protest. J. Espinas of Bellegarde, identified as a Protestant, thought the laws "revolting in their iniquity" and confessed his shame that a "French government could lower itself by decreeing such unjust and dishonest measures."[59] A second Protestant, Albert Gaillard of Beauvoisin, referred to the decision taken at the annual national synod, held in 1941 at Alès, to send a letter of protest to Darlan, and commented: "This undoubtedly will create a stir!"[60]

However, it is possible that many Gardois agreed with the belief, as expressed in a circular from the ministry of interior, that the law was a necessary "measure of public order."[61] The defeat and its train of material consequences irritated the xenophobic reflex, if not the persistent strain of anti-Semitism, in French politics and thought. Even an individual as humane and broad-minded as Marc Boegner affirmed in late 1940 that "there is a Jewish problem for certain states at certain periods in their history."[62] And, as we saw in the reaction of the Nîmois Jews to

56. This is the opinion of Lucien Simon; see his *Les Juifs à Nîmes et dans le Gard durant la deuxième guerre mondiale,* 16.

57. . CA 566, commissaire spécial to préfet, 23 May 1941.

58. G 354, commission de contrôle postal, May 1941. Letter sent 10 May 1941.

59. G 360, commission de contrôle postal, December 1941. Letter sent 31 December 1941.

60. G 354, commission de contrôle postal, May 1941. Letter sent 10 May 1941.

61. CA 1473, letter marked "très urgent" from interior to préfets, 12 July 1941. Containing the instructions for the census, the letter emphasized that given the "importance which is attributed to this . . . measure of public order, that it be executed with all possible care and control."

62. In a letter sent by Boegner on 23 December to the regional presidents of the Reformed Churches of France and quoted in Mehl, *Le Pasteur Marc Boegner,* 142. In fact, in the several letters of protest he sent to the Vichy authorities in 1941, Boegner stressed that he was speaking solely on the

the arrival of their co-religionists in the summer of 1940, even many French Jews agreed that there was a problem.[63] Hence, when the searchlight was in turn concentrated on the native Jews, there were few calls from their Christian neighbors to dim the beam.

Further evidence of public impatience with the "Jewish question" is found in the early spring of 1941, when a series of acts of vandalism was directed at various stores in Nîmes owned, or thought to be owned, by Jews. After having reported the breaking of shopwindows in Nîmes, the central commissioner noted that the public had "condemned these acts." But what they actually condemned was less the motivation behind the act than the method in which it was carried out: the Nîmois "do not accept that any individual should take the place of those authorities empowered to solve the problem of the Jewish race."[64] This echoed the commissioner's report the week before, which noted a few "manifestations" of anti-Semitic violence—acts that "everyone has deplored since the government alone is considered qualified to find the right solution to the Jewish question."[65]

The hooligans were not always social misfits or marginals. For example, the five youths who terrorized the Goldenberg family on two separate occasions in December 1941—first having left death messages and then breaking into their apartment and roughing up two of the Goldenberg women—were all children of well-respected Nîmois. The group's leader was the son of a lawyer, a second the son of a former judge; as the prefect noted, they all belonged to "honorable and respected families incapable, in my advice, of pushing them by their opinions or attitudes to such acts."[66] Chiappe's observation was passing strange. First, he seemed oblivious to the fact that there were respectable as well as gutter varieties of anti-Semitism, and that being "bien-pensant" was not necessarily antithetical to hatred of the Jews. Second, and even more disturbing, was his echo of the teenagers' claim that they were influenced by the "anti-Jewish campaign that has been led by certain journals for a long time." He thus ignored the regime's very institutionalization of anti-Semitism. This was a remarkable oversight, given his own official functions and, as we shall see in the next chapter, his participation in

---

behalf of French Jews, as foreign Jews, in his eyes, *did* pose a problem for the state. Mehl defends Boegner's position as the only practical one: since any protest in favor of non-French Jews "was doomed to fail, it was reasonable to obtain what seemed still possible" (145).

63. Marrus and Paxton make this point, as well. For a discussion of the ambivalences expressed even by opponents to Vichy's anti-Semitism, see *Vichy France and the Jews*, 186–91.

64. CA 776, commissioner central to préfet, 28 March 1941.

65. CA 776, commissioner central to préfet, 22 March 1941.

66. CA 300(1), préfet to interior, 18 April 1942. It is interesting to note that while the police commissioner in his report termed these acts "reprehensible," Chiappe avoided any such judgement in his report.

groups such as Collaboration, a virulently anti-Semitic organization founded by Alphonse de Chateaubriant and devoted to the cause of ideological collaboration with Nazi Germany.[67]

A less "respectable" personality involved in anti-Semitic rabble-rousing was Louis Guiraud. Founder of the Gardois section of the Jeunesse de France et d'outre-mer (JFOM), Guiraud had already won local notoriety in the late thirties by hawking issues of *Action Française* and leading street brawls against the left. In February 1942 Guiraud led a series of anti-Semitic acts, from the breaking of Jewish shopwindows to protesting against the appearance of the singer Reda Caire, whom he accused of being Jewish. The JFOM leader identified himself as a devoted follower of Pétain—a claim that clearly worried the police inspector assigned to his case, who observed that Guiraud's activities annoyed respectable citizens and led them to confound his deeds with the policies of the marshal.[68] Guiraud's claims of loyalty were perhaps sincere, the official concluded, but his "tactlessness" was alienating the public.

There was, at the same time, an increasing number of anti-Semitic activities under official patronage. For example, the Colisée cinema in Nîmes showed "The Jew Süss," the notorious Nazi anti-Semitic movie which, provided with a French soundtrack, was run in a number of French cities in 1941. After the film's initial showing, the central commissioner, who had assigned two inspectors to the cinema, reported that it provoked "unanimous applause at each showing, [which] is very symptomatic of the evolution of France's attitude towards the Jewish race."[69] Yet, the value of the police official's report is dubious, thanks not only to his critical appreciation of the film (he described it as a "remarkable realization of German cinematographic art"), but also because he does not provide hard statistics. We are not told the number of those who attended, or who they were. We learn little more when, the following year, Nîmes hosted a conference of the Cercles Populaires Français, a group devoted to anti-Semitic and anti-Masonic propaganda. A representative harangue was given by Noël Roger, a Nîmois lawyer and local collaborationist. He declared that Léon Blum "deserved to be

---

67. CA 300(1), préfet to interior, 18 April 1942. In this same report, Chiappe referred to the official representative of state anti-Semitism in Nîmes, M. D'Ornano, delegate to the police of Jewish Affairs. According to a letter sent to a bureaucrat at the Ministry of Education, it seems that Chiappe officially joined Collaboration in June, 1942. Chiappe noted that he "would take advantage of every occasion to encourage the group in Nîmes" (G 258, 9 July 1942). Concerning the relationship between respectability and anti-Semitism, it is of some relevance that Chiappe's son Jean-François was an anti-Semitic ringleader in primary school and today is an honorary vice-president of the extreme-right Front National (interview with Mme Benfredj by author, November 1987).

68. CA 300(1), commissaire de police to préfet, 4 May 1942.

69. CA 785, commissioner central to préfet, 7 June 1941.

shot, incinerated, and his ashes dispersed so that his corpse would not rot in French soil." Between six to eight hundred people "from all social classes" attended the conference, but we are not told their reaction to Roger's modest proposal. Moreover, we do not know the motivations of the relatively small number who did attend. Curiosity, idleness, the promise of refreshments and distraction, and plain rubbernecking, no less than ideological or political conviction, may have explained the presence of many in the audience.[70]

From such sparse evidence, we can only suggest that the Gard was no exception to the argument that Vichy's anti-Semitic efforts found a response mostly among the already converted.[71] The great majority of the inhabitants seem to have been indifferent to the official tours of anti-Semitic celebrities and the rantings of journals like *L'Eclair* and *L'Eveil du Gard*. Moreover, by 1942, many Gardois gradually came to understand the specious distinction made between state anti-Semitism and popular acts of violence directed at the Jews. The increasing violence of the regime's acts against the Jewish population, far eclipsing that of local vandals, forced the Gardois to question the political and moral legitimacy of Vichy.

An early example of the population's changing attitude was provided by the aryanization of the textile business owned by M. Landauer. A veteran of World War I, Landauer was a local personality, sitting on the Conseil de l'Association des Israélites and president of the Syndicat des confectionners of Nîmes. Due to his charitable activities, described by a police official as "undeniably generous," Landauer had earned the city's widespread respect and sympathy, "especially among the workers." As a result, the population "was somewhat disturbed" by the seizure of Landauer's business. However, the police official assured the prefect that the public's reaction would not go beyond petitions and personal interventions.[72] The official was right, but later that summer the regime further tested the public's tolerance of state anti-Semitism.

In July, Vichy and Germany struck an agreement to deport all foreign Jews from the unoccupied as well as the occupied zones.[73] This led to the capture, and eventual deportation to Drancy (the grim suburban Parisian complex that served as the transit camp for Auschwitz), of fifty-nine men, women, and

70. CA 776, commissaire principal to préfet, 28 April 1942. It should be noted that a similar conference given by the same group two weeks later at Saint Gilles, a town located on the southern plain of the department, attracted "a limited audience" (CA 766, commissaire principal to préfet, 26 May 1942).
71. See survey in Marrus and Paxton, *Vichy France and the Jews*, 209–14; and for a local case, Laborie, *Résistants, Vichyssois et autres*, 199–201.
72. CA 776, commissaire central to préfet, 13 June 1942.
73. The initial campaign set a quota of 32,000 deportees and was aimed at all foreign Jews who

children from the Gard on 25 and 26 August.[74] In a profound sense, this *rafle* crystallized the public's shifting perceptions of the "Jewish question." Until this point, and despite the questions that earlier measures may have raised, certain illusions concerning the nature of the regime remained possible. The difficulties of everyday life, along with the enduring popularity of Pétain, had hindered a full understanding of the government's policies. The events of the last week of August, however, could not be concealed by even the broadest of blinders: the Gardois were confronted with the real nature of the Marshal's regime. It had been relatively easy to rationalize or minimize the "abstract" and "limited" measures contained in the two *statuts des juifs*. However, with the regime's brutal rounding-up of men, women, and children, Vichy might summon support or provoke dismay or even deepen indifference, but its nature could no longer be ignored or misunderstood.

The police action in Nîmes had been anticipated not only in late June in Paris by the infamous *vel d'hiver* roundup (so-called as the more than 12,000 victims were kept for several days in inhuman conditions at the *vélodrome d'hiver*, a Parisian bicycling stadium), but also by the arrest in early August of all Jews enrolled in the Gardois brigades of foreign workers.[75] The foreign workers' camp located in Beaucaire, for example, was quietly surrounded by the gendarmes. In a telephone conversation, the camp's director, taken unawares, described the action as a "kidnapping."[76] The impact of these earlier dragnets, and the rumors of yet others about to be cast, struck public opinion and tormented the life of the local Jews. "It's food for thought," noted a woman, who had witnessed the arrest of the Jewish workers in La Grande-Combe.[77] In mid-August, a woman in Nîmes wrote to a Jewish friend in Ganges (a town in the neighboring Hérault) that she had just learned (mistakenly) that new *rafles* were planned for November. She

---

had entered France after 1 January 1936, singling out Germans, Austrians, Poles, Letts, Czechs, Russians, and Estonians. Moreover, exceptions were made for war veterans, unaccompanied children under eighteen, and pregnant women. After the initial *rafles* and the realization that the quota would not be met, the criteria were considerably loosened; see Paxton and Marrus, *Vichy France and the Jews*, 256–62.

74. This represented one half of those Jews designated to be arrested in the Gard and does not include those individuals enrolled in the Groupements des travailleurs étrangers. See Simon, *Les Juifs à Nîmes*, 33–35.

75. The Groupements de travailleurs étrangers were created in 1939 largely in order to incorporate the refugees from Spain and other countries who did not enlist in the French Army. Simon estimates that there were slightly more than two hundred Jews enrolled in these brigades in 1942 (*Les Juifs à Nîmes*, 21–27).

76. CA 646, commission de contrôle postal, August 1942. Telephone conversation, 28 August 1942.

77. CA 650, commission de contrôle postal, September 1942. Letter sent by Juliette Martin, 11 September 1942.

begged him not to visit her: "David, this is all so incomprehensible. Forgive me, but I beg you to answer me."[78] A resident of Aulas, though he "hardly like[s] this race," found the details on the roundups "painful." He thought that "the measures taken against [the Jews] are much too exaggerated. Excess in anything is a fault."[79]

The subsequent "excesses" of 25–26 August seem to have overwhelmed the majority of Gardois. Reluctance was expressed even by policemen involved in the hunt. "We've a good deal of work at the moment," wrote one gendarme: "We were woken up this morning in order to arrest all the foreign Jews. There are a lot of them and the work is scarcely interesting and sometimes pretty painful, since some of them are decent sorts."[80] The sentiment that the Jews are undesirable as a "race," but as individuals are as "decent" as the next man and woman, is one that was often expressed in the wake of the roundup. The fashion in which the Jews were arrested, wrote a good woman of Nîmes, was simply "excessive." Everywhere, she exclaimed, "heartbreaking family scenes are taking place, and there have even been suicides . . . as unpleasant as the Jews may be, one feels sorry for them all the same for being subjected to such treatment. It is really inhuman."[81] A fellow Nîmoise did not find the Jews' fate too tragic: after all, a spell in the work camps in the East "can only do them a great deal of good." The problem was that "the parents were being sent off and the children left to look after themselves."[82]

It is clear that cultural and religious stereotypes had a long life. Even when confronted by the brute reality of the police actions, numerous Gardois distinguished between the individual Jews they knew and the Jew as an abstract notion. Tragically, this ambivalence toward the "Jewish question" had helped set the scene for the roundups. Had the two Jewish statutes and the official efforts at rallying public opinion to such policies provoked resistance and revulsion rather than indifference or tepid support, Vichy may have hesitated to take any further measures. In sum, the conflicted attitude of many Gardois toward the victims of

78. CA 646, commission de contrôle postal, August 1942. Letter sent by Suzanne X (Nîmes), 19 August 1942.

79. CA 646, commission de contrôle postal, August 1942. Letter sent 18 August (Aulas), 1942.

80. CA 646, commission de contrôle postal, August 1942. Letter sent by Pierrot X (Nîmes), 27 August 1942 (obviously, the letter was written a day or two before its date).

81. CA 646, commission de contrôle postal, August 1942. Letter sent 28 August 1942. The correspondent, Mme Manon, lived on the same street as the city's synagogue.

82. CA 356, commission de contrôle postal, September 1942. Letter sent by Micheline Lombard (Nîmes), 10 September 1942. A certain Teissier of Alès thought the problem lay in the Frenchman's inconsistency: he can "allow his father to die of hunger, [yet] revolts at the idea of separating a little Yid from his parents." CA 356, commission de contrôle postal, September 1942. Letter sent 22 September 1942.

the *rafles* was no less invidious than their previous acceptance of the Jewish statutes. The law, like humanity, is indivisible: the moment categories are imposed, so too are inequalities.

In truth, those who welcomed official efforts against Jews were probably a small minority. Given the imprecise and general nature of the documentation, no firm statistics can be offered. Yet of the hundreds of letters and reports I have examined, those that praised the roundups are in a clear minority. On the eve of the roundup, a writer from Bagnols complained that "Isaac and Co. are everywhere. You cannot walk a hundred feet without stepping on one. In the search for butter or cheese, these animals are always there first." The correspondent sighed, "What a life! The Good Lord is testing us sorely."[83] A native of Concoules praised Vichy's action, wishing that "for the sake of world peace this cursed race be destroyed and that it disappear forever."[84] And a third, having dwelt on the danger posed by the Jew's natural drive to monopolize and hoard, regretted "the human impulses that surface when one speaks of the measures to which they are subjected."[85] Lamenting the ugliness of the world, yet another Nîmois placed the blame for the black market on the shoulders of the Jew: "We have not succeeded to get rid of all these Jew-masons. The majority have no homeland, or rather, money is their nation."[86]

Nearly all the letters expressing such sentiments return time and again to the theme of food. This is not a coincidence since, in a time of material hardship, the foreigner often becomes the focus of fear and suspicion. The very embodiment of the foreigner, the local Jews found themselves increasingly vulnerable. As one Nîmois reflected, "the Jew really has roots nowhere and has no country."[87] Second, the civil disabilities imposed by Vichy pushed the Jews, both materially and mythically, into the public's consciousness. Few French seemed to understand that if the Jews had money, it was because they were forced to sell their property; and if they spent their money, it was because they found themselves isolated in villages, bereft of family or connections that could help them resolve their difficulties. Instead, the "signs of distress among the Jews were misread, accord-

83. CA 356, commission de contrôle postal, August 1942. Letter sent by Delepine (Nîmes), 11 September 1942.

84. CA 356, commission de contrôle postal, September 1942. Letter sent by Dehan Bailly (Concoules), 2 September 1942.

85. CA 354, commission de contrôle postal, September 1942. Letter sent by Boulanger (Nîmes), 26 September 1942.

86. CA 356, commission de contrôle postal, September 1942. Letter sent by Vigouroux (Nîmes), 7 September 1942.

87. CA 356, commission de contrôle postal, September 1942. Letter sent by X (Nîmes), 7 September 1942.

ing to an ancient symbolism, as signs of privilege."[88] The xenophobic tendencies of a part of the population were sharpened to the point that even the brutality of the roundups could not eclipse the mythic image of the Jew.

Still, that many, perhaps most, Gardois were shocked and revulsed by the events is the clear impression left by the intercepted letters. "I was depressed all day yesterday," wrote a woman from Uzès: "The Jews have all been shipped off to concentration camps. They were woken up at five o'clock in the morning by the gendarmes and packed off. . . . We are just as badly off as the occupied zone. I wonder why we just are not baptized as Germans, for this would avoid two different police forces and a lot of fuss. We haven't much reason to be proud of being French."[89] A Nîmoise recounted that "Jews were arrested all day and all night. . . . It is a terrible thing to see in our good and gentle France. We wonder what is in store for them. It is terrible that men can be so evil and unfair."[90] A third Nîmois had no doubts as to what was in store: "A fit of murderous insanity has overcome mankind. (I hope that it is insanity, as that would make it less horrible.) Are the Jewish persecutions reaching their climax? Thousands and thousands of these poor wretches are being hunted down like animals and taken to concentration camps. And to what end? To work in Polish mines? A number of them have been killed." This same correspondent then told the story of a departmental leader of the Compagnons de France, a Vichy-inspired youth movement. Described as "reflective and humane, a Protestant in the mold of Pastor Brunel," this official found himself at the train station of Montpellier at the moment when the victims of the *rafle* were being shipped out. Overwhelmed by the sight, the Vichy official cried out the word "Courage" to the prisoners and fled the station.[91]

In general, the letters culled by postal control officials speak of widespread "consternation," "indignation," even "revolution" in the wake of the roundup. The police and prefectoral reports confirmed the state of shock that swept over the public. The Gardois, reported one official, while "recognizing that there are too many foreigners in our country at a moment when food supplies are growing scarce, [still] took pity on the arrested Jewish families."[92] In a subsequent report, however, this same official insisted that it was less the measure itself than its appli-

88. Marrus and Paxton, *Vichy France and the Jews,* 184.
89. CA 646, commission de contrôle postal, August 1942. Letter sent by Jeanne X (Uzès), 27 August 1942.
90. CA 356, commission de contrôle postal, August 1942. Letter sent by Gilberte X (Nîmes), 27 August 1942.
91. CA 356, commission de contrôle postal, September 1942. Letter sent by X (Nîmes), 2 September 1942.
92. CA 776, commissaire principal to préfet, 29 August 1942.

cation, especially the separation of family members, that stirred the population.[93] Clearly, the sight of parents struggling with the dilemma of either leaving their children behind at the train station or staying together for a voyage to a vague yet menacing terminus was the most heartrending aspect to the roundup.[94] Yet, public opinion clearly questioned the legitimacy of the operation itself. According to the departmental military commander, the arrests were condemned for two reasons. First, it was thought to be the result of German coercion, and thus proof that Vichy was no longer master in its own house. Second, the concession to German pressure was all the more inexcusable since the public could not "understand the necessity of arresting people who do not seem a priori dangerous."[95]

The durability of the public's concern is difficult to ascertain. One report, written on 16 September, affirmed that "apathy has quickly reasserted itself and it seems, for the moment, that the event has been forgotten."[96] At the end of September, however, a summary from the postal control commission emphasized that the roundup and other anti-Semitic measures "provoked an indignation that, far from calming down, seems to have been largely kept alive."[97] The situation was especially tense in and around Alès. The subprefect claimed that the already existing hostility of the populace toward Germany and Vichy was so great that "twenty-four hours after the resettling [sic] of the families of foreign Jews, the entire population was repeating the lie [sic] that mothers were separated from their children." He worried that popular discontent was so great that, if an Allied invasion of the continent were to take place at that moment, a popular uprising would follow.[98] A popular uprising did not take place, in Alès or elsewhere in the Gard. The initial shock could not be maintained indefinitely; the minor crises of everyday life eventually drew the Gardois back to their private affairs.

---

93. CA 776, commissaire principal to préfet, 9 October 1942.

94. Many of the intercepted letters refer to the separations. One Jewish woman living in Nîmes, momentarily untouched by the *rafle* as she was a French citizen, sought to answer the question that must have been asked by nearly all women: "I believe that if I had a child I would prefer to die with him than be separated. Well, let us hope that, for the French, things will not go so far." CA 646, commission de contrôle postal, August 1942. Letter sent by Mme Goldenberg, 26 August 1942.

95. CA 776, commandant de 15ème division militaire to préfet, 16 September 1942.

96. CA 776, commandant de 15ème division militaire to préfet, 16 September 1942.

97. G 354, rapport mensuel of commission de contrôle postal, 30 September 1942. It ought to be noted that the central commissioner affirmed on 6 September that the roundup of Jews (whom, revealingly, he neglects to qualify as foreign) "has not provoked any apparent reaction (CA 776)." This observation flies in the face of the other police reports we have already cited, as well as the mass of intercepted letters. It appears that Legrand was becoming less and less objective in his reports (his piece on "The Jew Süss" being just one sign); as a consequence his observations need to be used carefully.

98. CA 776, sous-préfet of Alès to préfet, 28 September 1942.

Nonetheless, the widespread indignation did not disappear without a trace. This is manifest in the individual and institutional reactions of the department's Catholics and Protestants.

Following the arrests, there was a natural reflex to turn to the churches for guidance. Yet, the local Catholic hierarchy maintained a near total silence. As one Nîmois exclaimed, "Not a sole protest is heard—and yet, there are priests and bishops!"[99] The silence was not sudden, however; from the promulgation of the first Jewish statute in October 1940 to the events of August 1942, the departmental representatives of the Catholic Church had not uttered a single word of protest. Neither Girbeau nor *La Semaine Religieuse* had commented, in either direct or oblique fashion, on the series of juridical and civil disabilities placed on their Jewish compatriots. This silence had already been addressed in early 1942 by a Protestant tract that circulated through the Gard. It criticized the "equivocations and incomprehension" of the church in the face of events that called for a "revolt against the violations of the Christian rules of justice and goodness." Underlining the enormity of this failure, the tract warned that at "the moment of liberation, the church will risk suffering the hard consequences."[100] Yet, in the two issues of *La Semaine Religieuse* that followed the arrests, not even the most indirect of references appeared to what Monsignor Théas of Montauban had described, in his famous protest, "as painful and sometimes horrifying scenes."[101] Instead, there was a reminder from the bishop about the upcoming grape harvest and his warning against the "grave dangers" of promiscuity among the young participants.[102]

Girbeau's silence on these events, as will be shown in Chapter 5, contrasted sharply with his drumbeating for Vichy. From the very beginning, the bishop sought to rally the Gardois Catholics to the regime. Girbeau's fervent support of Vichy was not in itself exceptional; during the first year of the regime, the Catholic hierarchy was unsparing in its praise of Pétain's government. What is

99. CA 646, commission de contrôle postal, August 1942. Intercepted telephone conversation of 28 August between unidentified representatives of the groupement des travailleurs étrangers at Beaucaire and the Commissariat de la lutte contre le chômage in Nîmes.

100. CA 646, commission de contrôle postal, March 1942. The anonymous authors of the tract, which had been mailed from Montpellier to St. Laurent d'Aigouze, specified that it would be the last number and that they would be collaborating henceforth with *Cahiers de Témoignage Chrétien*.

101. For the texts of Théas and other protesting bishops like Monsignor Saliège of Toulouse, along with a critical commentary, see Xavier de Montclos, "Des Voix d'évêques et de prêtres en Europe," in *Spiritualité, théologie et résistance*, ed. Bolle and Godel, 130–46. In one of his telephone conversations, M. Salem, the local representative of Vichy's office of propaganda, notes that the reason he attended the church ceremony where Girbeau spoke was because of the protests already delivered by Saliège and Monsignor Gerlier, the archbishop of Lyon.

102. *La Semaine religieuse* (6 September 1942).

striking about Girbeau's zeal is its constancy. During the career of Vichy, even those events, such as the second Jewish statute and the roundups that provoked the first doubts and veiled criticisms among some other members of the ecclesiastical hierarchy, gave no pause to the bishop of Nîmes.

We already have had occasion to mark the bishop's concern with sexual morality at moments of national crisis. A second and more important strand of continuity, however, was Girbeau's anti-Semitism. His attitude toward Jews and Judaism had little in common with the ideological stew of an Xavier Vallat or Charles Maurras (though we must not forget the former ties between Girbeau and Action française). Girbeau instead shared the traditional Christian anti-Semitism of many of his peers. By the 1930s, the hierarchy of the Catholic Church and many of its lay representatives had condemned anti-Semitism. As early as 1928, Pius XI criticized that "hatred commonly described as anti-Semitism." A decade later, in his encyclical *Mit brennender Sorge,* Pius issued a sharp rebuttal of Nazi racist and anti-Semitic doctrines, asserting that "spiritually we are all semites."[103] Similar declarations were made by French representatives of the church, while Cardinals Verdier, Saliège, and Gerlier, and Catholic journals like *La Croix* and *Etudes* all renounced their earlier anti-Semitism.

Yet the evolution was slow and uneven. François Delpech has pointed out that while the church had "clearly reacted against racism and anti-Semitism, it remained a prisoner of a burdensome political and theological past."[104] This historical burden was carried by that segment of the French ecclesiastical hierarchy that had been formed by the violent battles between the Republic and the church at the turn of the century, and which was sympathetic to the doctrines of Charles Maurras and Action française. These men contrasted sharply to the new generation of ecclesiastics who participated in the renewal of the French episcopacy during the interwar period and the return to evangelical and pastoral concerns.[105]

Girbeau's age thus helps explain his attitude toward Vichy's anti-Semitism, for he belonged to this older and deeply conservative generation. Born in 1870, the bishop of Nîmes was twenty years older than the average age (51 years) of those bishops appointed during the interwar changing of the guard, and five years

---

103. Quoted in Duquesne, *Les Catholiques français sous l'occupation,* 244.

104. François Delpech, "Les Eglises et la persecution raciale," in *Eglises et chrétiens,* ed. Montclos et al., 261.

105. Mayeur has observed that between 1926 and 1936, thirty-nine new French bishops—many of whom, like Cardinal Saliège, had participated in the various Catholic youth movements such as Action catholique and Sillon—were appointed by Rome. Girbeau predated this renewal, having been named to the bishopric of Nîmes in 1924. See Mayeur's "Les Evêques dans l'avant-guerre," in *Eglises et chrétiens,* 11.

older than the average age of all French bishops.[106] In contrast to some of his peers, Girbeau never made any statements during the war that explicitly praised the anti-Semitic measures taken by Vichy.[107] Yet the comments uttered by Girbeau both before and after France's defeat reveal that he never succeeded in shedding the theological anti-Semitism that marked so many Catholics of his generation. The Jew remained, in Girbeau's mind, the killer of Christ. In a sermon given in 1936, Girbeau described Peter's arrival in Rome as the quest to "conquer the city from Caesar and render it the faith of the God attached to a cross by the Jews."[108] With the advent of Vichy, Girbeau avoided any mention of the Jews in his sermons. However, one of his official letters published in 1941 provided an oblique notion of his attitude toward the Jewish question. In commenting upon the purpose of Catholic faith and love, Girbeau offered a list of priorities. After having asserted that there is "neither Jew nor gentile, Greek nor barbarian" and that it is the Catholic's duty to love all men, Girbeau immediately spun around and added that to live one's faith implied the establishment of "a hierarchy of affections." It was a question of loving "the members of a family who have the same name and the same blood before loving foreigners. One must love the *patrie* before one can love mankind."[109]

Where did the archetypical foreigner, the Jew, fall in this hierarchy? Not very far from the bottom, given Girbeau's complete silence during the storm of anti-Semitic measures. Chiappe praised the "complete loyalism" shown by Girbeau and nearly all his clergy in the wake of the *rafles*. The prefect implicitly lauded the role played by Girbeau when he linked the absence of any reaction among the local Catholics to the fact that "no pastoral reading was made and the Jewish question was not treated in *La Semaine Religieuse*."[110] Applauded by Chiappe, Girbeau's silence was condemned by a scattered number of Catholics. He was sent one letter, signed by an "outraged Catholic," in which the writer recounted the brutal manner in which the gendarmes had carried out their orders. He wondered if "it was not already enough that we are sending people off to prison

---

106. See statistics in Mayeur, "Les Evêques dans l'avant-guerre," 11.

107. For example, the bishop of Grenoble welcomed the repression of that "harmful power, the *métèques,* of which the Jews are a particularly outstanding specimen" (Marrus and Paxton, *Vichy France and the Jews,* 199). Similarly, the Jesuit journal *Construire* praised the first Jewish statute as a measure of "moral purification" (Duquesne, *Les Catholiques français sous l'occupation,* 242–43).

108. *La Semaine Religieuse* (22 March 1936), 125. One month later, in the issue of 19 April, the paper carried an unsigned article that recounted the success of Father Coughlin's preaching in the United States. The article enthused over Coughlin's courage and noted the "great fuss" created by the priest's social commentary. Tellingly, the writer omitted the anti-Semitism that was central to Coughlin's "social commentary."

109. *La Semaine Religieuse* (5 October 1941), 460.

110. CA 776, préfet to conseiller d'état secrétaire général à la police (19 October 1942).

whom we ought to be protecting. . . . Must we also behave like brutes? Monsignor, I am waiting for you to give your answer from the pulpit."[111] The disheartened Catholic never received an answer—or, at least, not the one for which he hoped, since Girbeau's silence could only be construed as support for the regime's measures. As a resistance tract that made the rounds in late 1942 affirmed, the Church's "fearful silence and hope for material advantages can inspire only compromise and complicity."[112]

With one or two exceptions, the silence of Monsignor Girbeau was imitated by all his clergy. This was partly due to the church's emphasis upon authority and obedience; the rigid ecclesiastical structure and weight of tradition and theology dissuaded priests from voicing open disagreement with official policy. Besides, a number of Vichy's policies had substantial support among the local clergy. During a lecture given in 1941 at Marguerittes, Charles Maurras had occasion to observe approvingly that "numerous priests and religious officials are present, which proves that democratic ideas have not yet won over the French clergy."[113] At a second talk given by Maurras in St. Ambroise, a participant remarked with satisfaction that "a dozen priests were in attendance" and that the priest of St. Ambroise had "advertised the meeting from his pulpit."[114] Abbé Pons of Durfort, an active collaborator with the Service d'ordre légionnaire (SOL), showed even greater commitment to the values of the extreme right than his colleague in St. Ambroise. He gave a series of talks to the Légion de combattants in late 1942, discoursing on the dangers of *judéo-maconnerie,* and seeking to rally the "slumbering légionnaires" to the program of the SOL.[115]

By the end of 1942, most Gardois priests probably sympathized with the sigh of one of their colleagues: "It is up to us to defend the poor marshal against everything and everyone."[116] Yet, the impact Girbeau and his clergy had upon the mass of Catholic Gardois is difficult to determine. There is, on the one hand, the risk of exaggerating the clergy's influence, especially at a time when they were bemoaning declining church attendance. For example, Lasalle's priest lamented the empty pews in his church and the frequent cancellation of Sunday vespers

111. CA 1475. Copies of letter sent to commander of the gendarmerie, the prefect, and the apostolic nuncio. In a report to Chiappe, attached to the letter in question, the commander of the gendarmerie repudiated the charges of brutality and affirmed that the letter-writer was undoubtedly "an Israelite unhappy with the government's measures."

112. CA 745. Tract titled "Aux catholiques français."

113. G 353, commission de contrôle postal, April 1941. Letter sent by T. Bourneton, 27 April 1941.

114. G 480, commission de contrôle postal, September 1941. Letter from X (Besseges), 23 September 1941.

115. G 354, commission de contrôle postal, October 1942. Letter of Pons to Colonel Dire, departmental commander of S.O.L., 11 October 1942.

116. CA 646, summary of commission de contrôle postal, 5–19 December 1942.

"because there are not enough choral singers!"[117] Yet, on the other hand, Chiappe credited the bishop for the role he played to help assure public calm following the roundup. At the very least, the political account in which Girbeau and his quiescent clergy invested the moral capital of the church comforted those who either supported the state's measures or those—and they seem to have been far greater in number—who were disturbed by the events, but simply wanted to get on with their lives. The apathy of most Gardois was reinforced by the official sanction of the church's local representatives.

In addition, some Catholic journals were much less reticent than *La Semaine Religieuse* in regard to the *rafle.* For example, *Le Viganais,* which was generally more moderate than *L'Eveil du Gard,* aligned the regime's action with church doctrine. The paper reminded its readers that Saint Thomas had "closed public functions to all Jews and forbade Christians to be on familiar terms with Jews." It also pointed out that the wearing of the Jewish star (imposed only in the occupied zone) had historical antecedents dating back to the Lateran Council, quoted Pope Innocent III on the Christian's need to be constantly on his guard against the Jews, and warned that if "certain Catholics allow themselves to be shaken by the marshal's politics, they will become the dupes of those foreign powers seeking to undermine French unity."[118] The paper's defense may well have been a response to the unpopularity of the *rafle*—particularly, as a postal commission report observed, among the "denominational groups."[119]

A certain number of local Catholics, shaken by the measures and Girbeau's moral forfeiture, turned to other ecclesiastical figures, or even other churches, for guidance. As Pastor A. N. Bertrand had affirmed a year before, the Protestant churches were welcoming "people who are not Protestants and that pastors receive numerous and daily letters revealing the great distress in our hearts and souls. Men who have not found in their own church a satisfactory response to the problems they are asking themselves, are trying to see if they can find the answers elsewhere."[120] Tracts began to circulate through the department, "passed from hand to hand in Catholic and Protestant circles," which denounced the roundup and quoted the protests of Cardinals Gerlier and Saliège, as well as the Protestant

117. *L'Echo paroissial de Lasalle,* December 1942. This reference raises the broader issue of the level of religious practice and belief among local Catholics and Protestants. Unfortunately, there is no simple and clear answer. I have found no statistics on the frequency of church attendance—which is, of course, itself a potentially misleading indicator of religious practice. As a result, I have been forced to rely on the impressionistic evidence supplied by the sermons, reports, and letters of the period.

118. *Le Viganais* (12 September 1942).

119. G 354, commission de contrôle postal, 30 September 1942.

120. Address given at the national synod of Reformed Churches held at Alès in May 1941. Quoted in the Resistance tract "Aux catholiques français."

theologian Karl Barth and the contributors to the Christian resistance journal *Cahiers de témoignage Chrétien*. For example, a police official reported the existence of a tract titled "We Must Choose Between Hitler and Christ," which declared that the "time of equivocation and silence is over" and the time for the resistance of all Christians had begun.[121] Rumors blossomed in this atmosphere of fear and repression, and stories spread that both Gerlier and Saliège had been arrested and a new era of state-led repression of the church had begun.[122] The rumors and protests may well have influenced public opinion. One letter-writer, though noting that he knew too little about the matter to judge accurately, insisted that the protesting bishops "must know what they are doing, and in my opinion, have shown courage and ought to be thanked."[123]

Yet as the various prefectoral and police reports make clear, the Protestant community reacted more sharply than did the local Catholics to the regime's policies. Already uneasy with Vichy's clerical bent and the cult of Pétain, the Gardois Protestants considered the growing anti-Semitic activity to pose yet another affront to the moral imperatives of Christianity and a threat to all religious minorities in France. Given their spiritual emphasis upon the Hebrew Bible and the vivid memory of their own persecutions, the Protestants had powerful theological and historical reasons to resist Vichy's anti-Semitism. Although there were exceptions to this tendency, the misgivings first felt by certain Protestants toward Vichy from the fall of 1940 now began to grow and spread.

As already noted, Chiappe was aware of the potential problems posed by the department's Protestant community. Upon his arrival, the prefect harbored doubts concerning the "patriotism" of the local Protestants—doubts that were reinforced by the receipt of anonymous letters that, welcoming his arrival in Nîmes, denounced all Protestants as "Gaullist fanatics."[124] Moreover, Chiappe had been directed by the ministry of interior in late 1940 to "follow very closely" the state of Protestant opinion.[125] This partly explains the close tabs he kept on

121. CA 745, commissaire principal to préfet, 24 August 1942.
122. G 354, commission de contrôle postal, October 1942. The letter reporting this rumor was sent by a priest from the Alesian mining basin who qualified the roundup as "inhuman" and affirmed that France's religious restoration would not come from the "so-called National Revolution."
123. G 354, commission de contrôle postal, October 1942. Letter sent by X, 3 October 1942. The correspondent mentioned that the government, worried over the public's reaction to the measures, had sent the prefects to speak with the bishops in their respective departments. I have not come across any documents that report Chiappe's visit to Girbeau, or that the latter expressed in private any concern over the roundup.
124. CA 743, letter of denunciation to Chiappe, n.d. (probably late 1940).
125. CA 660, Direction général de la sûreté nationale to Chiappe, 20 December 1940.

them and his efforts to remain in frequent touch with the community's leaders.[126] Thus in a 1941 report, Chiappe included a clipping from a favorable story in *L'Eclair* on the national synod of French Protestants at Alès, adding that Boegner had himself confirmed the "loyalism" of the Reformed Church.[127]

It was at this same synod, however, that Pastor Bertrand observed the unique moral role played by the Protestant churches in these "troubled times." After the creation of the Commissariat General of Jewish Affairs in March 1941, Pastor Boegner sent letters to both Darlan and the Grand Rabbi of France denouncing the regime's racist legislation and declaring that the Protestant Church, "which has known the suffering of persecution, feels a sharp sympathy for [the Jewish people]"—a position that was formally approved by the national synod at Alès in early May.[128] The vote became rapidly known. Two days after the synod's conclusion, a Gardois wrote to an acquaintance of the unanimous vote to protest Vichy's anti-Semitism, remarking gleefully that it "undoubtedly will make a splash."[129] At roughly the same time, *Semailles,* seeking to underline the universal consequences of Vichy's actions, published Archbishop Saliège's Easter letter, in which the prelate of Toulouse asked his parishioners if God was in their hearts. Not just any god, but the "true God, by whom I mean the God of Abraham, Isaac, Jacob and the prophets, the true God to whom all men must answer, even those small men who pretend to usurp his place on earth. The true God to whom all the oppressed and all those who suffer seek solace. The just God."[130]

126. Vichy also had its doubts concerning the reliability of the Protestants. For example, a circular from the ministry of interior (7 December 1940) ordered the investigation of the Salvation Army, which was suspected to be a center of antigovernment activity. The authorities in the Gard absolved the organization of any wrongdoing, but observed in a suspicious tone that "the majority of leaders, officers, and members are recruited from among orthodox Protestants" (CA 300–302). Such suspicion was, in retrospect, perhaps justified. The national leader of the Armée de Salut, "Major" Georges Flandre, became an important resistance leader under the nom de guerre "Montcalm." He was arrested and shot by the Gestapo in August 1944. See W. D. Halls, "French Christians and the German Occupation," in *Collaboration in France,* ed. Hirschfeld and Marsh, 74.

127. CA 566, letter from préfet to Pétain, 11 May 1941. Similarly, in February of that same year, Boegner gave a talk at the Grand Temple of Nîmes on the subject of "French Protestantism and the National Revolution." The prefecture saw fit to include in its files a report in *Le Républicain du Gard* on the talk, which was given in front of an "imposing audience" that included M. and Mme Chiappe, and in which Boegner underlined the role Protestants needed to play in the remaking of a new France (CA 566, 18 February 1941).

128. Letter written 26 March 1941. Quoted in Pierre Bolle, "Les Protestants et leurs églises durant la seconde guerre mondiale," *Revue de l'histoire moderne et contemporaine* 27 (April–June 1979), 294. Interestingly, the letter was meant to be private, but the Parisian collaborationist journal *Au Pilori* obtained a copy and printed it. Though its goal was to embarrass Boegner, the journal instead succeeded in embarrassing the regime.

129. CA 273, commission de contrôle postal, May 1941. Letter sent by Albert Gaillard (Beauvoisin), 10 May 1941.

130. *Semailles* (August 1942).

The Gardois Protestants truly mobilized with the *rafles* of August 1942. A police report observed that the Reformed Church, through the multiplication of individual interventions and its official denunciation of Vichy, had assumed "a veritable fighting position."[131] The bulletin of the Reformed Church of Nîmes reprinted the message of the 1942 synod, which condemned the regime's measures and reminded Protestants that they were retainers of the moral imperative "to resist the assault of any doctrine and ideology, of any threat and any promise that undermines the teaching of the Bible.... [the Church] knows that all men are created equal, in perdition as well as in salvation, and that divine justice requires the respect of all human beings."[132]

The stand taken by the Protestant leadership had a powerful impact on the members of the various churches. One letter, posted at Nîmes on the eve of the roundup, sharply criticized the regime on the basis of biblical citations and pronouncements from Protestant leaders. The anonymous author declared that the church "recognized in Israel the people elected by God to give the Messiah to the world and to be ... a permanent witness to the mystery of faithfulness." Hence, though the state perhaps confronted a problem requiring a solution (an echo of the unhappy qualification used by Boegner), the church remained duty-bound to protest "any statute that places the Jews outside all human community."[133] The pastors, as the letter indicates, often played a critical role in recalling the moral and spiritual imperatives of Protestantism. "Our seven pastors," one Nîmois exclaimed with great satisfaction, "are spoiling us 'spiritually.' Such a difference from 1914–18 when we were fed patriotic sermons aimed at 'the swarthy and blood-thirsty enemy.' But now, such loftiness! Such spirituality!... All wrapped in humility and the consciousness of the personal responsibilities we must shoulder in this horrible affair.... We have good shepherds whom we ought listen to and follow."[134]

What is striking in the nature of the Protestant response is its lineage. This ancestry, which stretches back to the Camisard Rebellion and the "years of the

131. G 354, commission de contrôle postal, September 1942. There is already a large literature, scholarly, popular, and autobiographical, on the role played by French Protestants in the rescue of thousands of French and foreign Jews during the war. As a result, the work of Madeleine Barot and CIMADE (Comité d'Inter-Mouvement auprès des évacués), and the pastor Marc Boegner and the National Council of the Reformed Church of France, all of whom were located in Nîmes, have received a good deal of attention. For this reason, as well as the fact that these were national organizations and figures who were temporarily settled in Nîmes and not necessarily characteristic of the Gard, they will be discussed only when they touch directly upon departmental politics.

132. *Bulletin de l'Eglise Réformée de Nîmes* (July–August–September 1942).

133. G 357, commission de contrôle postal, July 1942. Letter sent 3 July 1942.

134. G 354, commission de contrôle postal, December 1942. Letter sent by J. Koch, 20 December 1942.

desert" following the revocation of the Edict of Nantes, caught the attention of André Siegfried. The great Protestant sociologist wrote in 1945 that no land resembled the Protestant strongholds of the Midi where "history is so present!" Quoting Auguste Comte, Siegfried asserted that "it is a region that is made up more of the dead than the living."[135] Allowance made for Siegfried's postwar jubilation, his observation is just: the factor of history was decisive in the moral calculus of the Gard's Protestants. The relevance of the past as a guide through the present turmoil was often and explicitly invoked. Thus a certain Monsieur Hours pondered the future of mankind in the wake of the roundup of foreign Jews. Such a question, he felt, "should be the theme of a profound meditation ... poor spectators whom we are, who knows if, as Protestants, we will not be next."[136] Yet, the deliberate allusions to past symbols and events was not neces- sary, for the notion of resistance had become reflexive among most Protestants. The Nîmois Protestant J. Monod emphasized that "one must always choose between dying and making concessions. We have chosen the latter course, which is why we still have enough to eat. If we want to have the right to criticize, we must first of all be prepared to accept the consequences."[137] By 1942, most Protestants seemed prepared to accept the consequences.

The overlapping of symbols and the confluence of past and present dramas were especially striking during the annual ceremony on 6 September at the Musée du désert in Mas Soubeyran. The ancient home of the Camisard leader Rolland, the museum was a memorial for the *galériens de la foi* — Protestants who had suffered exile, imprisonment, and death for their faith — and since 1911 sheltered an annual assembly of Protestants from across the nation. During the assembly of 1942 Marc Boegner presented a sermon on the theme "Be faithful unto death," in which he sought to underline the duty of all Christians to aid the Jews. Following his discourse, Boegner gathered some sixty-seven pastors around him to alert them to the situation they now confronted and to learn what measures the pastors had already taken. He learned that the majority had already begun to aid and hide fleeing Jews in their parishes. As Boegner himself noted, this moment marked the beginning of "the ministry that, up until France's liberation, helped thousands of French and foreign Jews escape from the French and German police."[138] Conferring under the ancient oaks and walnut trees of

135. Siegfried, in Siegfried and Boegner, *Le Protestantisme français,* 29.

136. G 356, commission de contrôle postal, August 1942. Letter sent from Nîmes, 29 August 1942.

137. G 480, commission de contrôle postal, September 1941. Letter sent from Nîmes 23 September 1941.

138. Quoted in *Cévennes: Terre de refuge,* ed. Joutard et al., 252. This book is entirely consecrated to the role played by the Cévenol Protestants in the assistance and shelter provided to Jews during the war and is an invaluable source of oral testimony. It should be noted that in a meeting with René Bousquet,

Mas Soubeyran, sheltering a patch of ground fertile with the memories of their own history of persecution, the pastors were keenly aware of the momentousness of their decision. George Gillier spoke for his fellow ministers when he noted that during this meeting they understood that "the Jewish question was no longer a mere biblical question, but a reality. From that moment on, we began to act."[139]

Yet not all the Protestants of the Gard agreed with Gillier. A minority committed to the person of Pétain, the ideas of the National Revolution, a conservative approach to Protestantism or simply the desire to avoid trouble, marked their disaccord with the Protestant leadership and the majority of their co-religionists. This minority judged illicit and dangerous the words and gestures of the pastors that other Protestants found "exhilarating" and "spiritual." Thus, in the wake of the roundup, one Protestant wrote that "several pastors have compromised themselves. The consequences will be heavy. We need to act like Christians, rather than degenerate into a political party."[140] A Cévenol Protestant, recounting the rumor that Pastor Elie Lauriol had been arrested following a sermon critical of the regime's anti-Semitic policies, exclaimed "It serves him right! His sort will finish up by destroying Protestantism."[141] Yet another correspondent echoed the fear that the official protest lodged by Boegner would confirm the popular stereotype of the unpatriotic Protestant, and moreover would complicate Pétain's tasks. He concluded that "our duty is to be quiet and obey."[142] The dissension within the ranks of the local Protestants became so noticeable that it attracted the attention of the local authorities. Chiappe reported that certain members of the Reformed Church warned Boegner that the publication of his letter could "spark the most extraordinary rumors and that an appeal to union ... should have instead been published." The prefect concluded that a "certain division reigns among the Protestants, some showing a certain reticence toward the government's politics, others giving proof of great loyalty to the marshal and his government."[143]

It is as difficult to ascertain the number of Protestants who were loyal to the regime as it is to grasp their motivations. One pastor, Marc Donadille, has

---

the prefect of police, Boegner protested against the actions of the state and warned about popular reaction. Bousquet's reply was that of the pure technocrat: "the role of public opinion is to be disturbed (s'émouvoir), while that of the government is to choose" (*Carnets du pasteur Boegner 1940–1945*, [Paris, 1993], 203). The marvelous irony is that public opinion *did* choose, as the subsequent actions of the Protestants attest.

139. "Table ronde," in *Cévennes: Terre de refuge*, ed. Joutard et al., 240.

140. G 354 commission de contrôle postal, September 1942. Quoted from report's summary.

141. G 354 commission de contrôle postal, October 1942. Letter sent by B. Mathieu (St. André de Valborgne) 2 October 1942.

142. CA 641, letter cited in summary of commission de contrôle postal, October 1942.

143. CA 776, préfet to conseiller d'état secrétaire général à la police, 19 October 1942.

insisted that the dividing line was that of class; those Protestants who clung to the policies of Vichy were from the local bourgeoisie. As Donadille exclaimed, "It was the same thing during the time of the Camisards! Who hesitated to follow them? The bourgeoisie, of course! There were not many nobles [sic] who went off to the prison galleys, far from it!"[144] Although the situation was not so neatly divided as Donadille suggests, and despite his confounding of the nobility with the bourgeoisie, it remains the case that the Protestant bourgeoisie of Nîmes had grown more conservative over the course of the twentieth century. In the phrase of André Siegfried, they had "slid more and more into a position of 'resistance', in the sense that this term is opposed to 'movement.' "[145] Certain members of the local *haute société protestante* undoubtedly feared the threat of social and political unrest as much as their Catholic counterparts. Moreover, given their history and the dubious activities of their co-religionists, these Protestants felt the additional burden of proving their political innocence in the eyes of Vichy. The fear of appearing unpatriotic was the principal motivation in their criticism of the Protestant Federation's letter of protest. Like the Jews who had been thrust outside the national community, these French Protestants were still haunted by the need to prove their Frenchness.

It is unlikely, however, that many of them found solace in the anti-Semitic ramblings of *Sully.* As the journal itself remarked in December 1942, "we have waited in vain . . . for messages of loyalty to the marshal from the various Protestant churches." Unsurprisingly, the journal had rallied to the anti-Semitic policies of the Vichy regime. In the issue of December, alongside extracts from the *Protocols of the Elders of Zion,* Noël Vesper published the second in a series of "Letters on the Jews." He made a murky distinction between the "true Israel" and the "racial Israel," asserting that the latter was of "flesh and circumcision . . . and rightfully delivered to the rigors of history, which will not cease to settle its accounts." For Vesper, a vigorous policy of anti-Semitism would rid France of this "synagogue of Satan."[146]

Vesper and his cronies pursued their idiosyncratic view of Protestantism until the very end; they remained, however, an isolated and marginal voice. By the late summer of 1942, the Protestants of the Gard had, by and large, crossed the Rubicon of resistance to Vichy. Chiappe underscored this point in the late fall of that year, on the occasion of the meeting in Nîmes of the national council of the Eclaireurs Unionistes, a Protestant youth movement. Invited to attend the ceremony, Chiappe at first considered refusing, in order to show his displeasure at the

---

144. "Table Ronde," in *Cévennes: Terre de refuge,* ed. Joutard et al., 238–39.
145. Siegfried, in Siegfried and Boegner, *Le Protestantisme français,* 48.
146. *Sully* (December 1942). This is the first extant copy of *Sully* after 1939.

"sentiments shown by certain Protestant circles in the department."[147] The prefect eventually did attend, which did not prevent the subsequent spread of rumors that "pro-English demonstrations" had taken place at the convention.

By the time of this scouting convention, a sharp difference existed in the way Catholics and Protestants of the Gard regarded Vichy—a divergence that was deepened by the snowballing of the state's anti-Semitic policies. The authorities repeatedly noted the absence of dissent or hesitation among the Catholic clergy and their parishioners, while the reactions of the Protestant community provided grounds for growing anxiety and suspicion. The Protestants did not, once again, have a patent on moral outrage and political resistance. Nevertheless, the historical, social, and theological factors for resistance to these events weighed more heavily in favor of the Protestants than the Catholics. André Siegfried declared that, in the midst of the twentieth century, the "moral separation" between Protestants and Catholics in the Midi remained so sharp that "despite oneself, one thinks of a river whose merging tributaries maintain different colors, densities, and consistencies, running together without mixing."[148] In light of the evidence concerning the evolution of the two communities' attitudes toward Vichy and its Jewish policy, the metaphor rings true.

---

147. CA 767, préfet to préfet régional, 20 October 1942.
148. Siegfried, in Siegfried and Boegner, *Le Protestantisme français*, 23, 28.

5

DEGREES OF COLLABORATION

Let us collaborate, collaborate, collaborate.
—Angelo Chiappe, prefect, 1941

The marshal has no greater admirer than me, but the people who are executing his program are idiots.

—anonymous Nîmois, 1941

In the winter of 1941, G. Ehrmann, a high-school student in Nîmes, penned a letter to a friend. In it, the young man, who by the sound of his name may well have been a refugee from Alsace-Lorraine, praised the "great Pétain" whose portrait, present in the classrooms, dining hall, and dormitories, "gives us courage and hope." Yet, in the following line, the student remarked that everybody "holds on to the hope, if not for an English victory, at least to see France once again become free and strong."[1]

These sentiments were neither unique to young Ehrmann nor so contradictory as they may first appear. The famous remark that, in 1940, there were forty million Pétainists actually tells us very little. Pétain was many things

1. CA 646, commission de contrôle postal, January 1941. Letter from G. Ehrmann (Nîmes), 15 January 1941.

to many people, and allegiance to his person did not always entail support of the regime's attempts at embarking on a collaborationist policy with Germany.[2] The invocation of Pétain's name could, among other things, serve as a call to neutrality, to inner exile, to reflexive patriotism or, at least for the first two years of the regime, to actual resistance to the Germans.

This confusion of symbols and aims, widespread during the war—and here the historian must exercise great caution—remains clouded today. Despite the scholarship devoted to this period, the questions of collaboration and collaborationism are still loaded concepts.[3] In this study, I am following Stanley Hoffmann's distinction between collaboration—cooperation with an occupying force in order to safeguard national interests—and collaborationism—the openly desired cooperation with, and admiration of, these forces.[4] Hoffmann's formulation will help in our examination of the many organizations and individuals that were compelled, at one time or another, to confront the moral and ideological issues raised by the policies of Vichy. As an example of the first category, we shall examine the evolution of the Veterans' Legion (Légion française des combattants), which was undermined by internecine conflict and diverging interpretations soon after its creation in the summer of 1940. We shall then study the positions taken by the departmental prefect, Angelo Chiappe, who engaged in the cause of collaboration, and Bishop Jean Girbeau, accused by certain resisters in the immediate postwar period of active collaboration. Finally, we shall

2. Robert Paxton long ago exploded the myth, popularized by Robert Aron in his *Histoire de Vichy* (Paris, 1954), that Pétain undertook a policy of subtle resistance to German demands and was ultimately bypassed by the outright collaborationism of Laval. Pétain was no puppet in the hands of a Laval or a Darlan, but was a moving force in the politics of collaboration. See *Vichy France*, chap. 1 and passim. See also Henri Michel, *Vichy: Année 40*, who anticipated Paxton's approach.

3. In a recent article, the American historian John Sweets claims that the historiographical consensus concerning Vichy France risks swinging from the extreme of seeing France as a nation of resisters to that of framing her as a country of collaborators. As Sweets notes, this is less a scholarly consensus than a popular one (though he warns that they seem to be merging). For example, two of the individuals he cites as responsible for this new myth are the filmmakers Marcel Ophuls and Louis Malle. Sweets's criticism of Ophuls in particular, and his landmark documentary film *The Sorrow and the Pity*, is telling and forceful. In fact, Sweets's *Choices in Vichy France*, which is based on Clermont-Ferrand, serves as an important and salutary corrective to Ophul's depiction of that same city. I would only suggest that the thrust of films that have appeared since the publication of Sweets's article, like Malle's *Au revoir les enfants* (which followed his controversial *Lacombe Lucien* by more than a decade) and Ophuls's *Hotel Terminus*, seem to indicate a more balanced view concerning this issue. See John Sweets, "Hold That Pendulum! Redefining Fascism, Collaborationism and Resistance in France," *French Historical Studies* (Fall 1988), 731–58.

4. Hoffmann, "Collaborationism in France during World War Two," *Journal of Modern History* (September 1968), 375–95. Reprinted in *Decline or Renewal? France Since the 1930s*.

plot the general evolution of public opinion from 1940 to 1942 in regard to the question of collaboration.

Signed into existence by Marshal Pétain at the end of August 1940, the Legion was the fusion of two World War I veterans' associations, the Union nationale des combattants (UNC) and the Union fédérale des combattants (UFC). Despite different political tendencies, both groups had a common distaste for the Third Republic. The advent of Vichy presented the veterans with the opportunity to fill the didactic and political roles they had been denied during the interwar years. The aims of the Legion thus went beyond the prewar role of mutual aid and support; they now included the goals of preserving the values of the nation, providing an open line between the state and the population, and broadcasting the principles and ideals of the National Revolution. In short, the Legion was conceived as a means to canalize the patriotism and energy of the mass of French war veterans, who would help propagate the cult of Pétain and inculcate and enforce the policies of the new regime.[5]

Launched on 29 August 1940, the Legion's beginnings were full of promise. By early the following year, it counted 18,000 departmental members, or approximately 4.5 percent of the population of the Gard.[6] The various reports and intercepted letters written during the first year all express great excitement and commitment on the part of the legionnaires. The movement's first anniversary in August 1941 drew six thousand participants whose "dignified" attitude favorably impressed those in attendance.[7] The Nîmois, exclaimed one participant, applauded the tricolored French flag with as much joy as they once cheered the "hideous rags of the communists."[8] A second veteran echoed this sentiment, adding that a "little bit of discipline satisfies everyone."[9]

The honeymoon between the Legion and both government and public,

5. On the Legion, see Cointet-Labrousse, *Vichy et le fascisme*, 104–14, and Jean-Paul Cointet, "La Légion français des combattants," in *Le Gouvernement de Vichy* (Paris, 1971).

6. This was the estimate of the Legion's president, Joseph Varin d'Ainvelle. See Armand Cosson, *Nîmes et le Gard dans la guerre 1939–1945* (Le Coteau, 1988), 34. Cosson's book appeared just as I completed the research for my own work. As befits a departmental correspondent for the Institut d'histoire du temps présent, Cosson presents a careful work based upon original archival research. Yet, for reasons imposed by the publisher (Horvath), the book has no scholarly apparatus. More important, the book's scope is limited—it begins in 1939 and follows a fairly narrow narrative line, with little reference to either the late interwar years or the historiography of Vichy. Lastly, Cosson does not concern himself with the Protestant-Catholic issue, which is one of the principal themes of this work.

7. CA 566, commissiare principal to préfet, rapport mensuel, 30 September 1941.

8. CA 646, commission de contrôle postal, synthèse of 20 August–5 September 1941.

9. CA 646, commission de contrôle postal, synthèse of 20 August–5 September 1941.

however, proved short-lived. The 1942 anniversary celebrations in Nîmes attracted a still substantial number of participants, yet as one legionnaire remarked in retrospect, "How old we have become!!"[10] This celebration was a last hurrah of sorts, for the Legion was racked by internal division and hampered by widespread public apathy. Chiappe had already warned, in the fall of 1941, that membership had failed to reach the level set by its leaders, attributing this failure to the appointment of individuals from the extreme right to leadership positions.[11] In early 1942 the subprefect of Le Vigan filed a series of discouraging reports on the inability of the local section of the Legion to mobilize its forces. Meetings were sparsely attended and a "certain lassitude" had overtaken the men; many of them, in fact, no longer wore the Legion badge in their lapels.[12] The news was hardly better from Alès where the subprefect was dismissive of the Legion: its moral influence, in his eyes, had been tainted by its support of a miners' strike in March 1942.[13] By May 1942, one dignitary considered the Legion to be afflicted by the same malaise found throughout France, citing as proof that only 30 percent of its members were now attending official functions.[14] These and similar reports indicate that the famous *vent mauvais* (ill wind), whose appearance was the subject of increasing official concern, was now sweeping over the Gard's section of the Legion.[15]

The Legion was undermined by several contradictions. First, though an explicitly political and ideological organization, it was formed largely by men who had no previous political experience and, indeed, often scorned politics. In the unoccupied zone, little more than a third of the Legion's departmental leaders had engaged in previous political activity; of this minority, more than half came from the ranks of movements like Action française and Colonel de La Rocque's Parti social français (PSF), with a quarter from the center parties and the remainder from the Radicals and SFIO.[16] This conforms roughly to the organization's profile in the Gard: of 222 officials, 161 had affiliations with various

10. G 356, commission de contrôle postal, August 1942. Letter sent by Dehan (Vergèze), 31 August 1942. *L'Eclair* estimated that there were some 15,000 legionnaires, a statistic that seems to have been inflated by the collaborationist paper.

11. CA 566, préfet to interior, rapport mensuel, 1 October 1941.

12. CA 776, sous-préfet of Le Vigan to préfet, rapports mensuels of February and March 1942.

13. CA 776, sous-préfet of Alès to préfet, rapport mensuel, 27 April 1942. This showing of solidarity occured despite a warning earlier in the year from Varin d'Ainvelle to a local Legion chief (Alinat of Sommières) that the Legion "must not support at any price the public criticism of the demonstrators," which would only result in disorder and weaken the work of Pétain (CA 279, letter from Varin d'Ainvelle to Alinat, 23 January 1942).

14. G 357, summary in rapport mensuel, commission de contrôle postal, May 1942.

15. This phrase marked a famous speech given by Pétain in August 1941, in which he identified and condemned all of those Frenchmen who questioned the wisdom of his regime's policies.

16. Jean-Paul Cointet, "Les Chevaliers du Maréchal," *L'Histoire,* no. 80 (1985), 112–13.

parties on the right, 23 belonged to the PSF, and 17 came from the left.[17] The departmental chief, Joseph Varin d'Ainvelle, a bureaucrat with the departmental Office of Forests and Waterways, was a practicing Catholic and political conservative. It is, in fact, arguable that Varin d'Ainvelle's sole merit was his lack of clear political activity and engagement during the interwar period. An indecisive and unremarkable individual, Varin d'Ainvelle belonged to that class of mediocrities who, thrown into prominence by France's defeat, were soon overwhelmed by the radicalization of the regime. The committee's vice president, Henri Cluzel-Duplan, a retired colonel, was also politically unengaged before 1940. However, Cluzel-Duplan and four other members of the committee— which, including the *tribunal d'honneur,* counted eighteen members—were royalist or Action française sympathizers. Among the remaining members of the committee, including the only two identified Protestants, were seven conservatives or moderates, two former Radical Socialists, and a former Socialist. The remaining members were innocent of all political identification.[18]

The composition of the Nîmois section of the Legion differed slightly from that of the departmental committee. First, the city's religious diversity was clearly reflected. At least two of the ten members were Protestants (including the committee's president, Ernest Ausset) and a third, René Horvilleur, was Jewish.[19] Second, its political associations was more varied. Only two members had been members of the PSF, while three others were moderate republicans, and a fourth a former sympathizer of the Radical Socialists (the remaining four apparently were not active enough to have earned political labels). In addition, two of the members, Joseph Poujol (one of the two vice presidents) and Pierre Quittard, were antimonarchists and, it was suspected, lukewarm supporters of the National Revolution.[20]

In late 1941, a legionnaire from Alès complained that his section was manned by representatives from the old guard—the very individuals, he claimed, responsible for France's current predicament. These men, he argued, refused "to participate in revolutionary propaganda" and were despised by the young.[21] This criticism, widespread by 1942, points to a second, generational contradiction

18. CA 279, note d'information to ministry of interior, 26 September 1941. These breakdowns and brief profiles were ordered by the minister of interior, Pierre Pucheu, in a circular of 27 August 1941. Yet it was easier said than done. In a letter to Chiappe, the commissaire principal reported that gathering information on these *notables* was a delicate affair and that, moreover, he was hobbled by a shortage of trustworthy personnel (CA 279, 10 September 1941).

19. The notes d'information, both in the case of the departmental and municipal committees, emphasized the religious affiliation of the members. As a result, it is fairly safe to assume that it identified all those members who were Protestant, not to mention Jewish.

20. CA 279, note d'information on Légion du Gard, section de Nîmes, 26 September 1941.

21. CA 279, letter sent by X to director of section de la réunion interdépartmentales des présidents, 22 October 1941.

inherent to the Legion. The average age of the departmental committee was fifty, and forty-six for the section in Nîmes. In the former group only two men were less than forty years of age, while only three Nîmois members fell below this line. These statistics point to a simple truth: the great majority of the leaders were veterans of the First World War. They were traditionalists mistrustful of revolutionary sloganeering and often disdainful of the veterans of the 1939–40 campaign. The younger generation, though outnumbered by their elders, apparently returned the scorn (which, along with the fact that many happened to be in German POW camps, helps account for the disparity). The nearly inevitable consequence was increasing friction and disaffection. This tension had, as early as the end of 1941, become manifest, leading Chiappe to report that the Legion was prey to growing discontent on the part of the younger members, who thought they were deprived of the roles and responsibilities which rightly belonged to them.[22]

The discontent also issued from Vichy's failure to assign a well-defined and specific administrative role to the Legion. In a directive of April 1941, the government declared that Legion officials "had the right and even the duty to enlighten" the local authorities on anything which contradicted the spirit of the National Revolution.[23] Yet the studied ambiguity of this assignment, as Robert Paxton has pointed out, amounted in practice to little more than vigilantism.[24] The collaboration of the legionnaires in the project of the National Revolution, as a result, often was reduced to petty and derisory tasks, like brawling with those who refused to show the proper deference to the flag or Pétain. For example, during a legionnaire parade on the Esplanade in Nîmes, a fight erupted between a participant and a reporter from Le Petit Provençal, the causus belli being the latter's refusal to remove a cigarette from his lips. The ensuing boxing match required the intervention of Chiappe.[25]

Even efforts at patriotic instruction often went awry, due either to the growing indifference of the public or the hostility of a local administration jealous of its prerogatives. One result was the uncertain fate of a Legion poster condemning the Gaullists at a school near Remoulins. The local teacher wrote to the departmental school inspector to learn if it was compulsory to hang it in his schoolroom. The inspector, M. Paganelli, referred the issue to Chiappe, reminding him of a recent circular from the ministry of education that forbade involving students in political affairs. The outcome of the affair is not reported, but it

22. CA 566, préfet to interior, rapport mensuel, 31 December 1941.
23. *Instruction* of 30 April 1941. Cited in Michèle Comtet-Labrousse, *Vichy et le fascisme,* 113.
24. Paxton, *Vichy France,* 190.
25. CA 279, préfet to interior, 12 July 1941.

certainly provided the prefect with yet another reason to question the "patriotism" of the inspector.[26]

The Legion's growing irrelevance is manifest in the days following the Allied invasion of North Africa. Colonel Dire, the chief of the Service d'ordre légionnaire (SOL) warned Varin d'Ainvelle of official fears over the possibility of popular demonstrations. The legionnaire chief, stunned at his rival's information, complained that he was not privy to discussions at the prefecture: "It's always the same: I'm the last one to learn about things."[27] This was a complaint echoed time and again in the correspondence of local and departmental Legion chiefs.

No less evident by mid-1942 is the younger generation's dissatisfaction with the numerical preponderance and political conservatism of their elders. In the spring of that year, a Legion meeting in Le Vigan, a section that had roughly two hundred and thirty-five members, attracted just twenty-five legionnaires, of whom only five were veterans of 1939–40.[28] Similarly, the section in Alès was plagued by the growing division between the veterans of the two wars. The younger members of the propaganda committees had become restless with the "inertia," "absence of authority," and "lack of initiative" on the part of Varin d'Ainvelle.[29] The director and his colleagues were labeled as "old caimans" and accused of sabotaging the goals of the regime, which aimed at nothing short of a National Revolution.[30]

The National Revolution: an ambiguous phrase coined by the men of Vichy to cover a multitude of often conflicting political beliefs and desires. The regime, it must be recalled, was a hybrid, pieced together in the haste and confusion of the sudden and humiliating defeat of 1940. There was a consensus that change was called for, that the laws and institutions of the Third Republic had failed France. But beyond this contempt for republican ideals and practices, and along with a turn toward xenophobia and anticommunism, there was little agreement on the

26. CA 279, inspecteur d'Académie du Gard to préfet, 21 November 1941. In an undated note to interior on the administrative purges he had undertaken in the Gard, Chiappe emphasized that he already had "reported several times the lack of zeal shown [by Paganelli] in supporting the work of the marshal" (CA 561). Chiappe's suspicions were well-founded: Paganelli would become the first prefect of the newly liberated Gard in 1944.

27. CA 641, commission de contrôle postal, transcript of phone conversation between Varin d'Ainvelle and Colonel Dire, 10 November 1942.

28. CA 279, inspecteur de police to sous-préfet of Le Vigan, 27 April 1942. The inspector concluded that this poor showing indicated that the National Revolution had "few fervent followers in our town."

29. CA 279, sous-préfet of Alès to préfet, 2 January 1942.

30. CA 279, intercepted letter of G. Etienne (Alès), 2 December 1941.

nature of the political transformation France required. At the outset, the regime had room enough for conservatives and reactionaries, technocrats and fascists, clericalists and former syndicalists, and opportunists of one sort or another. Hence the air of improvisation and oscillation that hung over Vichy. It was only over the course of its short life that the policies and men of the regime, increasingly pressured by economic and geopolitical realities, evolved and became closely identified with those of Nazi Germany.[31]

Thus, in 1940, the nature of this revolution was vague enough to permit most Gardois to rally, with little hesitation, to its standard and prompt the veterans to enroll in the Legion. It was only after Montoire and the promulgation of certain laws in late 1940 that the revolution's nature, if only to the most perceptive, became clearer. There nevertheless remained competing discourses among the legionnaires and other adherents to the National Revolution, opponents who were to square off against one another over the next two years. These tensions were nevertheless temporarily eclipsed by Pétain, who served as a unifying symbol during most of this period. In fact, the power of his image was such that it permitted the criticism of certain aspects of the regime while guaranteeing the continued loyalty of those uttering the criticism.[32]

It is in the shadow of Pétain that a telling confrontation took place between the SOL and the Legion. The Service d'ordre légionnaire was created by Vichy in January 1942 and placed under the command of Joseph Darnand. The original intent of the service was to provide a policing unit for legionnaire demonstrations and parades. From the outset, however, the SOL recruited its members from the ranks of war veterans, most often of 1939–40, who were driven by a thirst for action, ideological conviction, or plain opportunism.[33] Exactly one

31. The literature on this issue is extensive, and it is beyond this book to add to it. The interested reader is referred to the seminal works of Michel, Paxton, and Hoffmann listed in the Bibliography. It should be noted that the debate over the nature of Vichy has been fueled by the recent work of the Israeli historian Zeev Sternhell, especially in *Ni Droite, Ni Gauche: L'Idéologie fasciste en France* (Paris, 1983), which more or less claims that Vichy was the product of a distinct and autonomous strain of fascist thought in France dating from the late eighteenth century. For a critique of Sternhell's approach, see Shlomo Sand, "L'Idéologie fasciste en France," *Esprit* (August–September 1983) and Jacques Julliard, "Sur un fascisme imaginaire: A propos d'un livre de Zeev Sternhell," *Annales: ESC* (July–August 1984). See also René Remond's revised *Les Droites en France* (Paris, 1983), whose original formulation served as a foil for Sternhell's *démarche*. One may also refer to Jean-Marie Guillon's excellent summary, "La Philosophie politique de la Révolution nationale," in *Vichy et les Français*, ed. Azéma and Bédarida, 167–83; and John Sweets's succinct critique "Hold that Pendulum: Redefining Fascism, Collaborationism and Resistance in France."

32. This is a point emphasized by Roger Austin in his study of the Hérault, in which he argues that Pétain's role fostered a kind of "political integration" that helped assure public acquiescence to material sacrifices long after they had turned against the government; see his "Propaganda and Public Opinion in Vichy France: The Department of Hérault, 1940–1944."

33. The principal work on the SOL and its successor, the Milice, is Jacques Delperrié de Bayac, *L'Histoire de la Milice* (Paris, 1969).

year later, with the remorselessness of fallen fruit rotting in a noonday sun, this elite of marginals and zealots was transformed, by order of Pierre Laval, into the Milice, the autonomous police and paramilitary organization that, under the direction of Darnand, soon became the nemesis of the Resistance and the last rampart of collaborationism in southern France. This metamorphosis gave concrete expression to the divergent views between the traditionalist old guard and a more youthful and ideologically restless minority within the Legion.

Based on a report filed by the prefect Paganelli, who assumed office following the Gard's liberation in August 1944, 247 individuals were charged with membership in the Milice.[34] This figure must be used with care for a number of reasons. First, these were cases not yet brought to trial, and it is likely that not all of the accused were eventually found guilty as charged. Second, the total figures for those arrested by administrative measure rose from 736 in December 1944 to 1002 by the following month, yet the number of miliciens in this total was not specified.[35] Third, it conflicts with the estimate made by Colonel Dire that, in 1943, there were 700 men under his command.[36]

According to the local historian Armand Cosson, 41 percent of the miliciens had joined for ideological reasons.[37] This percentage, along with a handful of intercepted letters and occasional police reports on the organization's activity, is of some import. In light of a recent and mostly popular tendency to downplay the factor of ideological committment, these documents underscore a surprising degree of zeal and revolutionary ardor.[38] One member of the Nîmois section of the SOL, in a letter sent to the collaborationist journal Gringoire, excitedly described his unit's various activities and warned ominously that the "Gaullo-communists and Jews had better behave themselves."[39] A second young member affirmed his determination to "uphold the cause of the National Revolution," and complained that the veterans of 1914–18 rejected his interpretation of patriotic duty.[40] For the older legionnaires, propaganda and moral suasion were one thing, strong-arm tactics and vandalism quite another. During a Legion

34. C 482, préfet to interior, rapport mensuel, December 1944. Thirty-two of the miliciens held leadership posts.

35. C 482, préfet to interior, 23 January 1945.

36. Quoted in Cosson, Nîmes et le Gard dans la guerre, 1939–1945, 80. Unfortunately, given the absence of footnotes, it is difficult to ascertain Cosson's sources.

37. Cosson, Nîmes et le Gard dans la guerre, 1939–1945, 85.

38. This is the case of the controversial film of Louis Malle, Lacombe Lucien. Based on a screenplay by the novelist Patrick Modiano, it is the story of a young man who turns to the Milice for employment after having been rejected by the local Resistance. The historian Richard Cobb considers this novelistic turn in French and Germans, Germans and French (Hanover, N.H., 1984).

39. CA 279, intercepted letter of 19 September 1942.

40. CA 646, commission de contrôle postal, August 1942. Letter sent 18 August 1942.

parade in the summer of 1942, members of the SOL forcibly removed the hats of some spectators and roughed up several others, including legionnaires, the very individuals they were meant to protect. The publicity was predictably harsh; as one participant commented, "They are a bunch of idiots to think that they're going to maintain discipline by terrorizing people."[41]

The legionnaire's warning turned out to be accurate. An even greater stir was created when SOL members, in a series of attacks in May and August, damaged the busts of Marianne in the town halls of Roquemaure, Castillon-du-Gard, and Sommières. The public's reaction was overwhelmingly critical, especially in Sommières, whose population, described as "fundamentally republican" by a police official, had already been provoked by earlier acts of royalist propaganda undertaken by the local chapter of Action française.[42] In a candid letter to Chiappe, the mayor of Sommières, Raoul Gaussen, warned that the town's Socialist sympathies had not changed and that one of the comments heard in the wake of the attack was "Since the government cannot give us food, it prefers to demolish statues."[43] An effort by the departmental vice-president of the SOL, M. Montaud, to defend his group's actions only worsened matters. Introducing a lecture on Freemasonry given in Alès, Montaud thundered that the times called for "broken heads, hangings, and walls reddened with blood."[44] Despite the pro-Vichy sympathies of the audience— the meeting was held under the auspices of the regime's propaganda services—the violence of Montaud's exhortation shocked several individuals, leading Chiappe to strip Montaud of his official standing with the government bureau.[45] Interestingly, Montaud's phillipic led one witness to comment that "troubled days are in store for us if we are returning to the wars of religion."[46]

The great majority of Gardois legionnaires were clearly political and social conservatives who were as fearful of revolution from the right as from the left. For them, the National Revolution was less an ideological project to be undertaken than a newly won form of social recognition to be preserved. It most often amounted to little more than the regime's compensation—expressed through parades, medals, and the largely hollow duties assigned to them as the "eyes and ears of the marshal"—for the years of relative neglect and political impotence in which the veterans languished under the Third Republic. Wearing the ubiquitous beret and lapel pin of the Legion while marching in formation down the

41. G 356, commission de contrôle postal, August 1942. Telephone conversation of 16 August 1942.
42. CA 279, commissaire principal to préfet, 19 May 1942. The local president of the AF, M. Alinat, was also the chief of the local SOL.
43. CA 279, mayor of Sommières to préfet, 18 May 1942.
44. CA 279, mayor of Alès to sous-préfet of Alès, 23 May 1942.
45. CA 279, préfet to the délégué départementale à la propagande, 23 May 1942.
46. CA 279, anonymous letter sent to sous-préfet of Alès, 23 May 1942.

Esplanade, carrying large posters with heroic portraits of Pétain—this was the essence of the movement. As one legionnaire boasted, "For the first time in my life, I marched past the authorities at the cadence of a *chasseur* and with my head to the left. That brought back old desires and sentiments I hadn't felt in more than ten years."[47] As one of his colleagues declared, the National Revolution "for me is nothing other than obedience to the marshal. All of these political debates disgust me."[48]

As for those men who embraced the word "revolution" in the phrase "National Revolution," there was endless griping over the conservatism of the older members. A representative of the Francistes, a genuinely fascist organization under the command of Marcel Bucard, declared in a talk given at Nîmes that all those who truly supported the marshal had to "counter-attack against a French bourgeoisie" responsible for the "reactionary and rightist stigma" attached to the National Revolution.[49] This sentiment was shared by Jean Dire, departmental chief of the SOL. A fifty-five-year-old landowner from Redessan and a lieutenant colonel in the air reserve, Dire sought an increasingly active and independent role for his men—a desire hobbled by the timidity and hesitancy of his superior, Varin d'Ainvelle. Matters came to a climax during the demonstrations of 11 November 1942 in Nîmes. These events will be narrated in detail in Chapter 6; it will suffice for now to note that the Legion chief, much to the dismay of Dire, had dragged his feet on assigning men to patrol the streets. In several telephone conversations, Dire criticized Varin d'Ainvelle's reluctance to react, calling him a "moron" who gathered his men only after the emergency had passed.[50]

Although exasperated by the resistance of Varin d'Ainvelle, Dire only had words of praise for the role played that day by Chiappe. In a letter to the prefect, Dire praised the sang-froid of the prefect, who had placed himself "in the front line during the street battles."[51] In a report to Vichy, Chiappe himself boasted of his pivotal role in controlling the demonstrations, having taken in hand an "outnumbered and poorly trained SOL" in order to disperse the demonstrators.[52] The prefect's action that day reflected more than the desire to preserve order; it

47. G 356, commission de contrôle postal, August, 1942. Letter sent by Dehan (Vergèze), 31 August 1942.

48. G 356, commission de contrôle postal, August 1942. Letter sent by Francette (Aulas), 10 September, 1942.

49. CA 776, commissaire principal to préfet, 27 May 1942. Apart from a short-lived youth movement, the Francistes had no representation in the Gard.

50. CA 641, commission de contrôle postal, November 1942; and G 354, commission de contrôle postal, December 1942.

51. CA 760, Dire to Chiappe, 12 November 1942.

52. CA 563, Chiappe to ministry of interior (n.d.), report located in prosecution dossier for Chiappe's trial.

was the comportment of a man committed to an extreme interpretation of the National Revolution.

Corsican and Catholic, the Chiappes played a role in the political life of the Third Republic significant enough to earn the family name contemporary notoriety and the immortality of the scholarly footnote. It was the dismissal of Jean Chiappe, Paris's prefect of police, which played a crucial role in the events of 6 February 1934. Known for his rightist sympathies, Chiappe was accused by the Daladier ministry of laxity in controlling the Croix de feu (the earlier incarnation of the PSF), Action française, and various other leagues and was removed from office. This move sparked the street demonstrations and the *coup manqué* of 6 February, which led to Daladier's resignation and his replacement by the ministry of Gaston Doumergue. Jean Chiappe's second exit from French politics, though less consequential at a national level, was personally much more definitive. Assigned by Vichy to the governor-generalship of Algeria, Chiappe died somewhere over the Mediterranean on 27 November 1940, when the plane ferrying him to his new post was shot down by British fighters.

The impact on Angelo Chiappe of his elder brother's death was profound and lasting. In a letter to Colonel de la Rocque, thanking him for his note of condolence, the newly appointed prefect to the Gard recalled the colonel's words upon learning of his own son's death: "I gritted my teeth and pushed on."[53] The brothers had shared more than a common birth: their professional and ideological careers also bore great similarities. Like his older brother, Angelo Chiappe had carved out a career in the prefectoral service. Fifty-one years old when assigned to the Gard in 1940, Chiappe by then had served in the Ardèche from 1928 to 1931, the Aisne until 1936, the Manche until 1939, and then in the Basses-Pyrénées, where he had barely installed himself before the declaration of war.[54]

It was in this last post that Chiappe assumed responsibility for the notorious concentration camp of Gurs. Built shortly before his arrival in order to shelter refugees from the Spanish Civil War, Gurs served after September 1939 as a major center of internment for German Jewish refugees (Hannah Arendt was among the camp's more famous and fortunate residents). Chiappe left Pau, the departmental capital of the Basses-Pyrénées, at the end of September to take up his new

---

53. CA 561, Chiappe to de la Rocque, 9 November 1942.

54. CA 561, renseignements sur la carrière préfectorale de M. Angelo Chiappe, sent by Chiappe to interior (n.d., but probably some time in 1941). It ought to be noted that, apart from his own curriculum vitae and a 1944 liberation dossier compiled against him, I have been unable to find any biographical material on Chiappe. I sent two letters to his son, Jean-François Chiappe, for a possible interview, but never received a response.

duties in Nîmes. The subsequent horror stories of numerous deaths due to starvation and exposure thus cannot be directly attributed to his administration, and it would be unfair to tax Chiappe for the subsequent mass arrivals of German refugees that overwhelmed the camp's already strained capacity.[55] Nevertheless, there is an unsettling disingenousness in a report written by Chiappe on a visit paid to the camp by a German colonel following the armistice. The latter, according to Chiappe, "took pleasure in acknowledging the humanitarian regime that I had extended to the German internees, as well as to the 2,000 German citizens (women and children) driven from Paris in May 1940."[56] Given that the great majority of these internees were either political or religious refugees who now faced a less than brilliant fate, Chiappe's statement displays, at the very least, a remarkable insensitivity.

The prefectoral itinerary followed by Chiappe casts light on a second quality he shared with his brother: a pronounced sympathy for the political right. Chiappe's tenure in the Aisne was marked by a bitter struggle between the prefecture and the Socialists and Communists. The prefect played an important role in the repression of two major canal transportation strikes in Chauny in 1933, and also influenced the partial legislative elections in Laon in 1935. The ideological struggle was sharp enough that, following an official ceremony in St. Quentin in 1934, Chiappe and his wife were physically assaulted by Communist party members.[57] In a move that he attributed to a political settling of accounts, Chiappe was shifted to the Manche in September 1936 by Roger Salengro, the minister of interior in the Popular Front government of Léon Blum.

It is difficult to know where, in Chiappe's political worldview, professional and personal dissatisfactions leave off and ideology begins. The prefect thought he had been professionally stymied and mistreated by the interwar Radical and Popular Front governments, and the ink in his official and private correspondence carries the dull gloss of resentment. He dwelt repeatedly on the attacks he suffered in the pages of the Socialist Party's paper, Le Populaire, and blamed the Socialists for his transfer from the Aisne, as well as the failure to be assigned to the

---

55. See Marrus and Paxton, *Vichy France and the Jews,* 165–76, on Gurs and the other concentration camps. In recalling her experience at Gurs, where she was sent by the expiring Third Republic, Arendt noted that she and her fellow refugees had become a "new kind of human being created by contemporary history"—the kind that "are put into concentration camps by their foes and into internment camps by their friends"; quoted in Elizabeth Young-Bruehl, *Hannah Arendt: For Love of the World* (New Haven, 1982), 152.

56. CA 561, loose sheet to an undated document.

57. This, at least, is Chiappe's version of events, given in his personal dossier. In a separate note located in the same file, Chiappe elaborated that he was the target of his subprefect in Soissons, "a notorious Freemason," and his wife, an "Israelite in the worst sense of the term."

prestigious prefecture of the Loire.[58] He also repeatedly complained about his inordinately long passage at an inferior ranking in the civil service; it was only in 1939 that he received the promotion he thought he had earned long before. Georges Servigne, the state prosecutor at Chiappe's postwar trial, emphasized this aspect to the accused's character, charging that the former prefect was "above all dissatisfied and embittered, an eternal malcontent who always believes that he has been denied the posts and responsibilities that are his due."[59]

A victim, like his brother, of leftist intrigue, Chiappe welcomed the arrival of Vichy as the opportunity to exact revenge. That Chiappe's ambitions were, as Servigne argued, modeled after another Corsican's rise "from modest origins to the throne of France during a previous revolution," is nonsense. The prosecutor studiously avoided the question of ideology, probably because it ran counter to the already established myth of France as a nation of resisters, betrayed by a handful of corrupt and venal collaborators. But the ideological factor in Chiappe's fervent collaboration cannot be discounted. At first, most public authorities probably shared the belief of Yves Bouthillier, a finance minister at Vichy, that "orderly activity in the presence of the occupying authority was the best kind of civic spirit."[60] There is, however, a clear distinction between the establishment and maintenance of order and the deliberate and eager participation in an effort to impose an ideological agenda on a nation. The line between simple administration and active collaboration sharpened as time and policy distanced the regime and its representatives from the first confused and chaotic months of their existence. And it was this line that, without hesitation, Chiappe crossed.

This commitment was made manifest when, upon the amputation of the western half of the Basses-Pyrénées by the German occupying forces in the summer of 1940, Chiappe requested a transfer. This request, as the prefect makes clear, was not motivated by the desire for a more comfortable and secure post. To the contrary, he desired a "difficult assignment," one that would test his administrative competence and ideological mettle. He was offered the Gard, and when he arrived in Nîmes on 25 September 1940, it was with the intention to supervise the installation of a new order. The department provided

58. CA 561, mentioned in both the renseignements and in accompanying note.

59. *Le Procès Angelo Chiappe: Requisitoire de Georges Servigne, Commissaire du Gouvernement devant la cour de Justice du Gard* (Montpellier, n.d.), 13. It may be noted that Chiappe continued to agitate for a promotion well into the Vichy period. In a letter to Max Bonnafous, the Minister of Agriculture, Chiappe made a murky reference to the animosity of Pierre Pucheu, which prevented him from transferring to Limoges and kept him waiting for "the compensation I have coming to me" (CA 561, Chiappe to Bonnafous, 6 July 1942).

60. Quoted in Paxton, *Vichy France,* 17.

the challenge sought by this pioneer of the New Europe, where he would try to "make the principles of the National Revolution prevail" in a hostile and forbidding environment.[61]

In order to build new foundations, the old structures had to be razed: a thorough purge of the local administration was thus the first order of business. Since 1884, the mayors of towns and villages in France assumed office through local elections. However, a law of 16 November 1940 annulled the Third Republic's democratization of local politics by appointing mayors to all municipalities with more than 2,000 inhabitants, and investing the central government with the discretionary power to name mayors in towns below this limit. By 1941, Chiappe had dissolved sixty-three municipal councils, including those of the Gard's most populous towns (Nîmes, Alès, Besseges, Beaucaire, and La Grand-Combe).[62] He also dismissed the two departmental subprefects, thoroughly shook out the upper echelons of the police, nearly all of whom he accused of being former Freemasons or leftist sympathizers, and fired more than eighty departmental bureaucrats whom he judged hostile to the new regime.[63] The prefecture "still shelters a good number of people sympathetic to the old formulas," Chiappe wrote to his superiors soon after his arrival in Nîmes, but he assured them that he would "deal ruthlessly with the faint-hearted."[64]

Administrative efficiency was, for Chiappe, less an end than a means to guide the Gardois down the path of collaboration. At the inauguration of Groupe Collaboration's headquarters in Alès in the fall of 1942, Chiappe affirmed that France "must play the role which that great nation, Germany, has so generously offered us." Affirming the necessity of "unreservedly practicing" European cooperation, the prefect asked the audience, which included the German counsel general from Marseilles, to "bow with emotion and respect before the image of Marshal Pétain and Chancellor Hitler."[65] The symbol of Montoire figured in another speech by Chiappe, this time praising a lecture given by Dr. Friedrich

61. CA 561, curriculum vitae sent by Chiappe to préfet régional, 28 May 1942.

62. CA 561, renseignements from Chiappe to interior. Thus, just one year into his tenure, Chiappe had overturned more than 20 percent of all municipalities, a statistic that makes a telling comparison with a 14 percent turnover in Puy-de-Dôme over four years. See Sweets, *Choices in Vichy France,* 35.

63. CA 561, document titled "Action menée par M. Angelo Chiappe depuis son arrivée dans le département du Gard." The document is written in the first person and gives a good deal of detail on Chiappe's efforts to "purify" the department's politics. Unfortunately, there is no date on the document and the contents provide no clues to its time of origin.

64. CA 1861, préfet to interior, 7 October 1940.

65. G 262, copy of speech given in Alès, 12 September 1942. On the nature of the Groupe Collaboration, see Bertram Gordon, *Collaborationism in France during the Second World War* (Ithaca, 1980), 230–43; and Pascal Ory, *Les Collaborateurs* (Paris, 1976), 62–64.

Grimm, a Nazi emissary who barnstormed Vichy France to broadcast the gospel of national socialism and hail the future of Franco-German collaboration. Following Grimm's talk in Nîmes on Franco-German reconciliation, Chiappe stated that Montoire represented the spirit of Molière's remark that " 'I take my good where I find it' . . . the French shall take certain ideas from the Germans, and the Germans take yet others from the French." He concluded that the continuation of war between France and Germany would be fratricide: "There cannot be war between brothers in the New Europe."[66]

The prefect's sense of fraternity embraced not just the Germans, but also reached the bishop of Nîmes. Political and religious affinities drew these two men together. Chiappe, a practicing Catholic, was very active in church affairs. For example, when prefect of the Ardèche, he helped organize a Marian Congress in Liesse, and during the pilgrimage ceremonies at Notre Dame de la Blachère he was awarded the Cross of St. Gregory the Great by Monsignor Maglione, the papal nuncio to France. As Chiappe himself boasted, it was the first time since 1870 that a prefect had been so honored.[67] He also participated in the planning of a pilgrimage to Saragossa in 1940 while prefect of the Basses-Pyrénées, but the procession was cut short by the war.[68] State participation in such activities was perhaps routine, if only to provide security and routing. Chiappe's emphasis on his role, however, suggests that rather than a simple matter of official responsibility, it was also the work of a devout Catholic.

Chiappe's devotion to the church was mirrored by Girbeau's devotion to the state. There was, of course, the bishop's refusal to criticize the anti-Semitic legislation and *rafles* of 1942. No less eloquent than Girbeau's silence on the fate of the Gard's foreign Jews, were his words in praise of Vichy and the National Revolution. Thus, in his 1940 sermon commemorating Armistice Day, the bishop dwelt "on the horror inspired by the country's traitors, as well as those who, by their recklessness, wrought the humiliations of defeat."[69] The sermon so impressed Chiappe that he wrote an enthusiastic letter to Vichy underlining Girbeau's "praise for the work of *redressement* (recovery) undertaken by the government and his energetic criticism of traitors to the *patrie*."[70]

The official reviews of subsequent performances by Girbeau were no less laudatory. As late as 1942, Girbeau did not hesitate to launch political exhorta-

---

66. CA 561, concluding speech given by Chiappe at Nîmes public lecture of Grimm. There is no date on the document, but it was probably written for Grimm's appearance in Nîmes on 9 June 1942.
67. CA 561, renseignements sur la carrière préfectorale (n.d.).
68. CA 561, renseignements sur la carrière préfectorale (n.d.).
69. *La Semaine Religieuse* (17 November 1940). Contained in summary of articles in G 258.
70. CA 760, préfet to interior, 12 November 1940.

tions from the altar. According to Marcel Salem, the former bullfighting reporter of *Le Républicain du Gard* who had become the departmental representative of state propaganda, Girbeau transformed one particular religious ceremony "into a veritable political demonstration." The bishop asked that the Catholics support Pétain's policies and closed the sermon by leading his flock in a rousing rendition of the regime's anthem "Maréchal, Nous Voilà." Salem sought to give the event as much play as possible in the local papers and bubbled that Girbeau deserved promotion to the bishopric of Marseilles.[71] At a ceremony that same year at Rochefort-du-Gard, Girbeau's sermon was hailed by Chiappe. According to the prefect, the bishop turned a simple religious ceremony into a "great patriotic demonstration." He considered the event important enough to cite at length in letters to both Dr. Ménétrel, Pétain's personal physician and adviser, as well as the marshal himself. Chiappe emphasized that Girbeau had not "hesitated to demand in an energetic and very clear manner that all the faithful follow the government in its politics of National Restoration."[72]

The bishop's support of Vichy was evident not only in his sermons, but also through the selection of articles published in *La Semaine Religieuse*. For example, there appeared in 1941 an unsigned piece titled "A Frenchman of France and Not of Great Britain Speaks to You."[73] The anonymous author exhorted the reader to adhere to the National Revolution and "struggle against the adversaries of French renovation and foreign propagandists who seek to divide the French and erase France from the map of nations."[74] Later that same year the journal published a speech that Paul Marion, the minister of information, gave at Nîmes. The former director of propaganda for the fascist PPF (Parti populaire français) of Jacques Doriot, Marion warned his listeners that Pétain had understood the necessity to "terrorize the terrorists," combat the "Jewish lies broadcast over dissident radio," and gather enough devoted followers "ready to follow him regardless of the circumstances."[75] The article was introduced by the remark that the bishop had attended the speech and was seated in the officials' rostrum.

Girbeau's repeated incitements to collaboration and obedience did not slacken with the changing domestic and international situation. The bishop probably saw himself as a faithful interpreter of the declaration made in July 1941 by the Assembly of Cardinals and Archbishops. Did they not, after all, swear "a sincere and complete loyalty toward the established power [and] venerate the chief of

71. G 354, commission de contrôle postal, October 1942. Telephone conversations of 6 and 8 October 1942. It ought to be mentioned that the crowd also sung the *Marseillaise*.
72. CA 279, préfet to Ménétrel and Pétain, 5 October 1942.
73. A clumsy reference to the BBC program "The French Speak to the French," a mixture of commentary, songs, and reports broadcast by the Free French.
74. *La Semaine Religieuse* (15 June 1941).
75. *La Semaine Religieuse* (21 September 1941). Contained in summary of articles in G 258.

state and demand that all Frenchmen rally around him"? Yet, the French ecclesiastics also emphasized that the church would restrict itself to "the religious sphere"
and stand clear of all political parties. Finally, they condemned all "injustices and
excesses" that violated "the respect, dignity and essential liberties of man."[76] As
it turned out, the spheres of religion and politics overlapped for some bishops,
and yet others either ignored, or honored in the breach, violations against the
human person. Girbeau was among those ecclessiastics who maintained a damning silence on the regime's repeated blows against the Jews, and we shall see in the
next chapter that his attitude toward those called up for the *service du travail
obligatoire* (STO) was hardly more inspiring.

As for the ties between throne and altar in the Gard, some of Girbeau's
sermons violated the spirit, if not the letter, of the 1941 assembly's vow not to
meddle in state affairs. Clearly, the promises Vichy held out to the Church—such
as financial and administrative concessions, along with intangibles such as respect
and deference—proved no less a temptation for Girbeau than for most of his
peers. No less important a factor was the bishop's fear of communism. Robert
Paxton has suggested that if there was a single common denominator to Vichy, it
was antibolshevism.[77] We have seen that, threading through Girbeau's sermons
from the mid-1930s to the outbreak of the war, was an obsession with the
communist menace. We do not know whether Girbeau agreed with Paul
Thoulouze, political columnist of *L'Eveil du Gard,* the secular and quasi-official
voice of the departmental church authorities, who hailed Hitler's invasion of the
Soviet Union as the attempt to "rid Europe of the Bolshevik canker."[78] No such
statement was ever publicly uttered by the bishop; nonetheless, it would be
surprising had the bishop's obsessive fear of communism ended with France's
defeat.

At the very least, the bishop was held by Angelo Chiappe as an honorable
partner in the work of the National Revolution. In early 1943 the prefect
orchestrated the state's recognition of the bishop's efforts. Girbeau was recommended
for the *françisque,* the medal struck by Vichy to reward loyal service to the
regime. The bishop ultimately turned down the honor when he learned that,
along with the medal, he would have to "make a gift of his person to Marshal
Pétain." This was impossible, Girbeau explained to Chiappe, since as a man of the
church, he already had given his life to God. Girbeau nonetheless assured

76. Quoted in François Delpech, "Les Eglises et la persecution raciale," in *Eglises et chrétiens,* ed. Montclos, 266–67. This declaration was made on 24 July by those bishops and cardinals from the occupied zone; it was adopted two months later by those in the unoccupied zone.

77. Paxton, *Vichy France,* 249.

78. *L'Eveil du Gard* (July 1941), 2.

Chiappe that he never would forget the prefect's kind offer, and would continue to remind his flock that they would "fail both God and France if they refused to recognize that the marshal had been heaven sent."[79] Ultimately, whether the bishop actually pinned the *françisque* on his soutane was irrelevant. To paraphrase the old jibe about the French Legion of Honor, the one thing worse than receiving the *françisque* was to have actually earned it.

"Whether at Alès, Grau-du-Roi, or Nîmes, whatever the occasion, even for the festivities of 1 May, with every opportunity I repeat: let us collaborate, collaborate, collaborate."[80] Angelo Chiappe was, as we have seen, as good as his word. But how successful were his efforts to rally the Gardois to the standard of the National Revolution? What did the Gardois understand by the term "collaboration"? How open were they to the government's efforts to encourage this attitude? What factors favored — or hindered — such acceptance? And how was Pétain's role perceived in relation to this question?

In methodological, no less than existential terms, the issue of collaboration is freighted with difficulties. As Stanley Hoffmann pointed out more than twenty years ago, there were as many forms of collaboration as there were collaborators.[81] The very use of the term, it has been argued, imposes a simplistic and misleading interpretive grid on this period.[82] Roger Austin contends that the analysis of public reactions in terms of collaboration and resistance not only forces moral judgments upon the actors, but also leads the historian to confuse acquiescence with collaboration and discontent with resistance.[83] Moreover, there is a multitude of shades and nuances to the everyday acts of men and women. The effort at neat and orderly classification may well do violence to the unbounded nature of history and an injustice to the perceptions and intentions of the actors.[84]

The resistance of life to categorization is found in the case of the Gaussen family. The family's eighteen-year-old daughter, Yvonne, was a secretary at the Nestlé milk office in Nîmes, respected by her colleagues and employer. The girl lived at home with her parents; her mother was incapacitated by a nervous

79. G 258, letter from Girbeau to préfet, 3 December 1943.
80. CA 561, "note" (n.d., probably 1941).
81. Hoffmann, "Collaborationism in France during World War Two," 375. This observation, perhaps self-evident today, was much less so when Hoffmann first uttered it.
82. This is the welcome thrust of John Sweets's work. See both his *Choices in Vichy France* and "Hold That Pendulum."
83. Austin, "Propaganda and Public Opinion," 455–456.
84. As the late Detlev Peukert demonstrated in his study of everyday life in Nazi Germany, the "experiences of separate individuals cannot be neatly and mechanically categorized under the labels of 'dissent,' 'passive consent' and 'active participation.'" See his *Inside Nazi Germany: Conformity, Opposition and Racism in Everyday Life* (New Haven, 1987), 79.

disorder, and her father, a guard at the museum of natural history, was a *grand mutilé* of the First World War. Yvonne added another shade to this portrait of prosaic misery: the young girl was having an affair with a member of the German Armistice commission. Her father, a "good patriot" who would never tolerate such a relationship, had been kept in the dark by his daughter. It was due to her frequent trips to Lyon, where the commission was permanently located, that the curiosity of the police was sparked. The commissioner concluded that it seemed to be nothing more than a "sentimental liaison."[85]

Three years later, on the eve of the liberation of the Gard, the prefect Papinot, who had replaced Chiappe after the latter's promotion to Orléans, reported that a certain François Paul Gaussen had been executed in Montpellier. Called up by the STO, the young man fled to the neighboring Lozère, where he was working clandestinely on an isolated farm. Found and arrested by the German police, he was brought to Montpellier and subsequently shot on 30 May. The prefect asked the central commissioner to contact the boy's family, adding that the German pastor at the execution had given the young Gaussen last communion. The family's address noted by Papinot was the same as that of Yvonne's.[86]

The story of the Gaussens underlines the poverty of concepts like collaboration and resistance—if not the insufficiency of words in general—to depict the maddening ambiguities and tragedies of this period. Was Yvonne—a young, serious, and responsible woman—a collaborator, horizontal or otherwise? Was her brother, having fled Nîmes to escape being sent to Germany as a forced laborer, a resister? How did their father, veteran of a previous war and a "good patriot," react to the news about his daughter and his son? How, in fact, is a "good patriot" supposed to react? Did he "lose" a daughter in addition to his son? More generally, what was the young girl's fate? And how had the young man's death been remembered and commemorated?

This one example reminds us that the torrents of history often overwhelm the dams of language meant to tame them, and that hidden reefs threaten the most experienced pilots of narrative. Nevertheless, the historian has no choice but to use "collaboration" and "resistance" as guiding concepts. First, with his task of portraying a certain time and place, the historian's conceptual palette is limited. The concepts and terms can be—must be—qualified and nuanced, but their basic content remains. Second, the fact that these terms were common currency among the actors themselves obliges the historian to confront them as well. Even if he ultimately disagrees with the fashion in which they were used, he at least is obliged to understand his protagonists' reasons for doing so.

85. CA 367, commissaire speciale to préfet, 18 June 1941.
86. CA 367, préfet to interior, 16 August 1944.

It first needs to be emphasized that, throughout this period, the popularity of Pétain in the Gard seems to have only slightly diminished—an observation which runs counter to that of some notable local studies which argue that the public's attitude toward Pétain was less enduring than commonly held. John Sweets, for example, affirms that Pétain's popularity in Puy-de-Dôme began to decline in the first half of 1941.[87] Pierre Laborie's contention, based upon his findings in the Lot, is even more radical. He claims that the popular picture of the general frenzy surrounding Pétain as early as the summer of 1940 corresponds less to reality than to hagiographic press accounts.[88] He also asserts that mainstream, *attentiste* opinion, although respectful of Pétain, was, by the end of 1941, critical of his decisions.[89]

These reservations were, to a certain degree, true in the Gard as well: adherence to the person of Pétain did not prevent, and perhaps even encouraged, a critical attitude toward the regime. Nevertheless, based on the available police reports from this period, it appears that there existed a spontaneous and popular attachment to Pétain that lasted well into 1942. Reports from the winter of 1941 attest to fairly strong support and respect for Pétain. In January, Chiappe reported that despite increasing public skepticism concerning the course of the war, Pétain "remains above dissension [and] everyone agrees that, whatever may happen, the marshal's policies must be blindly followed."[90] Allowance made for the prefect's hyperbole, it does seem that Pétain did have the support of the Gardois. Proof was offered on 13 February when Pétain, following a meeting in Montpellier with Francisco Franco, stopped briefly at the train station in Nîmes. According to the central commissioner's report, the popular enthusiasm expressed in the "spontaneous and fervent cheers...reached a level, during these brief moments, that never before has been seen in our city."[91] This impression was confirmed by Albert-Gondrand, the usually blunt and hard-nosed commander of the gendarmerie, who remarked that Pétain's stopover left a "deep impression" on the populace.[92]

87. Sweets, *Choices in Vichy France*, 155.
88. Laborie, *Résistants, Vichyssois et autres*, 169.
89. Laborie, *Résistants, Vichyssois et autres*, 189. Some other studies, however, seem to parallel my findings in locating a significant streak of abiding respect and attachement to the marshal at least through 1943. See the articles of Christian Bougeard on Brittany, Marie-Thérèse Viaud on the Dordogne, and Jean-Louis Pinicacci on the Alpes-Maritimes in *Vichy et les Français*, ed. Azéma et Bédarida, 535–60.
90. CA 566, préfet to interior, 16 January 1941. This observation is confirmed by a January report from the commissaire special, who noted that "the great majority of French have complete confidence in Marshal Pétain" (CA 566, commissaire special to préfet, 27 January 1941).
91. CA 566, commissaire central to préfet, 15 February 1941.
92. CA 566, commandant de gendarmerie departmentale to the préfet, 15 February 1941.

The opinion of one Gardois who went to see Pétain was thus probably shared by the great majority of spectators: the marshal was "splendid and strikingly young," indeed, "a little cocky."[93]

By the same time the following year, the marshal's popularity remained high. In early 1942, the central commissioner—whose reports, punctuated with fawning nods to the policies and personalities of the regime, become increasingly suspect over this period—affirmed that confidence in Pétain continued to grow.[94] Yet his observation is confirmed by the more dependable postal commission summary, which noted that of those correspondents who wrote about other than material cares, "nearly all express confidence in the marshal."[95] Typical of the many letters intercepted and cited by the commission during this period was one written by a resident of St. Hippolyte-du-Fort. Hailing Pétain's 1942 New Year's address, the correspondent exclaimed: "As usual, [Pétain] points out our errors to help us improve ourselves.... Such greatness, such strength radiates from this old man."[96] This sentiment was echoed by the widow of Gaston Doumergue, the former prime minister and native son of the Gard. Madame Doumergue declared to a native of Aigues-Vives (Doumergue's birthplace) that France's salvation resided in the union of all Frenchmen around the marshal, and that one must hope "that he yet be preserved for a long time."[97]

In sum, Pétain's continued popularity with the public through early 1942 appears genuine and fairly widespread. His image reassured not only the urban middle class, but initially the farmers and workers as well.[98] As late as mid-1942, reports attest to his enduring popularity. Despite the defacing of the marshal's poster at a local town hall, the sub-prefect of Le Vigan observed that Pétain's prestige remained intact.[99] Pétain remained above criticism in this densely Protestant region a few months later; in fact, those elements opposed to the government studiously avoided attacking the marshal and instead aimed their criticism at the other members of the government.[100] In a report to Vichy at roughly the same time, Chiappe remarked that Pétain continued to attract as

93. CA 646, commission de contrôle postal, February 1941. Letter from Charles Malige (Uzès), 27 February 1941.

94. CA 776, commissionaire central to préfet, 10 January 1942.

95. CA 776, commission de contrôle postal, 28 February 1942.

96. G 360, commission de contrôle postal, January 1942. Letter from Miquette, 2 January 1942.

97. G 360, commission de contrôle postal, February 1942. Letter from Mme Doumergue (Haute-Garonne), 19 February 1942. Of course, one must keep in mind that the ties between Mme Doumergue's husband and Pétain stretched back to 1934, when the marshal was named minister of war by the veteran politician.

98. CA 566, commandant de gendarmerie nationale to préfet, 15 February 1941. Albert-Gondrand reported that Pétain's popularity "continues to grow among the working class."

99. CA 776, sous-préfet of Le Vigan to préfet, rapport mensuel, 24 February 1942.

100. CA 776, sous-préfet of Le Vigan to préfet, rapport mensuel, 24 April 1942.

much confidence as ever: "It is generally considered that he alone can save France from the perils which threaten it."[101]

It is telling that support for Pétain, which seems to have remained constant, contrasted with the increasingly critical attitude of the Gardois toward the policy of collaboration. At the same time that a number of police reports assured the prefect of Pétain's popularity, they also warned of the government's crumbling support. The peasantry, asserted one official in early 1942, were no longer supportive of the regime's policies and warned that "the National Revolution seems to be on the decline."[102] As for the bourgeoisie, this same official placed them under three categories: those confident in Pétain but hostile to collaboration, those who remained under the influence of the left, and finally the merchants who were in search of profits and only had "an opportunistic attachment to the politics of the marshal."[103] Lastly, the disaffection of the workers deepened; like the peasants, they "held the government responsible for all of their difficulties."[104] In sum, the state of public opinion in the Gard toward the regime seems largely to have reflected that of the rest of the unoccupied zone. In a synthesis of prefectoral reports for December 1941, the ministry of interior drily concluded that the prospect for collaboration "is losing more and more ground," and ominously remarked that "anti-German sentiment is deepening even among those Frenchmen who are free from foreign influence and deny all political motives."[105]

Clearly, the public's embrace of Pétain must not be confounded with the acceptance of his politics and policies. The public's largely negative reaction to Montoire had indicated the limits of collaboration; the prospect of a military and diplomatic alignment with Germany aroused more anxiety than enthusiasm in the Gard. There was, moreover, a widespread optimism, following the Battle of Britain, that Germany was less than invincible. The postal commission reports in the spring of 1941 affirmed that only a minority believed in Germany's ultimate triumph, while the great majority "kept all their hopes in an English victory."[106] Even the central police commissioner, who seemed determined to put the most optimistic glosses on his reports— thus insisting that the French now knew that "their true interest lies in fully collaborating with our closest and most powerful neighbors [the official often betrayed a certain reluctance in writing the name 'Germany']"—admitted

101. C 359, préfet to interior, rapport mensuel, March 1942.
102. CA 776, commandant militaire de la 15ème division militaire to préfet, 7 February 1942.
103. CA 776, commandant militaire de la 15ème division militaire to préfet, 23 February 1942.
104. C 359, summary of commission de contrôle postal, April 1942.
105. CA 566, synthèse des rapports des préfets de la zone libre, December 1941.
106. CA 566, synthesis of public opinion in commission de contrôle postal report, 2 May 1941.

that "yesterday's enemies" had not yet found the same place in the hearts of the Nîmois that their "ex-allies" once held.[107]

This image had little in common with the Pétain who was pursuing a policy of active collaboration with Germany. Instead, the public's imagination fixed on an ideal image—the Pétain who, just as he broke the German offensive at Verdun twenty-five years before, would now stem the rising tide of material want and ideological zealotry. As a summary from the postal commission warned, there was a general fear that were Pétain to die, there would be no one else capable of maintaining unity. The report observed a "marked distrust" shown toward the composition of the new National Council; it was held that it was weighted with too many figures from the extreme right.[108] Clearly, homage paid to Pétain was not always synonymous with support for his policies; it was, in fact, occasionally a method to criticize those same policies. Albert-Gondrand astutely pointed out that not only was the policy of collaboration criticized by many Gardois, but that they found justification for their position in certain phrases uttered by Pétain himself.[109] Similarly, the very adhesion to the person of Pétain was thought to sanction criticism of the regime. Thus, one Gardois, after having been lectured by an acquaintance for voicing defeatist opinions, replied that "the marshal has no greater admirer than me, but the people who are executing his program are idiots."[110]

The showing of a propaganda film, *A Year of the National Revolution,* later that same year sparked a similar reaction. Enthusiasm was much in evidence, and the scenes with Pétain were "the object of lasting ovations." There was, however, one exception to the audience's rapturous reception: a scene of the handshake with Hitler at Montoire "was welcomed by whistles."[111] The multivalent symbolism of Pétain was again apparent. When the marshal represented a France free of German occupation or influence—where he remained the Pétain of Verdun, the guarantor of the nation—he was warmly cheered. But in those scenes that conflicted with this view, the marshal carried the negative symbolic charge of collaboration. When the audience cheered Pétain, their applause was not only based on an authentic reaction of gratitude and respect. It also served as a

---

107. CA 566, commissaire central to préfet, 17 May 1941.

108. CA 566, commission de contrôle postal, 17 April 1941. It should be noted that this summary was not based exclusively on letters from the Gard.

109. CA 776, commandant de la gendarmerie nationale to the préfet, 22 January 1942.

110. CA 646, commission de contrôle postal, January 1941. Telephone conversation between M. Durand and X, 30 January 1941.

111. CA 300, commissaire principal to préfet, 10 November 1941. A similar incident took place a few weeks later during a newsreel of General Huntziger's funeral. A scene showing Darlan shaking hands with the German ambassador Otto Abetz sparked "isolated whistling" (CA 566, commissaire central to préfet, 30 November 1941).

broadside to the authorities. In a society where the normal channels of free expression were corked up, the public took those opportunities as they came to express their displeasure. In the safety of a darkened theater and with the complicity of one's neighbors, public opinion willed out. Clearly, the audience was less taken by the prospect of close collaboration with Germany than with France somehow remaining France.

A certain number of Gardois nevertheless did respond to Vichy's calls to collaboration with Nazi Germany. In mid-1941 an anonymous Nîmois wrote that his sole regret concerning the marshal's decision to collaborate was that it came "twenty-three years too late." So much death and destruction, he lamented, could have been avoided if France had sought such a collaboration in 1918. He concluded that "a loyal enemy is preferable to a selfish ally: at least you know where you stand."[112] Whereas collaboration for this individual reflected the tradition of the legionnaires, for others it implied a revolutionary commitment. A Nîmois syndicalist, André Nicholas, also praised Pétain's leadership, but for different reasons: the marshal and his National Revolution represented a new life for France. Commitment to the National Revolution entailed the breaking of old friendships and the "braving of scorn and hatred from others." Hence, he accepted the price of isolation and mockery, since "to attain the summit there must be an avant-garde of revolutionaries."[113]

It was as an avant-garde that the collaborationists remained: relatively few Gardois, as Nicholas' self-portrayal suggests, were won over to the idea of a renewed and fascist France taking her place in Hitler's New European Order. The stubborn efforts at proselytization by the local Groupe Collaboration, under the leadership of Joseph Garette, a failed medical student and former traveling salesman, were fruitless. Public presentations sponsored by the group rarely attracted more than two to three hundred spectators and its membership (approximately 270, most of whom were from Nîmes) was derisory. By the spring of 1942, the organization was forced to acknowledge that its original expectations had not been met.[114] Their marginality was demonstrated during a public demonstration in March 1942. Though Garette's troops joined members of the Parti populaire français (PPF), the Legion des volontaires français contre le

112. CA 646, commission de contrôle postal, May 1941. Letter from X (Nîmes), 26 May 1941. Though in favor of Pétain's foreign policy, the correspondent was critical of one of the traits to domestic policy; that is, "the reappearance of [religious] processions in our good city of Nîmes!!!! Still, it is the less of evils."

113. G 354, commission de contrôle postal, October 1942. Letter from André Nicholas (Nîmes), 4 October 1942.

114. CA 776, commissaire principal to préfet, rapport mensuel, 27 April 1942.

bolchévisme (LVF) and Action française for the occasion, the total number of participants was only two hundred. To boot, their repeated calls of "Down with the Jews" and "Hang de Gaulle" annoyed "certain nationalists" in attendance.[115] Eventually, the organization threw over its didactic concerns, and devoted its energies to pillaging local Jewish businesses that had been "aryanized."[116]

The PPF was by far the most active of the various collaborationist groups in the Gard. As specific membership lists are lacking, it is difficult to gauge the movement's actual strength. However, we do know that the PPF congress held in Paris in 1942 attracted 113 members and sympathizers from the Gard.[117] This number corresponds to a police report from the same month that declared that there were 112 members in the departmental chapter.[118] Led by the Nîmois lawyer Noël Roger, the movement posed a growing problem for the other collaborationist groups and the departmental authorities. Formed by ideological zealots, as well as those with more material motives—men far more dynamic than the greybeards of Action française and the vaguely literary clique of Groupe Collaboration—the PPF was active not only in combating subversion, but also in challenging the other movements for local leadership. The departmental head of Vichy propaganda complained that he was having problems with Noël's group, for it was trying to infiltrate not just Collaboration and the SOL, but even his own office.[119] In fact, one departmental official feared that the PPF was beginning to assume a "quasi-official" status in the Gard.[120]

Compared to its competitors, the PPF played a disproportionately active role. For example, several members of the group were pivotal in suppressing the 14 July 1942 demonstrations in Nîmes. It was during this anti-Vichy protest, which will be discussed in greater detail in Chapter 6, that Noël's followers rushed in where the police and even the SOL feared to tread. About thirty party members, led by Noël, descended upon the demonstrators, roughing up a few and tearing from their lapels the resistance symbols par excellence—the Cross of Lorraine and tricolored cockade. Noël, greatly impressed by his own leadership and bravery under the ire of the demonstrators, telegraphed Doriot to report that the "orders had been executed and a few Crosses of Lorraine snatched away."[121]

---

115. CA 776, commissaire principal to préfet, rapport mensuel, 27 March 1942.
116. Cosson, Nîmes et le Gard dans la guerre, 82.
117. CA 641, commission de contrôle postal, October, 1942.
118. According to Cosson, there were 167 members in 1943, and just 74 by August of the following year; Nîmes et le Gard dans la guerre, 81.
119. CA 641, commission de contrôle postal, October 1942.
120. G 356, summary of commission de contrôle postal, August 1942.
121. G 356, summary of commission de contrôle postal, August 1942.

The PPF's isolated role during this demonstration bespeaks the absence of general support for the regime. Noël bitterly complained to Chiappe that the regular police forces had harassed the PPF militants, considering *them* to be the agitators, rather than the demonstrators.[122] This lack of zeal on the part of the very men responsible for the regime's safeguard points to a more general phenomenon— growing public indifference to the project of the National Revolution. As Albert-Gondrand warned in the winter of 1941, the overwhelming majority of men and women cared not a whit about the goals of the National Revolution. The marshal's work, he concluded, "is not yet understood."[123] The themes of indifference and incomprehension appear regularly in the police reports by this period. The public, local officials agreed, did not understand that they belonged to a vanquished nation.[124]

Apparently, the "fact of defeat" was within the ken of understanding only of the *la couche saine,* or "sound portion" of the population—a phrase that begins to occur in official reports with the same numbing frequency as "We aren't yet understood." The meaning of the phrase varied over the course of time and context. For example, with the increase of resistance activity after late 1942, it usually referred to those Gardois who, for a variety of reasons, criticized these acts of "terrorism." Before this period, however, *la couche saine* of the department instead referred to those who supported the policies of the regime. Thus the mayor of Genolhac praised the "right-thinking population" which "approves without hesitation the justness" of Darlan's politics.[125] Similarly, a Nîmes police commissioner observed that the "sound portion" of the population supported the collaborationist policies of men like Marion and Pierre Pucheu, the minister of interior.[126] The phrase helped straddle the gap between bleak truth and professional reassurance. By resorting to this euphemism, officials could both depict a decaying base of popular support, all the while maintaining an optimistic gloss for the benefit of their superiors.

By the spring of 1942, the great majority of Gardois began to understand only too well the direction in which the regime was headed: the path of collaboration was one way and led east to Germany. Popular resistance to this political itinerary first appeared with the news of Montoire; it became even more pronounced with the policies of Admiral François Darlan. In the aftermath of Laval's removal from

122. G 357, Noel to préfet, 17 July 1942.
123. CA 566, commandant de la compagnie de gendarmerie départmentale to the préfet, 15 February 1941.
124. CA 776, sous-préfet of Le Vigan to préfet, rapport mensuel, 26 January 1942.
125. CA 785, mayor of Genolhac to préfet, 10 June 1941.
126. CA 566, commissaire principal to préfet, 29 August 1941.

power on 13 December 1940 and Pierre-Etienne Flandin's subsequent and very brief tenure as foreign minister, Darlan not only moved into the latter's office but also laid claim to the ministries of interior, defense, and information and vice presidency of the council. Convinced that Great Britain could not win the war, preoccupied with the French empire and her fleet, and obsessed by France's future role in what he anticipated to be a German-dominated Europe, Darlan bent his considerable authority toward reviving the policy of collaboration first sketched at Montoire. The Protocols of Paris marked the climax of this new and sustained effort at state collaboration. Signed on 28 May 1941, the agreement gave significant military concessions to Germany in North Africa and the Near East; in return, France would benefit from a slight reduction in occupation costs, a loosening of the Demarcation Line and the liberation of those French POWs who were World War I veterans.[127]

The protocols became a dead letter following the combined British-Gaullist occupation of Syria and the German invasion of the Soviet Union one month later. As the concrete expression of the regime's political intentions, however, the agreements lived long enough to trouble a good number of Gardois. According to Chiappe, a speech given by Darlan toward the end of the Paris negotiations "went right to the hearts" of the listeners, "putting an end to all of the fantastic hypotheses" abounding in the department.[128] The prefect did not provide details, but it is obvious that these "wild hypotheses" were spawned by a less-than-wild fear, given the nature of the protocols, that Vichy's leadership was signing away France's neutrality. Resistance to this collaborationist policy deepened after another foreign-policy speech given in mid-June by Darlan. Following the usual practice, loudspeakers were erected on the main square of all the towns in the department, and a local official (sometimes a police commissioner, sometimes the mayor) filed the reactions of the assembled crowd. Reports from nine localities still exist; and of these nine, only two—Le Vigan and Molières-sur-Cèze—are unabashedly positive in their interpretation of the public reaction. The others range from the predictable appeal to "la couche saine" (Genolhac) to the ambiguous allowance that the speech "produced a deep impression" without specifying the *type* of impression (Pont Saint-Esprit) to a candidly pessimistic account from the mining town of Bessèges. The latter's mayor wrote that four to five hundred locals listened to the speech "in the deepest silence," and, after it ended, simply went

---

127. For the details of negotiation and motivations, as well as a succinct narrative of Darlan's passage through power, see Paxton, *Vichy France*, 109–31. See also the recent biography by Hervé Coutau-Bégarie and Claude Huan, *Darlan* (Paris, 1989) and Henri Michel, *Pétain, Laval, Darlan: Trois Politiques?* (Paris, 1972).

128. CA 566, préfet to interior, 26 May 1941.

about their business. He concluded that it was futile to try to prod the least sign of agreement or disagreement from the public: "One has the clear impression that [they] are withdrawing into themselves."[129] It is tempting to argue that most Gardois agreed with the reaction of an anonymous correspondent from St. André-de-Valborgne: "Darlan's speech threw me for a loop. All in all, [he is] a downright servant, a fine *Gauleiter* for Hitler."[130] Though exceptional in the strength of its language, the sentiment expressed in this letter seems widespread. Be it under Darlan, Laval, or Pétain, the Gardois refused to buy the goods of collaboration.

This growing reluctance and fear over the consequences of collaboration became even clearer with Pierre Laval's return to power on 18 April 1942. The palace coup of 13 December 1940, which had unseated the resilient Auvergnat, led to a period of great tension between Laval's German patrons and Vichy. This, in turn, provoked a good deal of anguish among the Gardois; one month after the events, Albert-Gondrand remarked that "a certain uneasiness" persisted. All in all, however, Laval's departure sparked more satisfaction than surprise since "the population had always been very reserved toward him."[131] Hence, the majority of Gardois regarded Darlan's replacement by Laval, brought back from his Parisian exile in the hope that he could win material and political concessions that his predecessors could not, as a harbinger of more of the same—only worse. The public attentively followed the spring negotiations between Laval and Pétain over the terms for the former's return to Vichy. As the central commissioner remarked, everyone was aware of Laval's desire for a closer collaboration with Germany—a perspective that "is far from sparking the enthusiasm of our fellow citizens."[132] One correspondent exclaimed that "only one cry is heard: if Laval comes to power, it means war."[133] It is not surprising that the population, convinced that the old horse-dealer (*maquignon*) had been imposed by the Nazis, was "clearly unfavorable" to his reappearance.[134]

The reaction in Alès, where Laval's "inaugural" address fell on hostile ears, was particularly worrisome. There were too many "anglophiles and Gaullists,

---

129. CA 785, dossier of municipal and communal reports to préfet, 10 June 1941.

130. G 352, commision de contrôle postal, May 1941. Letter from X, 20 May 1941.

131. CA 566, commandant de la compagnie de gendarmerie départementale to the préfet, 14 January 1941.

132. CA 776, commissionaire central to préfet, 4 April 1942.

133. C 359, letter quoted in summary of commission de contrôle postal, rapport mensuel, April 1942.

134. C 359, summary of commission de contrôle postal, rapport mensuel, April 1942. The official writing the summary, forced to look for a silver lining in this particularly threatening cloud, noted that Laval's very unpopularity was considered by some to be a guarantee of success as he would be in no one's thrall.

especially among certain Protestant elements," declared the subprefect, "to hope that [Laval] could win complete and unreserved support." Not only were workers and farmers markedly antagonistic to the new regime; so too were the local pillars of the community. More ominously, even the brief introductory speech by Pétain "did not have an impact," and the marshal's claim that France's situation was even more dangerous than it had been in June 1940 "was not taken seriously."[135] On the other hand, Nîmes' central commissioner affirmed that Laval's speech had a great effect, and that a word of confidence from Pétain sufficed to have all Frenchmen "of good faith to follow the government without hesitation."[136] In light of reports from elsewhere in the department and the commissioner's own earlier reports, one hesitates to credit his veracity. The key phrase, however, in his report may be "Frenchmen of good faith." Like "healthy layer," this qualification undermined the very argument it sought to make.

The events of 18 April 1942 are a watershed in the evolution of public opinion and collaboration in the Gard. For the populace, it not only buried any remaining illusions about the regime's intentions, but it also marked the demise of Pétain as a symbol of independence and a source of protection against German demands. The police authorities were well aware of this state of affairs; their reports, either through honest assessments or the use of euphemism, bear sharp testimony to the decay of public support. The subsequent events of that year—Laval's publicly expressed wish for a German victory; the creation of the "voluntary" labor exchange with Germany known as the *relève,* inexorably transformed into a forced labor draft (*service du travail obligatoire*); and the German invasion of the unoccupied zone in November—were all, as Gérard Miller argues, heralded by Laval's reassumption of power.[137] On 18 April, both watchers and the watched knew that the regime was more isolated than ever before, and that alienation from its policies was, on occasion, another word for resistance.

135. CA 776, sous-préfet of Alès to préfet, 27 April 1942.
136. CA 776, commissaire central to préfet, 27 April 1942.
137. Miller, *Les Pousse-au-jouir du maréchal Pétain,* 199–200.

6
DEGREES OF RESISTANCE

It's awful, you know! Climbing into lofts to look for hidden feed . . . this isn't work. I'm burnt out! There's nothing left in my region. And I've had enough! I'm tired and overworked . . . all of these demands . . . problems of all sorts . . . at this very moment in my office I've a poor bugger who's crying.

> —M. Pellegrin, agent of the Food Distribution Board, 1942

For the last three days it's the women who are demanding food. Roundups and arrests are useless. Their kids are hungry, and the only way to calm the women is to meet their demands. *Vive les femmes!*

> —Henri Brot, miner, 1942

In the late spring of 1941, a blind accordionist, Antonio Chabard, was asked to play the *Marseillaise* at the terrace of the Café de la Bourse, which stood in the shadow of the massive walls of the Roman arena. Unknown to the musician, a group of German officers was passing by at that same moment. His rendition received a wildly enthusiastic wave of applause, echoing down the broad boulevard and along the traffic circle. The response of the laughing and smiling crowd convinced an investigating officer that the request was a "useless and poorly-timed provocation" directed at the Germans.[1]

The story of Antonio Chabard raises the critical issue of resistance, the reverse side to the coin of collaboration. In his pioneering work on Vichy, Robert

---

1. CA 367, secrétaire principal de commissaire central à Nîmes, 26 May 1941.

Paxton introduced the concept of "functional collaboration." Apart from those Frenchmen and women who actively supported the Vichy regime and the National Revolution, there were also those citizens who, in Paxton's words, "grumbled at the regime without doubting its basic legality or doing anything positive against it." It was this large swath of the population, labeled "functional collaborators" by the American historian, who created "the broad public climate of acceptance that lent legitimacy to a more active participation."[2]

Paxton's evaluation of the political consequences of public opinion in Vichy France has not gone unchallenged. France's doyen of World War II historians, Henri Michel, wrote that Paxton's approach carried "a certain odor of hostility toward France."[3] More recently, another American historian, John Sweets, has questioned the legitimacy of Paxton's morphology of public attitudes and moral responsibility. In his subtle study of Clermont-Ferrand and the department of Puy-de-Dôme, Sweets convincingly argues that, by the end of 1942, the inhabitants had lost much, if not all, of their sympathy for Vichy. To thus emphasize the *attentisme,* apparent indifference, and apathy of most French, as does Paxton, "fails to make a sufficient distinction between thought and action and distorts the usual meaning of conventional language."[4] Suggesting that indifference could be better interpreted as opposition rather than support of the regime, Sweets broadens the notion of resistance to include sympathizers and supporters. He admits that such a concept is unwieldy, but is "also truer to the complex reality of the resistance in France."[5]

The complexity of this particular reality is undeniable. Yet Sweets's perspective does offer a more accurate portrayal. The historian must, of course, be extremely cautious: *depending upon the context,* it could prove no less distorting to interpret the *attentisme* of the great majority of French through the prism of resistance as through that of collaboration. Roger Austin's distinction, already noted, between acquiescence and collaboration, discontent and resistance, is salutary.[6] If this distinction is not acknowledged, the historian risks including a variety of dubious candidates in the pantheon of resistance, from the hundreds of thousands of Frenchmen joining the great exodus of 1940

2. Paxton, *Vichy France,* 235.
3. Quoted by Rousso, *Le Syndrome de Vichy: 1944–198...,* 270. Michel nonetheless praised the work as a "maître livre." J.-P. Azéma echoes Michel's ambivalence when he observes that some historians "suspected that Paxton was attacking not only the France of Vichy, but was also critical of the French under Vichy"; see "Vichy et la mémoire savante," in *Vichy et les Français,* ed. Azéma and Bédarida, 29.
4. Sweets, *Choices in Vichy France,* 169.
5. Sweets, *Choices in Vichy France,* 224.
6. Austin, "Propaganda and Public Opinion," 455.

to the deliberate giving of wrong street directions by a Parisian grocer to a bewildered German soldier.[7]

It is terribly difficult to draw the line between *attentisme* and resistance, endurance and refusal—between saying nothing at all and saying no. Could it be otherwise when the participants themselves were occasionally unable to know an act of resistance when they read one? For example, the delayed publication in 1942 of one of the first literary expressions of the Resistance, Vercors's *Le Silence de la mer*, was interpreted by some resisters as an implicit defense of *attentisme*.[8] The very notion of "the silence of the sea" is, of course, ambiguous. Must the refusal to rally to the propaganda of Vichy, turning a deaf ear to the politics of collaboration, be understood as an act of resistance? Such an attitude, as Jean-Pierre Rioux asserts, did not necessarily signal a proclivity for active engagement in the Resistance. Instead, this brand of passive resistance had "the traits of the self-conservation and inwardness of a people that had run and panted too much in 1940."[9]

Must we, on the other hand, apply to the concept of resistance the distinction employed by moral philosophers between the ethic of refusal and the ethic of positive action? According to the philosopher Philip P. Hallie, the latter form of ethical behavior affirms that "clean hands that do no harm, and harmless passions and language are not enough; the decent person must have working hands, he must be his brother's keeper."[10] What, then, of those Gardois who greeted the increasingly frantic propagandizing of the regime with skepticism and silence— and nothing but skepticism and silence? Was turning on a radio to listen to the BBC broadcast the work of idle or active hands? Did it suffice to be quietly disgusted at the racial politics of the regime? Was the reading of a resistance tract an act of positive resistance?

Such questions, by their very nature, will never be answered to the satisfaction of all. Moreover, we must keep in mind René Rémond's plea that choices that seem clear-cut today, were moral thickets for the men and women living under Vichy. The question of resistance was then posed in extraordinary circumstances: we must "understand the spirit of the time, to avoid giving in to the temptation

7. Jean Vidalenc has made the case for the former in *L'Exode de mai–juin 1940* (Paris, 1957). For the latter, the best portrayal of such *résistants* is found in Jean Dutourd's cynical and funny novel *Au bon beurre* (Paris, 1952).

8. See Azéma, *De Munich à la libération*, 262.

9. Jean-Pierre Rioux, "Survivre," *L'Histoire*, no. 80 (1985), 100.

10. Philip P. Hallie, *Lest Innocent Blood Be Shed* (New York, 1979), 282–83. The last chapter of this moving history of Chambon-sur-Lignon, the Protestant village in the Haute-Loire that saved the lives of countless Jews during the war, is an attempt to understand, in Hallie's phrase, "how goodness happened" there.

of hasty appraisals, to recognize the lucidity and willpower of those who knew where their duties lay, and also, perhaps, to be ready for situations that will demand of us choices no less difficult."[11]

Such will be the intent of this chapter. The organized Resistance in the Gard has been extensively discussed in the work of Aimé Vielzeuf and other local historians. Hence, this chapter, by examining the communities, motives, and methods of resistance, will focus on the everyday and spontaneous forms of departmental resistance (though we will consider in some detail the work of the very organized and clandestine PCF (Parti communist français), for it under-scores the peculiarities of the department).[12] Clearly, these categories are arbitrary and occasionally overlap—for example, the very nature of a particular "community" of resistance, like the refugees from Alsace-Lorraine, could provide both its reason for resistance and even the form such resistance took. Or, again, the brief study of the "community" of Gardois Communists necessarily entails some discussion of one of their principal forms of "expression": propaganda. With these caveats, this chapter will seek to make sense of a complex issue and confused period.

In April 1941, the head of government, Admiral Darlan, directed all prefects in the unoccupied zone to pay particular attention to the relations between the Alsatian and Lorrain refugees and the native populations among whom they were relocated. The latter, Darlan observed, "have not always understood the duties of solidarity and assistance that are imposed by the unhappy lot of our fellow citizens expelled from Alsace and Lorraine."[13] We have already seen that the Gard's welcome in 1940 was warmly and gratefully acknowledged by the northern refugees.[14] Yet even at this early stage the *patriotisme á fleur de peau* (the easily ruffled patriotism) of the Alsace-Lorrainers was obvious. For example, in September 1940 two German nationals who had been living in France and were on their way back home, passed through Nîmes and were directed to spend the evening at the Garage Perrault, which happened to be a camp of refugees

11. René Rémond, "Devoir de desobéissance à l'autorité?" in *Spiritualité, théologie et résistance,* ed. Bolle and Godel, 259.

12. An actor in the events he would subsequently recount, Vielzeuf has written several works of popular history on the Resistance in the Gard. See, in particular, *La Résistance dans le Gard* (Nîmes, 1979), *Au Temps des longues nuits* (Uzès, 1967), and *Compagnons de la liberté* (Nîmes, 1976). See also Bourderon, *La Libération du Languedoc Méditerranéen* (Paris, 1974); Jacques Poujol's succinct summary, "Histoire abrégée des maquis cévenols," *Causses et Cévennes,* no. 4 (1980), 231–42, and Cosson, *Nîmes et le Gard dans la guerre 1939–1945,* 119–40.

13. CA 687, circulaire from Darlan to préfets de la zone libre, 19 April 1941.

14. The prefect noted that, as of 25 November 1940, there were nearly 3,000 Lorrainers in the Gard alone (CA 686, préfet to interior, n.d.).

from Lorraine. One of the Germans became slightly drunk and began singing the German national hymn *Deutschland über alles*, to which the Lorrainers responded by bursting into the *Marseillaise*. The director of the camp intervened before the singing contest turned into a slugging match, and a police official suggested that all future German travelers be lodged in those camps where there were no Alsace-Lorrainers.[15]

The patriotism of the refugees from Alsace-Lorraine grew more pronounced with time. In mid-1942, it was observed that the refugees harbored "violent" anti-German sentiments and that they were "implacably hostile" to pro-collaboration propaganda.[16] The uncompromising patriotism of these men and women led, as we have already seen, to the creation of a refugee association, the Groupement des évacués et réfugiés d'Alsace et Lorraine (GERAL), dedicated to preserving the memory of the lost provinces. Unhappily, this organization did not lessen the friction between the Alsace-Lorrainers and Gardois. It was nearly inevitable that differences in culture, language, and religion, all catalyzed by divergent historical experiences, would lead to a mutual lack of understanding and sympathy.[17] As one refugee wrote, it was often "surprising to hear others discuss the situation in a manner which contrasts so with our own aspirations, since for us refugees the enemy remains the *boche*."[18] Another voiced hope that they soon would be able to return "chez nous," adding that the hardest thing "is to live with a population that understands us poorly or not at all, and shares neither our opinions nor our ideas. Even if our stay lasts longer than we hope, we will never be assimilated or become 'good' Southerners."[19] In much stronger terms, an Alsatian held that the natives' *attentisme* was tantamount to collaboration: "I'm anxious to leave this region, where people don't understand our situation. This is especially so in the Midi where everyone is a collaborator; it pains me to see the French side with our greatest enemy. Vive l'Alsace. Vive la France."[20]

Strangers in a strange land, the refugees were often placed in the untenable position of having their own "Frenchness" questioned. This was the case, for example, with German agents scouring the Gard for miners from the northern departments of the Meurthe-et-Moselle and the Meuse who were now working

15. CA 686, commissionaire divisionnaire to préfet, 26 September 1940.
16. CA 646, summary of commission de contrôle postal, rapport mensuel, July 1942.
17. There is a certain historical continuity in this mutual incomprehension. As early as World War I, *les gens du nord* taxed the French of the Midi for their pallid patriotism and ignorance of the realities of the war. See Richard Cobb, *French and Germans, Germans and French*, passim.
18. CA 646, commission de contrôle postal, 5–19 May 1942 (unattributed).
19. G 357, commission de contrôle postal, 5–19 June 1942, Letter from X (Nîmes), 12 June 1942.
20. G 357, commission de contrôle postal, 5–19 June 1942. Letter from G. Grandheuzie, 9 June 1942.

in the mines of Alès. A certain Ludwig Heeb, a German-born, naturalized Frenchman, employed by the German authorities of the Meuse, was apprehended by the departmental authorities for illegally hiring workers to return to the mines of Alsace. Heeb was finally nabbed when, approaching an Alsatian miner in an Alèsian bar, he introduced himself as a fellow *Reichsdeutscher.* Unmoved by Heeb's claim of shared racial roots, the miner reported the agent to the local police.[21]

"We Alsatians have become obstacles in the [regime's] new politics."[22] This observation made by a refugee was increasingly true not only at the level of foreign policy, but also at the level of local events. The 14 July 1942 antigovernment demonstration in Nîmes, in which the Alsace-Lorrainers played a significant role, was particularly telling. Long suspected by the authorities of being "Gaullist," a number of the demonstrators carrying the tricolor cockade were identified as "refugees"—presumably from Alsace and Lorraine. Moreover, a month earlier, Edouard Dammert, president of GERAL, had been accused of disseminating Gaullist tracts and was arrested by the police. Several Alsatian notables, including F. Hecker, the former editor-in-chief of *La République de Strasbourg,* rallied to Dammert's defense, attesting to his patriotic devotion and sacrifices.[23] Though there were some refugees who welcomed the move, they were in a minority; a clear majority seemed to agree with one Alsatian's opinion that Dammert had been imprisoned for "excessive patriotism."[24]

Heterodox interpretations of patriotism were not confined to the refugees from Alsace and Lorraine; they had a growing audience among Protestants, as well. As early as the winter of 1940, the so-called "Keller affair" underscored official suspicion of the Protestant community. Pastor Keller was editor of evangelical tracts published under the auspices of the Société des missions évangéliques of Nîmes. In a tract published in December 1940, an article on the future of missionary activity concluded that, though "no one knows the future . . . the French flag still waves above our colonies and the gospel is not bound to any one flag." The censor in Nîmes, Marcel Pays, who ordered the confiscation of the leaflet, thought the phrase an implicit critique of the regime and a defense of

---

21. CA 790, préfet of Ardèche to préfet of the Gard, 23 January 1942.

22. G 356, commission de contrôle postal, August 1942 (unattributed).

23. G 357, commission de contrôle postal, rapport mensuel, June 1942. Letter from Hecker to Mme Dammert, 17 June 1942. A second letter, from Eugène Imbs, affirmed that Dammert's party, the SFIO (Section française de l'international ouvrière) was the sole party in Alsace to "proudly brandish the colors of the French flag while combatting Karl Roos's party, the puppet of Hitler, the Bolshevik party of Stalin and the clerical, autonomist party."

24. G 357, commission de contrôle postal, rapport mensuel, June 1942 (unattributed).

rebellious acts.[25] There followed discussions between Pays and Marc Boegner, who accompanied Keller and defended his article. Pays insisted that the censors had the duty to transpose all phrases from the spiritual to the temporal level, and to suppress even religious commentaries when they conflicted with governmental directives. Besides, Pays added, in the context of the "alarming activities" of local Gaullist propagandists, one could not let pass allusions to the "support that evangelical missions located in the French colonies previously received from foreign countries." Boegner replied that he appreciated the difficulties that, in this respect, confronted censors—who, after all, are rarely theologians—but insisted upon the universal and inviolable nature of the gospel. He thus justified Keller's concluding line, which, Boegner added, was no less applicable to Catholics than Protestants. The censor parried Boegner's attempt to align the attitudes of the two churches by remarking that the Catholic press in the Gard had itself already taken the initiative of "free collaboration" (that is, submission of galleys before being sent to press) with the censors and he would welcome a similar arrangement with the Protestant press.[26]

A modus vivendi was eventually worked out between Boegner and Pays, where it was agreed that Pastor Lestringnant of Nîmes would serve as liaison with the censors. Nonetheless, the affair's resolution was not so neat as the compromise may suggest. Pastor Brunel, the leader of Nîmes' Protestant community, had written a letter to Chiappe in which he insisted that Keller's phrase had been misinterpreted; added (somewhat cravenly) that Keller "apparently doesn't like the English"; and assured the prefect that he would henceforth "ask his colleagues to be extremely prudent in their choice of words."[27] However, Brunel's attempt to appease the authorities went for naught. In a report sent to Vichy two days after having received the pastor's letter, the prefect warned that Keller's phrase, whether intentional or not, revealed a "state of mind prevalent among a certain Protestant milieu." Chiappe then partially erased the distinction he had just made between "certain" Protestants and Protestants in general when he asserted that the Gard still "conserves the imprint of the religious wars and the Protestant fraction—notably in bourgeois circles—doesn't hide its sympathy for the England that supported the Huguenot movement over the course of history." Brunel's assurances of good faith notwithstanding, Chiappe asserted that the

25. Pays had been the diplomatic editor of *L'Excelsior* before being appointed to the censorship department of the ministry of information. In December 1941 he left Nîmes upon his promotion to the post of regional censor in Limoges, where he won the reputation for great zeal on behalf of Vichy; see John Dixon, "Manipulators of Vichy Propaganda: A Case Study in Personality," in H. R. Kedward and Roger Austin, eds., *Vichy France and the Resistance* (London, 1985), 48–72.

26. This narrative is based upon letter sent by Pays to préfet, CA 660, 18 December 1940.

27. CA 660, Brunel to Chiappe, 7 December 1940.

regime found "itself in the presence of a very special (*tout particulière*) conception" in regard to the Protestants. It is unclear to what this "conception"
referred, but it probably had to do with duty and patriotism, since Chiappe
warned Vichy that it would be prudent to keep an eye out for other "manifestations" of this spirit.[28]

The report evidently stirred some concern at Vichy, for the prefect was directed
by the Sûreté Nationale to "follow very closely all manifestations of the Protestant
state of mind in [his] department."[29] Chiappe obeyed his orders closely. Several
months after the incident, he informed Vichy that the case against Keller had finally
been withdrawn and was apparently closed. He then went on to remark that he had
been trying to rally the Protestants to the regime—an effort that included Boegner's
address at the Grand Temple in Nîmes—and that though their opinions remained
unchanged, they were more circumspect in expressing them. Nevertheless, Chiappe
added, "an active surveillance is being exercised on this milieu."[30]

Despite the state's watchfulness, some of the Protestant journals still occasionally succeeded to broadcast their message. One method was to avoid all reference
to Pétain and the regime. The press, it must be recalled, was not simply censored,
but also directed in the tenor and actual wording of many of its articles.[31] Thus
Chiappe's proud declaration that all the departmental papers "are edited in a
spirit of perfect loyalism toward the government."[32] As a result, when one
examines these journals, both secular and Roman Catholic, and measures their
general level of bombast and *bourrage* (eyewash), the Protestant silences and gaps
become less modest and more daring than it first appears. Contrast, for example,
the December 1941 issues of *L'Eveil du Gard* and *Semailles.* The former extensively
quoted a speech given by Pétain, contained a typically egregious column by
Thoulouze on the Riom trial, and celebrated (rather belatedly) the first anniversary of Montoire.[33] *Semailles,* on the other hand, carried a piece titled "Message
to the Young." Apart from a single call to serve "our wounded country," the
message dwelt exclusively on the imperative need to serve God. The beneficiaries
of such service, the message affirmed, are "all those who suffer" and they "must

28. CA 660, préfet to interior, 9 December 1940.
29. CA 660, Direction générale de la Sûreté Nationale to préfet, 20 December 1940.
30. CA 660, préfet to interior, 2 July 1941.
31. According to Paul Marion, who was appointed in 1941 to direct the Office français d'information,
his bureau "was to the newspapers what a chemist is to the pharmacies" and he demanded "the strictest
conformity"; quoted in Lévy and Veillon, "Propagande et modelage des espirits," in *Vichy et les
français,* ed. Azéma and Bédarida, 187.
32. CA 566, préfet to Interior, rapport mensuel, 1 October 1941. Chiappe went on to note that *Le
Républicain du Gard* is "in particular completely behind the National Revolution."
33. *L'Eveil du Gard* (November–December 1941).

be saved from the shadows which are the very symbol of death."[34] Hence, beyond the striking omission of any mention of civic duties toward Vichy, there was also an elliptical reference to those individuals persecuted by that same regime praised in the Catholic *L'Eveil du Gard*.

This summoning to resistance in the pages of *Semailles* becomes even clearer a few months later. In a front-page meditation based upon the parable of the Good Samaritan, the question was posed whether the two men, seeing a wounded man lying on the side of the road, were right to pass by rather than stop to help. The reasons for this decision were reviewed: legitimate doubts as to the wounded man's merit, the danger the men would have run if they had stopped, the need to reach their destination, and so on. But what, asked the writer, is the ultimate end of life? Is it not to "obey the law of love"? He condemned the travelers for ignoring their true duty, not to be found in such excuses, but which is instead "both simpler and higher."[35] The reader did not have to be versed in casuistry in order to identify those "victims" he passed every day and know, despite the risks, where his duties lay in regard to them.

Or, again, there is an early 1942 meditation in *Foi et éducation*. The writer, G. Siguier, wondered if the "spirit of truth pushes us to 'protest' at every occasion 'against the character of this century, as well as the one to come,' as Karl Barth writes."[36] Both the nature of the question and the citation of Barth, known for his prescient resistance to the Nazis, were freighted with meaning for the paper's readers. Such articles justified Marcel Pays's determination to censure ostensibly spiritual sentiments; as he well knew, they redirected the reader's eye from eternal concerns above to worldly problems below—or, more precisely, sought to focus on profane concerns through the lens of Christian ethics.

That the Protestant press was more likely than its Catholic counterpart to question the regime's policies was reflected in the official concern over a resistance tract that appeared in the late summer of 1941. Titled "To French Catholics," the tract was sent to the majority of departmental ecclesiastics, including Bishop Girbeau. A long and powerfully argued condemnation of the church's silence in face of Vichy's anti-Semitic policies and politics of collaboration, the appeal was considered the work of Gardois Protestants.[37] Yet there were no damning hints

34. *Semailles* (December 1941), 2. It should be noted that the issues of this journal from February 1940 to November 1941 are missing from the collection at the departmental archives.

35. *Semailles* (February 1942).

36. *Foi et éducation* (March 1942). One may justifiably wonder how familiar most Protestants were with the name and thought of Barth, but the thrust of the quotation retains its power even if the reader was ignorant of the Protestant thinker's work.

37. CA 745, interior to préfet du Gard, 19 September 1941. The tract created a good deal of excitement in Vichy and was treated with much urgency.

in the text to support such a suspicion. Instead, the mere fact that it revealed a critical attitude—an attitude of resistance—sufficed to cast the burden of guilt upon the Protestants rather than the Catholics. Girbeau dismissed the tract, affirming that apart "from one or two exceptions," it would not have an "unhealthy influence" upon his clergy. The Protestant leaders, on the other hand, denied playing a role in its creation and instead linked it with "a dissident Catholic order, like the one which existed in Lyon [a reference to *Témoinage Chrétien*]." Although the local police officials concluded that there was no evidence to tie the Protestant community to the tract, one commissioner made the leading comment that the text nevertheless "reflects in part the views and ideas expressed by Pastor Boegner."[38] Lacking hard evidence, the authorities stopped short of making explicit charges, but the tenor of the reports made it clear that the Protestants remained under a cloud of suspicion.

Perhaps the most significant act of Protestant resistance dating from this period was the rescue of foreign and native Jews. Among the reasons that led many French Protestants to protest and actively subvert the anti-Semitic legislation and actions of the Vichy regime were the importance of the Old Testament in Protestant theology, the lucidity shown by Protestant thinkers and leaders from the mid-1930s concerning the nature of Nazism, the impact on French Protestants of the writings of Karl Barth, and the activity of Martin Niemoller and Dietrich Bonhoeffer, and the Protestant community's own minority fears concerning the character and intentions of the clericalist regime installed in Vichy. But as Philippe Joutard claims, the deciding factor for the Protestants, at least for those in the Cévennes, was the "living memory of their persecuted ancestors that established an instinctive solidarity with other persecuted peoples, first and foremost the Jews." This affinity was not new; the Cévenol city of Anduze had been the seat of massive Dreyfusard demonstrations at the turn of the century. As one resident recalled, the reason for their activity was simple: Dreyfus "was Jewish and was condemned because of his Jewishness. The Protestants were for him because like him, they too had suffered."[39]

These factors helped transform the Cévennes, by mid-1942, into a haven for Jews fleeing the French police. Although not so well known as the activities of the Protestant town Chambon-sur-Lignon, the valleys and villages of the Cévennes—which spill over into the Lozère and the Hérault as well as the Gard—constituted a formidable "underground railway."[40] Because of the nature of the subject, it is impossible to determine the exact number of Jews (as well as

38. CA 745, commissaire principale to préfet, 1 October 1941.
39. Philippe Joutard, "Postface," in his *Cévennes: Terre de Refuge, 1940–1944*, 331–32.
40. Among the works which treat Chambon is Hallie's *Lest Innocent Blood Be Shed*, as well as the powerful documentary film by Pierre Sauvage, "Weapons of the Spirit." In her just-published work

German political refugees and French youths fleeing the STO [service du travail obligatoire]) whose lives were saved by the network of Protestant villages. Basing himself upon a comprehensive survey, Philippe Joutard affirms that at least 1,200 refugees were rescued by the Cévenol Protestant community.[41] However, shared affinities and pasts alone were not enough; certain administrative and topographical features specific to the Protestant Church and the Cévennes were also essential for the success of the operation. The horizontal structure of the Protestant Church, in which a pastor simply contacted a colleague rather than first seeking the approval of a superior, provided the administrative flexibility so important to the success of such an undertaking. In addition, the harshness of the land benefited the rescue operation. The countryside is to this day wild and forbidding, and its polyculture, contrasting sharply with the rest of the Gard, provided the wherewithal to feed a refugee population. Even the area's shrinking population, as Jacques Poujol points out, suddenly became an asset: not only was there enough food to go around, but also enough houses to shelter the refugees.[42]

Of course, the safety found in the Cévennes by the refugees was not exclusively the work of Protestants. Catholics, here as elsewhere in France, participated in the growing efforts to help the Jews escape the dragnets of the French and German police. Nonetheless, the Catholic presence remained essentially marginal; it was the work of exceptional individuals, rather than the expression of entire communities as with the Cévenol Protestants. In fact, in certain areas the activity of the Protestants sharpened the traditional animosities between the two religious communities. Jacques Poujol recounts that he encountered especially reticent natives in the area around Le Vigan when trying to interview participants in the rescue operations. Such an inquiry, it was feared, would revive old resentments between the local Protestants and Catholics. Poujol even observed that, at least with the older generation, "a certain tension" between the two communities was still perceptible and that the "old grievances dating from the Occupation and the Liberation are still not effaced."[43]

Still, Catholic devotion to Vichy was not unanimous. Père Francois Alary was undoubtedly one of the "exceptions" earlier referred to by Monsignor Girbeau. At least until the end of 1942, Alary was one of the exceptions who proved the

---

The Holocaust, the French and the Jews (New York, 1993), Susan Zuccotti also refers, if only briefly, to this neglected aspect of the French Resistance.

41. Joutard, "Postface," in his *Cévennes: Terre de Refuge, 1940–1944*, 331.

42. Jacques Poujol, "Filières, répartition, caractéristiques du refuge juif," in *Cévennes: Terre de refuge, 1940–1944*, ed. Joutard et al., 140. Poujol estimates that the Cévennes lost 16 percent of its population between 1921 to 1936.

43. Poujol, "Filières, répartition, caractéristiques du refuge juif," 146.

rule that the Catholic clergy was far more reluctant than its Protestant peers to resist. Born in 1873, Alary had been for some twenty years parish priest of Arre—a town no less exceptional than its curé. It was a village of approximately 450 inhabitants, nearly all of whom worked for Monsieur Brun d'Arre, the local nabob and owner of the textile company "Bas-Lys." The townspeople worked together, lived together, and, overwhelmingly Catholic, they also followed the advice of their priest together.

A reputed Gaullist, Father Alary was investigated by a local police inspector in the summer of 1942. The crusty old curate admitted that he listened to BBC broadcasts, but this was his own affair since he was "maître chez lui." He acknowledged, moreover, that he occasionally discussed politics, but that his sermons were based on news he heard only over legal stations (for example, Radio Vatican), which "narrow-minded and poorly informed sources attributed to Gaullism." In fact, the father continued, he had no wish to engage in politics— which was precisely why he refused to sound the church bells to mark the anniversary of the "political" Legion. Apparently warming to his subject, the good priest then took the offensive. He lectured the inspector that all political acts were human acts that fell in the domain of the spiritual. For the benefit of his flock, it was his duty to comment upon these events. Showing the bemused inspector to the door, Alary concluded that he would "not hesitate to give his point of view to his parishioners, as in these matters he was accountable only to his superiors, Monsignor [Girbeau] and the Pope."[44]

Alary's activity nevertheless earned a warning from the prefecture: if he failed to "assume the correct attitude" toward the government, he would be placed under house arrest. Bishop Girbeau, moreover, was asked to intervene. The request almost certainly came from Chiappe, for Girbeau wrote the prefect to inform him that he had spoken to Alary and reminded him of his duties, on which "our Catholic doctrine is very clear," toward the government. Girbeau promised to write Alary a second letter emphasizing the risk he was running, and assured Chiappe that as "fear is the beginning of wisdom, you will not have to intervene." The bishop's concern was less for the well-being of his stubborn priest than for the sensibilities of the prefect: "It is always disagreeable to act against an ecclesiastic, but especially so when the official who is obliged to intervene has a Catholic soul like you."[45]

But the various threats had their desired effect for only a few weeks. On 11 November, the curé was again under investigation. Fearful of Gaullist agitation, Vichy had forbidden all celebration of Armistice Day. Father Alary ignored

44. CA 660, inspecteur to commissaire principal, 17 August 1942.
45. CA 660, Girbeau to préfet, 30 August 1942.

this order and held a ceremony at the *monument aux morts,* having fixed the time so that all the workers could attend. Although his sermon did not carry an overtly political message, the subprefect of Le Vigan remarked that if Alary's gesture "had been that of a normal [*sic*] individual, [it] would have led to his internment." Since Alary was not "normal" and was widely respected, the subprefect, unwilling to create a martyr, asked that the bishop order the recalcitrant priest to "celebrate a mass for those Frenchmen who recently fell on the Algerian coast in the defense of their territory against the English and American invaders."[46]

Father Alary went on to become chaplain for the Aigoual-Cévennes maquis. Other priests would also be identified with the Resistance by the time of the Gard's liberation in the summer of 1944. Yet their number was still limited at that late date; at the time of Alary's activity, in the summer and fall of 1942, their ranks were even more sparse. There are sporadic comments culled by the postal commission made by priests dissatisfied with the drift of the regime. For example, Abbé Veyrunnes grieved over the working conditions of the Alesian miners and criticized "the same injustices, the same lack of social sense" continued by Vichy that, presumably, were found under the Third Republic. He concluded with the wish to see "Lille liberated from our 'friends' within the next two years."[47] Yet these ecclesiastics remained the exceptions. Neither Girbeau nor Chiappe doubted the "loyalism" of the departmental priests through 1942, and it would only be after the institution of the STO that certain cracks would appear in the ranks.

Among the various groups identified with the resistance in the Gard, the Communists soon assumed a pivotal role. It has been estimated that more than half the individuals arrested for subversive and "terrorist" acts between 1940 and 1942 were members of the PCF (Parti communist français).[48] However, these statistics must be used with caution, for the Communists were pursued more relentlessly by the French police during this period than were the Gaullist resisters.[49] There was a tendency to consider the latter as wayward patriots, whereas the former, by their very nature, were held to be implacable enemies of France. As a result, the percentage of arrests may not provide an accurate reflection of the actual degree of resistance activity among the non-Communist movements.

46. CA 760, sous-préfet to préfet, 18 November 1942.
47. G 357, commission de contrôle postal, June 1942. Letter from Abbé Veyrunnes (Nîmes), 12 June 1942.
48. Bourderon, *Libération du Languedoc Méditerranéen,* 71. For example, 42 of 97 individuals arrested in Nîmes, 11 of 13 in Beaucaire, 32 of 62 in Alès and 20 of 39 in La Grand-Combe were PCF members.
49. A point made by Sweets, *Choices in Vichy France,* 205.

Nevertheless, the activity of the local Communists did occupy a significant portion of the police reports. Despite the arrest of the great majority of the local leaders, already begun under the Third Republic, and the great administrative and moral confusion that reigned in the rank and file, the Gardois Communists managed to maintain a certain degree of activity throughout 1940. A typical police report from this period remarked that the PCF "continues to propagandize . . . and to deliberately work against the government."[50] By the spring of 1941, the profile of the PCF, largely through its propaganda efforts, became even more prominent. In March 1941 Chiappe reported to his superiors that there had occurred a "new and more serious outburst" of Communist activity, especially in Nîmes and Alès. Not only was there a striking increase in the distribution of tracts and leaflets, but a red flag had even been raised over the mines at Rochebelle.[51]

A commonplace of Vichy historiography is that, between the fall of France and the German invasion of the Soviet Union in June 1941, the French Communist Party, hamstrung by the Non-Aggression Pact, was more active against Great Britain and the Gaullists than Nazi Germany. The principal target of Communist propaganda was international capitalism rather than the Germans, with the result that Pétain, de Gaulle, and Churchill were all lumped in the same enemy camp. Recent historical research, however, has nuanced this generalization and distinguishes between the official party line and the activity of individuals and regional organizations, thus reinforcing the observation made by the former Communist Charles Tillon that there were "two parties according to the regions and the cadres."[52]

Does the evidence that exists for the Gardois Communists from this period support such a distinction? Based on the extant copies of tracts and posters from the months prior to June 1941, it does appear that the primary target of the Gardois Communists was not Germany, but the international capitalist class, and that they concentrated on the evils of Vichy at the cost of relegating the Nazis to the background. As early as December 1940, the residents of Alès came across Communist stickers attacking Pétain.[53] A leaflet distributed in Nîmes later that same month criticized Pétain for busying himself with the transfer to France of the ashes of Napoleon's son, the duc de Reichstadt, while the "suffering of the

50. CA 566, commissaire divisionnaire to préfet, 30 November 1940.
51. CA 745, préfet to interior, 10 March 1941. Chiappe tactfully omitted that the flag had written across it "Down with Pétain." (See report of inspection générale des services de police administrative, CA 716, 19 March 1941.)
52. Quoted in Azéma, *De Munich à la libération,* 134.
53. CA 566, commandant de la compagnie de gendarmerie départmentale to préfet, 14 December 1940.

prisoners of war has only just begun."[54] A poster from early 1941, adorned with a hammer and sickle against a tricolored backdrop, called on the workers and peasants to struggle for the liberation of imprisoned Communists, the free publication of *L'Humanité,* and the removal of "Pétain's clique, Laval's crooks, and all the corrupt capitalist agents in favor of a government of the people and for the people."[55] And a tract distributed at roughly the same time by the Nîmois section of the PCF also directed its hostility more at the "adventurers at Vichy," and the mythic "two hundred families" that ran France, than at Nazi Germany. The tract did acknowledge, though, that the "two hundred" counted upon "Hitlerian Germany to safeguard its domination, in exchange for which they are willing to transform France into a vassal of German imperialism."[56]

Police reports from 1940 observed that local Communists were at odds over the direction of the party's policy toward Nazi Germany. As early as the end of August it was remarked that the local Communists were riven between those who willingly accepted the establishment of a National Socialist state in France and those who, despite the official party line, were "fiercely anti-German."[57] This face-off continued through the following month when it was reported that the rank and file were divided between Germanophiles and Germanophobes. The latter, it was observed, hoped for an English victory "even though it is a capitalist state."[58]

Germany's invasion of the Soviet Union simplified matters dramatically. Not only did it immediately bury the former differences among the local Communists, but it also removed the greatest obstacle between the collaboration of the Communist and non-Communist resistance movements. More immediately, it appears to have led to a significant increase in the amount of Communist propaganda. From the late summer of 1941, there is a striking growth of Communist activity, reflected in the police reports and the sheer amount of impounded flyers and tracts.[59] The distribution of tracts was a risky enterprise, but conditions clearly favored the forces of resistance. The distribution of broadsheets and posting of flyers was always done under the cover of night, an activity aided by a sharp reduction in public lighting, imposed for reasons of conservation. In fact, in the fall of 1941, Nîmes' central commissioner vainly

54. CA 566, commission de contrôle postal, 31 December 1940.
55. CA 569, poster dating from 10 March 1941.
56. CA 569, tract (undated).
57. CA 565, commissaire divisionnaire to préfet, rapport mensuel, 28 August 1940.
58. CA 565, commissaire divisionnaire to préfet, rapport mensuel, 30 September 1940.
59. For example, the police superintendent of Nîmes reported that the activity of the PCF had increased "since the Russian invasion," citing the profusion of printed and mimeographed tracts found in most of the Gard's major towns (CA 566, commissaire principal to préfet, 29 August 1941).

asked the prefect to increase the amount of lighting. The sorely tried official was no less hobbled by a shortage of manpower than wattage: between 10:00 P.M. and 4:00 A.M. he had just twelve men to cover a city of 90,000 inhabitants that covered more than 30 square kilometers.[60] The nearly Sisyphean task was worsened by the city's labyrinthine topography. Apart from the handful of large boulevards cutting across the city, Nîmes was an intricate patchwork of winding alleyways and narrow streets that facilitated the clandestine dissemination of resistance tracts.

Various methods were used to distribute clandestine journals. In the region of Alès, for example, entire bundles were sometimes left at the entrance to the mines. A more daring approach was to shower copies of an issue on a movie audience from the safety and darkness of the theater's balcony.[61] The most common form of delivery, however, was to simply leave the tract in mailboxes. But this did not mean that the distribution was done randomly; to the contrary, groups and individuals were often targeted. In Sommières, members of the Legion and Action française woke one morning to find copies of *L'Humanité* and a tract titled *Vive la France, Vive l'URSS* placed in their boxes or pasted to their doors.[62] Clearly, such deliveries were less attempts at political conversion than provocations and a show of force. One Nîmois, like Chiappe a Corsican, who unexpectedly found himself on *L'Humanité*'s mailing list explained in a note to the prefect that his wife had found "this vile rag in our letter box this morning." The outraged recipient of the paper boasted that his experience in "tracking down bandits in Corsica" provided insight into ways to stamp out "this Communist vermin." Chiappe, unfortunately, would have to wait for the solution: the correspondent had a serious case of the flu and was unable to leave the house.[63]

The clandestine press of the local PCF also addressed more receptive audiences. Apart from the principal organ of the party, *Le Cri du Gard*, there was a variety of tracts aimed at different social and economic classes in the department. Small businessmen, artisans, farmers, miners, young Christian workers, and soldiers were all targeted by distinct leaflets. For example, the first issue of *La Tribune des mineurs* was printed—or, rather, mimeographed—in November 1941. The issue

60. CA 300, commissaire central to préfet, 22 September 1941. Perhaps the most constant refrain of the police commissioners during these four years was that they were handicapped by an insufficient number of personnel.

61. CA 745, commissaire principal to préfet, 28 August 1942. It should be noted that this particular "delivery" concerned issues of *Libération* and *Combat*, the journals of the two principal non-Communist resistance organizations.

62. CA 783, commandant de la compagnie de gendarmerie départmentale to préfet, 18 August 1941.

63. CA 267, anonymous letter to préfet, 11 February 1941.

lambasted the Labor Charter (*Charte du travail*)—Vichy's failed attempt, officially introduced in October 1941, to institutionalize and codify a form of national corporatism—as an "iron yoke passed over the neck of the working class." Significantly, the paper encouraged the miners to unite in their struggle, regardless of their "political and religious conceptions"—an exhortation suggesting that confessional differences in the Gard remained significant.[64] In this context, the Communist Youth organization also made overtures to its Christian peers. In a 1941 pamphlet, the usual economic and class definition of fascism was replaced by an interpretation that condemned it as the "very negation of morality and of the ideal of human fraternity that is no less ours than yours." Having affirmed that the moment to unite had come, for "tomorrow may be too late," the leaflet announced the creation of a National Front, the PCF-inspired resistance organization dedicated to "saving our human dignity, our liberty as Frenchmen and our lives."[65]

The PCF showed a good deal of acumen in its attempts to rally the Gardois to the resistance. One approach was to appropriate those very themes, like the sacredness and centrality of the family, that were dearest to Vichy. *Le Cri du Gard* carried an article on a recent scandal concerning the death of four infants at a local nursery, leading to the trial and ten-month sentences for the director and his assistant. The Communist paper blasted the length of the sentences as woefully inadequate, especially in light of testimony that revealed horrendous hygienic and emotional conditions at the nursery. Is it just, demanded the paper, to give these guilty parties such light sentences when individuals like Arthur Vigne, the former secretary of the miners' union and the father of a child, and Paul Planque, a miner from Alès and a father of three children, "are condemned to twenty years of hard labor for having acted as French patriots"?[66]

By the summer of 1942, the activity of the Communist press had become an unremitting headache for the departmental authorities. First, as already noted, the distribution was done under the cover of night, which rendered nearly hopeless any effort to catch the participants red-handed. Second, it was extremely difficult to uncover the printing facilities. The police were unsure if the tracts were printed in Nîmes, another town in the Gard, or in a neighboring department.[67] On occasion, the police did succeed in finding a clandestine printing press. For example, one important operation in March and April 1941 led to the arrest of the regional leaders of the Jeunesses Communistes, including six individuals in

64. CA 745, *La Tribune des Mineurs* (November 1941).
65. CA 783, untitled tract (n.d. but probably September 1941).
66. CA 745, *Le Cri du Gard* (30 December 1941).
67. CA 745, commissaire central to préfet, 7 March 1941.

Nîmes. In the same operation Robert Imbert of Alès was caught in the possession of numerous tracts as well as the offending mimeograph machine, prodding the prefect to express the hope that the core of the organization had been "completely dismantled."[68]

One strand of continuity between the final days of the Third Republic and Vichy is the difficulties faced by the police to suppress a resilient and many-faceted PCF. At the end of 1939, the subprefect from Alès reported that the struggle against Communist propaganda continued, but that the organization, though weakened, "had not been killed." Noting that Alès remained a center of Communist propaganda, he plaintively asked: "What can we do?"[69] The same note of despair can be detected in the reports of Vichy officials. In early 1942, for example, the police superintendent of Beaucaire noted that his town, which had been a Communist stronghold before the war, was still a center for illegal propaganda. The imprisonment of several well-known local militants, he concluded, had not put an end to this clandestine activity, and that there was an unbroken distribution of *L'Humanité, La Tribune des cheminots, La Voix des femmes, L'Avant-garde,* and so on.[70] By mid-June 1942, in a report to the central commissioner of Nîmes from the regional prefect of Marseilles, it was observed with some desperation that not only was the distribution of tracts growing larger and the distributors growing bolder, but that the process of printing and the very nature of the articles were increasingly varied.[71]

The local officials were no less preoccupied by the growth of "Gaullist" propaganda as by the Communist activity. As John Sweets has pointed out, the term "Gaullist" is slippery and was often a catchall for a variety of comportments.[72] Most often, at least through 1942, it seems to have been understood as a synonym for hostility toward the Germans and the politics of collaboration, rather than adherence to a specific and clear political program. For example, in many of the police reports, the terms "Gaullist" and "germanophobe" (and to a lesser extent "anglophile") form a nearly inseparable pair. Even if Gaullism's meaning remained ambiguous, its increasing popularity by the summer of 1941 is manifest. In late

68. CA 300, préfet to interior, April, 1941.
69. IZ 37, sous-préfet to préfet, 9 December 1939.
70. CA 745, commissaire principal to préfet, 6 January 1942.
71. CA 328, intendant de police à la préfecture de Marseilles to commissaires centraux de la région, 11 June 1942. Of course, the PCF was not the only organized resistance movement in the Gard. In fact, of the three principal resistance organizations in the unoccupied zone—Libération, Franc-Tireur, and Combat—it was the last group that played the most important role. The local presence of the first two movements was relatively negligible. Combat was the most conservative of the groups; in fact, it remained mildly pro-Pétainist through 1941. See Bourderon, *Libération du Languedoc Méditerranéen;* and Cosson, *Nîmes et le Gard dans la guerre, 1939–1945* for detailed narratives.
72. Sweets, *Choices in Vichy France,* 166.

May, many of the city walls in St. Gilles were marked by the "V" sign, as well as slogans like "Down with Darlan," "Darlan is a boche," and "Long live England." The most common slogan, however, was "Vive de Gaulle."[73] Similar inscriptions were reported in Nîmes, but the police official asserted that it was the work of isolated youths looking to provoke the authorities.[74] The arrest of two youngsters in Bagnols-sur-Cèze, caught marking a city wall with Gaullist slogans, seemed to confirm such an observation.[75]

However, the commissioner's claim missed the mark. Gaullist sloganeering on public facades may have been a minority activity, but the audience for such sentiments was a large one. One indication was the growing number of Gardois listening to the Free French broadcasts over the BBC. Albert-Gondrand reported in the late summer of 1941 that the "Gaullist radio was widely listened to," though listeners took care that the broadcasts were not overheard.[76] Captain Orsatelli, the representative of worker propaganda, was no less preoccupied by the popularity of the BBC news and propaganda broadcasts, asserting that the radio was "very damaging for the national recovery and exercises a tremendous influence over public opinion." He advocated that laws punishing such activity be strengthened and efforts redoubled to catch those guilty of tuning in to the broadcasts.[77]

How does one gauge the significance of listening to "dissident radio"? Undoubtedly, its appeal was partially attributable to the pitiable quality of the official programs and news dispatches. The regime's broadcasting network was decentralized, leaving a good deal of autonomy to the local authorities. But neither the local selections nor those of Radio-Paris claimed the interest or won the trust of the Gardois; the famous BBC ditty, sung to the tune of *La Cucaracha*, "Radio-Paris ment, Radio-Paris est allemand" (Radio-Paris lies, Radio-Paris is German), accurately describes the Gardois' attitude toward the programming. The ministry of the interior itself acknowledged the failure of French radio, citing the monotony of the programming, sluggishness in news dispatches, and the "partiality of the editorials and discretion shown [in reporting] the major domestic and foreign events."[78] But was the act of listening to the BBC in itself

73. CA 785, commissaire de police, St. Gilles to préfet, rapport mensuel, 31 May 1941.

74. CA 566, commissaire central to préfet, 13 April 1941.

75. CA 566, commandant de la compagnie de la gendarmerie départmentale to préfet, 22 September 1941.

76. CA 566, commandant de la compagnie de la gendarmerie départmentale to préfet, 21 August 1941.

77. CA 566, commandant de la compagnie de la gendarmerie départmentale to préfet, 22 September 1941.

78. CA 566, synthèse mensuel de l'Interieur aux préfets de la zone libre, November 1941.

an act of resistance? This question shall be raised in the Conclusion but it can be noted here that even if such an activity did not, in Jean-Pierre Rioux's phrase, merit a certificate of resistance, it nevertheless nurtured the public's skepticism and disaffection for Vichy.[79] The refusal to swallow official bombast and the obstinate interest in accounts of political and military events from "subversive" sources—which were crimes under Vichy—measured just how far the regime had failed in its attempt to mobilize support.

We have considered some of the motives fueling the Gard's various "communities of resistance": patriotism in the case of the Alsace-Lorrainers, a blend of patriotism and ideology (though the former quality seems to have been dominant) among the Communists, and a mixture of historical identification and religious ideals with the Protestants. The force of each of these elements in the makeup of the local resistance must not be underestimated. However, the most widespread cause of discontent, which in turn deepened the *potential* for resistance, was the food shortage. To paraphrase Bertolt Brecht, the four-year-long crisis of food distribution and availability in the Gard underscored the pertinence of "Food first, politics second."

The issue of *ravitaillement,* or food provisioning, was a relentless concern for the French under Vichy. The impact of German economic and material demands worsened an already precarious situation in France. The entire country was subject to a growing gap between stagnant salaries and rising food prices, increasing shortages and black marketeering, and failing supply structures. The German requisitioning of vehicles and fuel, as well the increasing drain of French manpower (already hobbled by the 1,500,000 French POWs, representing about 4 percent of the French workforce), took an enormous toll. The daily caloric intake, during this period, shrank by one-quarter to one-half. The French were consuming no more than 1,200 calories a day, and during the winter of 1942–43, their daily intake actually dropped to 1,100 to 1,000 calories.[80]

The situation, though desperate through all of France, was especially critical in the Gard. Despite the slight variations across the department due to the hazards of distribution or local subsistence farming, official reports were unanimous in their concern over the food deficits and the fear that the crisis would sooner or later achieve critical mass. Their fears were well founded, as the situation in the monocultural Gard was even more desperate than most depart-

---

79. Jean-Pierre Rioux, "Survivre," 96.
80. Statistics quoted in Sarah Fishman, *We Will Wait: Wives of French Prisoners of War, 1940–1945* (New Haven, 1991), 60. Fishman notes that in 1936 the Organisation d'hygiène of the League of Nations estimated that adults needed 2,400 to 2,800 calories a day.

ments in the unoccupied zone. The reports from 1941 convey a monotonous and bleak litany of shortages faced by the Gardois. That spring saw the Nîmois lining up in front of stores as early as three or four o'clock in the morning, creating the fear among city officials that a "food shortage psychosis" was establishing itself.[81]

"Psychosis" was an odd choice of words, for it was painfully clear that the fears of the populace, far from marking a withdrawal from reality, were very much rooted in it. For those in line, there was no guarantee that they would find what they had been waiting for by the time they reached the counter. By late April it was reported from Nîmes that there was no pork, beef, chicken, fish, or eggs; moreover, the price of vegetables and certain other foodstuffs was prohibitively high.[82] The situation was nearly identical elsewhere in the Gard. Apologizing for the repetitiousness of his reports, the police commissioner of Beaucaire warned that his message had not changed: "I must say that the food situation remains the heart of the urban population's preoccupations and that it ought to be the object of the administration's entire attention."[83] According to Albert-Gondrand, most Gardois were suffering so from hunger that they would rally to any government that could feed them. If, he warned, the "workers, petty bureaucrats and owners are forced to endure their hardships much longer, the situation could become worrisome."[84]

Clearly, the crisis was grave even at this early stage. In April, a resident of Uzès wrote that the available food was "barely sufficient to keep oneself going, but we are not dying of hunger."[85] Yet even if hunger was not claiming lives at this point, the unending efforts to keep one's head above water was. For example, a month before the above letter was posted, a woman from St. Gilles hanged herself from her bedroom window. In a note left for her children, she wrote that she was "tired standing in line outside the market." An exceptional act, it nevertheless struck the imagination of the town's residents, underscoring the precariousness of their lives and harshness of their struggle. As the town's police commissioner reported, this "act of despair has left a very strong impression upon the populace."[86]

81. CA 566, commissioner central to préfet, 26 April 1941. The prefecture issued a law the following month forbidding lines to form before 6:00 AM, but the ordinance was generally ignored.

82. CA 566, commission de contrôle téléphonique, 15–30 April 1941.

83. CA 566, commissionaire de police de Beaucaire to préfet, 20 May 1941.

84. CA 566, commandant de la compagnie de la gendarmerie départmentale to préfet, 21 May 1941.

85. CA 566, commission de contrôle postal, April 1941. Letter from Georges Rey (Uzès), 20 April 1941.

86. CA 566, commissioner de police de St. Gilles to préfet, 29 March 1941. I have not found any comprehensive figures on the number of suicides during these four years; it would be interesting to compare the numbers with that of Paris, for example, where the level declined from 2,354 in 1938 to 720 in 1944. (See Jean-Pierre Rioux, "Survivre," 90.)

The administration of the Gard showed a serious lack of competence and imagination in dealing with the shortages; in particular, the unequal and chaotic fashion in which the limited foodstuffs were distributed simply exacerbated the tense situation. To a significant degree, however, matters were beyond the control of the local authorities. The material demands of the German home economy and occupying forces, the interruption of traditional exchanges (not just across the demarcation line, but also between town and countryside), and the English blockade of sea routes were all responsible for the critical situation in the Gard, as elsewhere in France.[87] And, of course, there was the Gard's specialized economy: in a period of growing scarcity and departmental autarchy, an agro-economy based almost exclusively upon wine growing proved especially vulnerable. The officials responsible for food distribution, caught between insufficient stocks and unyielding demand, were often confronted with an impossible task. The case of M. Pellegrin, a bureaucrat assigned to Alès' food distribution board (*commission du ravitaillement*), is illustrative of the tension inherent to the job. In a phone call to the departmental director of food distribution, Pellegrin appeared on the edge of a nervous breakdown: "It's awful, you know! Climbing into lofts to look for hidden feed . . . this isn't work. I'm burnt out! There's nothing left in my region. And I've had enough! I'm tired and overworked . . . all of these demands . . . problems of all sorts . . . at this very moment in my office I've a poor bugger who's crying." The director reminded Pellegrin that tears would not create additional animal feed and advised him to get a grip on himself.[88]

Nevertheless, the impact of the food shortages upon the image of the National Revolution was fatal. The flourishing black market and deepening misery of most Gardois furnished an increasingly intolerable contrast with state propaganda. A particularly grotesque example was the emphasis placed by Vichy propagandists on the cult of youth and exercise, despite the growing malnourishment of the children. As one correspondent exclaimed, "the tired eyes and sunken chests of these unhappy kids returning from their training sessions make for a pitiful sight! They're hungry, yet are asked to make a disproportionate physical effort."[89] For many who had previously devoted themselves to the National Revolution, the worsening food situation provoked disgust with the regime. Dr. Pibre of Beaucaire, who had actively propagandized on behalf of Vichy, sent a letter of resignation to Chiappe. He portrayed a town in which indifference had given

87. On the state of agriculture and supply under Vichy, see Michel Cépède, *Agriculture et alimentation en France durant la deuxième guerre mondiale* (Paris, 1961). The best overview of the state of the French economy remains Alan Milward's *The New Order and the French Economy* (Oxford, 1970).

88. C 360, commission de contrôle téléphonique, 31 January 1942.

89. CA 646, synthèse de la commission de contrôle postal, 5–19 January 1942.

way to hostility and where legionnaires removed their official pins and savagely criticized the government. This change, according to Pibre, was due "solely to the food situation. We are literally dying of hunger in the cities and towns of the plain."[90]

The black market had become, by this time, a source of constant preoccupation for both the inhabitants and officials. For the great majority of city dwellers who had neither a *maset*, relations, nor friends in the countryside, the black market was a necessity. Yet its existence, and those who profited from it, embittered the locals. Albert-Gondrand reported with some urgency that the local black market was expanding "and would continue to do so as long as the Draconian measures demanded for months are not taken." This state of affairs, he warned, was "the principal source of the malaise that holds sway over the population and is the butt of very sarcastic criticisms."[91] Certain establishments, moreover, monopolized the food supply. For example, one Nîmois recounted that a shopowner had a windfall of 1,200 eggs, which he put out for sale. A line of four to five hundred people quickly formed outside his store, but after the first forty had been served, a buyer from the Hotel Imperator arrived and bought up the rest.[92] The prestigious Imperator itself came to stand as the symbol of privilege, collaboration, and black marketeering. One Nîmoise, having described the lot of the city's poor, declared that it was all the more "appalling" when one saw the "undesirables at the Imperator who lack nothing at all."[93] In a flash of Jacobinical anger, Albert-Gondrand declared that the black market was growing, but that "it would be easy to strangle it with a pitiless repression. Exceptional periods demand exceptional measures."[94]

By the autumn of 1941, the situation grew even more desperate. Never one to mince words, Albert-Gondrand affirmed that there was "more and more misery with people suffering from hunger." He decried the local bourgeoisie's "egotism"— clearly a reference to the black market—and warned that their "awakening could be brutal."[95] There were shocking shortages in milk rations for infants, with supply unable to keep up with the *authorized* demand. In late November, the health inspector reported that despite his request that doctors limit the

90. CA 560, letter from Pibre to préfet, 6 August 1941.
91. CA 566, commandant de la compagnie de la gendarmerie départmentale to préfet, 22 November 1941.
92. G 353, commission de contrôle postal, May 1941. Letter from X, 8 May 1941.
93. G 353, commission de contrôle postal, May 1941. Letter from Mme de la Poterie, 9 May 1941.
94. CA 566, commandant de la compagnie de la gendarmerie départmentale to préfet, 21 May 1941.
95. CA 566, commandant de la compagnie de la gendarmerie départmentale to préfet, 25 September 1941. In this same report he advocated that the "wallets of the wealthy ought to be forced open" in order to relieve the burdens of the poor.

number of authorizations to nursing mothers, the situation had become "harrowing" and estimated that the Gard was 4,500 liters short of its weekly quota.[96] More generally, the Gardois were, with little or no success, scrambling to lay in winter supplies. One official observed that, at this same time last year there was an adequate supply of canned goods, but now "absolutely nothing can be found."[97] As one Nîmois wrote, the food supply was "becoming impossible and we are in a state of anguish over this winter. For the moment we are becoming tomatoes — that is all there is to eat."[98] Although *his* diet of tomatos was supplemented by carrots, a resident of Lasalle echoed the same fear: "We spend the entire day trying to assure that we have enough food. What will this winter bring?"[99] To the dismay of the local administration, the answer was soon forthcoming: the winter of 1942 brought a tide of discontent that rose and cascaded into the streets in the form of popular demonstrations.

The situation by January 1942 had clearly become critical. The combination of a particularly bitter winter, an insufficient diet, and inadequate heating took its toll, especially on the old and infirm. One letter recounted that "the number of people between 58 and 70 years of age who are dying is frightening."[100] A woman from Vauvert wrote that during just one week in February, four townspeople have died of starvation.[101] In order to fend off hunger, the Nîmois had recourse to unusual sources of food. One resident observed that cats had disappeared from the city streets — they "had all been eaten like rabbits."[102] At the main marketplace, the lines "form very early in the morning and there is a great rush the moment the doors open. . . . Yet these women have to remain on their feet for another several hours, waiting for uncertain items. You should hear the comments made by the crowd!"[103]

And heard they were. Police reports carried increasingly sharp warnings of public resentment over the nearly hopeless food situation. It was noted that the residents of Uzès were completely indifferent to international news; instead, their "eyes are turned toward one sole object: the food supply."[104] The subprefect of

96. CA 566, inspecteur de la santé to préfet, 25 November 1941.
97. CA 566, commandant militaire du département du Gard (XVème division militaire) to préfet, 25 July 1941.
98. CA 646, synthèse de commission de contrôle postal, 5–19 September 1941.
99. CA 646, synthèse de commission de contrôle postal, 5–19 September 1941.
100. CA 646, synthèse, commission de contrôle postal, 20 January–4 February 1942.
101. C 360, commission de contrôle postal, February 1942. Letter from Mme Figon, 12 February 1942.
102. C 360, commission de contrôle postal, January 1942. Letter from Mme. Brunel, 1 January 1942.
103. CA 646, synthèse, commission de contrôle postal, 5–19 January 1942.
104. CA 776, inspecteur principal d'Uzès to préfet, 9 February 1942.

Alès was especially apprehensive over the mood of his region, where PCF stickers were more plentiful than turnips. In late January there was a good deal of agitation among the population; the "scarcity of vegetables [and] the delay in the distribution of certain rationed foodstuffs . . . have sparked rather strong reactions among a part of the population."[105]

On 23 January, the departmental military commander wrote bluntly of the "real dearth" of food afflicting the Gard, and worried that "extremists" were trying to exploit the general discontent. He concluded, however, that the public "was not necessarily ready to riot."[106] An odd conclusion, since food demonstrations already had broken out two days before in Nîmes. On the eve of the riot, a few civic leaders had tried to collect signatures for a petition criticizing the distribution of food. In fact, one of the group's leaders, M. Bourguet, insisted he had received permission from the mayor's office. After two days of canvassing, however, his harvest proved too bountiful for the mayor and Bourguet was ordered to curtail his activities. Faced with the threat of internment in a concentration camp, Bourguet complied, but insisted that he had only sought to defuse the tense situation.[107] Bourguet's motivation soon became a moot point, for the day after he was visited by the gendarmes, the city was shaken by what one witness called "le grabuge."[108]

Nearly all of the approximately 1,000 individuals who took part in the so-called "ruction" were women.[109] This is not surprising: it was the women, after all, who were milling in lines every morning with no guarantee of filling their baskets, women who were feeding families on turnips and Jerusalem artichokes, and women who lacked milk for their infants. One excited miner from Alès commented to a friend on a similar demonstration in his city. Whereas the previous great demonstrations and strikes had been the work of men, "for the last three days it is the women who are demanding food. Roundups and arrests are useless. Their kids are hungry, and the only way to calm the women is to meet their demands. *Vive les femmes!*"[110]

The demonstrations broke out not just in Nîmes, but in nearly all the major

105. CA 776, sous-préfet d'Alès to préfet, rapport mensuel, 26 January 1942.
106. CA 776, commandant militaire du département du Gard (XVème division militaire), to préfet, 23 January 1942.
107. C 360, commission de contrôle postal, January 1942. Letter from Bourguet, 20 January 1942.
108. C 360, commission de contrôle postal, February 1942. Letter from Mme Agnel, (Nîmes), 21 January 1942.
109. CA 776, clandestine leaflet titled "Ménagères en avant." I have not found any official estimates of the size of the crowd.
110. C 360, commission de contrôle postal, February 1942. Letter from Henri Brot (Alès), 21 January 1942.

towns in the Gard. Alès, Beaucaire, Vauvert, Le Vigan, Vergèze, Bellegarde, Pont St. Esprit, Aigues-Mortes, and Sommières were all shaken by protest movements from January through March. The protests all followed the same general pattern. First, the leaders and rank and file were almost always women, often accompanied by their children—a detail rendering the response of the security forces yet more delicate. It is difficult to determine their social background, but according to a witness at Vauvert, the great majority of the two hundred demonstrators were "not from the lower class, but were women of breeding (*des femmes honnêtes*)." In fact, the Vauvert demonstrators were led by Mme Meisonnet, a former teacher.[111] It is probable, though, that the great majority of the women, in Vauvert and elsewhere, were the spouses of workers, artisans, and even petty bureaucrats (most especially those of schoolteachers and other politically active professions) since all of these classes, with the exception of the miners, were hobbled by grossly inadequate salaries.

The focal point of the demonstrations invariably was the administrative center of the locality—the prefecture, subprefecture, or city hall. In general, the protesters avoided making explicit political demands or slogans, and limited themselves to bread and butter issues. For example, during the first day of demonstrations at Alès about two hundred women, with their "little nippers" (*leurs mioches*) in tow, formed outside the subprefecture and chanted "Bread! Bread!" Having received no answer from the officials, the women returned the following day with a catchier slogan: "Death to the subprefect. We want bread to eat."[112] In Vauvert, a group of women, seeking to shame the administration, demanded, if not meat, at least turnips and carrots.[113] Explicit attacks against the government were rare. The shouts of "A bas Pétain," heard at the Nîmes demonstration, were exceptional (though similar slogans directed at the prefect were more common).[114] As the women of Le Vigan explained to the gendarmes guarding the subprefecture, "We mean no harm to the subprefect, but simply want enough to eat."[115]

The singing of the *Internationale* and the structural similarities to the various protests reveal the hand of the local PCF. The Communists helped organize many of these protests, investing them with a degree of cohesion, and perhaps political direction, that they otherwise would have lacked. For example, one tract written

111. C 360, commission de contrôle postal, February 1942. Letter from Gilberte Blanquet, 24 February 1942.

112. C 360, commission de contrôle postal, February 1942. Letter from X (Alès), 21 February 1942.

113. C 360, commission de contrôle postal, January 1942. Letter from Mme Pigon (Vauvert), 1 January 1942.

114. C 360, commission de contrôle postal, January 1942. Letter from Léone (Redessan), 21 January 1942.

115. C 359, commission de contrôle postal, March 1942. Letter from Vassas (Le Vigan), 7 March 1942.

and printed by the PCF that circulated through Alès in early 1942 exhorted the women to march on the subprefecture and city hall, and demand that the "wheat and products from our soil remain in France and be distributed to Frenchmen and women."[116] A second tract blasted recent increases in the price of staples, affirming that since the imposition of food restrictions men and women "have lost between five to ten kilograms, tuberculosis has increased by 30 percent and infant mortality is growing."[117] But even if the Communists helped fan the flame of protest, the tinder for the fire had been long piling up. Moreover, the PCF does not seem to have played a significant role in mobilizing the demonstrations in the smaller towns. These movements, to the contrary, seem to have often been spontaneous and organized on an ad hoc basis.[118] The protests were, in the broadest sense of the term, political—given the close ties between the legitimacy of the regime and its ability to secure an adequate level of provisioning for the French, they could hardly be otherwise. Yet there is little direct evidence that these movements were uniquely the work of the PCF. As was the case in the strikes of 1936 (or the student movement of 1968), the Communists seem to have instead been playing catch-up with spasms of popular anger.

The response of the authorities varied from town to town. In Nîmes, Chiappe refused to meet with the demonstrators, as did the subprefects of Le Vigan and Alès. The women were instead greeted by gendarmes who, with varying degrees of force, set about dispersing the crowd. In Alès the streets were blocked by the gendarmerie, who then collected the names and addresses of those who participated in the demonstration.[119] At Le Vigan, the gendarmes contented themselves with guarding the door to the subprefecture and serving as intermediaries between the subprefect and the demonstrators. After a standoff of more than five hours, the crowd finally dispersed late that same evening.[120] At Salindres, on the other hand, the protesters were hosed down by the firemen; as one witness remarked, the women, given the cold weather, "were obliged to change their clothing and warm themselves."[121] Finally, at Nîmes, a clandestine tract affirmed that the police used their bicycles to intimidate the women and arrested several participants.[122] On the other hand, a Nîmois asserted that "the cops and gendarmes

116. CA 745, resistance leaflet (n.d., probably early 1942).
117. CA 745, resistance leaflet (n.d., probably early 1942).
118. For example, tracts were distributed in mid-February to mobilize a protest march in Beaucaire; yet, as the police official reported, the call went unheeded and there was calm the following day (CA 745, commissaire principal to préfet, 12 February 1942).
119. C 360, commission de contrôle postal, January 1942. Letter from X (Alès), 21 January 1942.
120. C 359, commission de contrôle postal, March 1942. Letter from Vassas, 7 March 1942.
121. C 360, commission de contrôle postal, February 1942. Letter from Eugène X, (Salindres), 26 February 1942.
122. CA 776, commissaire principal to préfet, 23 February 1942.

said nothing at all" to the demonstrating women.[123] The general impression is that the forces of order were sympathetic to the protestors' demands. One officer stationed in Nîmes, whose regiment had been placed on alert, observed in a letter: "It's a fact that the population is starving." He went on to allow that but for the "seditious cries" during the protest—undoubtedly referring to the "Down with Pétain" calls—the demonstration "would have been legitimate."[124]

The mayors, unlike the prefectoral officials, usually met with the protesters and attempted to address their demands. Even those mayors who had been appointed to their office by the prefecture most often were natives of the towns they administered, and so were more vulnerable to local pressures than were state officials. Indeed, the mayors occasionally found themselves pushed into the role of advocates for the demonstrators, confronting Vichy's representatives on the issue of the food supply. For example, the mayor of Vauvert, after a two-hour parley with protesters, agreed to provide them with potatoes. At one o'clock in the afternoon he drove to Nîmes in order to secure the promised provisions, and was met by the demonstrators upon his return early that same evening. After some unexplained difficulties, a half-pound of potatoes was distributed to each of the women.[125] During a similar demonstration at Beaucaire, the mayor left his office to meet with the women and declared that he had done everything in his power to provide for the townspeople, but "the prefect refused all of his demands." Skeptical of his claim, the women insisted that he telephone the prefecture in their presence. He did so, and was vindicated when an official in Nîmes told him that "the prefect had nothing to say to *Monsieur le maire.*" Clearly inspired by this victory, the mayor promised the women that he would go directly to Vichy and Marshal Pétain. He apparently fulfilled his promise, for at least one resident affirmed that ever since that day "we have had something to eat, even if it isn't much."[126]

At Bellegarde, the mayor also sought to meet the grievances of the demonstrators. He waded into the crowd outside his office, selected six women (we are left in the dark as to the criteria), and brought them back inside with him. He then promised this group of representatives that if he did not receive satisfaction from the

123. C 360, commission de contrôle postal, January 1942. Letter from A. Loubière (Nîmes), 23 January 1942.

124. C 360, commission de contrôle postal, January 1942. Letter from H. Berleat, 22 January 1942.

125. C 360, commission de contrôle postal, February 1942. Letter from Gilberte Blanquet (Vauvert), 24 February 1942.

126. C 359, commission de contrôle postal, February 1942. Letter from J. Ginot (Beaucaire), 27 February 1942.

authorities, he would hand in his resignation.[127] Similarly, the mayor of St. Gilles received a delegation of five mothers—whose children, the police official observed, totaled a remarkable thirty-four—representing a group of some fifty protesting housewives, and detailed the many efforts he already had made to improve the situation.[128] In neither case, however, do the records tell us how successful these these officials were in their subsequent efforts to address the situation.

The demonstrations often succeeded in prying concessions from the authorities. One of the protests in Beaucaire, for example, forced the authorities to deliver chestnuts and a little jam, while an Alesian protest led to the delivery of a kilogram of turnips and a half kilogram of beans.[129] Even the protests in Nîmes obliged the prefecture to "débloquer" certain food stocks; one clandestine tract praised the concerted action of the Nîmois housewives, which pushed Chiappe into delivering dried vegetables.[130] Yet the amounts were invariably paltry and made available only after the women had taken to the streets. This unacceptable state of affairs was compounded by numerous stories of official food-hoarding and extravagant dinners given by the very authorities accused of bureaucratic incompetence or indifference. Jean Pacotte, the subprefect of Le Vigan, was excoriated for a series of soirées, one of which, ostensibly given for a charitable cause, included champagne and continued into the wee hours of the morning.[131] Other residents also wrote about Pacotte's extravagances. One Viganais described a "big blow-out with leg of lamb" that Pacotte threw for the mayor (yet "another piece of riffraff"). Recounting the rumor that twenty liters of milk were delivered each day to the subprefect's home, the writer wisecracked that Mme Pacotte "must take daily milk baths." He concluded bitterly, "A few more jokes of this sort and we are going to wake one morning with a Communist government."[132]

That such rumors took root and flowered in the public imagination underscored the incompetency of the regime. The significance of such gossip resided less in whether twenty liters of milk were, in fact, delivered daily *chez Pacotte*, than in the objectively critical material situation of the populace. The need for direct action in order to resolve, if only temporarily, the food supply crisis, further

127. C 360, commission de contrôle postal, February 1942. Letter from X (Bellegarde), 25 February 1942.
128. CA 745, inspecteur principal de St. Gilles to préfet, 10 February 1942.
129. C 360, commission de contrôle postal, February 1942, letter from Blanquet; and commission de contrôle postal, January 1942. Letter from X, 21 January 1942.
130. CA 776, commissaire principal to préfet, 23 February 1942. The tract was signed "A group of housewifes."
131. C 359, commission de contrôle postal, March 1942. Letter from X (Le Vigan), 7 March 1942.
132. C 359, commission de contrôle postal, March 1942. Letter from X (Le Vigan), 27 February 1942.

accentuated the divorce between the regime and the population. Throughout the winter of 1942, there is a muddled quality to relations between the populace and the authorities. A protest movement in a particular town would jolt the food supply system into a frantic response alternating between repression and concession. But due to a combination of nearly insuperable external obstacles and internal incompetence, the bureaucracy would relapse into its former state of inert desperation. This state of affairs continued through (and, in fact, beyond) the summer of 1944 and the Gard's liberation. The consequences of this remorseless crisis for the regime were incalculable. The corollary to Albert-Gondrand's remark that the Gardois would follow any government that maintained an adequate food supply was, of course, that they would be indifferent or hostile to one incapable of fulfilling such a task. By the late winter of 1942, this manifestly had become the case in the Gard.

The food demonstrations were but one of the many ways in which the population expressed its discontentment and alienation from the regime. Perhaps an even greater jolt to the local administration, both for its economic and political implications, was the general strike called by the miners of Alès in March 1942. There had been earlier work actions in the Alesian basin. For example, in late April 1941 there was a daylong strike in the mines of Bessèges by the surface rather than the underground workers. (It was generally the underground workers who were the more militant. But the facility at Bessèges was exceptional in that the antiquated condition of its surface equipment for sifting and washing the coal made the labor far more onerous than it normally was. As the subprefect of Alès remarked, Bessèges was the only mine in the region where underground miners did *not* want to work on the surface.)[133]

Moreover, various officials had been preoccupied since the first days of the Vichy regime with the material and moral situation of the Alesian miners. A critical report written by an inspector from the Inspection générale des services de police administrative, deemed sensitive enough to be stamped "Secret," depicted a workforce as attached to the PCF and CGT (Confédération générale du travail) as it had been during the days of the "ancien régime" (the phrase used by Vichy officials to describe the Third Republic). The investigator, struck by the negative attitude of the miners, argued that though the Communists no longer openly propagandized and organized, "they retain all of their influence and have lost none of their former supporters." In addition, he worried over the presence of a sizable number of Spanish refugees working in the mines. Most of them apparently

133. CA 716, sous-préfet of Alès to préfet, 29 April 1941.

hailed from the province of Asturias, reputed for its militant syndicalism and communist sympathies, and were a priori opponents "of any regime based upon order and discipline." All in all, it was a situation that demanded constant surveillance and vigilance.[134]

This report was forwarded by Chiappe to André Chassaigne, the subprefect of Alès, and ignited the latter's ire. He affirmed that morale had grown appreciably in the wake of increased food rations and dismissed as "completely unwarranted and unverifiable" the claim that the PCF had retained its influence. He acknowledged that the Spanish refugees could pose a threat during periods of agitation, but insisted that they had so far kept to themselves. As for the endurance of Communist propaganda, Chassaigne noted with much asperity that it "would be futile to deny it, but how could it be otherwise when one recalls that the two Communist deputies of Alès won 18,755 votes in 1936." Priding himself on the number of militants (at least forty-seven) who had been interned in his *arrondissement,* he concluded that though it "would be childish to affirm that all the former Communists admire Marshal Pétain and follow the government, I nevertheless believe that positive changes are now taking place among the workers of the mining basin."[135]

Chassaigne's heated response may have been due in part to professional pride, as well as to his impatience with official ignorance of the region's political past and unrealistic belief that the New Order could be built in a single day. He may also have been aware that his ideological sincerity was questioned by his immediate superior, Chiappe, and thus sought to defend himself against the suspicion of leniency.[136] In any case, though the officials differed on the danger represented by Communist propaganda among the miners, they agreed that the situation was far from stable. In fact, a report from Chassaigne later that same year was perhaps more pessimistic than the police inspector's earlier review. To explain the worrisome drop in coal output during the past six months—from 275,000 tons in May to 212,000 tons in November—Chassaigne went to the heart of the matter, emphasizing the material conditions of the miners. Workers *were* putting in fewer

134. CA 716, rapport secret de l'inspection générale des services de police administrative to préfet, 19 March 1941.

135. CA 716, sous-préfet of Alès to préfet, 24 April 1941.

136. In a report to the regional prefect in 1942, Chiappe noted that Chassaigne was a former Freemason, and that though he fulfilled his functions, he did not consider the subprefect "to be completely won over to the work of the National Revolution" (CA 787, préfet to préfet régional de Marseilles, 22 May 1942). Of course, since this report was sent a year after the reports in question, it is possible that we are putting the cart before the horse and that Chiappe's suspicions in fact were sparked by the inspector's opinion. In any case, Chassaigne could not win: in a report drawn up by the president of the departmental liberation committee in the fall of 1944, the former subprefect was described as a "collaborationist" (CA 1861, rapport sur l'attitude de certains fonctionnaires de la préfecture pendant la guerre, 26 October 1944).

hours and claiming more sick days, but this was due less to Communist propaganda than sheer physical exhaustion, the product of "intensive labor and insufficient nourishment." The subprefect acknowledged the "harmful action" of the PCF, but insisted that "it's impossible to use force against work slowdowns." A far more effective response, he argued, would be to improve the material situation of the workers. Among the reforms suggested by Chassaigne were annual vacations ("even if only for limited periods"); increased food rations (for example, the miners in the north of France received 550 grams of bread per day, whereas those in the Gard collected just 350 grams); more and better clothing (this was an issue already brought up several times by the subprefect, who deplored the lot of miners forced to work "shoeless and clad in rags"); and revising the rule according to which miners were financially penalized for reporting late to work. It is a psychological error, Chassaigne concluded, "to treat French workers like children whom one deprives of dessert because they have not done their homework."[137]

This remarkably honest and enlightened report, depicting a situation not far removed from that in Zola's *Germinal,* may have confirmed Chiappe's suspicions of his subprefect's ideological purity. Chassaigne's practicality and plainspokenness contrasted disagreeably with the social chimeras and fairy tales propagated, if not believed, by Vichy propagandists. How difficult it must have been for Chiappe to reconcile Chassaigne's analysis with a letter sent to Pétain just a few months before, in which he included an engraving given to him by a miners' delegation, proof of the latter's "loyal attachment to the government and its leader."[138] Still, one cannot accuse Chiappe of total blindness on this issue. After a visit to Alès in November 1940, he reported that the miners lacked "the food that is absolutely indispensable for them."[139] It was as if Chiappe at times actually confused illusion with reality, and thought that the workers needed only their devotion to Pétain to maintain their physical strength and productivity.

The subprefect's realism also contrasted sharply with the view of Henri Corsaletti, the Gard's delegate for worker propaganda. In a report analyzing the sources of the March strike, Corsaletti showed an extraordinary disdain for the material conditions of the miners, and attributed the strike to poor ideological management on the part of the regime, as well as the agitation of the PCF and Gaullists. In a near caricature of Vichy's paternalistic attitude toward the working class, Corsaletti reminded Chiappe that the workers were like children—both have violent tempers and impulses, but "both are basically good." Neither, he continued, "will long resent a severe, but deserved punishment if they see that

137. CA 716, sous-préfet of Alès to préfet, 12 December 1941.
138. CA 716, préfet to Pétain, 29 December 1940.
139. CA 716, préfet to interior, 12 November 1940.

they are still loved." Corsaletti concluded that despite the strike, the workers remained open to the message of the National Revolution and that the regime needed to "re-create a mentality, to liberate the worker from the constraints that hinder him from showing his better sentiments."[140]

The kindest interpretation of Corsaletti's fatuous analysis is that it was the effort of a bureaucrat to justify a post whose very raison d'être was undermined by the miners' strike of 12 March 1942. On that day, more than one thousand workers at La Grand-Combe refused to report to their morning shift; the strike was followed at most other mines in the region. The stated causes were a reduction in the miner's wine ration and insufficient food supplies. The prefect refused to credit either of these grievances, insisting that the wine ration was the same as it had been in February and that the authorities were doing all in their power to maintain the miners' supplements of potatoes and dried vegetables. Affirming that the strike was politically motivated by "Moscow's agents," Chiappe moved quickly to repress it by arresting the alleged leaders and instigators of the action; at least seventy individuals were taken in by the police.[141]

By 17 March, the workers had returned to the mine pits and the situation was reported to be "back to normal." Yet, the criteria for "normality" had clearly shifted and the strike had several disturbing elements for the local officials. First, there was the organizing role played by the PCF. Unlike the demonstrations of housewives, which were largely spontaneous, the miners' strike displayed a degree of coordination and cohesion that pointed to PCF and CGT participation. Though the authorities had had little illusion as to the quiescence of the PCF, the magnitude and duration of the strike was nevertheless a sharp jolt. Second, the strike underscored the irrelevance of the various intermediary bodies created by Vichy in its attempt to create a corporatist society. The worker-delegates appointed by Vichy, as well as the local members of the Legion, were hopelessly unprepared for the strike and unable to exercise the slightest degree of influence on the miners.[142] The role of the Legion pointed to a third problem for the authorities. Not only were the local leaders overwhelmed by the strike, but more than five hundred of the miners who were also legionnaires actually participated in it. Given the fact that these men had sworn allegiance directly to Pétain and were considered the guardians of the National Revolution, their participation in the strike helped bury most of the remaining illusions concerning the success of Vichy's ideological enterprise. Lastly, the strike's success was partly due to the collaboration not just of those miners who belonged to the Legion, but also

140. CA 716, délégué à la propagande ouvrière à Vichy to préfet, 10 April 1942.
141. CA 716, préfet to interior, 17 March 1942.
142. CA 716, préfet to interior, 17 March 1942.

miners who had formerly belonged to the moderate wing of the CGT and the
Catholic unions. Chiappe observed that the latter's hostility against the Labor
Charter and single labor union "was not the least of the causes for their joining
the movement."[143] The fact that Catholic workers—nominally one of the pillars
of the Vichy regime—were willing to collaborate with the other miners revealed
the sharp erosion at the core of Vichy's popular basis.

Any remaining illusions that disaffection was limited to those socioeconomic
groups that had long been under Communist sway were shredded by the
demonstrations of 14 July 1942. They marked the first major mass and organized
resistance to Vichy.[144] The local authorities, by mixing threats with great efforts
to increase the food supply, tried to discourage the announced demonstrations.[145]
Yet the carrots and sticks were waved in vain: at six-thirty that evening, approximately one thousand individuals obeyed the calls of the Gaullist broadcasts and
gathered around the war memorial, a site forming one of the points of a triangle
along with the Esplanade and Roman arena. The crowd sang the *Marseillaise,* but
was then dispersed by members of the SOL (Service d'ordre légionnaire) and
PPF.[146] We have already noted the complaints lodged by Roger Noël, the PPF
leader, about the police's lack of zeal. Chiappe confirmed Noël's suspicions about
the police, believing them "well founded," and promised to take the necessary
measures to repair the situation.[147] The evident distaste felt by the forces of order
to assume the role assigned them for Bastille Day was undoubtedly no less worrisome for Chiappe than the fact that one thousand individuals were willing to risk
injury and imprisonment to demonstrate their hostility to the Vichy regime.

    Though there were no similar demonstrations at Alès, several small groups of
men, totaling seventy-five, converged on the Place de la République that same
evening. They neither sang the *Marseillaise* nor chanted slogans, but they all
"conspicuously sported on their left lapel a small tricolored cockade." After half
an hour, the crowd dispersed, with several of the "nondemonstrators" retiring for
a well-earned apéritif at the nearby Café du Luxembourg. The leaders of this
"platonic movement," (according to one police inspector) formed mostly of
Freemasons, Communists, and a handful of students from the local lycée, were

    143. CA 716, préfet to interior, 17 March 1942.
    144. A number of historians have focused on this date as a watershed in public opinion. See
Sweets, *Choices in Vichy France,* 208–10; Kedward, *Resistance in Vichy France,* 215–19; and Laborie,
Résistants, Vichyssois et autres, 233–34.
    145. CA 563, préfet to interior, 4 July 1942.
    146. G 356, commission de contrôle postal, July 1942. Letter from "Homme Libre 171," 17 July 1942.
    147. G 357, commission de contrôle postal, July 1942. Letter from R. Noël, 17 July 1942, in which
he recounted his exploits and conversation with Chiappe.

Mssrs Balmel and Piquemal, both of whom were municipal tax collectors. Brought in for questioning, both men denied participation in subversive activity or knowledge of the Gaullist calls for a show of strength. Both men, who were wounded veterans of World War I, affirmed that it was the times, and not their behavior, that had changed—after all, they had been wearing the cockade every Bastille Day since 1919, and had been taking their apéritif at the Luxembourg every Sunday evening well before that date. Besides, M. Piquemal added defiantly, "suffering as I do every day, every instant from the enemy dum-dum bullet still lodged in my battered flesh, I wear the cockade as a silent and personal act of faith and hope in the immortal destinies of our homeland, France!"[148] Piquemal's fate is unknown. As for Balmelle, the subprefect advised that though no clear proof of subversive activity existed, the tax collector be relieved of his post "pour encourager les autres."

Apart from these mounting signs of organized resistance, there was an increasing number of local incidents that may be described as freelance resistance. These events were most often spontaneous and discrete; though having no serious political or social impact, they stand as examples of men and women who had the courage to say no. There was, for example, the case of a young gardener named Marie Begot. In the presence of a retired gendarme, she declared that all legion-naires were "bastards and *cagoulards* who ought to take the place of the workers in Germany." Her tirade ended with the flourish that Pétain was a "coward, sellout, and traitor." Questioned by the police, the young woman refused to recant her description of the Legion; as for Pétain, she affirmed that she was misrepresented. She simply said that the unoccupied zone was lousy with Germans, and that "the marshal should not tolerate it."[149]

Or there was the case of Emilie Barrès, a sixty-nine-year-old housewife from Aimargues. Standing in line outside a foodstore one morning in late 1941, Mme Barrès announced that the officials in charge of the food distribution were "nitwits" (*andouilles*). Rather than applauding the prefect during his recent visit to Aimargues, she continued, "we should have thrown him into the mud."[150]

148. CA 756, sous-préfet of Alès to préfet, 20 July 1942.

149. CA 300, procès-verbal de la gendarmerie à Nîmes, 18 August 1942. I have not been able to discover Marie Begot's judicial fate. "Cagoulard" refers to the Organisation secrète d'action révolutionnaire et nationale, a shadowy extreme-rightist movement during the 1930s which in 1940, under its leader Eugène Deloncle, transformed itself into the ultra-collaborationist hit group known as the Mouvement social révolutionnaire (MSF) and was responsible, among other things, for the assassination in 1941 of the former Socialist minister Marx Dormoy. See Pascal Ory, *Les Collaborateurs, 1940–1945*, 98–100 and passim.

150. CA 300, procès-verbal de la gendarmerie à Aimargues, 19 December 1941.

Though she denied having made this observation, Mme Barrès was fined 1,200 francs—an enormous sum even for an undervalued currency.[151] We do not know if the guilty party was able to meet the fine, nor do we know her subsequent fate. But that of another housewife, Mme Auzéby, who also protested against the deficiencies in the food supply, is instructive. The good woman simply remarked that certain individuals were giving potatoes to their pigs while the people went hungry. The harshness of her punishment, a fine of 300 francs, was probably because Mme Auzéby had the tactlessness to utter this pronouncement right in front of the prefecture. Unable to pay the fine, she was interned for thirteen months in a concentration camp in the Tarn.[152]

In the fall of 1941 a young man named Alexandre Beaumont was arrested by the police of Uzès. It seems that during the showing of a newsreel, Beaumont glossed a scene of Pétain attending a legionnaire ceremony with the comment that the government "would do better to give me a bread ration card. I've heard the ration is going to be reduced again." When apprehended by the local gendarmes and brought in for questioning, Beaumont admitted that he had uttered the comment, but hadn't "raised his voice too high."[153] A similar case of lèse-majesté in Uzès involved a local woman with the wonderfully appropriate name of Berthe Chauvin. Passing two young girls admiring a portrait of Darlan in a store window, Mme Chauvin snapped, "Admiring your dictator, are you?" Several days later an unrepentant Mme Chauvin upped the ante. Gazing upon a photograph of Pétain in yet another storewindow, she was overheard wondering when the old man would "kick the bucket." Mme Chauvin, for the record, admitted the first accusation, but denied the second.[154]

No less discomforting for the authorities were the patriotic pokes at visiting German soldiers and officials. We have already cited the baiting of a German contingent by the unsuspecting accordionist Antonio Chabard. Music was put to a similar subversive use by a troop from a *chantier de la jeunesse* (youth work camp). According to one youth, during an outing his group marched by a

151. Mme Barrès possibly misinterpreted the applause for Chiappe during his visit, for on at least one other occasion it was used as a weapon of derision. In late 1942, a Nîmois student reported that a speech given by the diminutive prefect took a vaudevillian turn. The combination of Chiappe's Corsican accent ("the prefect doesn't have perfect diction") and his attempt to cut an imposing figure ("he gave two or three shouts") made the respectable women in the audience smile and sparked much laughter among the students (G 354, commission de contrôle postal, October 1942. Letter from Jean Dhombres, 21 October 1942).

152. This and similar cases were recounted by the state prosecutor Georges Servigne in his closing speech in the Chiappe trial. *Le Procès Angelo Chiappe: Réquisitoire de Georges Servigne, Commissaire du Gouvernement devant la Cour de Justice du Gard* (Montpellier, n.d.), 22 and passim.

153. CA 569, inspecteur principal à Uzès to commissaire central à Nîmes, 29 September 1941.

154. CA 569, rapport de la gendarmerie nationale à Uzès, 5 September 1941.

German military car. As the latter passed by, the teenagers struck up a chorus of *"Vive la France,* You Will Be Rebuilt," and laughed at the car's passengers. The officers "frowned," stopped the car, and stared at the youths. The perpetrators were secure in the knowledge, however, that their troop leaders "were all just as annoyed to see these fine-looking officers."[155]

There are numerous other examples of this genre, plus the innumerable instances that inevitably went unreported or unrecounted. But what does it tell us about the Gardois and the existence of resistance in the department? Clearly, it would be wrong to equate such behavior with traditional notions of the Resistance. Though there were, for example, real risks in criticizing the handling of the food crisis, they did not entail in a systematic or continuous manner the dangers that confronted actual resisters. The acts of these men, women, and children may have, in fact, occasionally represented the "resistance on the cheap" that Jean Dutourd so cruelly mocked in his great novel of occupied Paris, *Au Bon Beurre.* Nevertheless, it can be argued that such incidents, though not resistance acts per se, represented weathervanes of the changing political climate and provided an increasingly hospitable atmosphere for the operations of the organized resistance.

Of course, certain professional groups had a greater proclivity for resistance. The *instituteurs* (primary school teachers) were among the most prominent. As was true throughout the rest of France, these men and women of the Gard had served since the last years of the nineteenth century as the shock troops in the battle to consolidate the institutions and values of the Third Republic. It was thus predictable that they would be unenthusiastic over the Republic's demise and its replacement by Vichy. No less predictably, the local authorities kept a close eye on the teachers, wary of the influence they could exercise over their students. For example, Chiappe sought the transfer of a married couple who were teachers at St. Quentin-la-Poterie. Although Chiappe acknowledged that they were well respected and innocent of subversive activity, their former allegiance to the extreme left of the SFIO (Section française de l'international ouvrière) made them suspect.[156] The subprefect of Alès was particularly sensitive to the danger. In the summer of 1941, he investigated rumors that the city's high schools had become a breeding ground for Gaullist propaganda. Although the inquiries proved fruitless, Chassaigne insisted nevertheless that "a certain number of professors are notoriously and openly Gaullist."[157] A few months later he reported that

155. CA 566, commission de contrôle postal, April 1941. Letter from Jeannot Oules (Le Vigan), 25 April 1941.
156. CA 279, préfet to inspecteur d'académie, 18 March 1941.
157. CA 659, sous-préfet of Alès to préfet, 27 June 1941.

though the primary school teachers were showing no outward signs of resistance, they were far from converted to the politics of Vichy. He regretted that these teachers had not been replaced much earlier: "A total change would have yielded very happy results. But now it is a little too late."[158]

The resistance among the teachers was, by necessity, most often veiled and muted. A representative instance was the flag ceremony at the local secondary school of St. Gilles. The practice, according to a police inspector, left much to be desired. The ritual was "very ordinary," the teachers lacked "patriotic passion," and the local priest had not been invited. It was obvious, sighed the inspector, that "the noble personality of Marshal Pétain is not universally admired."[159] The school's headmaster also came in for a good deal of criticism from other residents of St. Gilles. One recounted that the headmaster kept mum while the *Marseillaise* was sung, but once the flag was raised, he turned with a mocking air to the students and announced: "Please observe that the rope has worked quite well!"[160]

Of course, not all *instituteurs* and professors had the courage of their cynicism. In fact, in the postwar purge of civil servants, several cases of straightforward collaboration among the teachers came to light. The director of one school in St. Hilaire de Brethmas, a village near Alès, was accused of forcing her students to attend church services (devotion to the church clearly interpreted as support for the regime), while a professor of English in Nîmes was held to be a "dedicated anti-Gaullist" who continued to work clandestinely against the provisional government. (The latter denied the charge, citing as evidence of his resistance credentials that he "often visited a colleague whose wife was Jewish and was hunted by the Gestapo" and that he "kept the luggage of some Jews in my home." This is an especially egregious example of Richard Cobb's observation that many collaborators sought to have a Jew in their pocket in case the winds of fortune turned.) A certain Marcel Déat, a lycée professor in Alès, was charged with acts of collaboration (accused, among other things, with membership in the Milice). One's name may well be one's destiny: the accused was a nephew of *the* Marcel Déat, the fascist politician, inexhaustible columnist and editor of the collaborationist newspaper *L'Oeuvre,* and founder of the Nazi-fronted Rassemblement national populaire. Unlike his young relative, the elder Déat had the foresight to flee to Italy following the fall of Vichy.[161]

158. CA 566, sous-préfet of Alès to préfet, rapport mensuel, 26 September 1941.
159. CA 566, commissaire de police, St. Gilles to préfet, 29 March 1941. In contrast, the official praised the ceremony at the Roman Catholic school, which "quivered with a sincere and ardent patriotism."
160. CA 566, commission de contrôle postal, March 1941. Letter from S. Vedel (Uzès), 23 March 1941.
161. CA 779, dossier sur les instituteurs, December 1944.

But those teachers who actively worked on behalf of the National Revolution were as exceptional as the sarcastic headmaster at St. Gilles. Whether or not the regime was to their taste, most teachers seemed to have conformed, at least outwardly, to the demands of Vichy. In this regard, M. Faure, a schoolteacher in Bessèges, was representative. One resident wrote that it was "funny to see M. Faure sing the national hymn when, just last year, he was belting out the *Internationale* with his students."[162] Nevertheless, the hypocrisy of such transformations, or the indifference shown by the very men and women assigned to implant the values of the New Order, served to tarnish Vichy's image and encourage greater openness to intellectual resistance.

The social category undoubtedly most hostile to the regime and most resistant to its propaganda was the working class. The burgeoning strike activity of the miners and industrial workers in the region around Alès, the demonstrations of the wives of workers throughout the department, the persistence of the organizing and propaganda efforts of the PCF, and the widespread scorn and indifference reserved for the regime's much-heralded Labor Charter all indicated that, by the fall of 1942, Vichy's attempt to rally the working class had failed miserably. The discontent felt by most workers did not, however, necessarily translate into active resistance. Very often it led to sheer apathy and resignation. Yet it also prodded, on occasion, workers into various forms of organized and unorganized resistance.

One indicator of worker resistance is found in the statistics of individuals arrested for "antinational activities" (*menées antinationales*). After mid-1942 the records grow confused, but the first two years do offer a clear balance sheet of the Gardois working class and their receptivity to the National Revolution. The social and economic breakdown of those arrested and charged with antinational activity shows that the overwhelming majority were urban and rural workers. For example, between September and December 1940, of the fifteen individuals arrested by the police, ten were workers (almost all either miners or SNCF [Société nationale des chemins de fer] workers); the others were clerks, a secretary, and an engineer. Through 1941, although the percentages do not change significantly, a growing number of farmworkers join the ranks of "antinationals." There is, moreover, an increase in the number of students and artisans caught in the dragnet. The roll call for September 1941 is typical: four agricultural workers, one winegrower, a butcher, a painter, a postal clerk, a judge on leave, a stonemason, a plasterer, a mechanic, a female worker (unspecified), a seamstress, three miners, a painter's assistant, and an apprentice electrician. Apart from the magistrate and

162. CA 566, commission de contrôle postal, 30 March 1941.

winegrower, all of those arrested belonged to either the working class or petite bourgeoisie.[163] Vichy, in sum, had clearly lost the affection of the working class long before the event that is often cited—and will be discussed in Chapter 7—as the single greatest cause of worker disaffection, the creation of the forced labor draft, or Service du travail obligatoire (STO), in early 1943.

The food demonstrations, miners' strikes, Bastille Day demonstrations, and the growth of Communist and Gaullist propaganda were symptoms of a serious hemorrhaging of the public's adhesion to the Vichy regime. A majority of Gardois were still no more attracted to the cause of the Resistance than they were to that of collaboration. Yet, the blossoming of increasingly indiscreet acts of discrete resistance, from pinning a cockade to one's lapel and listening to a BBC broadcast to mockery and grumbling, informed local officials that they had lost the battle for the hearts and minds of the populace. No less important, it also served as a sign that the region's tradition of disrespect for and resistance to authority was alive and well. The German invasion of the unoccupied zone in November 1942 and the events that followed were thus, in an important sense, anticlimactic: despite the drama and hardship of the next two years, they merely accentuated those tendencies that had come into being by the fall of that year.

163. CA 569, état numérique des arrestations opérées et des affaires judiciares traités par le commissariat spécial de Nîmes, November 1942.

7
WAITING FOR LIBERATION

I admit that I'm ashamed to be French. The poor Marshal! . . . He wanted to rebuild a healthy France, but alas, society is still too rotten, and his beautiful edifice is collapsing. Now there is nothing left. Nothing, nothing at all!
—resident of Le Grau-du-roi, 1942

I still cannot take myself seriously. In this line of police work, I still have the impression of playing at Cowboys and Indians, and when I "scalp" someone, I'm much more bothered over it than he is.
—police agent of Nîmes, 1944

All that I have left are a few barbers.
—STO official, 1942

On 8 November 1942 the Allies landed in North Africa. Three days later, to protect its Mediterranean flank, the German army occupied southern France. This act threw a glaring light on the chiaroscuro of reality to Vichy sovereignty. Bereft of its fleet (scuttled at its base in Toulon), its North African possessions (now under the control of the Allies) and the leverage provided by a threat to join the Allies (undermined by Pétain's refusal to leave Vichy after the German invasion), the France of Laval and Pétain, which henceforth sought to confirm a fictitious independence by exceeding the demands made by the occupier, came under the near total control of Germany.

Shorn of the few assets it claimed during the first two years of its existence, Vichy's claims of legitimacy foundered under the stubborn assault of Charles de

Gaulle. Though he had been deliberately snubbed by the Allies in the planning of the North African invasion, de Gaulle was nevertheless well on the way in establishing the Free French as the legitimate representative of the French people. In Algiers, the effort made by Roosevelt and Churchill to promote General Henri Giraud as an alternative to the imperious and irritating de Gaulle failed: though Giraud showed great courage and skill in escaping from a POW camp, he proved no match for the Lorrainer's brilliant inside maneuvering. Equally important, de Gaulle had also now claimed the leadership of a unified resistance movement within France. His representative Jean Moulin, who had been parachuted into France in January 1942, worked tirelessly for both unification and acknowledgment of London's leadership. The creation of the Mouvements unis de la Résistance (MUR) a year later (January 1943), would crown Moulin's efforts.

Did the invasion and its immediate consequences, though, mark a watershed at the level of local affairs and attitudes? The answer is a qualified no. Public opinion was undeniably galvanized by the arrival of German troops in the Gard; for two years, despite their everyday cares and problems, the Gardois had been spared the even greater material sacrifices and moral issues imposed by the physical presence of an occupying army. The mere presence and increasingly brutal activities of the German Army, the Waffen SS, and the Gestapo forced the Gardois to face the reality of occupation and repression. As one resident of Uzès affirmed, "Don't think that I deplore this invasion, for I believe it was necessary. The Midi had to make the acquaintance of our collaborators so as to [better] appreciate the collaboration."[1]

But the German invasion did not radically transform the political and psychological landscape of the Gard. The various trends whose common source is often placed with the events of 11 November 1942, in fact predate the arrival of the Germans. As we have suggested, public disenchantment and the birth and growth of acts of resistance became manifest well before this date. Administrative incompetence, religious sectarianism, growing brutality, and fatuous ideological posturing by the local authorities had already discredited the National Revolution in the eyes of most Gardois. The German occupation, the launching of the STO and the concomitant birth and growth of the *maquis* (the name given to the resistance groups that formed in the brushland, or *maquis,* of the Midi) largely confirmed and reinforced these tendencies.

It would be simplistic, however, to force these tendencies into the categories of resistance and collaboration. Undeniably, the size of the Resistance and public sympathy for its aims did grow between 1940 and 1942. Similarly, public distaste

1. C 361, commission de contrôle postal, March 1943. Letter from J. Pelanque (Uzès), 8 March 1943.

for the very idea of collaboration, coupled with increasingly bold resistance activity, gradually reduced the collaborationist groups to a hardcore of ideological zealots and mercenaries. But these trends were neither immediate nor obvious. Though the prospect of collaboration quickly lost what little attraction it still held, support for the organized resistance did not automatically take its place. Instead, the attitude of a solid majority of the Gardois remained *attentiste*. In fact, it is, arguably, this tendency of wait-and-see that the events of November 1942 most immediately and forcefully encouraged. Pierre Laborie's assertion that, even if public opinion "was henceforth freed from its sentimental ties to Pétain and becomes politically detached from the regime and options of the Laval government, it nonetheless was not prepared to join the current of the Resistance," applies, with qualification, to the Gard.[2] By 1944, most Gardois still were not prepared to actively resist. However, a good number had come to actively *sympathize* with the Resistance, thus providing it with an immeasurably important base for their operations.

The blow to Vichy's image in the Gard delivered by the German occupation was immediately preceded by the equally jarring shock of the 11 November demonstrations. In a BBC broadcast on 10 November, Charles de Gaulle had called upon the French to publicly celebrate Armistice Day in order to protest against Vichy's policy of collaboration. Yet even before this appeal, the local authorities had anticipated that the date would provide an excellent rallying point for the Resistance and forbade all public demonstrations. An announcement carried in all the local papers declared that any attempt to demonstrate "would be immediately repressed" and that the "government counts on the patriotism of all concerned to see that this day passes calmly and with dignity."[3]

Despite the warnings, the day in Nîmes was tempestuous. The first storm warnings appeared at noon when a crowd of 100 to 150 formed around the *monument aux morts* with the intention of laying a spray of flowers. The site was guarded by a large number of gardes mobiles (*gardes mobiles de réserve*, or GMR), commanded by the prefect himself. There was a series of confrontations and scuffles between the police and demonstrators in front of the monument, which reached a climax when two bouquets of flowers were thrown over the fence and onto the crypt. One demonstrator was arrested when, while pitching his bouquet, a revolver fell out of his pocket. The crowd, which by then had grown to three hundred, most of whom were young men, women, and students, regrouped in front of the nearby courthouse and marched up the Boulevard

2. Laborie, *Résistants, Vichyssois et autres,* 247.
3. CA 563, 9 November 1942.

Victor Hugo, singing the *Marseillaise* (highlighted by calls to "Lynch Laval") and finally dispersed along the narrow streets leading off the boulevard.[4]

This represented but a rehearsal for events later the same day. At six-thirty that evening, a crowd—estimated by Chiappe to be six to eight hundred, and by René Rascalon, the head of the departmental *Armée secrète,* as "several thousand"—again formed at the war memorial.[5] The memorial, whose symbolic stake had grown for both sides, was again guarded by a large contingent of police led by Chiappe. In addition, there was now a SOL (Service d'ordre légionnaire) contingent. Under the covering fire of waterhoses, the miliciens attempted to drive back the demonstrators by butting against them with their bicycles, but sorely outnumbered, they were soon overwhelmed by the crowd. Chiappe, for whom discretion became the better part of valor, dove into his car and fled the scene, leaving in his wake a demoralized and fragmenting police force. One policeman later acknowledged that he and his colleagues received "a good thrashing," complaining that the "bastards [that is, demonstrators] didn't let us off easily" and that more than two hours passed before the arrival of reinforcements.[6] The crowd, temporarily masters of the street, marched across the city towards the Jardin de la Fontaine, singing the *Marseillaise* and *Chant du Départ.* Between choruses, the crowd bellowed chants to free the political prisoners, as well as that old chestnut, "Laval au poteau!" It was not until eight that evening that a greatly reinforced SOL succeeded in clearing the boulevards and arrested some thirty men and women.

The gauge of the demonstration's success was not only the size of the crowd and its tenacity in front of the SOL. There was also the reluctance on the part of the police to intervene, manifesting a possible form of complicity and, perhaps, sympathy with the demonstrators. Jean Dire, the chief of the SOL, described the bitterness his men felt for the diffident behavior of the "great majority" of the city police during the demonstration, particularly by the inspectors and agents of the Sûreté nationale. He complained that rather than breaking up the crowds, the police "protected and channeled," and at certain points even assisted them.[7] Chiappe echoed this criticism, faulting the commanding personnel who "acted sluggishly and seemed to prefer channeling the demonstrators rather than dispersing

4. The day's activities are based on the accounts of Chiappe, in his report to Vichy (CA 563, préfet to interior, 12 November 1942), and Vielzeuf, *En Cévennes et Languedoc au temps des longues nuits,* 50–60. The two accounts fundamentally agree, though Chiappe tended to omit sensitive facts—for example, the calls to hang Laval—and dramatize his role in suppressing the demonstrations.

5. Rascalon's account is contained in Vielzeuf, *En Cévennes et Languedoc,* 55–60.

6. CA 641, commission de contrôle postal, November 1942. Letter from Noel Guerillot, 13 November 1942.

7. CA 760, Dire to préfet, 12 November 1942.

them."[8] Whether or not there was active police complicity, the fact that they played a secondary and relatively modest role during the demonstration points to a disinclination to intervene—an unhappy detail for the local administration and its active collaborators.

Following the Armistice Day demonstrations, one local resident complained that "all the Gaullists and Jews can be proud of what they've accomplished. *Ah, le pauvre maréchal, la pauvre France.* Now that there are German soldiers, [the demonstrators] are making less noise."[9] Few other Gardois found a causal link between the demonstrations and the German occupation, but the latter event did eclipse the former in the eyes of the populace. The excitement sparked by the Allied invasion of North Africa and the events of 11 November was rapidly dampened by the arrival of German soldiers. According to one postal commission report, the "succession of reversals reveals the profound disarray of public opinion, tossed between hope and pessimism." Disoriented by the chain of events, the Gardois again looked to Pétain as the "one fixed point" on which they could pin their hopes.[10] As one Nîmois affirmed, "I do not pretend to be for either the Germans, the Americans or the English: I am French and wish to follow the marshal."[11] In terms of political acumen, this remark leaves much to be desired; but it was representative of the confused and anxious frame of mind among the locals.

The Gard, along with the other departments of lower Languedoc, was occupied by elements of the Fourth Army Air Corps under the command of General Petersen. The Fourth Army Corps in turn belonged to the Nineteenth Army under the control of General Wiese, who established his headquarters in Villeneuve-les-Avignon, a Gardois town built on the western bank of the Rhône. These forces were supplemented in February 1944 by the armored Ninth SS Panzer Division of SS General W. Bittrich, which set up headquarters both in Nîmes and in the strategic Cévenol outpost of St. Jean-du-Gard. Apart from Nîmes, Alès, Le Vigan, and a handful of other principal towns in the center and north of the department that were continuously occupied, the German occupation forces, their eyes turned toward the Mediterranean, tended to concentrate along the Gard's coastal plain. The great majority of towns in this sector were to play host, at one time or another, to rotating companies of German troops.[12]

8. CA 760, préfet to Interior (n.d., most probably 12 or 13 November 1942).

9. CA 646, synthèse de commission de contrôle postal, 5–19 November 1942.

10. G 354, commission de contrôle postal, rapport mensuel, November 1942.

11. CA 641, commission de contrôle postal, November, 1942. Letter from X (Nîmes), 15 November 1942.

12. Bourderon, *Libération du Languedoc Méditerranéen*, 17–18.

The German soldiers in the Gard were under the immediate control of the German departmental commander, who communicated with the prefecture through a liaison service. It was through this service that the commanding officer transmitted his demands concerning local manpower, police, and security activities. Relations between Chiappe and the various German departmental commanders appear to have been very amicable. For example, General Bottcher, first in a series of German commanders, was presented by Chiappe with a history book on Nîmes. In a note of thanks, Bottcher wrote that his "interest in the charms and beauty of the city were increased by the book, which will always be a beautiful and enduring souvenir of the time I spent in Nîmes."[13] In the early fall of 1943 the prefect received a letter of farewell from Bottcher's replacement, General Kohlermann, who was being transferred to another command. The German officer apologized for not having the time to personally say good-bye, and wrote that "I must tell you of my gratitude for the friendly welcome you gave to me and my troops."[14]

After the initial shock, the arrival of the German troops led to an array of reactions. A number of Gardois welcomed the presence of the Wehrmacht. Certain conservatives thought that the Germans would reestablish order and serve as a bulwark against communism. A notary praised their arrival as the lesser of two evils, the greater one being the possibility that the French otherwise "would now be tearing one another apart."[15] For some vague reason, a Nîmois thought the occupation would lead to the liberation of the French POWs, while another hoped that the Germans would at least guarantee a steady and adequate food supply.[16] Many others noted the "correctness" of the troops, relieved to discover, in the words of one sarcastic correspondent, that the "Fritz are not the ogres everyone thought."[17]

There were even instances of spontaneous collaboration between the Gardois and German troops. In the small port town of Le Grau-du-Roi, a fire that broke out in a building next to a munitions depot and hotel lodging the German garrison was extinguished by an impromptu Franco-German fire brigade. The grateful commander of the German garrison supported the town's request for the

---

13. CA 367, General Bottcher to Chiappe, 19 January 1943. On 1 December 1942, there were 1,560 German soldiers stationed in Alès, 2,158 in Nîmes, and slightly more than 6,000 in twenty-nine other communes in the department.

14. CA 367, General Kohlermann to Chiappe, 23 September 1943.

15. G 354, commission de contrôle postal, December 1942. Letter from D. Armand (Vauvert), 9 December 1942.

16. G 354, commission de contrôle postal, December 1942. Letters from E. Dhombres (Nîmes), 17 December 1942; and X (Nîmes), 10 December 1942.

17. G 354, commission de contrôle postal, November 1942. Letter from Mlle Armanini (Nîmes), 25 November 1942.

liberation of some local residents who were POWs.[18] Short of such notable and perhaps self-interested actions, relations between the Gardois and the Germans remained relatively relaxed during the first few months of the occupation. Every Sunday during the spring of 1943, for example, the Roman arena hosted not just the traditional bullfights, but the less customary mingling of German officers and soldiers with local residents. According to one police report, the behavior of both groups was exemplary.[19] In general, during this period the attitude of the populace seems to have remained what it had been in the immediate wake of the occupation — "calm and dignified."[20]

Yet there was a complex variety of reasons for "welcoming" the Germans. One Lorrainer admitted to wearing a "small smile" since the invasion, for now the Gardois "will see that the Lorrainers do not lie"—a sentiment that was probably widespread in the Alsatian and Lorrainer refugee communities.[21] However, discontent and resistance went beyond the refugee community: a good number of native Gardois were no less unhappy with the sudden turn of events. One Nîmois pledged that he would never forget those French "who are warmly welcoming" the Germans.[22] Another native affirmed that there were locals "stupid enough to gossip and have friendly chats" with the Germans, the very men who "probably will be shooting at us if the Americans land. It isn't worth our while to smile at them."[23] Others, such as Paul Brandt, agreed that the troops were "very polite," but wished nevertheless that he could "send them to the devil."[24] In fact, the German commandant in Nîmes complained of the public's attitude which, he warned, "sometimes verged on improper behavior." When he walked through town, certain individuals "did not show him the necessary courtesy, and forced him off the sidewalk."[25]

But perhaps the most widespread reaction was that of shame. As one resident of Le Grau-du-Roi, who was clearly a committed follower of Pétain, sighed: "I admit that I'm ashamed to be French. The poor marshal! . . . He wanted to rebuild a healthy France, but alas, society is still too rotten, and his beautiful

18. CA 777, commissaire principal to préfet, 5 December 1942.
19. CA 777, commissaire principal to préfet, 1 May 1943.
20. CA 777, commissaire principal to préfet, 5 December 1942.
21. G 354, commission de contrôle postal, December 1942. Letter from René Bigarel (Bagnols), 10 December 1942.
22. CA 641, commission de contrôle postal, November 1942. Letter from X (Nîmes), 17 November 1942.
23. CA 641, commission de contrôle postal, November 1942. Letter from Mme Pierre Dufay (Milhaud), 18 November 1942.
24. G 354, commission de contrôle postal, November 1942. Letter from Paul Brandt (Nîmes), 30 November 1942.
25. CA 367, préfet to mayor of Nîmes, 25 January 1943.

edifice is collapsing. Now there is nothing left. Nothing, nothing at all!"[26] But the local collaborationists would have begged to differ with this legionnaire's cry of despair. In fact, this period witnesses the final divorce between the Legion and the organization torn from its own flesh, the SOL. The prominent role played by Dire's men during the 11 November demonstrations revivified the organization, encouraging it "to push on with their activities."[27] By February of the following year, it was observed that the SOL, which had just metamorphosized into the Milice, still showed a good deal more energy than the Legion, producing fears that the two movements, fishing in the same waters, might become mutually antagonistic.[28]

This fear never materialized because by 1943 the Legion could scarcely keep itself together, much less keep up with the Milice. Reports and letters throughout 1943 attest to an irremediable decline in the organization's fortunes and popularity. In late 1942 Varin d'Aineville was replaced by a veteran of the 1940 campaign, Jean Sizaire. Younger and more energetic than his predecessor, Sizaire did his best to bolster the morale of his faltering troops, delivering numerous speeches as he crisscrossed the department. In a typical address, given to an assembly of communal leaders, Sizaire declared that "at a time in which incomprehension and apathy reign, you see united here that which is rare: courageous men." These men "having proved their military courage on the fields of battle, now show proof of a courage perhaps even more difficult—namely, civil courage."[29]

Yet this was bombast in the service of a lost cause. The occupation quickened the pace of disenchantment in the mission and raison d'être of the Legion. By January 1943 the subprefect of Le Vigan reported that though the 1914–18 veterans felt no sympathy for Great Britain, they betrayed a "reserved enmity" for Germany and a sharp preference for the United States. As for the veterans of 1940, they were described as "moderately Gaullist" and deeply hostile to Germany.[30] Alive to the collaborationism of the Laval–Pétain regime, yet having sworn their fidelity to an individual who, according to one's perspective, was either bypassed by events or betrayed by his subordinates, the more clear-sighted legionnaires thus found themselves caught on the horns of a political dilemma.

The horns were sharpened by the fact that the Legion was increasingly

26. G 354, Letter from X (Le Grau-du-Roi), 30 November 1942.

27. C 354, commission de contrôle postal, rapport mensuel, November 1942.

28. G 361, commission de contrôle postal, rapport mensuel, February 1943.

29. CA 1480, Sizaire to assemblée trimestrielle des chefs communaux du Gard, 10 May 1943. Reprinted in June 1943 issue of (the appropriately titled) Courage, the monthly journal of the Légion française des Combattants du Gard.

30. CA 777, sous-préfet du Vigan to préfet, rapport mensuel, 30 January 1943.

considered a collaborationist organization. One veteran remarked sadly that his own family was riven by this belief, noting that his own nephews were scornful of his membership. "They say that the Legion is completely for the Germans, an opinion they share with all young Frenchmen. In Nîmes, I only see a few legionnaires wearing their pins, and they are all old veterans of 1914–18. The young will not march."[31] The Legion, confronted by growing public disdain as well as threats from the Resistance, attempted to parry accusations of collaborationism. For example, in the daily *Le Petit Méridonial*, the departmental chapter took out an advertisement that declared that it had "nothing in common with either the French Milice or the Légion des volontaires français contre le bolchevisme (LVF), organizations that are placed under the authority of the head of the government [Laval, not Pétain, who was head of state] and whose status, recruitment, and methods of action and leaders are totally different from ours."[32] This poignant and pathetic appeal (given the pride and hubris of the movement two years before) had little effect. Two days after the notice was printed, a bomb explosion ripped through the Legion's headquarters in Nîmes, taking the life of one member.[33] Clearly, in the eyes of the Resistance, along with the general public, the advertisement had made a distinction without a difference.

For many legionnaires, the dilemma was resolved by a shrug of the shoulders and the retirement of one's uniform and pins to the closet. The celebrations for the Legion's third anniversary were funereal. Less than a thousand members turned out for the parade in Nîmes, and a journalist with *L'Eclair,* in a phone conversation with his wife, flatly described it as a "disaster."[34] This judgment was echoed by the police superintendent, who remarked that the crowd showed a "certain indifference and, at times, even hostility."[35] A police report confirmed that the Legion was entering a "grave crisis," despite its recent attempt to tack between the "ultra-collaborationists" and "Gaullists" and adhere to an "essentially French position."[36] The most generous description of this last position, urging the French to "Think French and nothing but French," is that of keeping one's eyes firmly shut. Hence, it is hardly surprising that, in a period rife with pitfalls

31. G 363, commission de contrôle postal, May 1943. Telephone conversation of M. Cepelier (Nîmes), 14 May 1943.

32. CA 662, clipped article titled "Do Not Confound," printed in *Le Petit Méridonial* (13 November 1943).

33. CA 662, commissaire principal to préfet, 16 November 1943.

34. G 364, commission de contrôle postal, August 1943. Telephone conversation between M. Soulier and Mme Soulier, 29 August 1943.

35. CA 777, commissaire principal to préfet, 4 September 1943.

36. CA 279, "note" on Legion activity, 6 September 1943.

whose negotiation demanded at least one open eye, the casualty rate was so high. As the same report observed, the Legion's activity was minimal and only its "social actions"—for example, soup-kitchens and aid for the French POWs and their families—continued to attract public interest.

An especially telling sign of the Legion's growing irrelevance was the organization's inability to fill communal leadership posts. Both the increasing number of resignations and the stubborn lack of candidates to replace them had a common source: fear of public disdain and, perhaps, useless martyrdom at the hands of the Resistance. The recruitment problems faced by the Legion were underscored in an account filed by a departmental official, Paul Brun. In his effort to find someone to appoint a president for the local legionnaire section in the town of Molières, Brun ran up against a chain of polite, but firm refusals. A certain M. Tuech declined for "reasons of health" which, according to Brun, were undoubtedly complicated by the fact that one brother had been arrested by the Gestapo for black-marketeering while a second had gone over to the Resistance. The next candidate, M. Pellet, described himself as "honored" by the offer, but unhappily could not accept. As he confided to Brun, a recent car accident had left him with a limp, making it impossible for him to "march in any kind of procession"—a phrase that reveals much about the increasingly symbolic role of the Legion. Stymied by these refusals, Brun sought the advice of the local sages, who suggested that he offer the position to M. Taulelle, a respected cabinetmaker. Yet M. Taulelle showed himself to be no less adroit in waxing on his inadequacy for such a post. Pleading extenuating circumstances and insisting upon the undoubted existence of worthier candidates, Taulelle gently showed Brun out the door of his workshop. The latter left town with empty hands and the distant hope that Taulelle's modesty could be overcome by neighboring Legion chiefs.[37]

If the Legion now inspired general indifference, the Milice drew increasing animosity from the public. In a letter written by a milicien to a comrade on the latter's promotion to Vichy, the former expressed his hope that the "closer contact with Darnand will instill the Milice's true principles, precise thinking, and intelligence." Yet the typist, in transcribing the missive, typed *inculper* (to charge with) rather than *inculquer* (to inculcate)—a Freudian slip that speaks long on the public's attitude toward the collaborationist organization.[38] According

---

37. CA 1480, rapport de l'inspecteur départemental to chef départemental du Légion, 31 December 1943.

38. C 364, commission de contrôle postal, August 1943. Letter from R. Potie (Nîmes), 21 August 1943.

to a police report, the creation of the Milice on 30 January 1943 was welcomed
only by the partisans of collaboration. The majority of the population "remained
skeptical and refrained from commenting upon it."[39] This silence was short-
lived. By the fall of 1943, the Milice had become the butt of explicit hostility
on the part of the public. At a talk given in mid-October in Nîmes by the
ineffable Dr. Grimm and Philippe Henriot, the zealous voice of the regime,
the Milice's presence was a topic of much commentary, all of which was negative.
It was reported that the miliciens' "method of marching" (a parody of the
already ludicrous goose-step) provoked "sharp criticism and ironic comments."
The result, noted the official, was that "hatred for the Milice has grown even
deeper."[40]

The Milice's isolation understandably demoralized many of its members.
Following the Allied invasion of Italy in July 1943, it was observed that while a
handful of Nîmois miliciens remained steadfast, many others were "disappointed
by the lack of directives and seem fearful of the future. The hostility against the
Milice grows at the same pace as does the approach of Allied soldiers to French
soil."[41] Alesians were no kinder than the Nîmois toward their local miliciens.
It was joked that the recruits were so young that they bent under the weight of
their guns, and so inexperienced that they wouldn't know which way to point
them. Rather than inspiring fear, the patrols only "provoke smiles of scorn and
pity."[42] The antagonism did not always remain at the level of sharp jibes and
cold glares; with increasing frequency it was translated into acts of violence. In
August 1943, for example, the Milice headquarters in Nîmes, located on Rue
Emile Jamais, was damaged by a bomb explosion.[43] A month later, a bomb was
thrown through the office window of M. Jourdan, a wine merchant and head of
the Bagnols section of the Milice.[44] These and numerous other acts of the
Resistance had a sobering impact upon members of the Milice. During the final
months of 1943 there was a steady stream of resignations from the Milice, while
many other members simply stowed away their uniforms and kept their heads
low.[45]

In fact, a few days after the bombing in Bagnols, an important changing of the
guard took place in the organization. Described as having been "hit very hard"

39. CA 777, commissaire principal to préfet, 6 February 1943. The inauguration of the Milice on
the anniversary of Hitler's taking of power in 1933 seems to have been coincidental.
40. CA 777, 23 October 1943.
41. CA 777, 7 August 1943.
42. CA 572, commissaire de renseignements généraux of Alès to préfet, 24 June 1944.
43. CA 777, commissaire principal to préfet, 14 August 1943.
44. CA 777, 18 September 1943.
45. CA 793, commissaire principal to préfet, 24 December 1943.

by the widespread hostility, Dire handed in his resignation and was replaced by M. Roumegous, a twenty-six-year-old notary from Anduze.[46] (The promotion pleased Mme Roumegous. In a letter to a friend, she admitted that she now worried a good deal more, but was proud of her husband and the role he was playing with those Frenchmen "who desire to safeguard order in France . . . the state prosecutors, judges, priests, miliciens, royalists.")[47] Yet Dire's example was not universally followed. Though there are no precise statistics for the number of miliciens in the Gard during the last year of Vichy's existence, one local historian places the figure at roughly 350.[48] A second indicator is the number of members who turned out for the funeral procession of Georges Masse, a colleague assassinated by resisters in April 1944. Along with members of other collaborationist movements, approximately one hundred and fifty miliciens joined the funeral cortege.[49] Surprisingly, comments made by various miliciens point to continued recruitment through the early months of 1944—a period during which most sensible men would have been edging toward the other camp. One local milicien observed that "We're still signing on blokes. There's been a real procession."[50] At roughly the same time, the local chief of Roquemaure confirmed the Milice's qualified success in attracting new members: "We've done some recruiting, and it seems to be coming along."[51]

Why did these men either join so late in the day or remain in the ranks of the Milice until the bitter end? For some, undoubtedly, the Milice offered one of the few options left to avoid the STO (Service du travail obligatoire) and legally remain in France. One young Nîmois thus advised a friend to sign up with the Milice since "rumor has it that they will not be affected by the call-up [for the STO]."[52] It also offered the certainty of a couple of square meals a day, since the Germans supplied the miliciens with special food tickets. For yet others, it represented a source of action and excitement, and perhaps an escape from the

46. CA 777, commissaire principal to préfet, 25 September 1943.

47. G 358, commission de contrôle postal, December, 1943. Letter sent 25 December 1943.

48. Cosson, *Nîmes et le Gard dans la guerre 1939–1945*, 87. For a comparison with other departments, see table of the Milice Française Membership (which omits that of the Gard) in Bertram Gordon, *Collaboration in France during the Second World War*, appendix A, 355–56. It should be noted that my figures correspond with those provided by John Sweets, who suggests that Gordon's global figure of 150,000 to 200,000 collaborators may be "much too high," see Sweets, *Choices in Vichy France*, 82–98.

49. CA 572, commissaire principal to préfet, 22 April 1944.

50. G 358, commission de contrôle postal, February 1944. Letter from Charles Piez, 15 February 1944.

51. G 358, commission de contrôle postal, February 1944. Telephone conversation between Roquemaure section chief and Nîmes headquarters, 15 February 1944.

52. G 361, commission de contrôle postal, February 1943. Letter from Alfred Verdelhan (Nîmes), 28 February 1943.

ennui of rural life. In this regard, it is significant that in early 1944 the Nîmois section of the Milice observed that the majority of its *franc-gardes* were farmers.[53]

Yet another important motivation seems to have been loosely ideological. As we have already seen with the testimony of Mme Roumegous, a number of miliciens saw themselves as the final guarantors of social order. They alone barred the way, in Mme Roumegous's evocative description, to those "young imbeciles who follow dangerous leaders and an entire army that lives solely on crimes and plunder in order to eat and clothe itself, and take themselves for patriots because they kill [other] Frenchmen." The belief that they were a bulwark against communism surfaces in the letters of miliciens as well. By dint of "rubbing shoulders with the bourgeois of Nîmes, who are filled with Communist principles [sic]," wrote one member, "I now find myself squarely in the opposite camp."[54] A second admitted to having had several disappointments since he began the "struggle for national ideas," but was committed to carry on the good fight: "I believe that there isn't a second to lose if we hope to strangle communism and save the country."[55] The opening of the Milice's ranks to women also managed to attract a certain number of young recruits. One aspiring milicienne wrote enthusiastically about a "splendid" meeting she had attended and affirmed that she "was not afraid to be 'caput' should the Americans land." In any case, she concluded, the miliciens "are not leaving for Germany, but are staying as police in France."[56]

Ideological conviction, combined with a good dollop of self-interest, was not the monopoly of the Milice. A handful of other collaborationist organizations in the Gard also continued their activity through the final days of Vichy. It was a level of activity, however, akin to the spasms of a rabid, dying animal. Among the various formations, perhaps the most important was the Groupe Collaboration. The group was at the heart of most collaborationist functions, from guest lectures (Dr. Grimm was a great favorite) and film showings to active cooperation with the German police. In the late winter of 1944 its membership was still estimated to be two hundred, three quarters of which came from Nîmes alone. With the exceptions of the PPF (Parti populaire française) the Tradition française (a royalist organization), and Action française (and there may well have been significant overlapping in the memberships of the two last groups), each of

53. C 358, commission de contrôle postal, February 1942. Telephone conversation between X and the Milice headquarters in Nîmes, 17 February 1944.

54. G 361, commission de contrôle postal, March 1943. Letter from L. Bernadou (Nîmes), 1 March 1943.

55. G 361, February 1943. Letter from Alfred Verdelhan (Nîmes), 28 February 1943.

56. G 361, March 1943. Letter from Josette (Nîmes), 12 March 1943. Given the gender of "milicien," it appears as if Josette was trying to convince a close male relative or boyfriend to sign up and so remain in Nîmes.

which were thought to have one hundred members, no other collaborationist group could boast more than a relative handful of followers. If one were to combine the membership rolls of these various movements, and then add the approximate number of miliciens, the total number of active collaborators in the Gard, at the most liberal estimate, did not exceed 850 men and women.[57]

Apart from the ideological collaborationism of these political movements, there is the issue of police and administrative collaboration. We have already noted the existence, on the one hand, of a certain reluctance on the part of the police to actively repress the Armistice Day demonstrations. On the other hand, the local police had carried out the notorious roundup of Jews just a few months before, and the gendarmerie had even been accused of brutality by at least one witness. The ambivalence felt by the police in regard to their role deepened after the arrival of the German occupation forces. Clearly, once they were working alongside or under their German counterparts, once the belief could no longer be plausibly maintained that they were safeguarding the existence of a sovereign France, once the calls for repression became more frequent and more severe, and once the organized and unorganized resistance began to make life as a state functionary uncomfortable and possibly fatal, local officials had second thoughts about the viability of their work.[58]

Though it is risky to leap from limited evidence to broad generalizations, the few extant letters written by members of the gardes mobiles, gendarmerie, and police, combined with a scattering of general reports on their morale, suggest that there was a good deal of soul-searching and irresolution throughout the ranks. A certain A. Anglade, a member of the gardes mobiles stationed in Uzès, may have been representative. Barely two weeks after the German occupation of the Gard, Anglade wrote a pessimistic letter to his wife, in which he confessed that he could not say what the future would bring, but if the present state of affairs continued, it would be "very bad." He criticized the "overly severe measures" taken by the Germans, and confided that "it won't be a minute too soon when this all comes to an end."[59] In a second letter written a few days later,

57. These statistics are based upon a police survey of political groupings in the Gard (CA 572 commissaire principal to préfet, 3 February 1944). Once again, it is important to recall that there undoubtedly was some overlapping between the various groups; moreover, the membership roles did not reflect the actual degree of participation of those listed. In this context, it is revealing that the activity of most of the groups was described as "nul" or "peu important."

58. See John Sweets, "La police et la population dans la France de Vichy: Une Etude de cas conformé et fidèle," *Guerres mondiales et conflits contemporains* (July 1989), 63–74, for a comparative examination.

59. G 354, commission de contrôle postal, November 1942. Letter from A. Anglade, 27 November 1942.

Anglade was no cheerier. He had been raked over the coals by his commanding officer for lax work, but what could he do? He just "didn't enjoy bothering people and throwing the book at them when they haven't done anything."[60]

The letters of colleagues attest to similar feelings of irritation and occasional despair. A fellow member of the gardes mobiles, having described the endless shifts of duty across the Gard, reported that his unit's morale had fallen to the point that "we now wish the Army's fate [that is, dissolution] would befall us!!!"[61] Following the bombing of a German truck parked near the Jardin de la Fontaine, a policeman complained that he and his colleagues now had to "walk hand in hand" with the Germans. "You'd laugh if you could see us," he told his friend: "We've got to frisk the men every which way, and we won't even speak about the women. . . . What a joke!! Thanks to the commies, we no longer sleep at night."[62] Sleepless nights also became the lot of the families of the policemen. It is difficult to conceive the constant fear and anxiety of the wives and children, especially as the Resistance became increasingly bold and experienced. In the winter of 1944, the daughter of a gendarme in Lasalle wrote that her family was "living in terror." Her father resigned the day after the rumor had spread that police headquarters "was to be blown up because Papa had locked up a terrorist. No use describing the night we passed; Mama is still ill."[63]

Yet not everyone found the job of law enforcement as nightmarish as the Lasallian gendarme. In a letter written in early 1944, and which deserves to be quoted at length, a police official in Nîmes glibly acknowledged that he was a convinced *attentiste* — a "petty bureaucrat completely won over to an easy wait-and-see attitude." He argued that "self-interest is the motivation of the vast majority of human actions" while patriotism was "an ingenious invention that people never defend to their death." As a result, he had "taken the position of having no position at all and living a life of mild skepticism." As for his everyday duties, the anonymous official showed himself to be no less cynical: he was on duty as he was writing this letter, waiting to relieve a colleague who was hidden at the train station in a rail car, spying on some unexplained activity. Somewhat

60. G 354, commission de contrôle postal, December 1942. Letter from A. Anglade (Uzès), 2 December 1942.

61. G 354, commission de contrôle postal, November 1942. Letter from H. P. (Nîmes) 28 November 1942.

62. G 354, commission de contrôle postal, December 1942. Letter from R. Blanc (Nîmes) 10 December 1942.

63. G 358, commission de contrôle postal, February 1944. Letter from Mlle Merel (Lasalle), 13 February 1944. If the gendarme did resign, he was luckier than some of his colleagues. In May, the commandant of the Lasalle gendarmerie was assassinated by the Resistance, an act that apparently was condemned by the town's population (CA 572, sous-préfet of Le Vigan to préfet, rapport mensuel, 24 May 1944).

blasé, he admitted that such assignments "relieve the boredom a bit," but that "I still cannot take myself seriously. In this line of police work, I still have the impression of playing at Cowboys and Indians, and when I 'scalp' someone, I'm much more bothered over it than he is."[64]

It is impossible to say how many others shared the Tartuffian cynicism and jaded honesty of our mysterious gendarme. Yet it does seem that by the final year of the war, the majority of gendarmes and police, caught in the middle between the Resistance and the German occupation authorities, were doing their best to simply survive. The balancing act spent great emotional reserves; the police, said one official, were "literally exhausted by the constant tact they had to show to the occupation authorities." He reported that "the police and municipal bureaucrats often must overcome serious obstacles in order to avoid compromising themselves. Although the agents execute their duties conscientiously, they look forward to their liberation from material cares and the enslavement of their consciences."[65]

"Execute one's duties conscientiously": a phrase bathed in ambiguity. Did it mean that the police arrested only those Jews who, figuratively speaking, turned up on their front doorstep? Or that the police actively collaborated in the Nazi hunt for those Jews who had gone into hiding? Given the paucity of documentation, it is impossible to say. Two observations are, however, essential. First, we must not forget that, though the lot of the police was difficult and grueling, it was a profession that was often called upon to accomplish morally indefensible actions. The repression of the Resistance, the roundup of Jews, the harassment and surveillance of those critical of the regime—such labor was dishonest and unworthy of our sympathy. *Tout comprendre, c'est tout pardonner* is a pitfall the historian must avoid.

Yet we have seen numerous instances where the gendarmerie, in particular, carried out their duties in desultory, sullen, and resistant ways. This tendency became even more marked during the closing months of the war, when there appeared numerous reports and sporadic letters critical of the laxity shown by the forces of order, taxed for their impotence or unwillingness to break the reign of terror.[66] In early 1944, for example, the prefect complained about the "absolute incompetence" shown by a brigade of gardes mobiles stationed in Pont St.-Esprit,

64. G 358, commission de contrôle postal, January 1944. Letter from X (Nîmes), 15 January 1944.

65. CA 572, commissaire principal to préfet, 6 May 1944.

66. In the closing months of the war, the police superintendent warned that "incompetence and incoherence" were widespread among the *fonctionnaires* (CA 777, commissaire principal to préfet, 1 May 1944), while a resident of St. Jean de Serres affirmed that the "hecatomb" could be stopped by seeing that a few heads rolled among the police officials (G 358, commission de contrôle postal, January, 1944; letter sent by X, 2 January 1944).

who had not uncovered the "slightest piece of interesting evidence" following the assassination of two prominent local collaborationists.[67] Similarly, the accounts of refugees and resisters from this period occasionally refer to local police officials who, either through sympathy or sheer prudence, turned a blind eye or actively participated in the activities of the Resistance.[68]

In the twilight of Vichy, the police betrayed so powerful an ambivalence in carrying out their duties that it captured the attention of national officials. The regional prefect, having learned of a "certain malaise" among the Gard's police force, due to the "especially onerous responsibilities that have fallen upon them," asked the departmental prefect to respond.[69] Yet such concern was largely academic: the Gard's liberation was just a few weeks away. In fact, one of the astonishing aspects of this period is that the departmental administrators and police, even if they were only shuffling papers, and unable in any real sense to direct or influence the lives of the Gardois, continued to operate at all. By the final months of the war and occupation, the Gard was no longer under even the nominal control of local French authorities (excepting, of course, the small number of Gardois in the ranks of the Milice and those collaborationist groups which were still active). The local representatives of the regime were no less impotent than their superiors in effecting the course of events, and had been relegated to mere observors of their own remorseless and imminent dénouement.[70]

The short-circuiting of the local representatives of Vichy was, of course, due not only to the interference of the Gestapo, but to the proximate cause for their increasingly bloody and indiscriminate activity, the local Resistance. Up through the fall of 1942, the resistance movements remained limited in both the scale of their membership and the nature of their activities. A comparatively small number of militants and sympathizers concentrated their energies on the publication and dissemination of resistance tracts and leaflets. As one participant has since written, at this early stage the most effective way to show the "true face of the enemy and its Vichyssois allies" was through a clandestine press: "Tracts and

67. CA 667, préfet to préfet régional de Marseilles, 17 January 1944.

68. For example, the Picard brothers at the prefecture of Nîmes played an important role in the saving of Jews and the lieutenant of the gendarmerie at Le Vigan was an active accomplice in the production of false identification cards. See Simon, *Les Juifs à Nîmes et dans le Gard durant la deuxième guerre mondiale de 1939 à 1944,* 52.

69. CA 764, préfet régional to préfet du Gard, 31 July 1944.

70. Even in the role of observer, the French authorities did not always have a privileged vantage point and were themselves often in the dark about resistance activity. For example, the departmental police superintendent complained that the arrival of numerous occupation troops and their subsequent police operations in the department made it impossible for him to evaluate the number, location, or importance of resisters (CA 663, commissaire principal to préfet, 2 March 1944).

journals proved that the Resistance was not a myth and that it was rooted in the region."[71]

It was only after the German occupation of the Gard and the institutionalization of the STO that the roots of the Resistance found a nearly inexhaustible source of nourishment. The "true face of the enemy" was now seen on street corners, touring the local sites of Roman antiquity, striding into *pâtisseries* and stumbling out of *maisons de tolérances* (brothels often catering exclusively to the German occupying troops). Although the Germans were thought to be "correct," and their presence, once established, became less remarkable and thus less remarked upon, the prevalence of empty vegetable stands and full German lorries ineluctably transformed the face of the occupier in the eyes of the occupied.[72] More important, the occupier was now making demands upon the Gard, especially its young men, that confronted the inhabitants with moral and political choices they theretofore could ignore. These demands were for manpower, for French backs and brawn to keep the fires of the German industrial war machine stoked while German workers were carted to the various fronts. The STO, the means to feed the maw of German industry and agriculture with French labor, was the last, fatal blow to the prestige of Vichy and the most important boost to the size and fortunes of the local Resistance.

The STO was the issue of earlier, failed efforts made by Vichy to meet the labor demands of Nazi Germany. Under increasing pressure, Laval had authorized in May 1942 the establishment of German labor recruitment offices in the unoccupied zone. This attempt to parry even greater German demands failed, however. In a meeting with Laval on 15 June 1942, Fritz Sauckel, the veteran Nazi who had the responsibility of coordinating foreign labor in Germany, said that France would have to supply him with 250,000 workers, including 150,000 skilled metal workers. In an effort to make the best of a bleak situation, Laval countered Sauckel's demand with an offer that, after it had been worked out by the two officials, was called the *relève*. The agreement stipulated that for every three *skilled* workers sent to Germany, one French POW would be freed. The great emotional value of the liberated prisoners notwithstanding, it was a deal struck with the devil. The quid pro quo applied only to skilled workers, yet France was still obliged to supply the 250,000 workers originally demanded by Sauckel. As a result, France had to supply five, and not three times the number of workers in

71. Vielzeuf, *En Cévennes et Languedoc*, 31.
72. It was observed that a "certain familiarity" in many towns had been established between the troops and the locals, and that the troops' relocation in the summer of 1943 disappointed "numerous peasants who profited in selling them their produce at prices superior to the official rates" (CA 367, "note" 7 August 1943).

order to secure the release of 50,000 POWs.[73] Moreover, France agreed to bleed herself of her skilled industrial labor and, given the background of the released POWs, replace it with a rural and unskilled workforce. As Robert Paxton remarks, Vichy "wound up doing Sauckel's job about as well as Sauckel could have done it himself."[74]

It is impossible to measure accurately the reaction of the public to the announcement of the *relève*, for the sole contemporary report is one filed by the police superintendent of Nîmes. He asserted that Laval's speech had created "an enormous sensation," declaring that no "discourse since those of Marshal Pétain has so stirred the crowds. [Laval's] show of confidence, his lucid exposé, were appreciated as they should be, even by those who do not share the conceptions of the chief of government."[75] The report's wording, simultaneously ambiguous and fawning, when added to the brute fact that precious few Gardois shared Laval's "conceptions," undermines the document's value. As for the initial number of volunteers for the *relève*, it was noted that though Nîmes did not have a large community of specialized workers, a "satisfactory" number of individuals had signed up.[76] Apparently no less satisfying were the departmental figures: the first seven weekly departures of volunteers totaled 122 Frenchmen (a handful of foreigners and Algerians also went along for the ride).[77]

The local authorities emphasized the patriotism and happy prospects of those departing, and the joy and relief of the families of those POWs returning. The labor placement office in Nîmes forwarded to the prefecture, with an eye on the local press, a letter one volunteer, Georges Vernande, had sent home. Vernande assured his mother that he was quite happy: "Good food, comfortable beds, well paid and work is easy and pleasant. . . . Everyone is very kind and polite, and they treat us as they treat their own: All in all, we are very content."[78] The

73. This ratio was, in fact, mentioned by Laval in his speech of 12 August, 1942, which followed the arrival at Compiègne the day before of the first train load of released POWs. However, the censors directed the press to elide this fact in their accounts: "You must not mention in the headline the relative figures of 150,000 and 50,000 concerning skilled workers and prisoners"; quoted in Sarah Fishman, *We Will Wait: Wives of French Prisoners of War, 1940–1945*, 187.

74. Paxton, *Vichy France*, 368.

75. CA 776, commissaire central to préfet, 27 June 1942.

76. CA 776, commissaire central to préfet, 2 August 1942.

77. CA 790, office de placement allemand to préfet (n.d., but probably late August 1942). My totals differ from those of Cosson, who counts 194 volunteers, including 47 foreigners. See *Nîmes et le Gard dans la guerre, 1939–1945*, 49. The enlistment peak was hit on 5 August, when 25 workers left the Gard. The curve then begins to descend, bottoming out at 14 workers on 26 August, the last recorded entry.

78. CA 561, office de placement allemand to préfet, 14 August 1942. Lucien Boyer, the official who sent the copy of Vernande's letter, glossed it with the recruitment appeal of his office: the workers "are very happy, they eat well and will have the opportunity to discover a new country and learn German, an appreciable advantage."

reception of such a letter (though it is the only one I have found, it does not mean that Vernande was exceptional in his reactions) was an obvious windfall for the *relève* authorities, and helped their well-orchestrated propaganda campaign. Following the passage of the first trainload of liberated POWs, Chiappe received a circular from the ministry of information that applied an additional coat of ecstatic patriotism to the already thick layer slapped on by the press. The propaganda officials directed the press to dwell "in a more emphatic and hearty manner than it previously has on the sacred character of the *relève*. . . . A mystique of the *relève* must be created in our country." The official specifically imposed silence on the actual statistics of departing workers and returning prisoners, as well as on the fact that only certain workers qualified to liberate the prisoners.[79]

By the end of the summer of 1942, the *relève* was a manifest failure. Despite massive press and radio campaigns, only 17,000 French workers had enrolled in the program.[80] Persuasion having failed, Vichy next tried coercion. In early September, the regime issued a law mobilizing all men between the ages of 18 and 50, as well as all single women between 20 and 35 years of age. According to the law, these individuals were eligible to be called upon to "undertake all work that the government judges essential for the superior needs of the nation."[81] A census of the working population was ordered and employers in the relevant industries were obliged to furnish lists of their workers. As Dominique Veillon has pointed out, the law was tantamount to forced labor: although the STO was not formally announced until February 1943, it was in the preceding September, following a new demand by Sauckel for yet another 250,000 workers, that "hunting season on workers was declared open."[82]

If there had been some initial excitement and hope inspired among the Gardois by the *relève*, it all but evaporated in the heat of the summer crackdown. As early as July, Alès was sadly lagging in enlistment. This was due partly to the fact that miners, essential to the nation's economy, were excluded from joining, and that there was little or no unemployment in the other regional industries. Yet the subprefect also allowed that the mass of workers "remained resolutely hostile to the government," one and all believing in the eventual defeat of Germany.[83] The sentiment among the working class in Nîmes, following the promulgation of the September decree, was similar. The workers were "frankly hostile," and a

79. CA 790, circulaire du ministère de l'information aux préfets, 30 July 1942.
80. Dominique Veillon, "La Vérité sur le STO," *L'Histoire*, no. 80 (1985), 106.
81. Quoted in Azéma, *De Munich à la libération*, 211.
82. Veillon, "La Vérité sur le STO," 106.
83. CA 776, sous-préfet of Alès to préfet, 29 July 1942.

"veiled, but unmistakable opposition" had become evident.[84] Following another speech by Laval on the *relève,* the police superintendent once again put the best possible spin on his report, insisting that the workers acknowledged Laval's "honesty" and did not hold him responsible for the regime's pickle. Yet despite the Auvergnat's "real [but unspecified] merits," the workers viewed the affair through "their personal interests, habits, and family life." Hence, the workers' obedience could be guaranteed "solely through the threat of harsh punishment."[85]

Discontent and anxiety metastasized throughout the Gard. One representative letter was written by the sister of a young man threatened by the call-up. A grammar school teacher in La Grand-Combe, she wrote to a friend that the "so-called *relève* is my great torment. I don't believe for a moment in the exchange of POWs for workers, and I'm afraid that my brother will be in the first tumbrel of 'involuntary volunteers.' I'm very worried because I know *le petit,* and since our 'brothers' on the other side of the Rhine don't inspire a great deal of sympathy in him, I fear that this will shatter him."[86] As for those families with members who had volunteered to work in Germany, they found themselves the target of spreading scorn and disapprobation. In the town of Montaren, local officials refused to furnish Mme Detaille, whose son had left for Germany in March, her monthly allotment of gas and bread. But this was just the latest incident in the daily travails of a woman who had become the object of an "underhanded hostility" of townspeople attempting to "make her life as difficult as possible."[87]

Workers left no legal stone unturned in the frantic scramble to avoid being called up.[88] One widespread rumor was that any man married *less* than two years would be deferred. Although such a law would have been perfectly illogical, the Gardois eagerly grasped at it. According to the local military commandant, there was a "multiplying" number of marriages. And where loopholes did in fact exist, there was no shortage of men and women waiting to leap through. One young Nîmoise wrote that she would never willingly go to Germany: "They will have to drag me, and even then I'll do all that I can to stay." But it might not come to that: "I'm going to set about looking for a boy who I'll find pleasant enough and get married. . . . I think I'll find one, but it isn't very

84. CA 776, commissaire central to préfet, 18 October 1942. The police official commented that the younger candidates seemed less worried over being called up, and suggested that it was due to a "taste for adventure and the desire to travel."

85. CA 776, commissaire central to préfet, 22 October 1942.

86. G 354, commission de contrôle postal, October 1942. Letter from Blanche (La Grand-Combe), 10 October 1942.

87. CA 790, office de placement allemand to préfet, 3 December 1942.

88. CA 776, commandant de la 15ème division militaire du Gard to préfet, 17 October 1942.

important if he is handsome or ugly—just think that I'll be 20 years old in three days . . . "[89]

In addition to numerous individual efforts to escape or protest the relève, there was a growing number of collective refusals. These acts of group insubordination were concentrated in the Alesian mining basin. As early as mid-October, the subprefect warned that the Forges d'Alès was the site of worker resistance to the relève. Although only 24 men out of 1,500 had been designated, there were rumors that there would be a collective work stoppage for twenty-four hours. The strike rumor turned out to be only that, a rumor, but the wretched candidates nevertheless refused to sign their contracts, go for their medical examinations, and pack their bags. The subprefect tried to reason with them, but reported glumly that he ran into a "mulish silence and total incomprehension."[90] Next month, following the designation of another sixty workers for the relève, the ironworks were rocked by a wave of protests. In a gesture of solidarity with those called up, 700 workers laid down their tools during the last three hours of their shift. Ten men were arrested, yet as the subprefect admitted, it was done "pour l'exemple" as he could not with any certainty identify the actual strike leaders.[91]

With the official inauguration of the STO in the wake of Sauckel's new demand in January 1943 for an additional 250,000 French workers, including 150,000 metallurgical specialists, the mulishness turned into active resistance. It is difficult to establish a definitive account, from the establishment of the relève through the final spasms of the STO, of the number of Gardois who ultimately were sent to Germany. The relevant documentation is riven with gaps; there are confusions between those designated for the relève and those for the STO; and the statistics are often undated. The local historian Armand Cosson estimates that 10,200 men were convoked, and approximately one-fifth (2,250) eventually departed for the factories and farms to the east.[92] This appears a reasonable tally,

89. CA 763, commission de contrôle postal, September 1942. Letter from Jeanette (Nîmes), 15 September 1942.

90. CA 790, sous-préfet of Alès to préfet, 24 October 1942.

91. CA 819, sous-préfet of Alès to préfet, 26 November 1942.

92. Cosson, Nîmes et le Gard dans la guerre, 1939–1945, 94. In an article devoted to this very question, based on studies done in several departments (the Gard was not included), Pierre Mermet warns of numerous obstacles. He notes that the archival dossiers are "often dense and plentiful, [but] unclassified and incomplete due to total or partial destruction." Moreover, he remarks that "confusion often reigns in the documents" and after citing obstacles identical to those I encountered, concludes that it is "practically impossible to establish a precise, clear and definitive list." See Pierre Mermet, "Enquête sur la main d'oeuvre française au service de l'Allemagne (1940–1944)," Bulletin de l'institut d'histoire du temps présent, no. 7 (March 1982), 40–54. One document from the office du travail in Nîmes lists 2,567 workers sent to Germany between June 1942 and May 1943. Titled "Départ de volontaires

given the available documentation. Much easier to establish, though, is the qualitative reaction of the Gardois.

The announcement of the STO ignited the smoldering fire of public anxiety and resistance. In late January, Alès's police were deployed at the train station in anticipation of possible "incidents" among departing workers—or rather, with those workers who bothered to appear, since the rate of *réfractaires* (evaders) already topped 30 percent.[93] In an earlier send-off from Alès, only half of the seventy-two designated workers actually left. The remainder had either been crossed off the list (for unexplained reasons), were judged unfit for service, or simply absented themselves at the train station.[94] The workers of Nîmes were no less recalcitrant. The police superintendent insisted that the program had not sparked "severe criticism," but confessed that "numerous youths and even their parents are looking for ways to avoid it." Many were trying to find work on the farms, and even in certain state positions, like the police and railway, that were still beyond Sauckel's reach.[95]

The alternative of mining was perhaps the most popular—if only in the sense of the number of men it attracted, for the sudden scramble was savored by neither the novices nor the old hands. The former, the great majority of whom were from the urban areas, were stunned by the backbreaking labor. One apprentice in Bessèges dreaded the "martyrdom of hard labor" he would face the following day. Though the prospect of the descent was numbing and he "suffered from all my pores from this painful labor, from the milieu and my aborted dreams and unquenched desire for a riskier and nobler adventure," he had no choice, because of "family duties," but to assume this burden.[96] The veteran miners—the "milieu" that this young man found so great a burden— were no happier than were the newcomers over the situation. The infusion of new laborers maintained or inflated the size of the mining teams—and hence their quotas; yet the youths' lack of training and skill forced the veterans to work even harder to meet the required yields. Moreover, the presence of these awkward newcomers, whose sole reason for being there was to avoid the STO, understandably irritated those families in the area whose sons had already been packed off to Germany.[97]

---

pour aller travailler en Allemagne," the word "volontaires" was struck out by an anonymous and frank bureaucrat (CA 790).

93. CA 777, sous-préfet of Alès to préfet, 1 February 1943.

94. CA 763, sous-préfet of Alès to préfet, 27 January 1943.

95. CA 777, commissaire principal to préfet, 27 February 1943.

96. G 364, commission de contrôle postal, June 1943. Letter from Felix Cassagne (Bessèges), 28 June 1943.

97. CA 716, sous-préfet of Alès to préfet, 2 June 1943.

These grievances exacerbated an already difficult material situation in the mines. A number of reports were filed during 1943 detailing the harsh conditions facing the miners. One engineer at Rochebelle, over whose pit the red flag had been hoisted, complained about the "vile atmosphere" underground, where the lack of aeration and buildup of carbon dioxide had led to a rash of headaches and nausea. The engineer had previously thought that all mines were more or less the same, but now saw his error: "It's no laughing matter here."[98] At nearby Le Martinet, a doctor did not find the low moral of the miners surprising. Among the men's quotidian hassles were a single shower room at the mouth of the pit, frequent cave-ins, inadequate aeration, and the concomitant danger of asphyxiation. Two miners, in fact, had died of suffocation the preceding week. In sum, concluded the doctor, "one understands why the worker has communist sympathies and hates the rich."[99]

It seems clear that the material situation of the miners had deteriorated since the late 1930s and the advances they had then made under the Popular Front. Perhaps more important, however, was the sobering contrast between Vichy's ideological pap, garnished with paternalistic concern for the worker's lot, and the harsh reality of the mines. The situation was so critical that even those ideologically committed to the regime were shocked by the conditions and warned their superiors of the untoward consequences. A congress of workers of the National Revolution, held in Alès in early 1943, composed a long list of grievances that included shortages of clothing, detergent, soap, and food rations, as well as the total lack of shoes. The inventory was sent to the authorities in Vichy, who forwarded it to Chiappe for his comments.[100] At the same time, the mining engineer in Alès wrote to Chiappe that there was a "general malaise" in the mining basin and that, "regardless of the cost and without delay," food rations to the miners had to be maintained.[101]

That the mines, despite their hellish character, were a serious alternative to the STO says a good deal about the latter's unpopularity. Yet, once again, there were other options. Those working in agriculture, the police, and the national railway benefitted from temporary deferments, as did students. At least in the early stages of the STO, the ability to take advantage of these alternatives was limited to the bourgeoisie and those who had the necessary *pistons*, or connections. As a

98. G 363, commission de contrôle postal, May 1943. Letter from M. Bros (Rochebelle/Alès), 7 May 1943.
99. C 364, commission de contrôle postal, August 1943. Letter from Dr. Maurice Lasserre (Le Martinet), 27 August 1943.
100. CA 716, directeur général de la propagande to préfet, 7 February 1943.
101. CA 716, ingénieur des mines d'Alès to préfet, 20 February 1943.

consequence, the working class bore the brunt of the initial demands for labor—a fact that did not escape their attention. In early 1944 a police official warned that if such favoritism continued, "serious problems will not fail to occur."[102] Perhaps the most eloquent comment on these inequalities was an impromptu question-and-answer session held by disenchanted conscripts in one of the departing trains. A voice asked if there were any employers in the crowd. Silence ensued. It then asked if there were any priests. Again, silence. Finally, the voice, wondering if there were any workers, was immediately overwhelmed by "an immense 'Present.' "[103]

By early March the official pretense that the STO was uncontroversial could no longer be maintained. The fractious departure in the wee hours of 6 March of 700 youths from Nîmes left no doubt as to the state of public opinion. As the young men gathered on the train platform toward midnight, they broke into a rendition of the *Internationale.* They were so taken by their performance that they proceeded to sing it several more times. The general effervescence became so worrisome that the police convinced a lone German soldier, who wanted to arrest a few youths for having sung the revolutionary anthem, to leave the platform. The song was interrupted by shouts of "Laval au poteau" and "A bas Chiappe," and for those hard of hearing, the sides of the rail cars were covered with slogans like "Vive de Gaulle," "Vive the USSR," and "Down with Angelo [Chiappe] the turncoat." Seen off at the platform by the object of this last piece of graffiti, the train finally pulled out at 1:30 in the morning, carrying off its cargo of chanting Gardois.[104]

Identical scenes were repeated elsewhere in the department. The first trainload of youths from Alès marked their departure by hostile shouts and slogans aimed at Laval, as well as by a rendition of the *Internationale.*[105] At Sommières the protesters added brawling to the by now de rigueur chanting and singing. While slouching toward the train station, the restive draftees passed some local miliciens, and decided to make their departure a memorable one. In the ensuing skirmish, three of the miliciens were seriously injured.[106] According to one spectator, the president of the local chapter of the Legion, who passed by at that very moment on his motorcycle, "nearly had his brains beat out"

102. CA 793, "note" to préfet, 17 January 1944.
103. CA 648, commission de contrôle postal, synthèse, March 1943.
104. CA 777, commissaire principal to préfet, 7 March 1943. Yet a week later, the police official strove to put the demonstrations in the best possible light, insisting that the chanting was the work of a "noisy minority" and that the graffiti was erased by the youths when the train reached the demarcation line (CA 777, commissaire principal to préfet, 13 March 1943).
105. CA 777, sous-préfet of Alès to préfet, 31 March 1943.
106. CA 777, commissaire principal to préfet, 20 March 1943. As the official remarked, "This organization [the Milice] is not liked."

by the STO youths. All in all, it made for "a fine show—and, to boot, it was free."[107]

The local press, which of course omitted mention of the demonstrations and instead depicted fanciful scenes of peaceful departures, was the butt of much scorn. The papers carried one press release dwelling on the munificence of the local administration, which in the person of Angelo Chiappe distributed bread, chocolate, eggs, sardines, and fruit paste to a group of departing youths. Yet, as the police superintendent himself remarked, this was the same convoy that demanded the head not only of Laval, but of the prefect as well. Also, the youths complained of the cold meal that was furnished and the poorly organized distribution of the rations.[108] L'Eclair was especially criticized by the locals for its report that the departures took place without hitch or controversy—a particularly flagrant lie for those Nîmois who, living near the train station, could clearly hear the chanting and hostile cries. The populace, the official drily concluded, "doesn't hesitate to say that brainwashing continues and that the papers aren't reporting the truth."[109]

Whether they lived hard by the station or in the wealthy and more distant quarters of the Jardin de la Fontaine, nearly all the social classes were ultimately alienated by the relentless demands of the STO. The Gardois industrialists, both owners and managers, were increasingly incensed over the drain of manpower and sought to protect their workers.[110] The farmers, hobbled by the lack of fieldhands after agricultural deferments were cancelled in late 1943, also directed their ire at the regime. At a conference of the departmental agricultural corporation, Roger Rouvière affirmed that the recent call-ups of both foreign and French workers had "seriously affected the winegrowing region where winter work is particularly important. Deferments have been given in only the most dire cases."[111] Rouvière was aware that channeling manpower away from the farms undermined Vichy's pretension as guarantor of agrarian values. Thus the warning of one local agrarian official about the widespread impression that the regime's measures are designed "to empty the land of its workers to the profit of the mines and factories."[112]

107. G 361, commission de contrôle postal, March 1943. Letter from X (Sommières), 15 March, 1943.

108. CA 763, commissaire principal to préfet, 13 March 1943.

109. CA 777, commissaire principal to préfet, 13 March 1943.

110. The sub-prefect of Alès observed that the local industrialists were not "applying the slightest pressure to their workers to encourage them to go to work in Germany" (CA 763, sous-préfet of Alès to préfet, 4 January 1943).

111. Speech reprinted in Le Vigneron du Sud-est (January–February 1944). In the speech, Rouvière portrayed the Gard's viticulture in the bleakest of terms.

112. CA 572, délégué départmental du Gard, quoted by sous-préfet of Le Vigan to préfet, February 1944.

Both the insatiable demands of the STO and the growing degree of official collaboration with the Nazis was demonstrated in the decision to include certain Jews for the labor convoys. In a circular sent to all the prefects, Vichy announced that all foreign Jews and French Jews born between 1912 and 1922, apart from Alsace-Lorrainers, were now liable for the STO. The circular cited the regime's "respect for the principle of equality, in accordance with French aspirations" as its justification.[113] That by late 1943 the great majority of Jews, both foreign and French, had either been arrested, deported, or gone into hiding only deepens the decree's Kafkaesque quality. As for the Jewish minority that had not yet taken one of these routes, they had done their very best to keep a low profile. The decree concerning their eligibility merely reinforced their efforts.

By the late spring of 1943, labor officials noted that the ratio of desertions to designations was nearly ninety percent. One bureaucrat, in despair over the battery of exemptions, sighed "All that I have left are a few barbers."[114] Even the barbers, however, were soon making themselves scarce. The police reports from Nîmes on this score are eloquent. On 17 April, only 5 of the original 120 men summoned for departure appeared at the train station.[115] The following month, the police tried a novel remedy: they would hand the recruits their convocation notice with one hand while collaring them with the other. Yet this method failed, too. Of the 180 men gathered in this summary fashion, all but 13, with the obvious complicity of doctors and various bureaucrats, obtained deferments of one sort or another.[116] The appeal of the Todt organization, (responsible for construction projects, including the building of the Atlantic Wall) was scarcely greater. For example, in early 1944, out of 714 draft calls by Todt enterprises, only 322 men responded. This number was then whittled down by the usual array of medical and administrative deferments, and just 82 individuals ultimately departed. To reach the contingent of 900 men demanded by the Germans, the local authorities would have had to undertake ten similar operations and issue some 6,000 notifications. As a police official remarked, "It's to be feared that if this situation continues, the German authorities will intervene."[117]

Of course, the active complicity of a good number of administrators reflected a broad sympathy for those young men who refused to serve in the STO. One departmental police official flatly asserted that the STO was sharply resented "even by those individuals who are not affected by it. Apart from a few

113. CA 763, circulaire du ministère de l'Intérieur aux préfets (n.d., but undoubtedly sometime in late 1943).
114. CA 648, commission de contrôle postal, synthèse, May 1943.
115. CA 777, commissaire principal to préfet, 17 April 1943.
116. CA 777, commissaire principal to préfet, 29 May 1943.
117. CA 793, "note" 17 January 1944.

exceptions, it must be acknowledged that the entire population is unanimous on this subject."[118] As the subprefect of Le Vigan warned in July 1943, the STO has "sharpened everyone's emotions and provoked an increasingly vast movement of *réfractaires,*" leading to incidents that "produce an unfortunate impression on the public."[119] The police superintendent of Nîmes echoed this report, admitting that the public "has a marked tendency to excuse the youths who shirk their [STO] obligations."[120]

In the same report, however, the superintendent hastened to add that the Nîmois "judge severely those who incite [the evaders] to desert, and especially those who give them the means to resist by force." The Resistance, the subject of this oblique reference, was one of the great consequences of the STO. But before its examination, we must first consider a second and equally momentous result; namely, the reaction of the Gard's Catholic and Protestant churches. Jacques Duquesne has written that, whereas the Jewish persecution had led to a cooling of ties between the church and Vichy, the STO provoked a final and complete rupture. Yet he distinguishes between the mass of lay Catholics and the hierarchy, emphasizing that the separation between the ecclesiastics and regime was much more tentative and never fully consummated.[121] This important qualification applies to the Gard. As we shall see, the departmental hierarchy, at least in the person of Bishop Girbeau, worked at cross-purposes with much of not just their flock, but many parish priests as well.

The Catholic Church's representatives in the Gard, as already noted, by and large maintained an obstinate silence over the fate of the Jews. But with the advent of the STO, a perceptible shift in the relationship between the church and state, particularly at the parish level, began to take place. This trend came to the attention of the authorities as early as the spring of 1943. In mid-April, it was reported that the clergy was still reticent to display its political sentiments. But in a clear reference to the STO, the official added that there was a "change taking place among them that is separating them from the politics of the government." More distressing, certain priests were voicing "their sentiments in favor of an American invasion."[122] The following week, the same official warned that a growing number of priests were "criticizing, sometimes openly, the measures taken by a government reproached

118. CA 569, rapport du chef d'escadron Duval de la gendarmerie nationale to préfet, 19 April 1943.
119. CA 777, sous-préfet of Le Vigan to préfet, 30 July 1943.
120. CA 777, commissaire principal to préfet, 10 July 1943.
121. Duquesne, *Les Catholiques français sous l'occupation,* 271–307.
122. CA 777, commissaire principal to préfet, 10 April 1943.

for being nothing more than a servant of Hitler."[123] The process of disaffection continued: two months later, the official again remarked that there were "numerous" priests who were critical both of Laval and the policy of collaboration.[124]

The STO played a pivotal role in the initial sundering of a part of the Catholic clergy from the regime. This gradual divorce of the lower clergy from Vichy's politics deepened over the course of 1943; by early 1944, the sentiments of the departmental clergy were no longer in doubt. The majority of the Gard's ecclesiastics, it was reported in March, were opposed to the "Franco-German politics of entente and are apparently more or less under the influence of clandestine propaganda like *Cahiers de témoignage Chrétien.*"[125] Yet many members of the higher clergy were still reluctant to deny Pétain, if not Vichy. According to a series of January 1944 police reports, the clergy showed a keen disappointment in the "muddle in which the government... had fallen."[126] The "influential members" of the clergy, however, remained partisans of Pétain, whereas those "ecclesiastics who hail from the lower classes are fairly divided." On the one hand, there were those who, though opposed to violent methods, were "fiercely Gaullist," while on the other hand were those who, at one time sympathetic to Action française, were now "undecided and no longer sure which policy to support."[127]

The growing discord between the higher and lower orders naturally held the attention of their flocks. A resident of Bagnols sur Cèze recounted a meeting she and a group of Catholics had with Girbeau and the diocesan inspector, in which they "earnestly advised us to keep the most complete silence concerning recent events. Several local priests have had problems because they could not keep quiet, and they aren't alone."[128] Though ambiguous, the phrase suggests that certain priests had protested against the STO, much to the local administration's resentment. A few months later, a Nîmois lamented that "half of the clergy are anglophile or Gaullist; even the Franciscans from the Rue d'Aquitane hope for an English victory." It is not clear what the correspondent meant by "half," for he concludes pathetically that "there is only the bishop of Nîmes who remains faithful to the Marshal."[129]

123. CA 777, commissaire principal to préfet, 17 April 1943.
124. CA 777, 26 June 1943.
125. CA 572, commissaire principal to préfet, 25 March 1944.
126. CA 793, commissaire principal to préfet, 22 January 1944.
127. CA 793, commissaire principal to préfet, 29 January 1944.
128. G 362, commission de contrôle postal, October–November 1943. Letter from Jeanne (Bagnols sur Cèze), 12 October 1943.
129. G 358, commission de contrôle postal, January 1944. Letter from M. Vedrines (Nîmes), 2 January 1944.

Even if an exaggeration, the remark nevertheless points to an undeniable movement away from Vichy by the bulk of the clergy, and the isolation of those who, led by Bishop Girbeau, remained Pétainist to the end.[130]

The bishop's fidelity to Pétain never wavered. One woman recounted a New Year's 1944 meeting with Girbeau, in which the bishop, after having referred to the difficult days to come, "spoke movingly of the marshal, for whom he has an admiration bordering on veneration."[131] This veneration for Pétain shone in the bishop's sermons to his flock, as well. At a period when Pétain was widely considered by public opinion to have been by-passed by events, and his name only mentioned with a cluck of pity, Girbeau treated the marshal with the same reverence he had in the summer of 1940. In his 1944 New Year's address, the bishop affirmed that "every French Catholic shares the invincible faith of the marshal of France and chief of state in the renaissance of our country."[132] It was not until the summer of that year that Girbeau finally conceded Pétain's irrevelance and the chimera of a renaissance that would be conjured by a wave of the marshal's baton. Brooding over the relentless chain of disasters striking France, Girbeau wondered where the country would find a voice persuasive enough to unite all Frenchmen. He concluded that "there no longer is any hope to be expected from men. It is only from heaven that we can expect help."[133] Pétain, the "providential man" of 1940, was clearly no longer up to the task.

Girbeau's constancy to Pétain, as well as to the increasingly dubious contention that Vichy remained a legitimate and independent government, manifested itself most clearly and damagingly in his attitude toward the STO. In this respect, the bishop differed little from the vast majority of his colleagues and the official position of the church. Wrestle though they might with the issue of forced labor, the leaders of French Catholicism never succeeded in pinning it down. Instead, the church twisted itself into an awkward position that satisfied few factions and discredited the institution in the eyes not just of many lay Catholics, but also a significant number of clergy and lay activists. In the spring of 1943, thanks to the

130. A representative of Jacques Doriot's Parti populaire français (PPF), Joseph Julian, reported on a series of conversations he held with the canons at the cathedral in Nîmes, as well as "several" of the diocese's priests. He asserted that they all "followed the example of their bishop, Msgr. Girbeau, who has advised them not to 'make' politics." He then affirmed that all of the priests were for Pétain and that "several even deeply sympathize with our party." On the other hand, "certain are anticollaborationist, but there are very few" (G 358, commission de contrôle postal, February, 1944; letter sent 2 February 1944). The accuracy of this report is dubious; at least in the case of the departmental priests, nearly all the police reports agree as to their alienation from the regime. Moreover, that the clergy could support the fascist and revolutionary party of Doriot stretches one's credulity.

131. G 358, commission de contrôle postal, January 1944. Letter from Reine X (Nîmes), 1 January 1944.

132. *La Semaine Religieuse* (9 January 1944), 22.

133. *La Semaine Religieuse* (21 May 1944), 150.

erasure of the demarcation line, the Assembly of Cardinals and Archbishops met in Paris for the first time in three years as a complete body. One of the burning issues facing them was the STO. What position must the church assume? In a text signed in early April by the three primates of France, Lienhart of Lille, Suhard of Paris, and Gerlier of Lyon, the church allowed that serving in the STO was not a matter of conscience, and one could thus evade it without committing a sin. The weight of the text, however, fell heavily upon the positive moral aspects in *acceptance* of the STO. Offering the figure of the suffering Christ as their model, the cardinals argued that Christian workers would "invest this trial with all of its redemptive value and be the support of their brothers." This new suffering imposed upon France would thus provide the occasion to "unite, love one another and prepare, in this burst of spiritual energy, the coming resurrection of France."[134] In the bishop's considered opinion, evasion of the STO was "tolerable, but not the preferable attitude to be adopted by a Christian."[135]

The text's recipe for moral rectitude, which carried conflicting instructions, caused much confusion. The German and Vichy authorities were irritated by its dash of rebelliousness, while many clergymen and lay Catholics, who had hoped for a more vigorous protest, were no less annoyed. Bishop Girbeau quickly sought to simplify the instructions. On 9 May, he read the assembly's text at the Church of Sainte Jeanne d'Arc. This was, in itself, noteworthy: many church officials had simply omitted reciting it to their parishioners. It was the *manner* in which it was read, however, that was telling. The rapidity of the bishop's reading was, it appears, matched only its feeble volume. As a result, observed an attending official, only those men and women sitting in the first rows could properly hear the bishop's muffled and slurred words.

Any questions that may have persisted as to why Girbeau dispatched the text in this way were answered two months later. In the face of the growing controversy over the issue of the STO, the bishop publicly reproved those who advocated that the young should not serve. In a letter published on the front page of *La Semaine Religieuse*, Girbeau "condemn[ed] those who are dissuading youths from submitting to this obligation and encouraging them to hide in the forests and mountains." This position, Girbeau asserted, was contrary to the dictates of both justice and charity. The first quality was violated because other men would be forced to replace the shirkers, the second because the shirkers were placing themselves and their families in a situation that could end in disaster for all concerned.[136]

---

134. Text quoted in Duquesne, *Les Catholiques français*, 282–83.
135. Duquesne, *Les Catholiques français*, 287.
136. *La Semaine Religieuse* (4 July 1943). Girbeau prefaced the announcement with the remark that he had already given specific instructions to his clergy on this issue, but that given their nature, they would appear in the *bulletin du clergé*. Unfortunately, neither the departmental nor diocesan archives has this particular issue.

Although only rare voices critical of the STO were heard from the ranks of French bishops (Monsignor Saliège of Toulouse was the most notable example), those voices raised in support were nearly as uncommon. The vast majority of bishops found repose in the equivocal nature of the cardinals' message and chose not to mine its ambiguities. Yet, one prominent historian of the Catholic Church has listed declarations made by five French bishops that, in their sharp condemnations of those who urged French youth to obey their consciences and dodge the STO, differed from the official position of the church and the mass of their colleagues. Girbeau is one of those named, and the fact that his was perhaps the least detailed and exhortative of sermons hardly lessens its gravity.[137] Of course, the dilemma faced by Girbeau must not be underestimated. To condone the acts of those who advised the young to flee the STO represented a form of double jeopardy, for it overthrew political authority and confounded religious authority. Bound to a government he considered legitimate and sovereign, nourished on a scriptural bias demanding obedience to temporal powers, supported by a hierarchy rebuking those "theologians without a mandate" for advocating resistance to the STO, and haunted by the political and social consequences of any form of rebellion, Bishop Girbeau's reaction was, in every sense of the word, fatal.

In addition to the confusing "screen" thrown up by Vichy's ostensible legitimacy, there also was the "screen" drawn between the church hierarchy and its base. The divergence between Girbeau and his clergy was, in part, due to the closer contact the village priests had with the faithful and their consequent involvement in the endless series of family trials provoked by the STO. As one police report noted, the clergy was "subject to the influence of the milieu in which they live. As a result, a fairly large number of priests . . . are opposed to the sending of workers to Germany."[138] Girbeau was certainly more detached from the daily lives of the Gardois Catholics, and so less aware of the traumatic impact of the STO. In fact, not only was the bishop's life relatively distant from the lives of his parishioners, but so too were the ties between the parish priests and him. Communication was not a straightforward matter, and Girbeau was undoubtedly sheltered by a body of canons and priests intent on maintaining their superior's peace of mind.[139]

<hr />

137. Duquesne, *Les Catholiques français*, 293–96. The other four bishops were those of Le Puy, Clermont-Ferrand, Mende, and Rodez. All four figured on the original list drawn up in the wake of the liberation by Georges Bidault of those bishops the French provisional government considered "undesirable."

138. CA 572, commissaire principal to préfet, 18 March 1944. The same report insisted that even if many Catholics were not favorable to the government, many clergymen still had great sympathy for Pétain; what they criticized was the "one-way street of Franco-German collaboration."

139. Pierre Danchin uses the term *écran* or "screen" in his account of a group of Parisian students who had stolen a pile of yellow stars with the intent to wear them as an act of protest against the

A number of sincere Catholics, both clerical and lay, agreed with the Church's interpretation. One seminarian in Nîmes held that "by obeying we are certain not to fall in error." Besides, the STO will enable Christians to "realize a more beautiful life, because separation, suffering, and work will steel our souls for a better future as priests."[140] But a second seminarian described the recent departures as "sickening" and declared that "it was enough to break the hardest heart. . . . How sad!"[141] This young man counseled prayer as the sole response to the confusion and torment of the times, but it is clear that fewer and fewer Gardois found his advice, not to mention Girbeau's position, adequate. To the bishop's call for justice, a growing number of youths replied that true justice resided in combatting the injustice of the STO. And to his plea for charity, his opponents countered that true charity lay in not merely advocating resistance, but actively aiding those who chose this path.[142]

This spiritual alternative is glimpsed in the reflections of a young Nîmois living under the shadow of the STO. What was most terrifying, he wrote, was the separation from loved ones and the forced collaboration with Nazi Germany. "The hardest part is this enslavement to national socialism, and the most painful part is the moral and spiritual suffering." Where did one's duties thus lie? Must one "leave and preach the gospel in Germany, or go spread it among 'others' who also have need of it? God must triumph everywhere." Though the youth did not furnish a clear answer to the question he and countless others were posing, his conclusion is suggestive: "We cannot adopt either national socialism or communism in France. [Yet] to be faithful to the sense of the Holy Scriptures means that the Christian must take a political position: the state, like the church, must submit to Christ."[143]

That this letter could just as easily have been written by a young Protestant as a Catholic underscores the convergence of views that occurred between important segments of the two communities by the end of 1943 and the early months of 1944. The position of French Protestantism on the STO had been defined and

---

anti-Semitic legislation of Vichy. Learning that the Germans intended to punish them if they carried out this threat, one sought the advice of Cardinal Suhard. The ecclesiastic's response was a confused: "What star?" Bishop Girbeau's blindness to the gravity of the STO was equal to Suhard's ignorance that French Jews in the occupied zone were obliged to wear a yellow star. Pierre Dachin, "Débat," in *Spiritualité, théologie et résistance,* ed. Bolle and Godel, 206–7.

140. G 363, commission de contrôle postal, June 1943. Letter from Labertrande (Nîmes), 4 June 1943.

141. G 361, commission de contrôle postal, March 1943. Letter from René X (Nîmes), 16 March 1943.

142. This, in part, was the platform that the Action Catholique des Jeunesses Françaises assumed in the spring of 1943. See Duquesne, *Les Catholiques français,* 287–92.

143. G 361, commission de contrôle postal, June 1943. Letter from Pierre Torreilles (Nîmes), 30 June 1943.

announced in a message by the Fédération Protestante de France on 14 April 1943. There was, it declared, an "insurmountable opposition" between the Gospel and any "conception of man or society that envisages labor as a commodity that can be bought or demanded at will, without regard for the person, conscience or most sacred beliefs of the worker." As the church could "neither ignore [this] nor be silent," the message concluded with the demand that its audience "remain entirely faithful to their Christian vocation [and] hold firm."[144]

In commenting upon this passage, the great historian of French Protestantism Pierre Bolle observes that the message was "clear enough for the majority of young Protestants."[145] In fact, the message, read and circulated through the Gard, was so clear that certain Protestants were astounded that it had not provoked a response from the regime.[146] Having heard it read at the temple in Uzès, one Protestant wrote "I cannot but wonder why [relations between] the Reformed Church and the government do not completely break off."[147] Moreover, the local ministers were not content simply to broadcast the messages of their national representatives. A few months after the reading of the federation's letter, the Protestants of Nîmes were treated to a sermon by Pastor Boisset of Montpellier, who dwelt on the imperativeness of remaining faithful "to God in the face of authoritarianism, in the midst of total war and deportations." The sermon, according to one church member, was particularly courageous since "pastors are now threatened and jailed for a yes or a no."[148]

The local administration, aware of the Protestant community's deepening hostility, kept close tabs on its activities. The Milice contributed, fingering certain pastors as actively subversive. For example, Paul Cadier, the pastor of Durfort, was accused of hiding Jewish fugitives and fabricating false identity cards for them. In a report to Chiappe, Colonel Dire declared that Cadier "was not qualified to spiritually instruct the youths confided to his charge."[149] In nearby Lasalle, the pastor Edgard Wasserfallen also fell under the baleful eyes of the Milice. Dire warned the prefect that the attitude and state of mind of the pastor—indeed, the town of Lasalle itself—"leave a good deal to be

144. Text quoted in full in *Spiritualité, théologie et résistance,* ed. Bolle and Godel, 180–81.

145. Pierre Bolle, "Des voix protestantes," in *Spiritualité, théologie et résistance,* ed. Bolle and Godel, 154.

146. There was at least one copy intercepted by the commission de contrôle postal (G 363, May 1943), which had been sent by Pastor Georges Crespy of Lasalle to his colleague Jacques Martin of Ganges (Hérault). Oddly, this particular copy is missing the phrase "hold firm."

147. G 361, commission de contrôle postal, May 1943. Letter from M. Bouer (Uzès), 11 May 1943.

148. C 364, commission de contrôle postal, September 1943. Letter from J. Koch (Nîmes), 5 September 1943.

149. CA 660, Dire to préfet, 1 May 1943.

desired." Wasserfallen was a convinced anglophile and "does not hide it from his parishioners."[150]

The problem for the local representatives of Vichy was that these and similar cases of rebelliousness were neither discrete nor limited to the clergy. Rather, it was an attitude rooted in the vast majority of Gardois, and most especially, Cévenol Protestants. In the case of Cadier, it was observed that he ministered to an "essentially Protestant region," and if he had a certain ascendancy over the population, it was because the latter shared his "religious conceptions."[151] There was, however, a "healthy fraction" of the town that, though a "small minority," was favorable to the regime and "astonished that MM. Cadier and Paux [an associate] are not troubled" by the authorities.[152] Similarly, Wasserfallen officiated in a town where the overwhelming majority of residents were Protestant and "hostile" to the regime's politics. Wasserfallen thus "finds himself in a particularly welcoming milieu, which explains why it is impossible to find a witness who will consent to file a written declaration."[153]

The defiance of the various Protestant churches was not, however, welcomed by all of the faithful. A minority of Protestants expressed ire and fear over the activities of the pastors. Cadier was taken to task by a member of Lasalle's Evangelical Church for having given a sermon in which "the audience must have easily grasped the rather transparent allusions." That the church should "push their sons to revolt against the authority of the marshal and enroll them with the Communist troops and the partisans of disorder and anarchy" was intolerable to some parents. Declaring that the pulpit was not a soapbox for political agitation and the "overexcitation of spirits," the correspondent promised that she would send Cadier the latest issue of Sully, "which expresses much better than I can these essential truths."[154] A second Protestant, from Le Cambon-par-Aumessas, also praised Sully's "remarkable" articles on the STO and state anti-Semitism, affirming that "our opinions are solidly represented, but we still are ignorant of one another's existence."[155]

This claim notwithstanding, the local Protestants who were faithful to Vichy

150. CA 660, Dire to préfet, 19 July 1943.
151. CA 760, inspecteur de police to commissaire de la police régionale de Marseilles, 5 August 1943.
152. CA 760, commissaire principal to interior, 13 August 1943.
153. CA 660, "note," 19 August 1943.
154. G 363, commission de contrôle postal, July 1943. Letter from Mme Dreysse (Lasalle), 7 July 1943.
155. G 364, commission de contrôle postal, September 1943. Letter from Madeleine Boisset (Le Cambon par Aumessas), 2 September 1943. Sully's position on the STO was predictable. It asserted that acceptance of the program was a "patriotic duty of the highest order" (July 1943, 6). In the same issue it asked if the "sectarians [those Protestants unwilling to obey the regime] were ready to assume the responsibility for just [sic] reprisals?"

or the political line of *Sully* were a very small minority. A resident of Anduze thought the German presence in their town would have been easily accepted "if the Protestants and especially the pastors did not maintain a fierce hatred against them." The correspondent noted that "in this region everyone knows one another and are in constant contact. It's the nest par excellence of Protestantism, its birthplace. It's unimaginable."[156] At nearby Lasalle, a resident declared that the atmosphere was "heating up and the Protestants are by and large Gaullist."[157] Yet another Lasallian complained that not one of the youths who had been called up by the STO had either reported or been punished. Incensed, the resident excoriated the spirit of Lasalle: "The stupidity and foolishness are nauseating and make one want to flee to another planet."[158]

Lasalle's atmosphere was a source of anxiety for yet other residents—the times, thought one woman, recalled "the wars of religion."[159] Was there a correspondence between the political and religious differences that existed among the Gardois? There exist a few intriguing documents which hint that such may well have been the case, permitting the historian to suggest that the increasingly violent and decaying situation tended to reaffirm old prejudices. For example, following the Allied capture of Rome, it was reported that the Gardois clergy were relieved that the religious buildings and Catholic practices were "untouched by the Anglo-Saxons, who are mostly Protestant."[160] More generally, there was, at least at an institutional level, a clear reflex of distrust, if not hostility. Under the headline "Case of Conscience," *La Semaine Religieuse* posed a leading question. If someone is a Catholic, yet participates in religious services organized at the temple or synagogue, as well as officiates at certain rites used by the "heterodox confession," what must one think of his conduct?[161] In a similar vein, Monsignor Girbeau, in a lengthy reflection upon the major cause for France's fall—the "disorganization and breaking up of the family"—inevitably raised the issue of the declining birthrate. Girbeau claimed that this decline was given a push in the nineteenth century by "the doctrine of Malthus, a Protestant pastor," preoccupied by the danger of overpopulation. Malthus's doctrine, declared Girbeau, was a "crime before society."[162]

156. G 363, commission de contrôle postal, July 1943. Letter from X (Anduze), 7 July 1943.

157. G 358, commission de contrôle postal, January 1944. Letter from M. Richard (Lasalle), 19 January 1944.

158. G 358, commission de contrôle postal, January 1944. Letter from X (Lasalle), 23 January 1944.

159. G 358, commission de contrôle postal, February 1944. Letter from Mme Dreysse (Lasalle), 3 February 1944.

160. CA 572, sous-préfet of Alès to préfet, 10 June 1944.

161. *La Semaine Religieuse* (7 February 1944), 38.

162. *La Semaine Religieuse* (14 March 1943), 83. Unsurprisingly, the Catholic Church remained

That a corresponding degree of mistrust existed among the Protestants is not surprising. The police reports assert that whereas the Protestants were uniformly hostile to Vichy, the Catholics were generally "less implacable."[163] For example, the subprefect of Le Vigan reported that support for "Gaullism" was located primarily in the cantons of Sauve, Quissac, and St. Hippolyte-du-Fort, whose population was mostly working class and Protestant. On the other hand, the northern part of the *arrondissement,* weighted toward Catholic farmers, "shows no hostility at all to the government."[164] As a result, the Protestants betrayed some mistrust for their Catholic neighbors. According to one resident of Le Vigan, the "holier-than-thous are for Pétain and the Germans" and the parish priest "gives entire sermons on the loyalty we owe to Pétain, etc. . . . to hear such things from the pulpit is unprecedented." The "ordinary people" on the other hand, "are for the English and naturally listen to the English radio."[165]

These differences may have had an impact on the progress made toward ecumenism. This topic will be taken up in the Conclusion, but it should be noted that in early 1944, *Le Messager,* the journal of Protestant refugees from Alsace-Lorraine, published an editorial on the implications of a rapprochement between Catholics and Protestants. Though the paper hailed the gradual shedding of old prejudices, it wondered if true unity was possible or even desirable. It asserted that the two branches of Christianity were founded on "two principles not only different, but opposed: authority and liberty." In order for unity to be realized, one of the two confessions "would have to abandon totally what had hitherto been its very reason for being." Could Protestantism "deny what has always been its raison d'être: the liberty of conscience?"[166] And could it do so in light of the positions taken during the previous four years?

For the great majority of Gardois Protestants, the answer was clearly "No." The anti-Semitic legislation and roundups of 1942 have already provided us with the occasion to furnish some of the theological and historical reasons for the

---

hostile to the trend in mixed marriages. Although the summer of 1944 was a period of great material deprivation and relentless emotional turmoil for the Gardois, the church found the time to lament the growing number of Catholics marrying outside of the faith. In an article on the Cévenol town of Sauve, *La Semaine Religieuse* asserted that mixed marriages were "raging like a plague through the parish," and that despite the priest's exhortations on the danger of such unions, he was unable to "remove the blindfold that the misty intoxication of being twenty years old places over the eyes of some youths" (16 July 1944), 213.

163. CA 572, commissaire principal to préfet, 18 March 1944.

164. CA 777, sous-préfet of Le Vigan, rapport mensuel, 30 January 1943.

165. G 361, commission de contrôle postal, January 1943. Letter from Marie-Louise X (Le Vigan), 2 January 1943.

166. *Le Messager* (15 February 1944).

resistance of the Protestant community to Vichy's rule. With the arrival of the Germans and the burgeoning of the resistance in the Cévennes, the *refus protéstant* became even more pronounced. In order to contextualize and understand the rapidly unfolding events, the Protestant Cévenols conjured up images and memories from their Huguenot past. A resident of Anduze thus likened the local youths who, refusing to enter the STO and joining the *maquis*, to "the camisards, and like them they are armed by the English. Nothing new under the sun, except that the dragoons of Villiers have been replaced by the Wehrmacht."[167] The same images leapt to the mind of Lasallians in the wake of a parade of more than one hundred resisters, uniformed and fully armed, through the streets of their town in February 1944. One resident, overcome by this courageous and moving display, exclaimed: "Poor camisards: they've the right to celebrate. But it is frightening since the dragoons are on the lookout and one still fears that something evil will come this way."[168]

Something evil had, in fact, already arrived: the Gard, like the rest of France, had become the arena for armed resistance and savage repression. The references to the camisards point to the second of the two great consequences of the STO: the birth of the *maquis* and the advent of armed resistance in the Gard. Throughout 1943, a growing number of young Gardois plumped for the *maquis* as an alternative to the STO. At first, the great majority of those choosing this path were workers; but with Vichy's eventual suppression of most deferments, formerly privileged classes helped to swell the ranks. This was particularly the case with students. As one young Nîmois declared, "all the students talk about joining the *maquis*. It will not be long in coming: the class of '44 has largely disappeared already, and for that of '45, it will happen in the next few weeks." He then concluded in a mischievous flourish, "We'll then be counted among the terrorists, thieves, robbers, assassins, and God knows what else!"[169]

The general attitude of the young Gardois to the STO was summed up by a resistance poster: "The youth of France say: '*Merde*.'" The sheet, distributed by Libération, urged those who were called up to "hide yourselves if necessary. France is big, and the countryside is still rich."[170] However, an important distinction existed between those who, in early 1943 were fleeing the STO, and the actual *maquisards*. There were *réfractaires*, or STO-dodgers, well before there were *maquisards*. The former, it has been pointed out, "at

167. G 363, commission de contrôle postal, July 1943. Letter from J. F. Van Der Waarden, 7 July 1943.
168. G 358, commission de contrôle postal, February 1944. Letter from X, 2 February 1944.
169. G 358, commission de contrôle postal, February 1944. Letter from X (Nîmes), 1 February 1944. The march seems to have been a response to a raid against the town planned and then aborted by the Milice.
170. CA 328, sticker dating from January 1943.

first only thought to escape from being sent to Germany."[171] It was only over the course of 1943 that the STO evaders, realizing that the Allied liberation of France would not take place before the onset of winter, began to elaborate plans for their long-term survival. This entailed "direct action"—namely, the forced requisition of food, ration cards, and clothing—which almost ineluctably led to armed struggle against both the Germans and Vichy, and thus to closer ties with the organized resistance. By the beginning of 1944, there were five principal *maquis* operating in the Cévennes: the Arphy-Mandagout, Ardaillès-Vallerauge (founded and led by the pastors Georges Gillier and Laurent Olivès), Lasalle, Vallée Française (located near St. Jean-du-Gard), and Mont-Lozère-Vallée Longue.

What were the relations between the populace and *maquis*? How were the latter perceived by the former? Clearly, it was not until mid-1943 that the Gardois had to confront these issues squarely, for until then the resistance organizations had mostly limited themselves to propaganda and intelligence-gathering activities. But with the creation of the STO and arrival of German troops in the Gard, and the consequent emphasis upon popular and armed struggle, the populace found itself directly concerned. Either as spectators or as participants, the men, women, and children of the Gard were henceforth implicated in the drama and dénouement of Vichy.

In the first four months following the German arrival in the Gard, more than thirty important raids were undertaken by the Francs-tireurs et Partisans français (FTP). These acts included the sabotaging of rail lines, electrical pylons, and telegraph and telephone lines.[172] There was also a growing number of bombings directed at the offices of collaborationist organizations, as well as stores owned by merchants accused of collaborationism. Individuals suspected of collaboration also became the target of reprisals. The case of the miliciens Georges Guez *père et fils*, owners of the cinema in Pont St. Esprit, is exemplary. Following the massacre at Les Crottes (a hamlet in the department of the Ardèche), in which sixteen innocent Frenchmen and immigrant Italians were executed by the SS and Feldgendarmerie, the local section of the Armée secrète condemned the Guez for having compiled the initial list of "suspects" used by the Gestapo in its manhunt. The two men were subsequently gunned down under the marquee of their movie house on 8 October 1943. The local residents, it was reported, were astonished by the reprisal, for though the Guez were known for their "very favorable sentiments for the government, they never showed themselves to be

171. Jacques Poujol, "Histoire abrégée des maquis Cévenols (1943–1944)," *Causses et Cévennes*, no. 4 (1980), 232.

172. See Vielzeuf, *En Cévennes et Languedoc*, 60–65.

ultra-collaborationists."[173] But, fittingly, the Guez did shuffle off with a flourish of theatrical irony: the film advertised on the marquee for that evening was "Twenty-Four Hours of Happiness."

Such acts of summary justice lent a jolt of veracity to the increasing number of warnings and death threats delivered by the Resistance. One form commonly taken by these mortal missives was an envelope containing a miniature wooden coffin, often secured by a noosed cord.[174] Or there were instances of public warnings, such as in Tavel. Posters were found there one day which, in purple and black print, declared: "Victory Is Near. Your Turn Will Be Next, SOL. *A bientôt.*" The warning was embellished by the primitive sketch of a man hanging from a gallows. The police suspected that M. Paret, the local chief of the Milice, was the object of the threat. Although recognized as a "good and honest man," he was "reproached for repeating too often, with a pride that could rub his adversaries the wrong way, that 'We [that is, the Milice] are the bosses here.' "[175] Overall, the threats were fairly successful. They frightened most local mayors and administrators into tendering their resignations, leaving the prefecture and subprefectures with an ever-widening administrative vacuum which few dared to fill. As the subprefect from Le Vigan reported in early 1944, many of the area's mayors were threatening to resign, while others had already done so, which could have "serious repercussions on the communal administration."[176]

Moreover, the Alesian mining basin, through the quickening pace of resistance activity, began to hemorrhage seriously. There were, on the one hand, sporadic instances of strike actions. For example, on 14 July 1943, anti-government demonstrations unsettled the entire region. At Le Martinet, the women once again took a leading role: despite an intimidating police presence, the wives gathered at the entrance to the pit and successfully prevented their men from descending.[177] On the other hand, there was a steady growth of

173. CA 777, commissaire principal to préfet, 9 October 1943. The account of the bloody events at Les Crottes can be found in Vielzeuf, *Au Temps des longues nuits,* 229–35. Vielzeuf mistakenly states that the Guez were executed on 8 November.

174. For example, Albert Pourreau of Beaucaire sent a letter to Laval to complain about having received just such a threat, and added that his was not an isolated case: "Dozens of Frenchmen are on the verge of being killed in cold blood by a category of men that is becoming stronger every day in front of completely ineffective police measures that are a prelude to the coming days of anarchy." The local police commissioner, observing that more active collaborationists in town had not received similar messages, concluded that a former political opponent of Pourreau was looking to settle an old score (CA 300, commissaire de police of Beaucaire to commissaire principal, 15 October 1943).

175. CA 300, commissaire principal to préfet, 10 July 1943.

176. 4Z 211, "note," 14 February 1944.

177. G 364, commission de contrôle postal, July 1943.

industrial sabotage. The police and prefectoral reports from Alès through 1943 and 1944 are laden with notices of deliberate floodings, setting of fires, and breakage of equipment in the mines. In July, it was reported that the basin had been "the theater of several acts of sabotage"—a remark repeated with numbing consistency by the local authorities until the department's liberation.[178]

But most disturbing for local officials was the intensification of attacks against German installations. The campaign was inaugurated when, in December 1942, a couple of German trucks stationed in the center of town were demolished by bombs placed by the FTP.[179] On 20 February 1943, a much more serious blow was landed by the Resistance. That evening the "Maison Caro," a brothel exclusively servicing German troops and officials, was blown up by Jean Robert and the brothers Vincent and Bernard Faïta, all three members of the FTP. The toll was high: five Germans and two French women were killed. The German authorities immediately demanded that the French police round up fifty hostages; after a month's imprisonment, forty-two were released, and the remaining eight were deported to work in various Todt enterprises.[180] In October, a bomb was thrown into a formation of German soldiers assembled on the Place des Carmes in Nîmes, killing three and wounding twenty-seven. As with past attacks, an eight o'clock curfew was imposed and the Germans carried out several arrests.[181]

The Germans quickly and brutally responded to the challenge presented by the *maquis*. A rehearsal of sorts had already been played out at Aire-de-Côte in early July 1943. An armored German column of between sixty to eighty soldiers fell upon a group of young evaders who had settled in an abandoned youth camp in Aire-de-Côte, a desolate site in the heart of the Cévennes. During the ensuing battle, seven Germans were wounded while nine Frenchmen were killed, twenty wounded, and thirty-five (including the wounded) taken prisoner. In the aftermath of the lopsided battle, the Germans

---

178. CA 648, commission de contrôle postal, synthèse, July 1943.

179. Two bombs were set off near the parked German trucks on the avenue Feuchères, the artery which leads to the train station, on 8 December, and two weeks later, on Christmas Day, it was the turn of a truck stationed outside the Hotel Cheval Blanc, which is located in the shadows of the Roman arena (CA 777, commissaire principal to préfet, 2 January 1944 and Vielzeuf, *Au Temps des longues nuits,* 62).

180. CA 662, commissaire principal to préfet, 22 February 1944. Vielzeuf gives a detailed account of the bombing and its aftermath in *Au Temps des longues nuits,* 65–68. Jean Robert and Vincent Faïta were subsequently arrested by the French police, tried, and executed on 22 April 1943. Today there hangs a plaque outside the municipal courthouse, commemorating the place where the two men were guillotined.

181. CA 622, "note" of 19 October 1943 and CA 777, commissaire principal to préfet, 23 October 1943.

arrested the mayor of the nearby town of Saumane, as well as the commandant of the gendarmerie in St. Jean-du-Gard, both of whom were accused of complicity with the STO evaders.[182]

Apart from the serious blow this bloody collision struck to the organization and morale of the *maquis,* it also delivered an equally potent shock to the populace, frightened by the German's savage response to the activity of the Resistance.[183] Prior to this encounter, many Gardois seem to have viewed the *maquis* with a good deal of tolerance and sympathy. In a report on the incident at Aire-de-Côte, a police official emphasized the "hospitality with which the evaders (*réfractaires*) had been welcomed by the peasants of the department's mountainous region."[184] To be sure, even after the events at Aire-de-Côte, the local population continued to furnish a haven for the *réfractaires* and *maquis.* The moral and material support supplied by the Cévenols was underlined repeatedly in the police reports. In early 1944 we learn that a number of *réfractaires* were living in the countryside around Lasalle, whose "inhabitants appear to willingly help them and come to [their] aid. In fact, it's easy to see that the majority of the population of the Cévennes is hostile to the policy of Franco-German collaboration and to the departure of young men for the STO."[185] As the subprefect of Le Vigan asserted a few months later, it was nearly impossible to combat the local Resistance due to the "lack of information." The locals, he complains, "say nothing, either because they are afraid or because they approve [of the Resistance]. In any case, we must not expect them to support our actions."[186]

As Chiappe himself conceded in a report to Vichy, the *maquis* were "walking the Cévenol streets fully armed . . . [but] it is difficult to obtain information not just from the population, but even from the local authorities and gendarmerie."[187] Yet the public was an often troubled audience to the activities of the Resistance. The label "terrorist," generally applied by the authorities to members of the Resistance, was one a number of civilians would themselves have used. First, there were individuals and groups in the Gard who, profiting from the deepening political and administrative anarchy, plied the age-old trades of theft and extor-

182. CA 763, préfet to interior (n.d., probably 5 July 1943). Jacques Poujol writes that thirty-nine men were taken prisoner, of whom only twenty returned alive from the concentration camps to which they were sent ("Histoire abrégée des maquis Cévenols," 233). It is important, moreover, to emphasize that the young men at Aire-de-Côte were not *maquisards,* having neither yet organized along such lines nor having received military equipment or training.

183. According to Poujol, the action at Aire-de-Côte overwhelmed the local residents and "gravely discredited the Resistance in the Cévennes" ("Histoire abrégée des maquis Cévenols," 233).

184. CA 777, commissaire principal to préfet, 10 July 1943.

185. CA 662, "note" of 14 January 1944.

186. CA 572, sous-préfet of Le Vigan to préfet, 25 March 1944.

187. CA 667, préfet to interior, 3 February 1944.

tion behind the mask of the Resistance. For example, there was the case of Léopold Fougairolle, his wife, and two of his sons of St. Bonnet. The family, under the guise of the *maquis,* looted a number of Cévenol farms, and their arrest in early February 1944 was widely hailed by the locals.[188] There is little reason to doubt the police superintendent's observation that the population was sympathetic toward the young *réfractaires,* but condemned those "lawbreakers who, under the cover of a counterfeit patriotism, devote themselves to a variety of crimes, of which pillage and murder are the most common."[189]

Even among the actual *maquis* there probably were instances of excess, where the line between necessity and luxury was sometimes blurred.[190] Yet, in general, they showed a keen sense of the local moral economy, fastidiously signing receipts, usually with the Cross of Lorraine (the symbol of the Free French), for commandeered rations and material. Hence, when five armed individuals burst into a tobacconist's shop in La Favède and "requisitioned" his stock of cigarettes and tobacco, they left a small number of packets to provide for the French POWs who were supplied by that particular store.[191] The Alesian resistance groups also burned payments destined for farmers as a warning against the inflated prices they demanded for their products, a form of popular justice that was praised by nearly the entire population.[192]

Second, many Gardois, though neither pro-German nor even pro-Vichy, were as unnerved by the political character and activity of the Resistance as they were by the forces of repression. A number of letters witness to the discomfort felt by a bourgeoisie fearful of the Communist presence and revolutionary posturing in the movements. According to one official inquiry in late 1943, all of the Gard, with the exception of the mining basin, was hostile to the possibility of the Communists gaining power and "generally takes a dim view of the concessions

188. G 358, commission de contrôle postal, February 1944.
189. CA 572, commissaire principal to préfet, 12 February 1944.
190. Vielzeuf recounts one episode where a new recruit to the *maquis* was dressed down for having suggested, during a raid of food ration tickets, to pocket a few for the team's own use (*Au Temps des longues nuits,* 49). The title of one of Vielzeuf's other works, *On les appelait "Les bandits"* (Nîmes, 1967), underscores the author's unswerving belief in the moral rectitude of the Gardois resistance.
191. CA 572, compte-rendu de police, June 1944. A week later, however, there was the theft of nine thousand francs worth of tobacco, but no receipt was left.
192. CA 572, compte-rendu de police of Alès, 8 May 1944. On this subject, see the article by H. Roderick Kedward, "The Maquis and the Culture of the Outlaw (With Particular Reference to the Cévennes)," in H. R. Kedward and Roger Austin, eds., *Vichy France and the Resistance: Culture and Ideology* (London, 1985), 232–51. It was only as I was finishing the final revisions to this book that Kedward's book *In Search of the Maquis: Rural Resistance in Southern France, 1942–1944* (Oxford, 1993), appeared. A sequel to his earlier monograph on the origins of the resistance, this work is an extraordinary mine of archival documentation, oral testimony, and great empathy and intelligence. My hope is that this monograph provides additional evidence for the wealth of insights in Kedward's work.

granted to the Communists in North Africa."[193] This was echoed in a police report that asserted that most Gardois, hitherto indifferent to the character of the Resistance, were becoming anxious: "The fear of revolution is showing itself almost everywhere."[194] The statement of one Nîmois that France "could not remain neutral in the conflict that is now deciding her and Europe's fate" and had to side with the Axis powers against the Bolshevist threat, was the credo of only a small minority. Nevertheless, for many Gardois, the success of the Soviet Army and the strength of French Communists in the Resistance did cast a gray pall over the future.

The specter of German reprisals deepened the public's ambivalence toward the Resistance. Though the presence of the Germans was, for one Nîmois, "rather annoying (it's a matter of self-respect)," he found no less irritating those "imbeciles who, by their misplaced acts, threaten to bring about serious consequences. . . . I don't like the Germans, but if I catch someone engaging in this little game [sabotaging German trucks], I will not hesitate to report him."[195] A good number of fellow townsmen were equally nettled: an act of sabotage two weeks later was "severely criticized" by the public, who "feared reprisals on the part of the German authorities."[196] Even the residents of La Grand-Combe, a hardened population sympathetic to the Resistance, followed the dizzying chain of acts of sabotage with increasing nervousness. This work of the Resistance, it was reported, "weighed heavily on a population [that] feared the probable consequences: denunciation, repression, and especially unemployment."[197]

Through 1943 the reprisals had been relatively selective and usually undertaken by the French authorities. For example, Jean Robert and Vincent Faïta, two of the principal agents in the bombing of the Maison Caro, had been tried and executed by the French.[198] Indiscriminate terror was unleashed, however, with the arrival of the Ninth SS Panzer Division in early 1944. On 1 March, the eve of the Ninth Panzer's bloodletting at Les Crottes, there unfolded the infamous *les pendus de Nîmes* (the hangings of Nîmes). Pursuing the *maquisards* of Bir Hakeim,

193. G 358, commission de contrôle postal, December 1942. Inquiry undertaken by the Association des Anciens des Chantiers de la jeunesse de Nîmes, 31 December 1943.

194. CA 777, "note," 30 October 1943.

195. G 354, commission de contrôle postal, December 1942. Letter from P. Theulon (Nîmes), 10 December 1942.

196. CA 777, commissaire principal to préfet, 26 December 1943.

197. CA 648, sondage de la commission de contrôle postal, La Grande-Combe, 17 November 1943.

198. This did not prevent the local German military commander, General Kohlermann, from writing to Chiappe after the executions and expressing the hope, anticipated by the prefect in an earlier letter, that "this heavy but necessary measure will provide a healthy example to unthinking individuals" (CA 367, Kohlermann to Chiappe, 24 April 1943).

the Germans swept across the Cévenol towns of St. Hippolyte-du-Fort, Driolle, and Lasalle. Failing to locate the men of Bir Hakeim, the SS randomly arrested fifteen residents and brought them to Nîmes that same night. At six o'clock the following evening, the men (only two of whom, both grievously wounded and torn from their hospital beds, were *maquisards*) were piled into a German truck. The tumbrel made four stops. At each of the halts, a few of the prisoners were pulled from the back and hanged, either from a bridge (as on the Routes d'Uzès and Beaucaire) or from trees (the case at the Avenue Jean Jaurès and the Route de Montpellier). Guarded by SS troops, the bodies swung from their impromptu gallows until eleven that night; a couple were draped with the advertisement "This is how French terrorists die."[199] The cords themselves, on orders of the SS, dangled from the trees until 24 August, the day the department was liberated.[200]

The bodies of the hanged men cast horrifying shadows across Nîmes. Rather than discouraging the Resistance, it was feared that the mass hangings would instead lead to a "recrudescence of terrorist attacks."[201] In fact, in the wake of the executions, the various resistance movements swore vengeance in their tracts and papers, and the Fédération Gard-Lozère des Jeunesses Communistes called for a general strike of miners for 10 March. The German authorities took the threat of demonstrations and strikes very seriously. The garrison commandant at Uzès distributed a poster that warned against heeding the call of those "imbeciles who have given proof of their narrow mindedness." Asserting that a general strike would be unpatriotic, foolish, and destructive of "the good relations I have tried to preserve between the German troops and local population," the commandant concluded: "Parents, I am warning you! Keep an eye on the activities of your children!!"[202] In the end, the strike call was only partly followed. The miners of Cessous were exceptional; following the call of the PCF tract, they walked out for two days.[203]

The hangings underscored the impotency of the local administration. The French authorities were almost always informed of German police actions, usually supported by local miliciens, only after the fact. Administrators in name only, these men were reduced to keeping a tally of the dead and wounded, and maintaining the pretense of power and sovereignty. The lie to this conceit was given not just by the German military and police, but also by the Resistance. By

199. CA 572, commissaire principal to préfet, 4 March 1944.
200. For an account of the tragedy, see Vielzeuf, *Au Temps des longues nuits,* 164–91.
201. CA 572, commissaire central to préfet, 4 March 1944.
202. CA 777, commissaire principal to préfet, 11 March 1944.
203. CA 667, sous-préfet of Alès to préfet, 12 March 1944.

the spring of 1944, the *maquis* had acquired effective control over most of the northern and western parts of the department.[204] Living under a state of siege, the subprefect of Le Vigan reported that the *maquis* controlled nearly all of his *arrondissement:* "A certain number of cantons live in an absolutely independent fashion, immune to all control."[205]

A number of Gardois complained of the police's feeble efforts, asserting that they were "closing their eyes in many places."[206] This impression was confirmed by at least one gendarme in Nîmes, who did his best to avoid getting mixed up in "ces histoires-là." Though he had always succeeded "in remaining outside all of this," he did not know how long he could continue: "I want to have nothing to do with them—I ask nothing more—but I don't want to get knocked off, either!"[207] Poorly armed and poorly motivated, many colleagues shared his opinion.[208] The growing ease with which the *maquis* executed their acts of sabotage and requisitioning pointed to the deepening paralysis of the French police. It is revealing that the police were usually disarmed by the resisters (an option usually plumped for by the un-combative and irresolute gendarmes), whereas the miliciens were generally fired upon.[209]

Caught in the vortex of anarchy and violence were the civilians of the Gard. By the late winter and spring of 1944, the Gardois were at the end of their tether. Food distribution was less satisfactory than ever and the population was increasingly dependent upon a still-flourishing black market, whose prices were further inflated by the buying power of the German occupation troops. In April, a police official from Alès insisted that the food situation was actually better than it had been at the same time the previous year. Yet he acknowledged that public opinion maintained that the Gard, along with the neighboring department of Bouches-du-Rhône, was the most poorly sup-

204. CA 663, commandant de la gendarmerie nationale to préfet, 4 March 1944. He reported that the activity of the *réfractaires* seemed limited to the northeastern and northwestern parts of the department, the most troubled region being to the north of Le Vigan.

205. CA 572, sous-préfet of Le Vigan to préfet, 22 July 1944.

206. CA 572, "note," 15 May 1944.

207. G 358, commission de contrôle postal, January 1944. Letter from Berthe (Nîmes), 26 January 1944.

208. On the question of firearms, the subprefect of Alès complained that the size of the police force was insufficient for the tasks they were called upon to undertake, and that the small pistol and four cartridges assigned to each inspector were useless (CA 777, sous-préfet of Alès to préfet, October–November 1943).

209. For example, on 11 June a force of between 300 to 400 *maquisards* attacked the gendarmerie posts in the region of Alès, easily disarming the men on duty (CA 572, compte-rendu des renseignements généraux, 11 June 1944).

plied in the southern zone. Moreover, the official admitted that there was a lack of meat and fats, and that the local bread was "if not toxic, at least a permanent source of illness."[210]

If the baker had now become a source of fear, how much more preoccupying and deadly were the activities of the Gestapo, German troops, and Milice. The police reports dating from the final six months of Vichy paint a bleak picture of endless arrests, repeated military sweeps, and frequent, often senseless killings. A forty-year-old housewife, Mme Hebrand, was shot by German soldiers in the hamlet of Mons after having refused to obey an order. Her refusal, it turned out, was because she was deaf.[211] Such incidents added a tragic twist to the daily fears of the brutal and indiscriminate efforts to root out and destroy the Resistance. The official policy was summarized in a letter from an assistant to the departmental military commandant to the prefect. No distinction, he declared, could be made "between the terrorists themselves and rural youths who often are not conscious of their behavior and the [consequent] danger." Hence, his troops were ordered to consider anyone found with arms or "in the midst of collaborating with armed terrorists as partisans."[212] This definition was as rambling as the Cévennes, which, by late spring, was largely controlled by the *maquis*.

The final, frenzied heaves of German violence were aggravated by the relentless activity of the *maquis*. In early 1944, the frequency of the attacks, and the impunity with which they were carried out, prodded the departmental SS commander Hauck to complain to the prefect. He inveighed against the "atmosphere of terror" created by the *maquis*, whose "number and frequency call for severe measures."[213] His threat was not idle, for the tragedies of Les Crottes and Nîmes were played out a few weeks later. Yet these "lessons" were not learned: in the subprefecture of Alès during June and July 1944 alone, 216 attacks were recorded by the police. One hundred and eighty-one were robberies, 11 were acts of sabotage, kidnappings accounted for 7, assault and battery for another 10, and 7 murders topped off the list.[214]

It is impossible to determine which of these attacks were the work of the Resistance and which the work of bandits exploiting the deepening chaos of the period. For the public, however, the consequences were largely indistinguishable.

210. CA 572, commission des renseignements généraux, bulletin hebdomadaire of Alès, 29 April 1944.
211. CA 572, commissaire principal to préfet, 14 May 1944.
212. CA 367, conseiller supérieure Stackbrandt to préfet, 28 June 1944.
213. CA 663, Hauck to préfet, 15 January 1944.
214. CA 367, sous-préfet of Alès to préfet, 25 July 1944.

"The civil war is in full swing," announced one Nîmois: "Bombs here, bombs there, without one knowing the point to it all. One moment communist, the next moment ultra-religious, it's anarchy."[215] To add to the general confusion and despair, the bombs issued even from Allied bombers. On 27 May, an aerial attack on Nîmes, whose rationale has never been explained, resulted in two hundred and sixty-five deaths and more than three hundred wounded. Condemned by Bishop Girbeau in language he had never succeeded in finding on the occasions of the Jewish *rafles* or the STO dragnets, the attack compounded the already immense misery of the urban population.[216]

The Gardois seemed to maintain a certain critical distance even in the chaos of the final months and weeks. Upon the showing in Nîmes of an animated propaganda film that attempted to exploit the widespread anxiety over the Allied bombings, several spectators grumbled that they had been suckered: they had paid good money for the sort of propaganda that was usually free.[217] No less revealing was the reaction of the crowd at a bicycle race in Alès. The winner of the race, having offered his bouquet of flowers to a troop of German soldiers in attendance, was greeted "by no applause and total silence."[218]

Nevertheless, the words that crop up most frequently in the police reports are those of anguish, fear, worry, and despair. The overpowering impression is that of lassitude, of a general numbing of the population. One official reported in June that the public was "deadened" and simply wanted "to be finished with a situation that had become untenable."[219] Transfixed by the violence of oppressors and liberators, simultaneously hoping for and fearing an Allied landing, prey to wild rumors and flourishing fears, the great majority of Gardois, in fear and trembling, spent the last weeks of August waiting for their liberation.

215. G 358, commission de contrôle postal, January 1944. Letter from J. Boyer (Nîmes), 30 January 1944.

216. The front page of *La Semaine Religieuse* (4 June 1944) carried the headline "The blind and inhuman attack against Nîmes by the Anglo-American aviation." In the following article, Girbeau lambasted the barbarism of "such accursed methods . . . which shed the blood of innocents." Clearly, some ethnic and religious groups did not, in the eyes of the bishop, qualify as innocents.

217. CA 572, "note," 27 March 1944.

218. CA 572, sous-préfet of Alès to préfet, 17 June 1944.

219. CA 572, commissaire principal to préfet, 18 June 1944.

CONCLUSION

When God's commandments are clearly violated by the established order, the church must officially state ... to the government and the people: You shall not ...

—*Semailles,* 1944

Vive la France!
—Angelo Chiappe, 1945

In the third week of August 1944, the German troops stationed in the Gard, along with the rest of the occupation army in southern France, began to fall back toward Germany.[1] By the evening of the 23d, nearly all the German soldiers who were stationed in Nîmes, having commandeered all possible forms of transportation, including bicycles, had left the city.[2] The men of the Francs-tireurs et Partisans français (FTP) entered the city that same evening. Eliminating a few remaining pockets of resistance, they presented themselves to the city the following morning in cars bedecked in the French tricolor. Given this stunning proof that the city was again their own, the Nîmois joined in an "explosion of joy and astonishment." Quite suddenly, the flags of France, Great Britain, and the United States were draped from countless windows

---

1. If not pivotal, the accompanying military engagements nevertheless were costly for the Germans. Jacques Poujol estimates that the approximately 2,700 members of the Forces françaises de l'Intérieur (FFI) accounted for 1,000 killed and 3,300 prisoners; he does not, however, specify if these figures include miliciens and other French collaborators. See Poujol, "L'Histoire abrégée des maquis cévenols, 1943–1944," 241.

2. In fact, the city was not yet fully liberated as over the next four days trailing columns of retreating German forces from the southwest continued to pass through the Gard and Nîmes, sparking additional combat. It was not until the 28th that the Gard was definitively liberated. For a detailed narrative of the battles, see Bourderon, *La Libération du Languedoc Méditerranéen,* 161–92.

and doorways, framing streets awash with the townspeople celebrating their liberation.[3]

In the Gard as elsewhere, the *épuration,* or purge, of those accused of collaboration constituted the dark side to the celebrations. Along with the bouyant militancy of the regulars of the Forces françaises de l'Intérieur (FFI), there was the problem posed by the so-called *résistants de la dernière heure.*[4] Opportunists who jumped on the bandwagon at the last moment, they lacked the discipline of the veteran resisters and seem to have been responsible for many of the excesses of the liberation. By the first days of September, public opinion was already divided over the issue of the purge. There were those, generally from the "popular classes," who thought the purge too tepid, and others, from the bourgeoisie, who were "frightened by [its] breadth and hoped to shorten this 'period of terror.' "[5]

Instances of this "terror" were not wanting. One historian, although sympathetic to the Communist resistance, allows that acts of summary and popular revenge were fairly widespread, that innocents were sometimes victimized, and that the leaders who "sought to canalize this explosion were overwhelmed."[6] On 25 August, while the Comité départemental de libération (CDL) was setting up shop in Nîmes and flag-waving, *Marseillaise*-singing parades were converging on city hall, local women accused of "horizontal collaboration" were having their heads shaved "to the great joy of the public." This practice continued over the next several days.[7] There were numerous other cases of hazings, hasty arrests, and abuse by certain resisters, for even the *Renaissance Républicaine du Gard,* the organ of the CDL that took over the offices of Pujoulas's discredited newspaper, warned against such incidents. The paper affirmed that liberty was prey to extremes from both sides: "Should liberty turn into license, it creates anarchy and disorder."[8] This warning came the day after the summary execution of nine miliciens inside the Roman arena. Over all, it is estimated that twenty-three Nîmois, including the nine miliciens, lost their lives in the first wave of popular fury and summary justice.[9]

3. CA 314, note d'information, commissaire des renseignements généraux de Nîmes, 19 September 1944.

4. For the intricacies of the local disputes, both personal and ideological, between the FTP, the departmental chief of the FFI, and the CDL, see Bourderon, *Libération du Landuedoc Méditerranéen,* 204–11.

5. CA 314, note d'information, commission des renseignements généraux de Nîmes, 21 September 1944.

6. Bourderon, *Libération du Languedoc Méditerranéen,* 209. He places the ultimate responsibility on the "former executioners," who created the thirst for vengeance.

7. Bourderon, *Libération du Languedoc Méditerranéen,* 209.

8. *La Renaissance Républicaine du Gard* (29 August 1944).

9. See Bourderon, *Libération du Languedoc Méditerranéen,* 209–10. The historian thus takes issue with Robert Aron's suspect claim in his *Histoire de l'Epuration* (Paris, 1974), that the number of

Still, the newspaper itself had earlier thundered that those guilty of collaboration "must be eliminated with vigor, rigor, and rapidity in order to provide an example and satisfy justice."[10] To be sure, by the winter of 1944, a number of Gardois, exasperated by the sluggish pace of the trials, had recourse to more peremptory methods. The most notable example was the lynching in Alès of four local miliciens on 28 December 1944. Angered by the news that the Provisional Government had commuted the death sentence handed down to Alès's former mayor, Marcel Farger, a crowd of some 5,000 Alesians massed in front of the municipal jail. Though Farger had already been transferred to Montpellier, there remained behind four miliciens who had also been condemned to death. Summoned to the scene, the subprefect tried to defuse the situation, but to no avail. The crowd's fury, he recalled, was terrifying: "The police forces were powerless and I was held under guard. The crowd was the master."[11] Having pushed their way past a cordon of gendarmes, the crowd, led by a company of men from the FFI, entered the prison and pulled the miserable quartet from their cells. They were led into the central courtyard of the prison, lined up against the wall and shot by a squadron of men. Following the execution, the crowd filed past the bodies sprawled in the courtyard and out of the prison; an hour later, the city streets were quiet and deserted.[12]

Overall, the Cour de justice for the Gard, which was assigned the responsibility of judging the most important cases, delivered 92 death sentences, 16 of which were eventually carried out.[13] The trial and execution of Angelo Chiappe was undoubtedly the most publicized. Brought back to Nîmes from Orléans, where he had assumed the duties of regional prefect in early 1944—a position he had long sought, and enjoyed for such a short time—Chiappe was charged and found guilty of collaboration and intelligence with the enemy. Among the specific charges leveled against Chiappe were his membership in Collaboration, his active support of the Milice, his zeal in enforcing the STO, and his composing

---

executions in Nîmes was significantly higher (1:549). Given the serious criticisms of Aron's work and estimates made by Peter Novick in his comprehensive study of the purge, *The Resistance versus Vichy* (New York, 1968), the benefit of the doubt must go to Bourderon.

10. *La Renaissance Républicaine du Gard* (6 September 1944).

11. CA 1512, sous-préfet of Alès to préfet, 29 December 1944.

12. CA 1512, préfet to Interior, 30 December 1944. In fact, the FFI seem to have played a pivotal role in the drama. They were accused by the prefect of having incited and managed the execution, and he demanded that they be brought to justice. As for Farger, the moment of reckoning was only delayed. Found guilty of numerous instances of collaboration, Farger was shot and killed as he was stepping out of a police car in Montpellier a few weeks later. Interestingly, Bourderon writes that the local PCF (Parti communist français) representatives tried to calm the crowd, but the report of the subprefect affirms that the PCF had earlier harangued the crowd, which responded by demanding the heads of the miliciens. See Bourderon, *Libération du Languedoc Méditerranéen*, 259.

13. Bourderon, *Libération du Languedoc Méditerranéen*, 259–60.

a list of hostages demanded by the Germans after "Maison Caro" incident. (His role in the *rafles* of Jews does not figure among the charges.) He was sentenced to death on 21 December, and the sentence was carried out a month later. As the condemned walked to the gallows, he uttered several times in a strong but halting voice "Vive la France."[14]

In general, the administrative purge was relatively mild. The moderation was partly due to a hierarchical decision-making process. Dossiers of individuals suspected of collaboration most often issued from written or oral denunciations (just one of the many continuities that the liberated Gard shared with its Vichy predecessor). They were then forwarded by local purge committees to the departmental purge committee, which was a branch of the CDL and generally examined the cases with greater objectivity and less passion than their local colleagues. Finally, the dossiers, carrying the committee's opinion and suggested punishment (or, indeed, acquittal) were then given to the prefect, who relayed them to the relevant judicial or administrative authorities. By August 1945 the administrative purge in the Gard was practically completed. The hardest hit category was the police: 15 of 39 dossiers were found serious enough to warrant dismissal of the men concerned.[15] Otherwise, the relatively small number of dossiers examined, the small fraction of those found guilty, and the general leniency of the sanctions all attest to the temperate nature of the administrative housecleaning.[16]

The windows were thrown open, then quickly and quietly shut, in the house of God as well. Of all the sectors of French society, the purge of the church was perhaps the most sensitive and the most complex. Specific proposals to purge the church were rare, and the few made, such as one which recommended that "patriotic priests establish Ecclesiastical Liberation Committees in each region, and that all cases [of collaboration] concerning the clergy be submitted to them," were filed away and promptly forgotten by the authorities.[17] Nevertheless, as

---

14. *Le Procès Angelo Chiappe: Requisitoire de Georges Servigne, commissaire du gouvernement devant la cour de justice du Gard* (Montpellier, n.d.). In his recently published war memoirs, Marc Boegner registers shock at the condemnation of Chiappe. "His chances for a pardon are slight; he is discredited by his familiarity with the Germans. But he wasn't a traitor! [*Mais ce n'était pas un traitre!*] His poor wife must be in terrible agony. Alas! Revolutions—real revolutions—are greedy for blood." *Carnets du Pasteur Boegner, 1940–1945,* annotated and introduced by Philippe Boegner (Paris, 1992).

15. CA 779, préfet to interior sur l'épuration administrative, 11 August 1945. This contains lists of the number of dossiers examined and their final adjudication among various categories of departmental employees.

16. For example, 31 Gardois teachers were ultimately struck by sanctions, only seven of which resulted in dismissal from their posts; see Roger Bourderon, *Libération du Languedoc Méditerranéen,* 256–57.

17. Peter Novick, *The Resistance versus Vichy,* 131.

André Latreille has written, even if ecclesiastical collaboration was not the most urgent question in the wake of the liberation, it was capable of taking "a very embarrassing political and moral turn if clear and rapid solutions were not found."[18]

The potential for such embarrassing turns clearly existed in the Gard. Following the liberation, Bishop Girbeau swung abruptly from his staunch support of Pétain and Vichy to enthusiasm for de Gaulle and the Resistance. In the bishop's sermons, the resisters were now heros rather than terrorists, and the FFI was praised for its "heroic sacrifices."[19] Yet even here Girbeau's moral perspective was oddly skewed. Of the "universal suffering" that afflicted all Frenchmen, the "largest and most crucifying (*crucifiante*) share belonged to the prisoners who in their stalags, factories, and concentration camps over there count the months and days to their deliverance."[20] There is a stunning moral obtuseness to this statement. Along with the sudden solicitude for not merely the POWs, but also those men of the STO who had gone "over there" at the bishop's explicit urging, there still reigns total silence about the Jews who were sent "over there" and for whom deliverance came too late.

To cover his volte-face, Girbeau scrambled in unlikely places for doctrinal allies. In early 1945, *La Semaine Religieuse* reprinted an address given by de Gaulle, dwelling on his "demand for *the union of all Frenchmen.*" The anonymous commentator underlined that apart from a "miniscule number of unfortunates who consciously preferred the victory of Germany to that of France . . . the *immense mass* of Frenchmen never wanted anything other than the good of the country."[21] It goes without saying that Girbeau neither worked for nor advocated the victory of Germany, but it is no less clear that the bishop, by his vocal support of the STO and his silence over the roundups, aided those who, like his close and respected parishioner Angelo Chiappe, did seek such a victory.

Yet Girbeau's apologia went neither unremarked nor unchallenged. The bishop's vicar general, in the traditional New Year's address to Girbeau, sped through the "frightening atrocities" of the Occupation and, unsurprisingly, concluded that it was "preferable to turn our hearts to hope and envisage the future destiny of our diocese."[22] But the effort to wrench the clergy's heads in

18. André Latreille, *De Gaulle, la libération et l'église catholique* (Paris, 1978), 13. See also Latreille's article "L'Episcopat de France dans la guerre," in *Eglises et chrétiens dans la deuxième guerre mondiale*, ed. Montclos et al., 475–92. Latreille's perspective is especially valuable, as he was *ministre des cultes* from 1944 to 1945.

19. *La Semaine religieuse* (31 December 1944), 664.

20. *La Semaine religieuse* (31 December 1944), 665.

21. *La Semaine religieuse* (7 January 1945). The emphasis is the paper's.

22. *La Semaine religieuse* (7 January 1945).

the direction of the future was unsuccessful. It was reported in early 1945 that a "good number" of the bishop's subordinates were critical of his past positions, particularly in regard to the STO. In fact, many priests wished to see the bishop replaced by a younger and more active prelate who would show himself "more diplomatic in this politically sensitive department."[23]

The clergy's discomfort reverberated among the parishioners. Among the Catholics, there were "fairly numerous elements [that] seem uncomfortable to have over them a prelate like Msgr. Girbeau, who clearly compromised himself during the occupation."[24] This widespread unease eventually flared into protest in the summer of 1945. Bishop Girbeau, in a stunning flourish of ignorance or gall, attended the official 14 July celebrations in Nîmes. His presence generated a good deal of unrest among the participants and the ceremony was interrupted when representatives of the Association nationale des anciens de la Résistance (ANAR) walked out in protest. The next day flyers were distributed throughout the city titled "Let there be no misunderstanding." It declared that the ANAR welcomed all veterans of the Resistance regardless of their religion or creed, and respectfully bowed toward those Catholics who had joined the clandestine struggle against the Nazis. However, the manifesto continued, it was unacceptable that a "bishop who had so deeply collaborated and propagandized in favor of the STO should participate in the commemoration of this national holiday." The tract concluded with the warning that for all future ceremonies, the ANAR "will prevent, *by all possible means* notorious collaborators from joining with those of us who have the duty to honor the martyrs and the dead."[25]

In a subsequent exchange of letters with the prefect, Girbeau attempted to quell the controversy by ignoring it. Silence, wrote the bishop, was the only dignified response to the charges of the ANAR.[26] Of course, silence was no more dignified or defensible here than during the roundup of the Jews. Girbeau was not, however, removed from his post. His survival was attributable, in part, to the Vatican's great reluctance to comply with the Provisional Government's demands for the replacement or retirement of politically compromised bishops. Moreover, there was the artful diplomacy of the new papal nuncio to France, Msgr. Angelo Roncalli (the future Pope John XXIII), who replaced Msgr. Valerio Valeri, having become persona non grata due to his close ties to Vichy. Moreover, the French government was preoccupied with more pressing political

---

23. G 402, commissaire principal to préfet, 11 January 1945.
24. G 402, commissaire principal to préfet, 11 January 1945.
25. CA 1861, mimeographed flyer (n.d.). Emphasis in original.
26. CA 1861, Girbeau to préfet, 16 July 1945.

and economic matters. In the end, just seven of the listed bishops were ultimately retired or removed by Rome.[27]

Second, Jean Girbeau's name did not appear on the so-called List A. The twenty-four bishops who figured on this list were those prelates the government wanted removed from their posts for especially flagrant support of Vichy's policies during the war. Yet this omission did not imply an official acquittal or whitewashing of Girbeau's behavior. As Latreille emphasizes, the list was hastily compiled and based less upon serious investigation than on hearsay and random denunciations. As a result, certain bishops found themselves on the list who, even if not card-carrying members of the Resistance, were far from collaborators. By the same token, certain bishops who richly deserved inclusion were overlooked in the rush to judgment. Two such individuals, according to Latreille, were the bishops of Poitiers and of Nîmes. Their behavior was "notoriously more revolting" than that of some of their colleagues who found themselves on the damning list.[28]

Although Bishop Girbeau was never officially troubled for his attitude under Vichy, during which he was silent when he ought to have spoken and spoke when he ought to have remained silent, several of his clergymen, lacking the shield of status and the excuse of age, found themselves targeted by the departmental authorities. By January 1945, five priests in the department had been arrested, a sixth was in hiding, and three more had either been warned or shifted to another parish because of past activities.[29] These men, however, seem to have been the exception rather than the rule. As we have seen, after November 1942 the overwhelming majority of priests, though they continued to respect Pétain, began to withdraw their support from a regime that had become badly collaborationist. As a consequence, though very few priests subsequently swung behind the Resistance, they, like the great majority of their *attentiste* parishioners, were not politically compromised.

The Protestant clergy played a more prominent role in the first days following the Gard's liberation. The subprefects of Le Vigan and Alès both reported that nearly all of the pastors in their respective *arrondissements* had been resisters, and that several of them figured on the local liberation committees.[30] Of course, not all the pastors played roles as notable and publicized as Olivès, Gillier, or Cadier.

27. Latreille, *De Gaulle, la libération et l'église catholique,* 65.
28. Latreille, *De Gaulle, la libération et l'église catholique,* 34.
29. G 402, préfet to interior, 17 January 1945.
30. G 402, sous-préfet of Le Vigan to préfet, 3 January 1945; and sous-préfet of Alès to préfet, 10 January 1945.

In fact, one young pastor from Alès, Jacques Bousquet, was found guilty of having served as chaplain in the Milice and was sentenced to a prison term of five years.[31] The term *résistant* seems to have most often been applied to those who were hostile to Vichy and sympathetic to, if not actively involved in, the organized Resistance.

As a result of the political and moral visibility of many of its pastors during the previous four years, the Protestant churches enjoyed a certain prestige denied to the Catholic Church. This distinction was emphasized in the Protestant press. *Semailles* published a piece on the future duties of the Reformed Church, which included serving as a judge and conscience for political leaders. "When God's commandments are clearly violated by the established order, the church must officially state . . . to the government and the people: You shall not . . . " "Yesterday," the piece continued, "it was deportation to Germany, the persecution of Jews and the unleashing of vengeance . . . tomorrow it will be the dictatorship of money or social violence, the criminal power of trusts, the lies and injustice of nationalism against which [the church] will protest."[32] Given this moral and religious momentum, the Protestants predictably assumed a prominent role in local political life. Thus it was reported that, in the upcoming municipal elections in Le Vigan, the local Protestant community was particularly powerful due to their attitude under Vichy: "The role played by Protestantism in our liberation confers a tremendous authority upon it."[33]

Yet the corollary that one may expect in such a situation—namely, scorn or hostility toward the Catholic Church for its more ambiguous wartime role—did not appear. To the contrary, the lay public remained respectful of the various confessions, and even those who did not belong to a church showed no hostility, merely asking that the various clergies limit themselves to their pastoral tasks.[34] It may well be, as Jacques Duquesne suggests, that the church's resiliency was partly due to the fairly low expectations the nonbelieving public had of it from the very beginning. There was, moreover, the gap between a good segment of the local clergy and the bishop: the good deeds or words of the former ultimately carried the day over the latter's sins of omission and commission. The fact that an abbé sat on the departmental liberation committee, and a significant number of priests either figured on local committees or supported the new provisional government, helped reinforce their church's public image.[35]

31. G 402, sous-préfet of Alès to préfet, 10 January 1945.
32. *Semailles* (n.d., but most probably late summer of 1944).
33. CA 325, "note d'information" (Le Vigan), 18 October 1944.
34. G 402, préfet to interior, 17 January 1945.
35. Abbé Duplan, who had been deported for resistance activities, sat on the CDL, while the abbé Guyon of Rochebelle, who was reported to have spoken out forcefully against the politics of collaboration, was named to the liberation committee of Alès.

Yet the absence of anticlericalism among the Gardois should not be confused with the death of religious particularism. The few reports from the immediate period of liberation that deal with this issue are very suggestive. For example, attendance at religious services was reported to have increased since the Liberation, attributable to the light that many thought the clergy could shed on contemporary political and social problems.[36] A police report filed less than two months after the Gard's liberation insisted upon the local importance of the "duality of religions." The report's author emphasized the enduring influence of the pastor and priest in a "region still closely tied to religion." Though he offered no percentages nor reveals how he came to this conclusion, the official predicted that in the upcoming elections Catholic communes would continue to vote for the right and Protestant communes for the left.[37]

The difficulties in examining postwar prefectural and police reports render impossible a definitive conclusion concerning enduring religious divisions in the Gard, and the historian can only speculate on the abiding social and political influence of the local churches. Nevertheless, a few observations are pertinent. At the beginning of this study I remarked that the relationship between the local Protestant and Catholic communities prior to the war was one of mutual ignorance and mistrust. Despite the tentative efforts at dialogue and rapprochement during the 1930s, the situation in the Gard was a prominent example of the Protestant thinker Pierre Burgelin's summation of Protestant-Catholic relations: "We scorn rather than know one another."[38] There was, in the summer of 1940, a certain rapprochement between local Catholic and Protestant figures. Both churches had to face the sudden twist in France's fate; the reasons proffered for France's fall, and the consequent duties of all Frenchmen, were shared by both Protestant and Catholic leaders. Less than three years later, with the onset of the German occupation and the institution of the STO, another stage in interconfessional accord seems to have been reached. At the local level, the Catholics no less than the Protestants were alienated from the Vichy regime by these events. Clearly, the forced labor program, the collaborationist politics of Laval, and (to a lesser extent) the continued persecution of the Jews revealed and perhaps reinforced a moral failsafe point common to both religious communities.

It is possible, as one eminent historian of religion has suggested, that the

36. G 402, commissaire principal to préfet, 11 January 1945.
37. CA 325, "note d'information," 18 October 1944. Once again, we confront the problem of measuring the accuracy of such reports. Unfortunately, I have found no documents that carry hard statistics on the voting patterns, much less the actual adhesion to their religious leaders, of Protestants and Catholics. As with the issues of confessional support of Vichy, the historian is left to sift and weigh the impressionistic and general remarks made by various officials.
38. Quoted in Etienne Fouilloux, "Une Épreuve tonique pour l'oecuménisme?" in *Eglises et chrétiens dans la deuxième guerre mondiale*, ed. Montclos et al., 527.

challenges both religious communities had to face helped spark a renewal of interest and effort in ecumenism.[39] There certainly existed signs of spontaneous interconfessional collaboration in the Gard—thus Girbeau's warning in September 1941 that all ecumenical activities had to be initiated from above and not below. Beyond such organized activities, there was also, as we have seen, a continued trend of intermarriage, which worried local Protestant leaders no less than the Catholic hierarchy. And, of course, there was an inevitable mixing between Catholics and Protestants in the various resistance movements. And yet, and yet . . . as the handful of liberation reports suggest, the political division between Catholics and Protestants remained well defined. To this we may add the already quoted observation of the Protestant sociologist André Siegfried, who in the immediate aftermath of the liberation wrote that the atmosphere of the Gard was still impregnated with the passions and emotions of the sixteenth century and that the "moral separation" between Catholics and Protestants was so sharp that it made one think of rivers whose waters, of different color and consistency, met but never mixed.[40]

Siegfried's remark applies to the history of the Gard during the four long years of Vichy's career. The series of national and local faux pas that ignited Protestant suspicion and fears, the growing wariness on the part of the local Vichy representatives concerning Protestant activity, and the undeniable divergences between local Catholics and Protestants in regard to the politics and ideology of the regime all attest to fundamental differences between the two communities—differences that were not completely surmounted between 1942 and 1944 when both confessions faced common threats and shared common concerns. The impact of these differences on departmental society and politics in the postwar period remains to be studied; but, for now, it can at least be affirmed that though the Vichy era did not rival the events of the sixteenth century in the Gard, it sharpened the latent mistrust and fear that each of the communities held for one another. The period 1940–44 offers, if not a new chapter in the wars of religion, at the very least a powerful and neglected coda.

The endurance of such religious particularism was just one among the many continuities that bridge the immediate postwar period with both the last years of the Third Republic and the Vichy era. A few of these strands marked nothing more than the rapid change in governments and the paucity of supplies and material. There was, for example, an unfortunate continuity in the critical state of the food situation. The prefect Paganelli warned in November 1944 that the Gard still lacked most basic foods and staples, and that an organization of

39. See Fouilloux, "Une épreuve tonique pour l'oecuménisme?"
40. Siegfried, Le Protestantisme français, 23.

housewives called "Femmes de France" had called for a demonstration outside Nîmes's central market. In addition, the public was making critical remarks about the material benefits received by the FFI, echoing previous complaints over the privileges bestowed upon the Milice.[41] The subprefect of Alès lamented that the Gard's status as an "orphan" was as pronounced under the Republic as it had been under Vichy.[42] The food situation, he wrote, was desperate and warned that the public wanted acts, not discourses—yet again another echo from Vichy.[43]

One other parallel worth noting was the lack of local enthusiasm over taking up arms against Nazi Germany. It was no easier for the local authorities to convince young men to risk their lives in battle after four years of relatively sharp material deprivation than it was to remedy the grave material difficulties under which the Gard had been laboring under Vichy. The population avidly followed the progress of the war, but was reluctant to actually join the fray. One official remarked that the local youth were "more taken with pleasures than with duties"—a remark that could just as easily have been made in 1938 or 1939. Moreover, as rumors began to circulate that miners would be exempt from the draft, applications for positions in the mines suddenly surged, provoking the all too familiar complaint that "the farmers will be the only ones to get themselves killed."[44]

The question of the purge is of course tied to the issues of collaboration and resistance. As I have suggested, these concepts often fail to cover the variety of behavior during the war. Either flung as an accusation or flaunted as an honor in the years following the liberation, the notions of resistance and collaboration have, even in the hands of many historians, been charged with confusing moral and political elements. A summary review of the evolution of public opinion under Vichy will help provide the means to gauge the comportment of the individuals who were subsequently praised or condemned by their neighbors and by history.

It has been the thesis of this study that in order to grasp French public opinion and behavior under Vichy, the historian must begin his narrative at least as early as 1938 and the Munich crisis. We have seen that it was between 1938 and 1939 that certain elements, often identified with Vichy, have their origin. The absence of strong political leadership during Munich was equalled by a general lack of understanding of the political and ideological stakes involved. Even as committed

41. G 483, préfet to commissaire de la République (Montpellier), 2 November 1944.
42. G 483, sous-préfet of Alès to préfet, rapport mensuel, 25 November 1944.
43. G 483, sous-préfet of Alès to préfet, rapport mensuel, December 1944.
44. G 482, chef de la gendarmerie nationale to préfet, 12 February 1945.

a republican as Georges Pujolas, the editor of *Le Républicain du Gard,* though initially willing to go to war for the Czechs, proved vulnerable to the mixture of Hitler's threats and Daladier's paralysis, and ultimately agreed to the betrayal of not just an ally, but also of the democratic values underlying the diplomatic relationship. In addition, the crisis helped fuel the already smoldering tension, dating from the Popular Front and the Spanish Civil War, between the political left and right. While the one portrayed fascism and national socialism as France's mortal enemies, the other instead emphasized the menace of communism. As a result, the right not only diabolized the Soviet Union, but tended to concentrate, under the very shadow of Nazi Germany, on the enemy within—namely, the French Communists.

Finally, the ambient confusion and fear, the diffuse sense that France was prepared neither materially nor spiritually for war—sentiments that suffused the religious and secular journals, as well as public opinion at large—were tributaries that eventually fed into the rapids of Pétainism in 1940. These tributaries deepened after the declaration of war in September 1939 and the subsequent *drôle de guerre.* The clear lack of resolution, of righteousness and ardor of the Gardois who were called to the colors, was matched by the equally mechanical and hollow exhortations on the part of the press. It is, in fact, revealing that the local newspapers devoted more attention to the chase after the outlawed Parti Communiste Français than it did to examining and justifying the reasons that France and Great Britain had gone to war against the Axis powers.

It was only with the great flood of refugees, fleeing before the lightning advance of the Germans in May and June 1940, that the Gardois were abruptly confronted with reality. It is against the background of ineffable confusion and shock, issuing from the collapse of venerable, if not venerated political institutions and illusions, that the Gard's rallying to Pétain must be understood. Initially, there was nearly unanimous support for the old marshal, as well as for the armistice he sought. However, as we have underlined throughout this narrative, Pétain was all things to all Gardois. He represented less a distinct political agenda than a vague promise of respite and security.

Many of the traits eventually acquired by Vichy were anticipated or adumbrated by the press and the public. (In fact, many of these motifs stretch back through the 1930s.) The call for a return to the soil, for example, found a sympathetic audience in a department whose principal industry was winegrowing. The other side to this coin of *la terre et les morts* was xenophobism, racism, and anti-Semitism. Elements of the local press, most notably the Catholic *L'Eveil du Gard* and *L'Eclair,* did not hesitate to take up where they had left off before the war; their anti-Semitic ravings and politics of paranoia were now given free rein.

Although it is difficult to determine the exact impact of the relentless anti-Semitism of these journals, it remains the case that until August 1942 and the *rafle* of foreign Jews, the majority of Gardois were either indifferent to or (though much less frequently) supportive of the regime's anti-Semitic laws and measures.

Similarly, the themes of moral decadence and social decay, cited by Pétain as major causes for the defeat, found a powerful echo among both the local Catholic and Protestant churches. However, though both confessions agreed on some of the fundamental reasons for France's defeat, they soon diverged on the prescriptions for the country's cure. With the exception of *Sully,* most Protestant journals were notably reticent over the cult of Pétain and the thrust to the National Revolution. The great majority of Gardois Protestants admired the person of Pétain and probably welcomed his arrival in power. However, they rejected his idolization and failed to rally to a regime that seemed unduly attentive to the claims and influence of the Catholic Church. We were, admittedly, often forced to argue that the silence of journals and organizations bespoke a nascent resistance on the part of the local Protestants. Yet, silence can be thunderous in particular contexts. When coupled with frequent sermons and meditations on the imperatives of the individual's conscience and his duties solely before God, these silences were catalyzed and expressed the age-old *refus protestant.*

Given the paucity of police reports from October 1940, we were also obliged to argue from silence concerning the public's reaction to Montoire. It was suggested that the meeting of Pétain and Hitler at the train station, and the marshal's subsequent call to France to follow him down the path of collaboration, were received by a deeply dubious audience in the Gard. Though the doubts would only later blossom into public discontent, it seems likely that they were first sown by the policies symbolized at Montoire. Thus, as early as the fall of 1940, the limits of the National Revolution, at least in the realm of collaboration, were first drawn.

Nevertheless, resistance remained largely the property of the Protestants through 1942. The police and prefectoral reports from this period underline the doubts that many Protestants maintained toward the regime. The moral tripwire was set off by missteps like the Joan of Arc affair in 1942, and more critically, the Jewish *rafle* in August of that same year. At both official and popular levels, the local Protestant community not only vigorously protested the police actions, but also began to organize in order to hide and help escape the remaining Jews in the department. The events of that summer galvanized the Gard's Protestants, who perforce recalled their own past, that of a threatened religious minority, and they prepared to resist state oppression. Of course, the Protestants did not have a monopoly on moral outrage or political resistance. Based upon the official reports, it appears that the roundup stirred misgivings and revulsion on the part of Catholics as well as Protestants, and one is tempted to argue that, despite the silence of the bishop and Catholic clergy, the event marked the moral threshold beyond which Catholics no less than Protestants refused to pass. Yet it is no less clear—and no less surprising, given the emphases peculiar to their theology and history—that the Protestants were more prompt, unified, and explicit in their condemnation of the regime's behavior.

The distinction that sociologists make between empathic and normocentric responses may, in this context, be helpful. The former is a reflexive reaction to a specific event, one that elicits the observor's sympathy and (perhaps) active response. This category seems to apply to the majority of Catholics in the Gard in 1942. The sight of Jewish men, women, and children hunted down and rounded up by French officials sparked spasms of revulsion and protest on the part of those who witnessed the events firsthand. Yet, for a significant number of Protestants, the response to the *rafles* was normocentric. Such a reaction is rooted in the rules and history of the particular social group with which the actor identifies and feels compelled to obey. As Samuel and Pearl Oliner emphasize in their study of the altruistic personality, such responses are not accidental, but based on a well-established moral economy. This form of "altruistic" behavior issues less from "explicit conscious choices than characteristic ways of attending to routine events. Already attuned to conferring meaning on events through their particular moral sensibilities, they depend on familiar patterns to discern the significance of the unprecedented events at hand."[45] When the time came to choose, the choice for many Protestants had already been made. The reply of local Protestants to the violent policies of Vichy had been rehearsed over the preceding years and generations.

The novelist and philosopher Iris Murdoch describes the same mechanism of moral decision making through the concept of "attention." By this term, Murdoch means that serious moral commitment entails *seeing* the ordinary world: a world made not of generalities and abstractions, but of distinct individuals perceived clearly and honestly. Such transparency of sight is not achieved overnight, but is the work of years and love. It is a habit that is conditioned over time and that may not always be evident to the seer; it is a form of sight that, whether focused on the banal or the extraordinary, is deep and imperious and the work of history. Murdoch is insistent that the exercise of this moral imagination is not a one-shot deal. It is "a small piecemeal business which goes on all the time and [is] not a grandiose leaping about unimpeded at important moments. The moral life, on

45. Samuel P. Oliner and Pearl M. Oliner, *The Altruistic Personality* (New York, 1988), 221. See also Ervin Staub, *The Roots of Evil: The Origins of Genocide and Other Group Violence* (Cambridge, 1989).

this view, is something that goes on continually, not something that is switched off in between the occurrence of explicit moral choices."[46]

The relevance of this insight to the behavior of the Gardois Protestants is obvious. As we have seen in the great majority of Protestant sermons, letters, and conversations, the moral comprehension of the events of 1940–44 required no great leap of imagination on the part of the Protestants. They acted rightly, to quote Murdoch one last time, not "out of strength of will but out of the quality of [their] usual attachments."[47] It was nearly as if the very performance of seeing shadowed that of acting. However, by the late spring and early summer of 1942, which was marked by Laval's return to power and the reaffirmation of an official policy of collaboration, the majority of Gardois, be they Catholic or Protestant (not to mention Jewish), began to see clearly. This lucidity was aided by chronic and severe food shortages, which earlier that same year had sparked food riots and demonstrations through the entire department. The public's alienation from a regime that could not guarantee the necessities of life was exhibited with éclat on 14 July, when hundreds of Nîmois defied repeated official warnings and security measures and publicly celebrated the holiday. These demonstrations, coupled with increasingly pessimistic police reports on public morale, confirm that the divorce between the Gardois and Vichy began well before the German invasion of the unoccupied zone and the advent of the STO.

Still, it was not until the institution of the STO in the winter of 1943 that a common point of resistance against Vichy was created. The anti-Semitic, anti-Communist, and anti-Masonic legislation aimed, by definition, at discrete political or ethnic groups that—at least those unaffected could tell themselves—were fundamentally anti-French. The STO, on the other hand, was nondiscriminating and eventually universal in its reach. Its insatiability and disregard for the social or political backgrounds of its subjects not only served to unify local resistance to the Vichy regime, but often forced those who had been sitting on the fence to jump down on one or the other side. Of course, not all *réfractaires* became *maquisards,* and many of the evaders, like the young Gaussen, sought only to pass unnoticed as farm laborers. Nonetheless, many did eventually find their way into the *maquis,* having evolved by small, nearly imperceptible steps from *réfractaires* into *résistants.* The growth of the *maquis,* in turn, led to the creation of an alternative society, especially in the Cévennes, where the representatives and supporters of Vichy soon found themselves in a distinct and isolated minority.

Does this mean that a majority of Gardois were active resisters? Far from it:

46. Iris Murdoch, *The Sovereignty of Good* (New York, 1971), 37. Oliner and Oliner refer to this work in their study.

47. Murdoch, *The Sovereignty of Good,* 91–92.

the great majority were no more card-carrying *résistants* than they were *collabos*. Instead, they mostly were men and women worn by the relentless cares of food scarcity, prey to forces beyond their control and trapped in a quickening spiral of violence. But must we stop here? Is it meaningful to say that they were irrevocably disaffected from the Vichy regime and overwhelmingly wished for an Allied victory? The answer is not simple. For some, there seems to be a signal difference between *wishing* to have the yoke thrown off and actually setting about to *do* it. Thus Robert Paxton essentially limits the latter category to those who literally were card-carrying resisters; namely, those who qualified after the war as official veterans of the Resistance.

Yet this seems an unjustly narrow approach to the question of resistance. It is doubtful, for example, that most of the individuals who participated in the Bastille Day demonstrations or the miners' strikes, or the numerous Emilie Barrès and Berthe Chauvins, or the Cévenol Protestants who are even today reluctant to discuss their heroic role in the saving of Jewish lives, applied for such cards after the war. Yet each of these men and women, though not full-time members of the Resistance, through their modest actions and uttered thoughts, their reflexes of revulsion and scorn, their obstinate embrace of humanity, helped remove a stone from the edifice of Vichy. We must not, it is agreed, confuse dissatisfaction, even disobedience, with resistance. Resistance, as I suggested in Chapter 4, entails an advanced form of opposition involving a certain complexity of organization and clarity of goals. Yet such "institutional" resistance, if it is to be effective, requires widespread and sympathetic support. Popular involvement, be it listening to the BBC, participating in demonstrations, wearing the *cocarde,* or criticizing the policies of the regime, is not a lesser form of opposition. To insist upon the moral or practical inferiority of such involvement would be no less perverse than to claim the relative insignificance of a cathedral's flying buttresses to its steeple. It has been recently and paradoxically argued, in fact, that the Resistance, in order to defend itself and act, required an "active non-resistance."[48] This web of sympathy and complicity not only provided the Resistance with the means, both material and moral, to carry out its activities, it also provided the inspiration for an alternate society, informed by opposing moral and political ideals. In fact, popular dissatisfaction had, by the last two years of the war, not only denied moral and political legitimacy to the regime of Vichy, but had itself frequently metamorphosed into forms of outright opposition.

In his life of Solon, Plutarch tells us that the great Athenian legislator intro-

---

48. Jacques Semelin, "Qu'est-ce que résister?" *Esprit* (January 1994), 59. Semelin provides a nuanced and sympathetic discussion of the varieties of resistance, both as a concept and a historical reality.

duced a law that required all Athenian citizens, on pain of disenfranchisement, to take one side or another in a revolution. The rationale, according to Plutarch, was that men should not remain indifferent to the public interest at times of national crises, all the while "congratulating themselves upon having nothing to do with the disorders and misfortunes of their country." Solon, he writes, wished to encourage the Athenians "to attach themselves at once to the better cause, share its dangers, and give it their support, not to sit back in safety waiting to see which side would win."[49]

It is impossible to say with certainty where Solon would have stood on the issue of French behavior during the war. It is noteworthy, however, that Solon himself, following the advent of Pisistratus's tyranny (admittedly a far more enlightened one than Pétain's), placed his arms on the path outside his door and retired from public life. Yet, at the risk of his life, Solon also refused to provide moral comfort to the tyranny and held both it and his fellow Athenians in contempt. Though he did not storm the Acropolis, Solon had *chosen*. Pisistratus certainly understood this as a choice, and well aware of the danger it represented, he spared no effort to win Solon over. (Pisistratus's eventual success in gaining Solon's support represents nothing more than his decision to uphold most of the venerable Athenian's reforms.) By 1942, and sometimes well before, many if not most Frenchmen had also chosen. The men of Vichy were well aware of this; but unlike the Pisistratid tyranny, Vichy had neither a program nor the humanity (nor, after 1942, the freedom) to convert its citizens. Charles de Gaulle notwithstanding, France was not a nation of *résistants*. Yet, based on our study of the Gard, it may well have been a nation of a good many *sympathisants* with the Resistance—a nation where most citizens rejected, on ideological and moral grounds, and earlier than generally held, the regime of Vichy. It is possible that the varieties of opposition shown by the Gardois allowed, to echo Goethe, the world to go forward.

49. Plutarch, *The Rise and Fall of Athens: Nine Greek Lives*, trans. Ian Scott-Kilvert (New York, 1960), 62.

SELECT BIBLIOGRAPHY

PRIMARY SOURCES

Archives départementales du Gard

Affairs militaires
    CA 771
Associations secrètes
    CA 753
Censure: Notes d'orientation
    CA 634
Collaboration
    CA 279, 1480–87
Commission de contrôle des PTT
    CA 636–55
Couriers des préfets
    CA 303, 384, 560–62, 564, 739, 754, 791
Enquêtes et renseignements
    CA 752
Epuration
    CA 755, 779–80, 1524, 1516
Fêtes et commémorations
    CA 760
Grèves et chômage
    CA 714–18
Israëlites: enquêtes et recensements; questions juives
    CA 1473–75, 1477, 1488

Menées anti-nationales
    CA 300, 351, 367, 511, 569, 748, 759, 787
Municipalités
    CA 388–90
Rapports mensuels de la police
    CA 314, 347, 565–66, 572, 776–77, 785, 793, 1279
Ravitaillement général
    CA 701–3
Réfugiés
    CA 682–89
Résistance
    CA 267, 328, 745, 758, 764, 783, 1861
Service du travail obligatoire
    CA 763, 790, 993
Surveillance des juifs
    4 Z 241
Terrorisme, attentats
    CA 661–63
Voyages et visites officielles
    CA 378, 575, 751, 1184–85, 1280

Tribunaux spéciaux

Cour de justice, section de Nîmes
    3 U 7/200–275
Cour d'appel
    4 U 2/355–90

Chambre civique
    3 U 7/307–17
Tribunal spécial
    3 U 7/476

Newspapers and Periodicals

CATHOLIC JOURNALS

Bulletin paroissial de Sauve
Bulletin paroissial de Sumène
Bulletin paroissial du Vigan
L'Echo paroissial de Lasalle

L'Eveil du Gard
La Semaine religieuse de la ville et du diocèse
  de Nîmes
Le Viganais

PROTESTANT JOURNALS

Association Sully: Bulletin du groupe du Bas-
  Languedoc
Bulletin de l'église chrétienne réformée de
  Nîmes
Christ et France
Foi et éducation

Le Foyer protestant
Les Mages
Le Messager
Le Reflet d'Anduze
Semailles
Le Soc

GENERAL JOURNALS

Le Combat social
Courage
Le Cri du Gard
L'Eclair
Le Journal du Midi

Le Languedoc socialiste
Le Républicain du Gard
La Vie nîmoise
Le Vigneron du sud-est

SECONDARY SOURCES

Austin, Roger. "The Chantiers de la Jeunesse in Languedoc, 1940–44." *French Historical Studies* (Spring 1983): 106–26.

——. "Propaganda and Public Opinion in Vichy France: The Department of the Hérault, 1940–1944." *European Studies Review* 13 (October 1983): 455–82.

Azéma, Jean-Pierre. *De Munich à la libération.* Paris: Editions du Seuil, 1979.

——. "Le Drame de Mers-el-Kébir." In *Etudes sur la France de 1939 à nos jours,* 38–53. Paris: Seuil, 1985.

——. "Vichy et la mémoire savante." In *Vichy et les Français,* ed. Jean-Pierre Azéma and François Bédarida, 23–44. Paris: Fayard, 1992.

——, et al., eds. *Le Parti communiste français des années sombres, 1938–1941.* Paris: Gallimard, 1986.

——, and François Bédarida, eds. *Vichy et les Français.* Paris: Fayard, 1992.

Barral, Pierre. "Idéal et pratique du régionalisme dans le régime de Vichy." *Revue française de science politique* (October 1974): 911–39.

Baubérot, Jean. "Les Principaux Thèmes anti-protestants et la réplique protestante." *Revue d'histoire et de philosophie religieuse,* no. 3 (1973): 178–221.

Baudot, Michel. *L'Opinion publique sous l'occupation: L'Exemple d'un département français, 1939–1945.* Paris: Presses universitaires de France, 1960.

Bayac, J. Delperrie de. *L'Histoire de la Milice, 1918–1945.* Paris: Fayard, 1969.

Bédarida, René. *Les Armes de l'esprit: Témoignage chrétien (1941–1944).* Paris: Editions ouvrières, 1977.

Bellanger, Claude, ed. *Histoire de la presse française.* 5 vols. Paris, 1972.

Bloch, Marc. *Strange Defeat.* Translated by Gerard Hopkins. New York: Norton, 1968.

Boegner, Marc. *The Long Road to Unity.* London: Collins, 1970.

———, and André Siegfried, eds. *Le Protestantisme français.* Paris: Plon, 1945.

Boegner, Philippe, ed. *Carnets du pasteur Boegner, 1940–1945.* Paris: Fayard, 1992.

Bolle, Pierre. "Des Voix Protestants." In *Spiritualité, théologie et résistance,* ed. Pierre Bolle and Jean Godel, 151–81. Grenoble: Presses universitaires de Grenoble, 1987.

———. "L'Influence du barthisme dans le protestantisme français." In *Eglises et chrétiens dans la deuxième guerre mondiale,* ed. Xavier de Montclos et al., 59–66. Lyon: Presses universitaires de Lyon, 1978–1982.

———. "Les Protestants et leurs églises durant la seconde guerre mondiale." *Revue d'histoire moderne et contemporaine* (April–June 1979): 286–97.

———, and Jean Godel, eds. *Spiritualité, théologie et résistance.* Grenoble: Presses universitaires de Grenoble, 1987.

Bourderon, Roger. *La Libération du Languedoc Méditerranéen.* Paris: Hachette, 1971.

———. "Mouvement de la main d'oeuvre et STO dans les mines du Gard." *Revue d'histoire de la deuxième guerre mondiale* (October, 1978): 47–66.

———. "Le Ravitaillement et les prix dans le département du Gard (été-automne 1940)." *Revue d'histoire de la deuxième guerre mondiale* (July 1970): 37–60.

"Bousquet: Les pièces du procès . . . qui n'aura pas lieu." *Le Nouvel Observateur* (10–16 June 1993): 28–33.

Cabanel, Patrick. "Veillée face à l'antisémitisme: Le Mouvement du christianisme social (1933–1940)." In *Cévennes: Terre de Refuge, 1940–1944,* ed. Philippe Joutard et al., 213–29. Montpellier: Presses du Languedoc, 1987.

Cairns, John C. "Along the Road Back to France, 1940." *American Historical Review* 64 (April 1959): 583–603.

Cépède, Michel. *Agriculture et alimentation en France durant la deuxième guerre mondiale.* Paris: Génin, 1961.

Cobb, Richard. *French and Germans, Germans and French.* Hanover, N.H.: University Press of New England, 1984.

Cointet, Jean-Paul. "Les Chevaliers du Maréchal." *L'Histoire* 80 (1985): 110–14.

———. "La Légion français des combattants." In *Le Gouvernement de Vichy, 1940–1942.* Paris: A. Colin, 1971.

Cointet-Labrousse, Michèle. *Vichy et le fascisme.* Brussels: Editions Complexe, 1987.

Combes, Gérard. "L'Esprit public en Haute-Loire, 1940–1942." *Revue d'histoire de la deuxième guerre mondiale* (January 1972): 51–71.

Conan, Eric. "Mort d'un collabo." *L'Express* (17 June 1993): 11–17.

Cone, Michèle C. *Artists Under Vichy: A Case of Prejudice and Persecution.* Princeton: Princeton University Press, 1992.

Cosson, Armand. *Nîmes et le Gard dans la guerre 1939–1945.* Le Coteau: Horvath, 1988.

Coutau-Bégarie, Hervé, and Claude Haun. *Darlan.* Paris: 1989.

Coutrot, Aline, and F.-G. Dreyfus. *Les Forces religieuses dans la société française.* Paris: A. Colin, 1965.

Dachin, Pierre. "Débat." In *Spiritualité, théologie, et résistance,* ed. Pierre Bolle and Jean Godel, 204–11. Grenoble: Presses universitaires de Grenoble, 1987.

Defrasne, Jean. *Histoire de la collaboration.* Paris: Presses universitaires de France, 1982.

Delpech, François. "Les Eglises et la persecution raciale." In *Eglises et chrétiens dans la deuxième guerre mondiale,* ed. Xavier de Montclos et al., 257–72. Lyon: Presses universitaires de Lyon, 1978–1982.

Dixon, John. "Manipulators of Vichy Propaganda: A Case Study in Personality." In *Vichy*

France and the Resistance: Culture and Ideology, ed. H. R. Kedward and Roger Austin, 48–72. London: Croom and Helm, 1985.

Droite et gauche de 1789 à nos jours en Languedoc-Roussillon. Montpellier: Presses universitaires de Montpellier, 1975.

Dubief, Henri. *Le Déclin de la IIIe république.* Paris: Editions du Seuil, 1976.

Dumas, André. "Courants théologiques dans le protestantisme français entre 1930 et 1939." In *Spiritualité, théologie, et résistance,* ed. Pierre Bolle and Jean Godel, 72–78. Grenoble: Presses universitaires de Grenoble, 1987.

Duquesne, Jacques. *Les Catholiques français sous l'occupation.* Rev. ed. Paris: Grasset, 1986.

Durand, Yves. *Vichy, 1940–1944.* Paris: Bordas, 1972.

Duroselle, Jean-Baptiste. *L'Abîme, 1939–1945.* Paris: Imprimerie nationale, 1982.

——. *La Décadence, 1932–1939.* Paris: Imprimerie nationale, 1979.

Dutourd, Jean. *Au bon beurre.* Paris: Gallimard, 1952.

——. *Les Taxis de la Marne.* Paris: Gallimard, 1956.

Encrevé, André. *Les Protestants en France de 1800 à nos jours.* Paris: Stock, 1985.

Etudes sur la France de 1939 à nos jours. Paris: Seuil, 1985.

Faure, Christian. *Le Projet culturel de Vichy.* Lyon: Presses universitaires de Lyon, 1989.

Ferro, Marc. *Pétain.* Paris: Fayard, 1987.

Finkielkraut, Alain. *La Mémoire vaine.* Paris: Gallimard, 1989. Translated by Roxanne Lapidus and Sima Godfrey as *Remembering in Vain.* New York: Columbia University Press, 1992.

Fishman, Sarah. *We Will Wait: Wives of French Prisoners of War, 1940–1945.* New Haven: Yale University Press, 1991.

Fitzpatrick, Brian. *Catholic Royalism in the Department of the Gard, 1814–1852.* Cambridge: Cambridge University Press, 1983.

Flonneau, Jean-Marie. "L'Evolution de l'opinion publique de 1940 à 1944." In *Vichy et les Français,* ed. Jean-Pierre Azéma and François Bédarida, 506–22. Paris: Fayard, 1992.

Fouilloux, Etienne. "Les Eglises contestées." In *L'Histoire religieuse de la France (19ème–20ème siècles): Problèmes et méthodes,* ed. Jean-Marie Mayeur, 143–83. Paris: A. Colin, 1975.

——. "Une épreuve tonique pour l'oecuménisme?" In *Eglises et chrétiens dans la deuxième guerre mondiale,* ed. Xavier de Montclos et al. Lyon: Presses universitaires de Lyon, 1982.

Garrisson, Janine. *L'Homme Protestant.* Brussels: Editions Complexe, 1986.

Gildea, Robert. *Education in Provincial France, 1800–1914: A Study of Three Departments.* Oxford: Oxford University Press, 1983.

Giran, Paul. "Le Régionalisme vu de la Tour Magne," *Mémoires d'Académie de Nîmes* 48 (1928–30).

Girardet, Raoul. *Mythes et mythologies politiques.* Paris: Editions du Seuil, 1986.

Gordon, Bertram. *Collaborationism in France during the Second World War.* Ithaca: Cornell University Press, 1980.

Le Gouvernement de Vichy, 1940–1942. Paris: A. Colin, 1971.

Graham, Helen, and Paul Preston, eds. *The Popular Front in Europe.* New York: St. Martin's Press, 1987.

Griffiths, Richard. *Marshal Pétain.* London: Constable, 1970.

Guéhenno, Jean. *Journal des années noires.* Paris: Gallimard, 1947.

Guillemin, Henri. *Nationalistes et nationaux, 1870–1940.* Paris: Gallimard, 1974.

Guillon, Jean-Marie. "La Philosophie politique de la Révolution nationale." In *Vichy et les Français,* ed. Jean-Pierre Azéma and François Bédarida, 167–83. Paris: Fayard, 1992.

Halimi, André. *La Délation sous l' occupation.* Paris: Editions Alain Moreau, 1983.

Hallie, Philip P. *Lest Innocent Blood Be Shed*. New York: Harper and Row, 1979.
Halls, W. D. "French Christians and the German Occupation." In *Collaboration in France: Politics and Culture during the Nazi Occupation, 1940–1944*, ed. Gerhard Hirschfield and Patrick Marsh, 72–91. New York: Berg, 1989.
———. *The Youth of Vichy France*. Oxford: Oxford University Press, 1981.
Hawes, Stephen, and Ralph White, eds. *Resistance in Europe, 1939–1945*. London: A. Lane, 1975.
Hirschfield, Gerhard, and Patrick Marsh, eds. *Collaboration in France: Politics and Culture during the Nazi Occupation, 1940–1944*. New York: Berg, 1989.
L'Histoire. No. 80 (1985). Special issue devoted to Vichy.
L'Histoire de Nîmes. Aix-en-Provence: Edisud, 1982.
Hoffmann, Stanley. "Collaborationism in France during World War Two." *Journal of Modern History* (September 1968): 375–95. Reprinted in his *Decline or Renewal? France Since the 1930s*.
———. *Decline or Renewal? France Since the 1930s*. New York: Viking, 1974.
———. "Le Désastre de 1940." In *Etudes sur la France de 1939 à nos jours*, 22–37. Paris: Seuil, 1985.
Horne, Alastair. *To Lose A Battle: France, 1940*. London: Macmillan, 1969.
Husson, Jean-Pierre. "L'Itinéraire d'un haut fonctionnaire: René Bousquet." In *Vichy et les français*, ed. Jean-Pierre Azéma and François Bédarida, 287–301. Paris: Fayard, 1992.
Joutard, Philippe, et al., eds. *Cévennes: Terre de refuge, 1940–1944*. Montpellier: Presses du ·Languedoc, 1987.
Juilliard, Jacques. "Sur un fascisme imaginaire: A propos d'un livre de Zeev Sternhell." *Annales: ESC* (July–August 1984): 849–61.
Kedward, H. R. *In Search of the Maquis: Rural Resistance in Southern France, 1942–1944*. Oxford: Oxford University Press, 1993.
———. "The Maquis and the Culture of the Outlaw (With Particular Reference to the Cévennes)." In *Vichy France and the Resistance: Culture and Ideology*, ed. H. R. Kedward and Roger Austin, 232–51. London: Croom and Helm, 1985.
———. "Patriots and Patriotism in Vichy France." *Transactions of the Royal Historical Society* 32 (1982): 175–92.
———. *Resistance in Vichy France: A Study of Ideas and Motivation in the Southern Zone, 1940–1942*. Oxford: Oxford University Press, 1978.
———, and Roger Austin, eds. *Vichy France and the Resistance: Culture and Ideology*. London: Croom and Helm, 1985.
Krumreich, Gerd. "The Cult of Joan under the Vichy Régime." In *Collaboration in France: Politics and Culture during the Nazi Occupation, 1940–44*, ed. Gerhard Hirschfield and Patrick Marsh, 92–102. New York: Berg, 1989.
Laborie, Pierre. "Historiens sous haute surveillance." *Esprit* (January 1994): 36–49.
———. "1942 et le sort des Juifs: quel tournant dans l'opinion?" *Annales: ESC* (May–June 1993): 655–66.
———. *L'Opinion française sous Vichy*. Paris: Editions du Seuil, 1990.
———. *Résistants, vichyssois et autres*. Paris: Editions du CNRS, 1980.
Lacouture, Jean. *De Gaulle: The Rebel, 1890–1944*. Translated by Patrick O'Brian. New York: Norton, 1991.
Laguerre, Bernard. "Les Biographies de Pétain." In *Vichy et les Français*, ed. Jean-Pierre Azéma and François Bédarida, 45–56. Paris: Fayard, 1992.
Langlois, Claude. "Le Régime de Vichy et le clergé d'aprés les 'Semaines religieuses' des diocèses de la zone libre." *Revue française de science politique* 22 (August 1972): 750–74.
Larkin, Maurice. *France Since the Popular Front*. Oxford: Oxford University Press, 1988.

Latreille, André. *De Gaulle, la libération et l'église catholique.* Paris: Cerf, 1978.

——. "L'Episcopat de France dans la guerre." In *Eglises et chrétiens dans la deuxième guerre mondiale,* ed. Xavier de Montclos et al., 475–92. Lyon: Presses universitaires de Lyon, 1982.

Lévy, Claude, and Dominique Veillon. "Propagande et modelage des esprits." In *Vichy et les français,* ed. Jean-Pierre Azéma and François Bédarida, 184–202. Paris: Fayard, 1992.

Levy, David A. L. "The French Popular Front, 1936–37." In *The Popular Front in Europe,* ed. Helen Graham and Paul Preston, 58–83. New York: St. Martin's Press, 1987.

Lewis, Gwynne. *The Second Vendée: The Continuity of Counterrevolution in the Department of the Gard, 1789–1815.* Oxford: Oxford University Press, 1978.

Lottman, Herbert. *Pétain: Hero or Traitor, the Untold Story.* New York: Morrow, 1985.

Marichal, W. "Des Belges en Cévennes." *Causses et Cévennes,* no. 4 (1976): 264–67.

Marrus, Michael. *The Politics of Assimilation: The French Jewish Community at the Time of the Dreyfus Affair.* New York: 1971.

——, and Robert O. Paxton. *Vichy France and the Jews.* New York: Basic Books, 1981.

Mayeur, Jean-Marie. "Les évêques dans l'avant guerre." In *Eglises et chrétiens dans la deuxième guerre mondiale,* ed. Xavier de Montclos et al., 11–16. Lyon: Presses universitaires de Lyon, 1982.

——, ed. *L'Histoire religieuse de la France (19ème–20ème siècles): Problèmes et méthodes.* Paris: A. Colin, 1975.

——, and Claude Langlois. "Les Eglises commes sociétés religieuses." In *L'Histoire religieuse de la France: Problèmes et méthodes,* ed. Jean-Marie Mayeur, 11–40. Paris: A. Colin, 1975.

Mehl, Roger. *Le Pasteur Marc Boegner.* Paris: Plon, 1987.

Mermet, Pierre. "Enquête sur la main d'oeuvre française au service de l'Allemagne (1940–1944)." *Bulletin de l'Institut d'histoire du temps présent,* no. 7 (March 1982): 40–54.

Michel, Henri. *Les Courants de pensée de la résistance.* Paris: Presses universitaires de France, 1962.

——. *La Défaite de la France.* Paris: Presses universitaires de France, 1980.

——. *Drôle de guerre.* Paris: Hachette, 1972.

——. *Pétain, Laval, Darlan: Trois Politiques?* Paris: Flammarion, 1972.

——. *Vichy: Année 40.* Paris: Robert Laffont, 1966.

Miller, Gérard. *Les Pousse-au-jouir du maréchal Pétain.* Paris: Editions du Seuil, 1975.

Milward, Alan. *The New Order and the French Economy.* Oxford: Clarendon Press, 1970.

Montclos, Xavier de. "Des Voix d'évêques et de prêtres en Europe." In *Spiritualité, théologie et résistance,* ed. Pierre Bolle and Jean Godel, 130–46. Grenoble: Presses universitaires de Grenoble, 1987.

——. *Eglises et chrétiens dans la deuxième guerre mondiale.* Lyon: Presses universitaires de Lyon, 1982.

Murdoch, Iris. *The Sovereignty of Good.* New York: Schocken, 1971.

Novick, Peter. *The Resistance Versus Vichy: The Purge of Collaborators in Liberated France.* New York: Columbia University Press, 1968.

Oliner, Samuel P., and Pearl M. Oliner. *The Altruistic Personality: Rescuers of Jews in Nazi Europe.* New York: Free Press, 1988.

Olivès, Laurent. "Valleraugue 1940–1944." *Causses et Cévennes,* no. 3 (1984): 208–11.

Ollier, Nicole. *L'Exode sur les routes de l' an 40.* Paris: Laffont, 1970.

Ory, Pascal. *Les Collaborateurs, 1940–1945.* Paris: Editions du Seuil, 1976.

Paxton, Robert O. *Vichy France: Old Order and New Guard, 1940–1944.* New York: Knopf, 1972.

Peukert, Detlev. *Inside Nazi Germany: Conformity, Opposition, and Racism in Everyday Life.* New Haven: Yale University Press, 1987.

Pierrard, Pierre. *Juifs et catholiques français.* Paris: Fayard, 1970.

Plutarch. *The Rise and Fall of Athens: Nine Greek Lives.* Translated by Ian Scott-Kilvert. New York: Penguin, 1960.

Ponson, C. "L'Information sur le nazisme dans la presse catholique française entre 1933 et 1938." In *Eglises et chrétiens dans la deuxième guerre mondiale,* ed. Xavier de Montclos et al., 17–32. Lyon: Presses universitaires de Lyon, 1987.

Posen, Barry R. *The Sources of Military Doctrine: France, Britain, and Germany Between the World Wars.* Ithaca: Cornell University Press, 1984.

Poujol, Jacques. "Filières, répartition, caractéristiques du refuge juif." In *Cévennes: Terre de refuge, 1940–1944,* ed. Philippe Joutard et al., 137–51. Montpellier: Presses de Languedoc, 1987.

———. "Histoire abrégée des maquis Cévenols (1943–1944)." *Causses et Cévennes,* no. 4 (1980): 231–42.

Rémond, René. "Devoir de desobéissance à l'autorité?" In *Spiritualité, théologie et résistance,* ed. Pierre Bolle and Jean Godel, 259–69. Grenoble: Presses universitaires de Grenoble, 1987.

———. *Les Droites en France.* Rev. ed. Paris: Aubier Montaigne, 1982.

———, Jean-Pierre Azéma, François Bédarida et al. *Paul Touvier et l'église. Rapport de la commission historique instituée par le Cardinal Decourtray.* Paris: Fayard, 1992.

Rioux, Jean-Pierre. "Survivre." *L'Histoire,* no. 80 (1985): 84–100.

Rossignol, Dominique. "La Franc-maçonnerie accusée et dissoute, 1940–44." *L'Histoire,* no. 49 (1982): 38–44.

———. *Vichy et les Francs-Maçons: La Liquidation des sociétés secrètes, 1940–1944.* Paris: J. C. Lattès, 1981.

Rousso, Henry. *La Collaboration.* Paris: Editions MA, 1987.

———. *Le Syndrome de Vichy, 1944–198 . . .* Paris: Editions de Seuil, 1987. Translated by Arthur Goldhammer as *The Vichy Syndrome: History and Memory in France since 1944.* Cambridge: Harvard University Press, 1991.

Sand, Shlomo. "L'Idéologie fasciste en France." *Esprit* (August–September 1983): 149–60.

Schram, Stuart R. *Protestantism and Politics in France.* Alençon: Corbière et Jugain, 1954.

Schuker, Stephen A. "France and the Remilitarization of the Rhineland, 1936." *French Historical Studies* (Spring 1986): 299–338.

Schwartz, Paula L. "*Partisanes* and Gender Politics in Vichy France." *French Historical Studies* 16, no. 1 (Spring 1989): 126–51.

Secondy, Louis. "Question religieuse et enseignement au lycée de Nîmes entre 1850 et 1900." *Annales du Midi* (October–December 1982): 387–402.

Semelin, Jacques. "Qu'est-ce que 'résister?' " *Esprit* (January 1994): 50–63.

Servigne, Georges. *Le Procès Angelo Chiappe: Requisitoire de Georges Servigne, Commissaire du gouvernement devant la cour de justice du Gard.* Montpellier: n.p., n.d.

Shennan, Andrew. *Rethinking France: Plans for Renewal, 1940–1946.* Oxford: Clarendon Press, 1989.

Simon, Lucien. *Les Juifs à Nîmes et dans le Gard durant la deuxième guerre mondiale de 1939 à 1944.* Nîmes: Lacour, 1987.

Staub, Ervin. *The Roots of Evil: The Origins of Genocide and Other Group Violence.* Cambridge: Cambridge University Press, 1989.

Sternhell, Zeev. *Ni Droite, Ni Gauche: L'Idéologie fasciste en France.* Paris: Editions de Seuil, 1983.

Strebel, Elizabeth. "Vichy Cinema and Propaganda." In *Film and Radio Propaganda in World War II,* edited by K. R. M. Short, 271–89. London: Croom Helm, 1983.

Sweets, John F. *Choices in Vichy France.* New York: Oxford University Press, 1986.
——. "Hold That Pendulum! Redefining Fascism, Collaborationism and Resistance in France." *French Historical Studies* (Fall 1988): 731–58.
——. "La police et la population dans la France de Vichy: Une Etude de cas conformé et fidèle." *Guerres mondiales et conflits contemporains* (July 1989): 63–74.
——. *The Politics of Resistance in France, 1940–1944: A History of the Mouvements Unis de la Résistance.* De Kalb: University of Southern Illinois Press, 1976.
Veillon, Dominique. *La Collaboration: Textes et débats.* Paris: Livre du poche, 1984.
——. "La Vérité sur le STO." *L'Histoire,* no. 80 (1985): 105–9.
Vidalenc, Jean. *L'Exode de mai–juin 1940.* Paris: Presses universitaires de France, 1957.
Vielzeuf, Aimé. *Au Temps des longues nuits.* Uzès: Lacour, 1967.
——. *Compagnons de la liberté.* Nîmes: Lacour, 1976.
——. *En Cévennes et Languedoc au temps des longues nuits.* Nîmes: Lacour, 1985.
——. *On les appelait "Les bandits."* Nîmes: Lacour, 1967.
——. *Et la Cévenne s'embrasa.* Uzès: Peladan, 1967.
——. *La Résistance dans le Gard (1940–1944).* Nîmes: Lacour, 1979.
Warner, Geoffrey. *Pierre Laval and the Eclipse of France.* London: Eyre and Spottiswoode, 1968.
Weber, Eugen. *Action Française.* Stanford: Stanford University Press, 1962.
Wilson, Nelly. *Bernard Lazare: Antisemitism and the Problem of Jewish Identity in Late Nineteenth-Century France.* Cambridge: Cambridge University Press, 1978.
Winock, Michel. *La Fièvre hexagonale.* Paris: Editions du Seuil, 1987.
Wright, Gordon. *France in Modern Times.* 3d ed. New York: Norton, 1981.
——. *Rural Revolution in France: The Peasantry in the Twentieth Century.* Stanford: Stanford University Press, 1964.
Young-Bruehl, Elizabeth. *Hannah Arendt: For Love of the World.* New Haven: Yale University Press, 1982.
Zaretsky, Robert. " 'Old Grudges and Atavistic Hatreds': Catholics and Protestants in the Department of the Gard, 1940–1942." *Historical Reflections/Réflexions historiques* (Fall 1991): 233–65.
——. "Nîmes and the Department of the Gard under Vichy." Ph.D. dissertation, University of Virginia, 1989.
Zuccotti, Susan. *The Holocaust, the French, and the Jews.* New York: Basic Books, 1993.

INDEX

www.ingramcontent.com/pod-product-compliance
Lightning Source LLC
Chambersburg PA
CBHW021854020426
42334CB00013B/322